P. F. Strawson and his Philosophical Legacy

P. F. Strawson and his Philosophical Legacy

Edited by
SYBREN HEYNDELS
AUDUN BENGTSON
and
BENJAMIN DE MESEL

OXFORD
UNIVERSITY PRESS

Great Clarendon Street, Oxford, OX2 6DP,
United Kingdom

Oxford University Press is a department of the University of Oxford.
It furthers the University's objective of excellence in research, scholarship,
and education by publishing worldwide. Oxford is a registered trade mark of
Oxford University Press in the UK and in certain other countries

© Oxford University Press 2024

The moral rights of the authors have been asserted

All rights reserved. No part of this publication may be reproduced, stored in
a retrieval system, or transmitted, in any form or by any means, without the
prior permission in writing of Oxford University Press, or as expressly permitted
by law, by licence or under terms agreed with the appropriate reprographics
rights organization. Enquiries concerning reproduction outside the scope of the
above should be sent to the Rights Department, Oxford University Press, at the
address above

You must not circulate this work in any other form
and you must impose this same condition on any acquirer

Published in the United States of America by Oxford University Press
198 Madison Avenue, New York, NY 10016, United States of America

British Library Cataloguing in Publication Data
Data available

Library of Congress Control Number: 2023941734

ISBN 978–0–19–285847–4

DOI: 10.1093/oso/9780192858474.001.0001

Printed and bound in the UK by
Clays Ltd, Elcograf S.p.A.

Links to third party websites are provided by Oxford in good faith and
for information only. Oxford disclaims any responsibility for the materials
contained in any third party website referenced in this work.

Contents

Acknowledgements	vii
List of Contributors	ix
Introduction *Sybren Heyndels, Audun Bengtson, and Benjamin De Mesel*	1
1. Strawson on False Presupposition and the Assertive Enterprise *Anne Bezuidenhout*	15
2. Meaning and Speech Acts *Ian Rumfitt*	38
3. Strawson's Basic Particulars *Paul Snowdon*	59
4. Strawson on Other Minds *Quassim Cassam*	79
5. P. F. Strawson and the 'Pseudo-Material Shadows' *Michelle Montague*	99
6. Concepts and Experience in *Bounds of Sense* and Beyond *Hans-Johann Glock*	120
7. Strawson's Metacritique *Anil Gomes*	146
8. Seeing (More than) What Meets the Eye: A Critical Engagement with P. F. Strawson *Lilian Alweiss*	169
9. To Reply, or Not to Reply, That Is the Question: Descriptive Metaphysics and the Sceptical Challenge *Giuseppina D'Oro*	192
10. P. F. Strawson and Connective Analysis *A.P. Martinich*	213
11. Responsibility After 'Morality': Strawson's Naturalism and Williams's Genealogy *Paul Russell*	234

12. Navigating 'Freedom and Resentment' 260
    Lucy Allais

13. Between Exemption and Excuse: Exploring the Developmental
    Dimensions of Responsible Agency 280
    Victoria McGeer

Index 311

Acknowledgements

We would like to express our gratitude to all those who have helped to make this volume possible. This collection originates in a conference that we organized at the Institute of Philosophy, KU Leuven, in November 2019, on the occasion of what would have been P. F. Strawson's 100th birthday. We would like to thank all conference participants and our sponsors, the Institute of Philosophy, the FWO (Research Foundation Flanders), and the Irish Research Council.

We are grateful to our Oxford University Press editor, Peter Momtchiloff, who believed in our project from the start and gave us helpful advice. Thanks to the entire OUP team involved in the production of this book, and to Lex Academic for providing excellent editorial assistance on the entire volume. Most importantly, we would like to thank our authors for their outstanding work and cooperation.

We dedicate this volume to Paul Snowdon, who sadly passed away while this book was in preparation, and to four people who taught us to appreciate Strawson's work and, more generally, to do philosophy: Arnold Burms, Stefaan Cuypers, Bart Pattyn, and Stefan Rummens. We have learnt a lot from you and we hope that our volume reflects this. Thank you very much.

Sybren Heyndels, KU Leuven
Audun Bengtson, Norwegian Defence University College
Benjamin De Mesel, KU Leuven

List of Contributors

Lucy Allais is Professor of Philosophy at the University of Witwatersrand and Johns Hopkins University

Lilian Alweiss is Assistant Professor of Philosophy at Trinity College Dublin

Audun Bengtson is Adviser at the Norwegian Defence University College

Anne Bezuidenhout is Professor of Philosophy and Linguistics at the University of South Carolina

Quassim Cassam is Professor of Philosophy at the University of Warwick

Benjamin De Mesel is Assistant Professor of Philosophy at KU Leuven

Giuseppina D'Oro is Reader in Philosophy at Keele University

Hans-Johann Glock is Professor of Philosophy at the University of Zurich

Anil Gomes is Fellow and Tutor in Philosophy at Trinity College, Oxford and Professor in Philosophy at the University of Oxford

Sybren Heyndels is Postdoctoral Fellow of the Research Foundation Flanders (FWO) at KU Leuven

Victoria McGeer is Senior Research Fellow at Princeton University and Professor of Philosophy at Australian National University

A.P. Martinich is Roy Vaughan Centennial Professor Emeritus in Philosophy at the University of Texas at Austin

Michelle Montague is Professor of Philosophy at the University of Texas at Austin

Ian Rumfitt is Senior Research Fellow at All Souls College, Oxford and Professor in Philosophy at the University of Oxford

Paul Russell is Professor of Philosophy at Lund University and the University of British Columbia (Emeritus)

Paul Snowdon was Emeritus Professor at University College London

Introduction

Sybren Heyndels, Audun Bengtson, and Benjamin De Mesel

This book aims to bring out the continuing relevance of the work of Sir Peter Frederick Strawson (1919–2006). Strawson was one of the most influential British philosophers in the second half of the twentieth century. He was elected to the British Academy in 1960 and received a knighthood in 1977. He never aimed at a comprehensive, integrated system, but he contributed to a wide range of debates in the philosophy of language and logic, metaphysics, epistemology, moral philosophy, the history of philosophy, and philosophical methodology. His writings were discussed by the world's leading philosophers, including Bertrand Russell, Wilfrid Sellars, Hilary Putnam, W.V.O. Quine, Donald Davidson, J.L. Austin, and Saul Kripke.

Strawson was born in London and went up to Oxford in 1937, where he studied Philosophy, Politics, and Economics (PPE). Immediately after having finished his studies, he was called up to the army in the summer of 1940. He attained the rank of captain and defended putatively delinquent soldiers facing court martial, an experience that may have triggered some of the ideas in his influential paper 'Freedom and Resentment'. After the war, Strawson was elected to the post of Assistant Lecturer in Philosophy at Bangor, in Wales. He won the prestigious John Locke Prize in Oxford in 1947 and impressed Gilbert Ryle, one of the examiners, who recommended him to University College. Strawson was elected a Fellow there in 1948 and remained in Oxford until his retirement in 1987. It did not take long before he achieved international fame through his influential criticism of Russell and Austin, two leading philosophers at the time.

Strawson's paper 'On Referring' (1950a), published in *Mind*, criticizes Russell's Theory of Descriptions. Russell's theory analyses sentences involving definite descriptions by capturing the logical form of such sentences in the language of first-order predicate logic. According to Russell, sentences such as 'The king of France is wise' are to be interpreted as expressing (1) the claim that there is a king of France, (2) the claim that there is at most one king of France, and (3) the claim that something that is a king of France is wise. In the language of first-order predicate logic, this means that sentences of the form 'The F is G' are analysed as having the following logical form: $\exists x(Fx \ \& \ \forall y(Fy \rightarrow x=y) \ \& \ Gx)$. This

---

Sybren Heyndels, Audun Bengtson, and Benjamin De Mesel, *Introduction* In: *P. F. Strawson and his Philosophical Legacy*.
Edited by: Sybren Heyndels, Audun Bengtson, and Benjamin De Mesel, Oxford University Press.
© Oxford University Press 2024. DOI: 10.1093/oso/9780192858474.003.0001

analysis allowed Russell to hold that sentences involving non-referring definite descriptions (such as 'the king of France') are both meaningful and false.

Strawson agrees with Russell that sentences involving non-referring definite descriptions are *meaningful*, but he disagrees that these sentences must be either true or false in all circumstances of use. Strawson criticizes Russell for failing to consistently distinguish between (a) the meaning of a word or sentence and (b) the object referred to by making *use* of a word or the truth or falsity of the statement made by *using* a sentence. This failure is the clearest, he thinks, in Russell's theory of logically proper names, where the meaning of such a name is identified with the object the name refers to. By clearly separating talk about *meaning* from talk about *reference*, Strawson argues that a sentence such as 'The king of France is wise' can be meaningful even though statements made by using that sentence can fail to have a truth-value (e.g. a use of that sentence at a time *t* where there is no king of France). Against Russell's analysis, Strawson argues that a speaker does not *assert* but rather *signals* or *presupposes* that there is a king of France when using 'The king of France is wise' to make an assertion. On occasions where such presupposition is not fulfilled (e.g. at times when there is no king of France), the speaker fails to make a statement with a truth-value even though the sentence is meaningful, which for Strawson means that there are certain general rules and conventions governing the proper use of the sentence on particular occasions.

In the same year as the above paper, the essay 'Truth' (1950b) was published, in which Strawson attacks Austin's correspondence theory of truth. Strawson criticizes 'Austin's account of the two terms of the truth-conferring relation', as well as his 'account of the relation itself' (Strawson 1950b, 129). For instance, Strawson agrees with Austin that it is *statements* that are properly said to be true, but he disagrees with Austin that such statements are to be understood as historic speech-episodes. And he agrees with Austin that it is *facts* that are what make statements true, but he criticizes Austin for assimilating facts to worldly events or things. The year before, Strawson had already published an essay with the same title (the 1949 paper 'Truth') where he develops his own account of truth. In this 1949 paper, Strawson defends an updated version of Ramsey's deflationary theory of truth while at the same time criticizing what he calls the 'meta-linguistic' or 'semantic' theory of truth. According to Strawson, the deflationist is right in claiming that to say that a statement S *is true* does not add any assertive content to S itself. Nevertheless, the linguistic occasions where it is appropriate to say that S *is true* are often quite different from the occasions where it is appropriate to say that S. To make this point, Strawson compares the use of 'true' with the use of 'yes' and 'ditto' to emphasize its typical *confirmatory* use; i.e. its use to confirm or underwrite a statement already made by another speaker. Strawson further argues that an analysis of the actual use of 'true' shows that it is not used as a device to talk *about* sentences at all. According to Strawson, '[t]he phrase "is true" is not *applied to* sentences; for it is not *applied to* anything. Truth is not a property of symbols; for it is not a property' (Strawson 1949, 84). Just as 'yes' or 'ditto' underwrite another speaker's statement, one of the main uses of 'true' is to *confirm* rather than *talk about* a sentence uttered by another speaker. According to Strawson, meta-linguistic theories about truth mistake truth for a property because they are tempted by grammatical constructions in which '... is true' is a grammatical predicate, which leads them to the idea that '... is true' is used to make a statement about a sentence rather than just confirming a statement that has, for instance, already been made by another speaker.

Strawson's first book, *Introduction to Logical Theory* (1952), not only serves as a useful introduction to standard logic, but also contains original philosophical discussions of some of the central concepts in the philosophy of logic, such as the concepts of logical necessity, logical form, and entailment. Furthermore, the book contains careful descriptions of the differences between the meaning of the truth-functional connectives and their counterparts in ordinary language, as well as a defence of traditional syllogistic logic. The latter was described by Quine as 'the best way of defending the traditional syllogistic' (Quine 1953, 439). The main methodological lesson Strawson teaches us in *Introduction to Logical Theory* is that formal logic is a sort of idealized abstraction, which does reveal certain fundamental features of our language and thought, but which also has some important limitations and therefore cannot do justice to the complexities of ordinary language use. These ideas were already in the background of Strawson's criticism of Russell's Theory of Descriptions. The thought that ordinary language use has a precise logic, or that the ordinary language counterparts of logical connectives have a precise logic (as Grice believed), often leads to philosophical confusion and misrepresentation.

In 1954, Strawson reviewed Wittgenstein's *Philosophical Investigations*, published posthumously one year earlier, for *Mind*. Strawson's lengthy review is critical of Wittgenstein at certain points (more so than many of his contemporaries, but less so than many philosophers today), especially when it comes to the alleged impossibility of doing philosophy in a systematic way, but he does not hesitate to call Wittgenstein 'a philosopher of genius' (Strawson 1974a, 147), and he ranks him, with Aristotle, Hume, and Kant, among the greatest philosophers of all time (Strawson 1995, 18).

The conflict between so-called 'ideal language philosophers' and 'ordinary language philosophers' became a central methodological debate in the 1950s and 1960s. In his 'Carnap's Views on Constructed Systems Versus Natural Languages in Analytic Philosophy', which was written in 1954 but published in 1963, Strawson discusses Carnap's method of explication, which aims at *replacing* our ordinary concepts by more exact concepts. Strawson contrasts this method with the method of *describing* the different, actual uses of our ordinary concepts. Given that Strawson thinks that philosophical problems arise through a failure to acknowledge the many different uses and purposes of the everyday concepts that we philosophize about, he argues that Carnap's method of explication cannot, in itself, be a sufficient method to solve philosophical problems. A Carnapian explication, after all, simply *replaces* the ordinary concepts that gave rise to the problem. By doing so, the same paradox or perplexity might indeed not arise anymore, but neither will the origin of the air of paradox or perplexity have been explained. This can be done only, Strawson argues, by giving a description of the actual uses of the concept or set of concepts that led to our philosophical puzzlement in the first place. Hence the idea that 'laying down the rules of use of exact and fruitful concepts' does not 'solve the typical philosophical problem' but simply 'change[s] the subject'; it is 'like offering a text-book on physiology to someone who says (with a sigh) that he wished he understood the workings of the human heart' (Strawson 1963, 505). Strawson's 'changing the subject' objection to ideal language philosophy has recently received renewed attention in the context of debates about conceptual engineering (Pinder 2020). Another remarkable achievement by Strawson in the 1950s was 'In Defence of a Dogma' (1956), co-authored with his former tutor H.P. Grice and published in *The Philosophical Review*, in which Strawson and Grice defend the analytic-synthetic distinction against Quine's famous attack on analyticity in 'Two Dogmas of Empiricism'.

Strawson's second book, *Individuals: An Essay in Descriptive Metaphysics*, appeared in 1959. It ambitiously addresses 'the question of what the most basic or primitive or fundamental objects of reference, or subjects of predication, are', and Strawson argues that they are 'relatively enduring space-occupying individuals' such as people, animals, and inanimate material objects (Strawson 1959, 9). In the introduction to *Individuals*, Strawson coins the distinction between descriptive and revisionary metaphysics: 'Descriptive metaphysics is content to describe the actual structure of our thought about the world, revisionary metaphysics is concerned to produce a better structure' (Strawson 1959, 9; on this distinction, see Haack 1979 and Snowdon 2008). Strawson conceives of himself as a descriptive metaphysician in the tradition of Aristotle and Kant, attempting to reveal the overall structure of our conceptual scheme, of our way of thinking about ourselves and the world. Especially the first half of the book, with chapters about bodies, sounds, and persons (including arguments against scepticism about other minds), has been widely discussed (Ayer 1963; Evans 1980; Ishiguro 1980; Williams 1973) and generated a range of essays on similar issues in descriptive metaphysics (Campbell 1994; Evans 1982; Wiggins 1980). Strawson's use of the term 'metaphysics', innocent as it may sound today, sets him apart from the then-influential anti-metaphysical and anti-theoretical pronouncements of Austin and his followers, but the extent to which Strawson departs from metaphysics as traditionally conceived is a matter of dispute (Glock 2012; Hacker 2001).

Strawson wrote two papers on moral philosophy in the early 1960s. In 'Social Morality and Individual Ideal', he distinguishes between the region of the ethical ('a region of diverse, certainly incompatible and possibly practically conflicting ideal images or pictures of a human life') and the sphere of morality (the sphere of 'rules or principles governing human behaviour which apply universally within a community or class') (Strawson 1974a, 33), and he outlines how both domains are related. In contrast to this relatively neglected paper, 'Freedom and Resentment' (1962) is Strawson's most-cited paper today. In it, he discusses the threat of determinism to our practices of holding each other morally responsible. These practices are marked by what Strawson calls 'the range of reactive feelings and attitudes which belong to involvement or participation with others in interpersonal human relationships', including resentment, gratitude, forgiveness, anger, and many other attitudes (Strawson 1974a, 10). Strawson believes that the truth of determinism cannot threaten moral responsibility, but there is a great deal of disagreement about the reconstruction of his argument(s). Classic discussions include Bennett (1980), Wallace (1994), and Watson (1987). Interpretations tend to emphasize Humean (Russell 1992), Kantian (Allais 2014), or Wittgensteinian (Bengtson 2019; De Mesel 2018) strands in the paper. Heyndels (2019) argues that 'Freedom and Resentment' is best understood as an application of Strawson's own philosophical methods; De Mesel (2022) shows that it can profitably be read in the light of some later remarks by Strawson. Many relevant papers are collected in McKenna and Russell (2008) and Shoemaker and Tognazzini (2014). The influence of 'Freedom and Resentment' on contemporary discussions of moral responsibility can hardly be overestimated.

Strawson began to lecture on Kant's *Critique of Pure Reason*, 'the greatest single work of modern Western philosophy' (Strawson 1998, 12), in the early 1960s. Strawson had studied Kant as an undergraduate (the only two options for PPE students specializing in philosophy in the late 1930s were logic and Kant; Strawson took both) and tutored students who chose to work on Kant. Strawson's lectures led to the publication of his third book, *The Bounds of Sense: An Essay on Kant's Critique of Pure Reason*, in 1966. Strawson describes the aim of his book as being:

> to separate Kant's brilliant and profound account of the structure of necessarily connected ideas and concepts which form the limiting framework of all human thought about the world and experience of the world from the overarching theory which he [Kant] saw as the explanation of the possibility of any such account; and at the same time to explain that explanation and to show why it should be rejected. (Strawson 1998, 12)

The explanation that Strawson rejects is Kant's transcendental idealism, which involves the idea that the nature of things as they really are is necessarily unknown to us. Strawson's work on Kant was impactful at the time (Harrison 1970; Matthews 1969); it is generally seen as crucial to the development of analytic Kantianism, and continues to be discussed (Glock 2003; Gomes 2016, 2017a,

2017b; and a special issue of the *European Journal of Philosophy* on the fiftieth anniversary of *The Bounds of Sense*, published in 2016). Strawson returned to Kant in some of his later essays (Strawson 1997). Among other things, *The Bounds of Sense* sparked a renewed interest in so-called 'transcendental arguments' (Rorty 1971; Stern 1999; Stroud 1968), which some take to have anti-sceptical implications, because they show that the sceptic's position presupposes the truth of claims which the sceptic claims to doubt.

In 1968, Strawson succeeded Ryle as Waynflete Professor of Metaphysical Philosophy at Magdalen College. His concern with language as an instrument of human communication took centre stage in his inaugural lecture, 'Meaning and Truth' (1970), in which he discusses the 'Homeric struggle' between 'theorists of formal semantics' and 'theorists of communication-intention' (Strawson 1970, 132). The former group analyses the notion of meaning in terms of truth-conditions, and the latter group argues that an elucidation of the notion of meaning is impossible without reference to the interaction between a speaker and a hearer, which includes the speaker's audience-directed intentions to communicate information. Strawson sides with the latter group, arguing that 'we know nothing of human *language* unless we understand human *speech*' (Strawson 1970, 145).

Strawson returned to reference and predication, issues that were at the centre of his philosophical interests throughout his career, in his fourth book, *Subject and Predicate in Logic and Grammar* (1974b). His aim in this book is twofold: 'first, to explain the foundation of the basic combination of predication on which our logic rests and, second, to reveal the general character of any adequate explanation of the grammatical structure of any type of natural language' (Strawson 1974b, ix). Also in the 1970s, Strawson wrote an influential paper on perception, 'Perception and Its Objects' (1979). In this paper, Strawson argues that our ordinary perceptual experiences are always already mediated by concepts, and that our ordinary perceptual judgements would be incorrectly described as being 'inferred from' or 'interpretations of' what sensible experience actually presents us with. Furthermore, he holds that we are pre-theoretically committed to a realist understanding of the nature of perception where we take our perceptual experiences to be causally dependent on independently existing physical objects. Lastly, he reconciles strong scientific realism about perception with commonsense realism by recognizing a certain relativity in our conception of the real properties of physical objects. Something may be a green leather table-top relative to the human perceptual standpoint, and nothing but a congeries of electric charges relative to the scientific standpoint.

Strawson delivered the Woodbridge Lectures at Columbia University in 1983. A book based on them was published in 1985 as *Scepticism and Naturalism: Some Varieties*. In the first chapter about scepticism, inspired by Hume and Wittgenstein, Strawson develops an anti-sceptical line of argument whose relation to his earlier Kantian, transcendental arguments is still being debated (Stern 2003;

Callanan 2011). Strawson argues that the attempt to combat sceptical doubts by rational argument is misguided, 'for we are dealing here with the presuppositions, the framework, of all human thought and enquiry' (Strawson 1998, 17). In subsequent chapters about morality and perception, the mental and the physical, and meaning, Strawson's target is a kind of reductive naturalism, which tends to 'discredit, or somehow to reduce to more scientifically acceptable, physicalistic terms, whole regions of ordinary human thought, language, and experience' (Strawson 1998, 17). His own form of realist naturalism is of another, 'humanistic' or 'liberal' variety that has been popular at Oxford. Snowdon and Gomes (2021) call it 'a *relaxed* realism that does not set its face against the claims of natural science, but rather refuses to take them as calling into question the legitimacy of our ordinary ways of thinking about the world'.

Strawson's last book, *Analysis and Metaphysics: An Introduction to Philosophy*, was published in 1992. From 1968 until his retirement in 1987, Strawson gave a series of introductory lectures in philosophy under the same title, and the book largely preserves the content of these lectures. It was published first in French in 1985 as *Analyse et Métaphysique*. In the second chapter, Strawson distinguishes between reductive and connective analysis, and he declares the latter 'more realistic and more fertile' (Strawson 1992, 19) than the former. Reductive analyses aim to reduce problematic concepts or explain them in terms of other concepts which are felt to be more perspicuous. Strawson, however, believes that philosophically important concepts 'tend to remain obstinately irreducible, in the sense that they cannot be defined away, without remainder or circularity, in terms of other concepts' (Strawson 1995, 16). Thus, another kind of analysis, connective analysis, is called for. Connective analyses aim to reveal the function of a concept 'by grasping its connections with the others, its place in the system' (Strawson 1992, 19). Strawson practises the method of connective analysis (whose relation to the method of descriptive metaphysics remains somewhat elusive) in subsequent chapters about experience and material objects, the inner and the outer, truth and knowledge, meaning and understanding, causation and explanation, and freedom and necessity.

In 'My Philosophy' (1995), Strawson summarizes his general philosophical aim as follows:

> it is possible to distinguish a certain number of fundamental, general, pervasive concepts or concept-types which together constitute the structural framework, as it were, within which all detailed thinking goes on. To name a few at random, I have in mind such ideas as those of space, time, object, event, mind and body, knowledge, truth, meaning, existence, identity, action, intention, causation, and explanation. I take the philosophical aim to be that of making clear, or elucidating, the character of such concepts as these and their interconnections.
>
> (Strawson 1995, 13–14)

Overview of Contributions

This volume opens with two chapters on Strawson's philosophy of language. In the first chapter, Anne Bezuidenhout develops and defends Strawson's view of presupposition, drawing on materials from 'On Referring' (1950a) and *Subject and Predicate in Logic and Grammar* (1974b). She connects Strawson's observations to recent work in linguistics and the philosophy of language. In the second chapter, Ian Rumfitt focuses on 'Meaning and Truth' (1970), Strawson's inaugural lecture at Oxford about the conflict between truth-conditional approaches and communication-intention theories of meaning. Rumfitt draws on recent work on the speech act of telling in order to criticize Strawson's argument in favour of the latter.

Chapters 3 to 5 deal with Strawson's ambitious project in *Individuals* (1959). Paul Snowdon scrutinizes and criticizes the first chapter of *Individuals*, where Strawson moves from claims about the nature of reference to the idea that material bodies are basic. Snowdon argues, contra Strawson, that understanding reference should not be analysed in terms of identification, and that it is not clear that material objects are the basic objects of reference for us. Quassim Cassam engages with Strawson's epistemology, and specifically with his account of the knowledge of other minds. He connects ideas from *Individuals* to Strawson's later *Scepticism and Naturalism* (1985a) and argues that Strawson's account of the grounds for ascriptions of mental states to others is too narrowly focused on behavioural criteria. By looking at the various grounds on which a biographer ascribes mental states to a deceased biographical subject, Cassam argues that *empathy* plays a crucial role in ascriptions of mental states to others as well. In the fifth chapter, Michelle Montague explores the second part of *Individuals* (which has often been neglected), where Strawson argues that there is a level of thought that is more fundamental than our thought about material bodies. According to Montague, a 'stuff ontology' most naturally corresponds to this fundamental level of thought.

Strawson's relation to Kant and his book *The Bounds of Sense* (1966) are at the heart of Chapters 6 and 7. Hans-Johann Glock explores the relation between concepts and experience, which is central to Strawson's descriptive metaphysics and to his analytic Kantianism. Glock argues that Strawson rightly believed that there are limits to the concept of a possible experience, but wrongly suggested that any conceivable experience must be conceptual. The insights offered by descriptive metaphysics are best conceived as conceptual truths of a special, mediated kind, not as synthetic a priori. Anil Gomes is also concerned with the status of Strawson's claims, specifically in relation to the status of Kant's claims in the *Critique of Pure Reason*. Gomes argues that Strawson did not understand and should not have understood Kant's claims as analytic. Rather, Strawson seems committed to our possessing non-analytic but a priori knowledge. Gomes extracts a model for understanding such knowledge from G.E. Moore's early writings on Kant.

Chapters 8 and 9 concern Strawson's naturalism and his response to scepticism. Lilian Alweiss compares Strawson's account of perceptual experience, as developed in 'Perception and Its Objects' (1979), with that of Edmund Husserl. Strawson defends a naive realist theory of perception, but why think that perceptual experiences represent the world as it is? Alweiss argues that Strawson's adherence to a Humean form of naturalism makes it difficult for him to dispel sceptical concerns about perception, while Husserl shows that we have evaluative reasons, and not merely natural ones, for sidestepping scepticism. Giuseppina D'Oro shows that Strawson's anti-sceptical arguments occupy an intermediate logical space between truth-directed transcendental arguments aimed at refuting the sceptic and naturalist-quietist responses of Humeans who decline to take up the sceptical challenge. Strawson's response to scepticism is neither quietist nor confrontational. It seeks to show primarily that the sceptic is not a genuine partner in conversation.

Chapter 10 is concerned with the philosophical methodology defended and developed by Strawson in his last book, *Analysis and Metaphysics* (1992). A.P. Martinich defends Strawson's conception of philosophy as connective analysis, according to which individual concepts are properly understood only by grasping their connections with others. Because connective analysis is not susceptible to the same criticisms as other forms of analysis, it should not have declined along with them.

Strawson did not see himself, at least not primarily, as a moral philosopher. It is somewhat ironic, then, that 'Freedom and Resentment' (1962) has become his most famous and widely discussed paper. In Chapter 11, Paul Russell asks whether Strawson's naturalism about moral responsibility is vulnerable to a genealogical critique of the kind that Bernard Williams presents. Lucy Allais, in Chapter 12, examines the key moves and claims in 'Freedom and Resentment', and discusses responses in the literature which go in different directions on these key points. She argues that the text is compatible with different interpretations and presents philosophical considerations in favour of one particular interpretation. In the final chapter, Victoria McGeer addresses Strawson's basic distinction between agents who are fit targets of our reactive attitudes and those who are not. She indicates how reactive attitudes may sometimes be appropriately directed to some types of non-responsible agents, and suggests that her elaboration of Strawson's view is congenial with his general approach to the problem of responsible agency.

Bibliography

Primary Literature

Books by Strawson

Strawson, Peter F. (1952), *Introduction to Logical Theory* (London: Methuen. Reprinted in 2011 by Routledge).

Strawson, Peter F. (1959), *Individuals: An Essay in Descriptive Metaphysics* (London: Methuen. Reprinted in 1990 by Routledge).

Strawson, Peter F. (1966), *The Bounds of Sense: An Essay on Kant's Critique of Pure Reason* (London: Methuen. Reprinted in 1989 by Routledge).

Strawson, Peter F. (1971), *Logico-Linguistic Papers* (London: Methuen. Reprinted in 2004 by Ashgate).

Strawson, Peter F. (1974a), *Freedom and Resentment and Other Essays* (London: Methuen. Reprinted in 2008 by Routledge).

Strawson, Peter F. (1974b), *Subject and Predicate in Logic and Grammar* (London: Methuen. Reprinted in 2016 by Routledge).

Strawson, Peter F. (1985a), *Scepticism and Naturalism: Some Varieties* (London: Methuen. Reprinted in 2008 by Routledge).

Strawson, Peter F. (1985b), *Analyse et Métaphysique* (Paris: Vrin).

Strawson, Peter F. (1992), *Analysis and Metaphysics* (Oxford: Oxford University Press).

Strawson, Peter F. (1997), *Entity and Identity and Other Essays* (Oxford: Oxford University Press).

Strawson, Peter F. (2011), *Philosophical Writings* (Oxford: Oxford University Press).

Selected Articles by Strawson

The list below contains only a selection of articles. For a full bibliography of his works, compiled by Strawson himself, see his (1998) 'Bibliography of P. F. Strawson', in Lewis Edwin Hahn (ed.), *The Philosophy of P. F. Strawson* (Chicago: Open Court), 405–17.

Strawson, Peter F. (1949), 'Truth', *Analysis* 9: 83–97.

Strawson, Peter F. (1950a), 'On Referring', *Mind* 59: 320–44. Reprinted in Strawson (1971), *Logico-Linguistic Papers* (London: Methuen).

Strawson, Peter F. (1950b), 'Truth', *Proceedings of the Aristotelian Society, Supplementary Volume* 24: 129–56. Reprinted in Strawson (1971), *Logico-Linguistic Papers* (London: Methuen).

Strawson, Peter F. (1954), 'Wittgenstein's *Philosophical Investigations*', *Mind* 63: 70-99. Reprinted in Strawson (1974a), *Freedom and Resentment and Other Essays* (London: Methuen).

Strawson, Peter F. (1956), 'In Defence of a Dogma', *The Philosophical Review* 65: 141–58. With H.P. Grice. Reprinted in Strawson (2011), *Philosophical Writings* (Oxford: Oxford University Press).

Strawson, Peter F. (1961), 'Social Morality and Individual Ideal', *Philosophy* 36: 1–17. Reprinted in Strawson (1974a), *Freedom and Resentment and Other Essays* (London: Methuen).

Strawson, Peter F. (1962), 'Freedom and Resentment', *Proceedings of the British Academy* 48: 1–25. Reprinted in Strawson (1974a), *Freedom and Resentment and Other Essays* (London: Methuen).

Strawson, Peter F. (1963), 'Carnap's Views on Constructed Systems Versus Natural Languages in Analytic Philosophy', in Paul Arthur Schilpp (ed.), *The Philosophy of Rudolf Carnap* (LaSalle, IL: Open Court), 503–18.

Strawson, Peter F. (1970), *Meaning and Truth* (Oxford: Clarendon Press). Reprinted in Strawson (1971), *Logico-Linguistic Papers* (London: Methuen).

Strawson, Peter F. (1979), 'Perception and Its Objects', in Graham F. Macdonald (ed.), *Perception and Identity: Essays Presented to A.J. Ayer* (London: Macmillan), 41–58. Reprinted in Strawson (2011), *Philosophical Writings* (Oxford: Oxford University Press).

Strawson, Peter F. (1995), 'My Philosophy', in Pranab Kumar Sen and Roop Rekha Verma (eds.), *The Philosophy of P. F. Strawson* (New Delhi: Indian Council of Philosophical Research), 1–18.

Strawson, Peter F. (1998), 'Intellectual Autobiography', in Lewis Edwin Hahn (ed.), *The Philosophy of P. F. Strawson* (Chicago, IL: Open Court), 1–21. Reprinted in Strawson (2011), *Philosophical Writings* (Oxford: Oxford University Press).

Strawson, Peter F. (2003), 'A Bit of Intellectual Autobiography', in Hans-Johann Glock (ed.), *Strawson and Kant* (Oxford: Clarendon Press), 7–14. Reprinted in Strawson (2011), *Philosophical Writings* (Oxford: Oxford University Press).

Videos

There are some interesting videos featuring Strawson on YouTube.
'P. F. Strawson on Imagination and Perception (1968)'.
https://www.youtube.com/watch?v=GOoC5osMNC0
'P. F. Strawson and Gareth Evans on Truth (Part 1 of 2)'.
https://www.youtube.com/watch?v=BLV-eYacfbE
'P. F. Strawson and Gareth Evans on Truth (Part 2 of 2)'.
https://www.youtube.com/watch?v=w__pIcl_1rs
'Gareth Evans and P. F. Strawson—Philosophy of Language'.
https://www.youtube.com/watch?v=nZXJ-aIHxt4
'Donald Davidson and Sir Peter Strawson in Conversation'.
https://www.youtube.com/watch?v=hE71QAOYav4
'Donald Davidson—The Davidson, Quine and Strawson Panel'.
https://www.youtube.com/watch?v=RjwY1vGBW4Y
'In Conversation: Peter Frederick Strawson (1992)'.
https://www.youtube.com/watch?v=clo2FReysBI
The television discussion between Strawson and Gareth Evans on truth from 1973, linked to above, is discussed in several essays, commissioned by Huw Price and published here: https://www.3-16am.co.uk/articles/.c/flickering-shadows-truth-in-16mm-edited-by-huw-price. The series contains essays by Crispin Wright, Ian Rumfitt, Anil Gomes, Amie Thomasson, Nikhil Krishnan, Mark Schroeder, Simon Blackburn, Paul Horwich, Cheryl Misak, and others.

Secondary Literature

Allais, Lucy (2014), 'Freedom and Forgiveness', in David Shoemaker and Neal Tognazzini (eds.), *Oxford Studies in Agency and Responsibility, Volume 2: 'Freedom and Resentment' at 50* (Oxford: Oxford University Press), 33–63.

Ayer, Alfred Jules (1963), 'The Concept of a Person', in *The Concept of a Person and Other Essays* (London: Macmillan), 82–128.

Bengtson, Audun (2019), 'Responsibility, Reactive Attitudes and Very General Facts of Human Nature', *Philosophical Investigations* 42: 281–304.

Bennett, Jonathan (1980), 'Accountability', in Zak Van Straaten (ed.), *Philosophical Subjects: Essays Presented to P. F. Strawson* (Oxford: Clarendon Press), 14–47.

Brown, Clifford (2006), *Peter Strawson* (Stocksfield, UK: Acumen).

Callanan, John J. (2011), 'Making Sense of Doubt: Strawson's Anti-Scepticism', *Theoria* 77: 261–78.

Campbell, John (1994), *Past, Space, and Self* (Cambridge, MA: MIT Press).

De Mesel, Benjamin (2018), 'Are Our Moral Responsibility Practices Justified? Wittgenstein, Strawson and Justification in "Freedom and Resentment"', *British Journal for the History of Philosophy* 26: 603–14.

De Mesel, Benjamin (2022), 'Taking the Straight Path: P. F. Strawson's Later Work on Freedom and Responsibility', *Philosophers' Imprint* 22: 1–17.

European Journal of Philosophy 24 (2016), Special Issue on the Fiftieth Anniversary of *The Bounds of Sense*.

Evans, Gareth (1980), 'Things Without the Mind: A Commentary Upon Chapter Two of Strawson's *Individuals*', in Zak Van Straaten (ed.), *Philosophical Subjects: Essays Presented to P. F. Strawson* (Oxford: Clarendon Press), 76–116.

Evans, Gareth (1982), *The Varieties of Reference* (Oxford: Clarendon Press).

Glock, Hans-Johann, ed. (2003), *Strawson and Kant* (Oxford: Clarendon Press).

Glock, Hans-Johann (2012), 'Strawson's Descriptive Metaphysics', in Leila Haaparanta and Heikki J. Koskinen (eds.), *Categories of Being: Essays on Metaphysics and Logic* (Oxford: Oxford University Press), 391–419.

Gomes, Anil (2016), 'Unity, Objectivity, and the Passivity of Experience', *European Journal of Philosophy* 24: 946–69.

Gomes, Anil (2017a), 'Perception and Reflection', *Philosophical Perspectives* 31: 131–52.

Gomes, Anil (2017b), 'Kant, the Philosophy of Mind, and Twentieth-Century Analytic Philosophy', in Anil Gomes and Andrew Stephenson (eds.), *Kant and the Philosophy of Mind: Perception, Reason, and the Self* (Oxford: Oxford University Press), 5–24.

Gomes, Anil (2019), 'Snapshot: P. F. Strawson', *The Philosophers' Magazine*. https://www.philosophersmag.com/essays/199-snapshot-p-f-strawson

Gomes, Anil (2022), 'P. F. Strawson', *Oxford Bibliographies Online*. https://www.oxfordbibliographies.com/display/document/obo-9780195396577/obo-9780195396577-0429.xml

Grice, Herbert Paul (1989), *Studies in the Way of Words* (Cambridge, MA: Harvard University Press).

Haack, Susan (1979), 'Descriptive and Revisionary Metaphysics', *Philosophical Studies* 35: 361–71.

Hacker, Peter Michael Stephan (2001), 'On Strawson's Rehabilitation of Metaphysics', in *Wittgenstein: Connections and Controversies* (Oxford: Oxford University Press), 345-70.

Hahn, Lewis Edwin, ed. (1998), *The Philosophy of P. F. Strawson* (LaSalle, IL: Open Court).

Harrison, Ross (1970), 'Strawson on Outer Objects', *The Philosophical Quarterly* 20: 213-21.

Heyndels, Sybren (2019), 'Strawson's Method in "Freedom and Resentment"', *The Journal of Ethics* 23: 407-23.

Ishiguro, Hidé (1980), 'The Primitiveness of the Concept of a Person', in Zak Van Straaten (ed.), *Philosophical Subjects: Essays Presented to P. F. Strawson* (Oxford: Clarendon Press), 62-75.

McKenna, Michael, and Paul Russell, eds. (2008), *Free Will and Reactive Attitudes: Perspectives on P. F. Strawson's 'Freedom and Resentment'* (Farnham: Ashgate). Reprinted in 2016 by Routledge.

Magee, Bryan (1971), 'Conversation with Peter Strawson', in *Modern British Philosophy* (New York: St. Martin's Press).

Matthews, H.E. (1969), 'Strawson on Transcendental Idealism', *The Philosophical Quarterly* 1969: 204-20.

Philosophia 10 (1981), 'Special Issue on the Philosophy of P. F. Strawson'.

Pinder, Mark (2020), 'On Strawson's Critique of Explication as a Method in Philosophy', *Synthese* 197: 955-81.

Pivcevic, Edo (1989), 'An Interview with Professor Sir Peter Strawson', *Cogito* 3: 3-8.

Quine, Willard Van Orman (1953), 'Mr. Strawson on Logical Theory', *Mind* 62: 433-51.

Rorty, Richard (1971), 'Verificationism and Transcendental Arguments', *Noûs* 5: 3-14.

Russell, Paul (1992), 'Strawson's Way of Naturalizing Responsibility', *Ethics* 102: 287-302.

Sen, Pranab Kumar, and Roop Rekha Verma, eds. (1995), *The Philosophy of P. F. Strawson* (New Delhi: Indian Council of Philosophical Research).

Shoemaker, David, and Neal Tognazzini, eds. (2014), *Oxford Studies in Agency and Responsibility, Volume 2: 'Freedom and Resentment' at 50* (Oxford: Oxford University Press).

Snowdon, Paul (2007), 'Peter Frederick Strawson: 1919-2006', *Proceedings of the British Academy* 150: 221-44. https://www.thebritishacademy.ac.uk/documents/1641/150p221.pdf

Snowdon, Paul (2008), 'Strawson on Philosophy: Three Episodes', *South African Journal of Philosophy* 27: 167-78.

Snowdon, Paul, and Anil Gomes (2021), 'Peter Frederick Strawson', in *The Stanford Encyclopedia of Philosophy* (Summer 2021 Edition), Edward N. Zalta (ed.), https://plato.stanford.edu/entries/strawson

Stern, Robert, ed. (1999), *Transcendental Arguments: Problems and Prospects* (Oxford: Oxford University Press).

Stern, Robert (2003), 'On Strawson's Naturalistic Turn', in Hans-Johann Glock (ed.), *Strawson and Kant* (Oxford: Clarendon Press), 219–34.

Stroud, Barry (1968), 'Transcendental Arguments', *The Journal of Philosophy* 65: 241–56.

Van Straaten, Zak, ed. (1980), *Philosophical Subjects: Essays Presented to P. F. Strawson* (Oxford: Clarendon Press).

Wallace, R. Jay (1994), *Responsibility and the Moral Sentiments* (Cambridge, MA: Harvard University Press).

Watson, Gary (1987), 'Responsibility and the Limits of Evil: Variations on a Strawsonian Theme', in Ferdinand Schoeman (ed.), *Responsibility, Character and the Emotions: New Essays in Moral Psychology* (Cambridge: Cambridge University Press), 256–86.

Wiggins, David (1980), *Sameness and Substance* (Oxford: Blackwell).

Williams, Bernard (1973), 'Mr. Strawson on Individuals', *Philosophy* 36: 309–22. Reprinted in Bernard Williams, *Problems of the Self* (Cambridge: Cambridge University Press), 101–26.

1
Strawson on False Presupposition and the Assertive Enterprise

Anne Bezuidenhout

1. Introduction

Strawson's view of presupposition has been assimilated to the view expressed by Frege (1892, 39–40). One often sees reference to the Frege-Strawson semantic conception of presupposition (e.g. Beaver and Geurts 2014, 9–12). According to this semantic conception, *p* is a presupposition of a sentence *S* if and only if the truth of *p* is a necessary condition for the truth or falsity of *S*, in the sense that the falsity of *p* means that *S* is neither true nor false. And indeed, in his 1950 essay 'On Referring', where Strawson first introduces his 'special and odd sense of "imply"', he writes: 'To say, "The king of France is wise" is, in some sense of "imply", to imply that there is a king of France' (Strawson 1950, 330). He goes on to claim that when we say in response to someone's utterance of 'The king of France is wise' that there is no king of France, we are not contradicting the statement that the king of France is wise or saying that it is false but rather 'giving a reason for saying that the question of whether it is true or false simply doesn't arise' (Strawson 1950, 330). Strawson wants to say that the sentence 'The king of France is wise' cannot be used in our current era to make an assertion. As he puts this in Strawson (1964), when we have a case of 'radical reference failure'—as we do with any attempt to use 'the king of France' in our current era—then the statement containing this description does not qualify for assessment as an assertion. '[I]t does not qualify for truth-or-falsity assessment at all. The whole assertive enterprise is wrecked by the falsity of its presupposition' (Strawson 1964, 106).[1]

In his 'Intellectual Autobiography', Strawson (1998, 7) says that he was surprised, although not displeased, to have his view referred to as the Frege-Strawson view of presupposition, as he had not read Frege's works at the time he wrote 'On Referring'. However, although there are parallels between Frege's and Strawson's

---

[1] As Soames (1989, 562) points out, there seem to be two notions of presupposition at play here; a logical and an expressivist one. The logical conception is Frege's semantic conception. The expressivist one places conditions on sentences for their felicitous assertive use. Strawson himself recognized this dual use of the notion of presupposition, as I will show in Section 2.

views, there are also differences. Strawson's views are tied to a conception of language-in-use whereas Frege's views are less obviously geared to the idea of 'an assertive enterprise' and to the idea of tailoring one's conversational contributions in a way that makes the assertive enterprise go smoothly. I shall show that Strawson's view of presupposition is intended to fit into a larger picture of the way in which conversational participants are engaged in 'conversational tailoring', which is a term I borrow from Grice (1981, 1989) and use to describe people's attempts to design their utterances in such a way as to focus on some issues and put others into the conversational background.

This aspect of Strawson's view is most clearly on display in his discussion of cases where the falsity of a presupposition does *not* wreck the assertive enterprise. Strawson gives 'The Exhibition was visited yesterday by the king of France' as an example where the assertive enterprise is not wrecked by radical reference failure, and in fact leads to a false assertion (Strawson 1964, 112). I develop arguments from Bezuidenhout (2010, 2016) to show how Strawson deals with such cases. I show, contrary to the claims of Atlas (2004) and Von Fintel (2004), that Strawson is not committed to a naive reliance on a topic-comment distinction. Strawson does not hold that false presuppositions wreck the assertive enterprise when and only when the presupposition trigger is used in topic position in a sentence.

Strawson's discussion of presupposition is largely confined to the case of the existence presuppositions associated with uses of definite descriptions and other referring expressions whose function is to provide identifying reference. He does not discuss the host of other expressions that other scholars have argued are presupposition triggers (e.g. factive verbs such as 'know', aspectual verbs such as 'stop', adverbs such as 'even' and 'too', it-cleft constructions). And he does not engage with the debate about presupposition projection that has been at the heart of discussions of presupposition for decades. I argue that this is because of Strawson's enduring and special interest in the subject-predicate distinction and in what he regards as the basic function of subject expressions, namely, to provide identifying reference to an entity that the predicate will then go on to say something about. Thus, it is natural that he would focus on the preconditions for the use of basic subject expressions, such as definite descriptions, demonstratives, and proper names.

In support of my claim that Strawson is interested the way in which we structure information in conversation, I will also refer to discussions in his book *Subject and Predicate in Logic and Grammar*, and in particular to his discussion of the notion of 'degrees of identificatory force' (Strawson 1974, 104–10), which he uses to explain why it would be more normal to describe a scene by saying 'A chair was overturned' than to say 'An overturned thing was a chair'. This book did not receive very favourable reviews when it first appeared (see e.g. McGinn 1978; Moravcsik 1976, 1981; Zemach 1981). Critics objected to its ontological commitment to individuals, to its characterization of modern logic as founded on the subject-predicate distinction, to its aprioristic speculations about the grammars of natural languages, and to the claim that the subject-predicate distinction is at the heart of such grammars. See Strawson (1981) for some replies to his critics. However, even if we have reasons to be sceptical of the book's larger project, Strawson does provide some interesting observations and discussions along the way.

I will argue that Strawson's observations can be connected to more contemporary discussions of information structuring in language (e.g. Birner 2013; Lambrecht 1994), the topic-focus distinction (Kadmon 2001), the distinction between sentence-level topic and discourse topic (Asher 2004; Reinhart 1981), and other discussions of ways in which information can be made at-issue or backgrounded, depending on one's conversational purposes (Abbott 2000; Lasersohn 1993; Schlenker 2008).

2. Moving Beyond 'On Referring'

If one confines one's reading of Strawson to his 1950 essay 'On Referring', it is easy to think that the debate between Russell and Strawson is about the most adequate formal representation of definite descriptions and about whether sentences containing such expressions express singular or general propositions. Are definite descriptions of the form 'the F' singular referring expressions, as they appear to be on the surface? Or are they incomplete symbols that only have meaning in the context of a complete sentence whose underlying form contains no expression purporting to refer to the F but only quantifiers, variables, and predicate expressions (or if it contains unanalysed singular terms, these refer to something other than the F, as would be the case for the Russellian analysis of 'The man visited John')? A great deal of subsequent work has been taken up with people arguing about whose view is correct. One argument is that Russell was correct about some uses (the attributive ones) and Strawson about others (the referential ones). Another line of reasoning claims that Russell's and Strawson's views can be accommodated in a single framework, since the Russellian general proposition captures what was said, whereas the Strawsonian singular proposition is a conversational implicature that arises in certain contexts. The *loci classici* of these two lines of reasoning are of course Donnellan (1966) and Kripke (1977) respectively.

Russell (1905) introduced his Theory of Descriptions to handle the cases in which there is no F or more than one F, as these appear to present problems for the view that definite descriptions are referring terms. Russell can say that the sentence 'The present King of France is wise' is false because it expresses a false proposition, namely that there is one and only one thing that currently reigns France and is wise. Those who hold that 'the F' is a referring expression, such as Frege (1892), have to say the sentence is neither true nor false, since the description lacks a referent. This failure of reference induces a truth-value gap. (One could try to preserve bivalence by positing subsistent but non-existent objects, as did Meinong (1904), but Russell is dismissive of such ontological profligacy.) The debate about truth-value gaps is also one that continues to the present day. Russell's view is not inevitable, as there are many responses available to someone who wants to preserve the idea that definite descriptions are referring terms. One could, as Frege proposed, supply dummy referents for non-referring terms, or one could accept the idea that truth functions are partial and are undefined in cases where the referring term has no referent, or one could give up the principle of bivalence and opt for a three-valued logic.

However, if one follows Strawson's development of his ideas beyond his 1950 essay 'On Referring', neither of these debates is one that Strawson seems much inclined to participate in.[2] One of the important points Strawson (1950) insists on is that referring and asserting are things people do by using referring terms or uttering sentences in contexts. Moreover, there are presuppositions for the felicitous use of definite descriptions and singular referring expressions more generally, including demonstratives, names, and pronouns (Strawson 1950, 14, 16). When these presuppositions fail, the description cannot be used to refer and hence sentences containing that description cannot be used to make true or false assertions. To use a way of talking from a later essay, we can say that the assertive enterprise will be wrecked in such cases (Strawson 1964, 84).

Strawson (1964) mentions the fact that scholars of language can have different interests. Some are interested in 'actual speech situations', while others take a more impersonal view of language 'in which the actual needs, purposes, and presumptions of speakers and hearers are of slight significance' (Strawson 1964, 109–10). It is clear that Strawson thinks his important contributions belong to a theory of actual language use. He blames himself for running together the debate about truth-value gaps on the one hand with a debate about the conversational function of definite expressions on the other. He writes:

> I feel bound to labour the point a little, since I may be partly responsible for the confusion of these two issues by making the word 'presupposition' carry simultaneously the burden both of the functional distinction and of the truth-value gap theory.   (Strawson 1964, 107–8)

Russell of course belongs to the camp of scholars who talk about true and false sentences and their underlying logical forms and who are unconcerned about how

---

[2] Strawson (1964, 108–9) does very briefly discuss some short arguments both pro and con the truth-value gap theory. He concludes that it is 'just an illusion to think that ether side's position can be carried by such swift little sallies as these' (Strawson 1964, 109).

definite descriptions function in actual speech situations.[3] However, were one to propose a Russellian view of the conversational function of definite descriptions, one would have to say that speakers can use them in the context of a sentence of the form 'The F is G' to make what Strawson calls a 'uniquely existential assertion'—i.e. an assertion that there is one and only one F and it is G. However, Strawson thinks it is clear that this is *not* the function of definite descriptions in ordinary discourse. On the contrary, speakers use them in appropriate conversational contexts to invoke identifying knowledge of these entities in their listeners, thereby enabling them to identify the speaker's reference. Such identifying references therefore presuppose that one's listeners already have (or can be presumed to have) knowledge of the existence of such entities. (I will be qualifying and elaborating on this in the following section.) If listeners already know of the existence of the (conversationally unique) F, it would be redundant to assert that there is one and only one F.

Snowdon and Gomes (2021, 7) give a nice example to illustrate Strawson's point. If you and your family are standing in front of your familiar family car and you say 'The car won't start', it does not seem that you are asserting that there is one and only one car (and that it won't start). Snowdon and Gomes (2021) go on to note that Strawson's objection collapses if it is not an implication of Russell's theory that 'The F is G' asserts that there is one and only one F. However, as noted in the previous paragraph, Russell himself was not in the camp of those interested in the 'assertive enterprise', and hence I was careful to attribute the implication not to Russell himself (or his view as articulated in 'On Denoting') but to someone who wants to adopt a Russellian perspective on the assertive enterprise. Against such a view, Strawson has a strong case.

Is there anyone who has explicitly proposed such a conversational function for definite descriptions (namely, that their function is to make uniquely existential assertions)? Someone who comes close to this is Grice (1989). He suggests that the unique existence of an F is a part of what is asserted by the utterance of 'The F is G'. However, when one opts to express oneself using the form 'The F is G', the claim of unique existence is backgrounded.[4] One can background this information if one assumes that it is uncontroversial or is unlikely to be challenged. The main point of one's utterance (what these days would be called the 'at-issue' content) is the fact that this uniquely existing thing has the property expressed by the

---

[3] The editors pointed me to an apt quote from Russell's (1957) response to Strawson. In this essay, Russell states clearly that he is not interested in analysing the circumstances under which it would be correct to assert a sentence containing a definite description. Instead, he writes, he is 'concerned to find a more accurate and analyzed thought to replace the somewhat confused thoughts which most people at most times have in their heads' (Russell 1957, 388).

[4] It is oxymoronic to talk of a backgrounded assertion. What is asserted is normally equated with the 'at-issue' or foregrounded content. This is why I hedged and said that Grice's view comes close to claiming that the conversational function of definite descriptions is to make uniquely existential assertions.

predicate 'is G'. If one thought the claim about the unique existence of an F might be challenged or was somehow controversial, one would opt for an alternative way of expressing oneself. One would say: 'There is a unique F and it is G'. A view similar to Grice's has more recently been proposed by Schlenker (2008). I will say more about this in the final section below.

3. The Assertive Enterprise and Presumptions of Knowledge and Ignorance

In the previous section I argued that Strawson's main interest in definite descriptions concerns their function in the assertive enterprise. He wishes to separate this from more formal concerns, such as the truth-value gap theory. He thinks that one can in principle reject the truth-value gap theory and still maintain his view that definite descriptions function to invoke identifying knowledge (Strawson 1964, 108). In this section I will elaborate on Strawson's notion of identifying knowledge.

Strawson assumes that assertive discourse has the primary purpose to inform one's interlocutors on some matter. (Of course, it may have other purposes too.) Such discourse is governed by several principles. Two of these are given below (a third will be introduced in Section 5):

PPI: The principle of the presumption of ignorance
PPK: The principle of the presumption of knowledge

If one rationale for making an assertion is to inform one's audience of something, one must be assuming that the audience antecedently lacks this knowledge—one is presuming ignorance. On the other hand, if one is informing them, they must know what it is one is informing them about—they must be able to identify the thing/event/situation that one's assertion is about.[5]

Strawson (1964) is interested in the special case in which a speaker invokes identifying knowledge in the audience by means of the use of a referring expression. This class of expression includes 'proper names, definite and possessive and demonstrative descriptions, demonstrative and personal pronouns' (Strawson 1964, 99). In his 1974 book *Subject and Predicate in Logic and Grammar*, Strawson calls these 'i-words' and talks of their use in acts of *individually identifying* (i.i.) substantiation (Strawson 1974, 100), since he wants to contrast this case with instances of *non*-individually identifying substantiation. I will say more about this later view in Section 6.

---

[5] Strawson is going to distinguish a weaker and a stronger sense of aboutness (Strawson 1964, 116–17). I will return to this in Section 5.

Strawson assumes that the speaker's choice of expression will depend on factors such as whether the entity to be identified is in the audience's current field of perception, whether the entity can be singled out in context by means of a description, or whether the entity is (known to be) known to the audience by name (Strawson 1964, 98).[6] Strawson also wishes to include cases in which it may not strictly be true that the audience has antecedent knowledge of the existence of a thing that can simply be invoked by the speaker's use of a referring expression. He has in mind cases where the listener has not yet noticed something in their field of perception but where a speaker can focus the listener's attention on the thing by the use of an appropriate referring expression (Strawson 1964, 100). We might say that in such cases, instead of *invoking* identifying knowledge, the speaker *evokes* identifying knowledge. Strawson puts this by saying that the speaker has brought it about that the audience can see for themselves that there is such an entity. These are cases in which some entity is mutually perceptually manifest to speaker and audience, in the sense of Sperber and Wilson (1986/1995, 39).

There is another sort of case that Strawson (1964) wants to include under the heading of identifying reference that he describes as follows: 'There are cases in which an audience cannot exactly be credited with knowledge of the existence of a certain item unique in a certain respect, but can be credited with a strong presumption to this effect' (Strawson 1964, 100). He does not give an example of what he has in mind by this sort of 'presumed presumption [of knowledge]' (Strawson 1964, 100). He might have in mind something along the lines of the presumed social knowledge that Clark (1992) claims interlocutors share in virtue of being socially co-present with one another.

Clark (1992) argues that in conversation we operate with 'co-presence heuristics' that allow us to make assumptions about the knowledge we share with our interlocutors. See also Clark and Marshall (1978). This includes what we share in virtue of being physically, linguistically, and socially co-present with each other. The case of knowledge evocation described above would be a case of some entity being available for an identifying reference because the speaker and audience are physically co-present. When the speaker and audience are linguistically co-present, entities already mentioned in the prior discourse can be assumed to be available for identifying reference. Clark (1992) also thinks that a speaker is entitled to make certain assumptions about what is already known to the audience on the basis of their social co-presence. For example, if the speaker and the audience are all faculty members in a departmental faculty meeting, the speaker will be licensed in assuming that the audience knows of the existence of some faculty policy that was decided on in the past. Possibly some junior faculty

---

[6] This idea that there are apt expressions to use in order to invoke identifying knowledge in the listener bears a family resemblance to the Givenness Hierarchy argued for by Gundel et al. (1993).

members were not involved in the earlier policy decision and others may have forgotten about it entirely. However, as faculty members they are obliged to inform themselves of policies governing them *qua* faculty members and that is why the speaker can presume knowledge of this particular policy.

4. Information Structure and the Contrast between Given and New Information

Strawson had an abiding interest in the subject-predicate distinction and in arguing that it (or its generalized version) is fundamental to the grammar of natural languages such as English. Arguing for this is one of Strawson's (1974) main aims. However, he argued for this in the special case of sentences containing referring expressions in many of his writings, including several of the essays collected in *Logico-Linguistic Papers* (1971). Strawson (1964, 110) argues that sentences containing referring expressions consist of two parts—the subject term and the predicate term. The subject term makes an identifying reference to an entity and the predicate term says something about that individual.

In light of the discussion in the previous section about the principles of knowledge and ignorance (PPK and PPI), we could say that the subject term presents an entity that is 'given' or 'presupposed' in the conversational context and the predicate term then presents information that is 'new' about this entity. Strawson does not himself mention the contrast between given and new information, although of course he does use the term 'presupposition'. He also uses the term 'topic' and notes that 'it often is the case that the placing of an expression at the beginning of the sentence, in the position of grammatical subject, serves, as it were, to announce the statement's topic' (Strawson 1964, 118). Strawson (1974, 139) speculates that the topic-comment distinction found in linguistics is related to the subject-predicate distinction. Since the notions of topic and aboutness play a rather large role in Strawson's (1964) discussion of cases of 'radical reference failure', and since Strawson (1974) indicates that he was aware of work in linguistics on the topic-comment distinction, I think is it useful to relate Strawson's ideas to discussions about information structure in language that were taking place in linguistics at the time.

Clark and Haviland (1977) discuss what they call the given-new contract or strategy, whereby speakers structure their utterances into two informational units. One unit contains information the speaker assumes the audience will take as 'given' and the other contains information that it is assumed the audience will take as 'new'. What is 'given' includes what can easily be inferred in context by means of a bridging inference. Thus, one will not violate the given-new contract by uttering something such as: 'A thief broke into a house. He tip-toed down the passageway towards the back of the house.' Even though the passageway has not previously been mentioned, it is inferable on the basis of a mental frame of the layout of a typical house that will be invoked in the minds of the audience at the speaker's initial mention of a house.

Clark (1992) attributes the given-new distinction to Halliday (1967), who writes that 'we can say that the system of information focus assigns to the information unit a structure in terms of the two functions "given" and "new"' (Halliday 1967, 204), where the 'new' is what is marked out as being the informative part of a message. He also mentions that what is new need not correspond to an element of the message's cognitive content. He writes: 'The focal information may be a feature of mood, not of cognitive content, as when the speaker confirms an asserted proposition; but the confirmation is itself still "new" in the sense intended' (Halliday 1967, 204). Halliday goes on to argue that his theme-rheme distinction is more fundamental and is not co-extensive with the given-new distinction, although he admits that the partial congruence between these two distinctions and the fact that information units often line up with clauses means that there is 'a tendency towards a left to right form of organization in the information unit with given, if present, preceding new' (Halliday 1967, 205). Halliday also prefers not to use the topic-comment distinction because he thinks that 'topic' has been 'used in a way which conflates what are here regarded as distinct functions, with "topic" meaning both "given" and "theme"' (Halliday 1967, 200).

Clark (1992) also mentions a similar distinction between 'old' and 'new' information in the writings of Chafe (1970) and Kuno (1972) and a related distinction between 'presupposition' and 'focus' in the writings of Akmajian (1973) and Jackendoff (1972). Thus, there was intense interest in the 1960s and 1970s in information structure and in the ways in which speakers design their utterances. Even though Strawson was not an active participant in these debates, his concerns with the 'assertive enterprise' are, I believe, helpfully framed as his grappling with ways in which people structure their conversational contributions so as to highlight what is new/informative and put what is old/presupposed in the background.

5. Radical Reference Failure, Topic-Hood, and Aboutness

We saw in Section 2 that Strawson wants to separate the truth-value gap theory from an account of the function of definite descriptions to invoke identifying knowledge. As one illustration of how these come apart, he discusses cases of 'radical reference failure' which do not result in truth-value gaps but instead result in false assertions. He provides the following two illustrations, where we are to assume that Jones and the Exhibition exist but that there is no local swimming pool and there is no present King of France (Strawson 1964, 112):

24 ANNE BEZUIDENHOUT

1. <u>Jones</u> spent the morning at *the local swimming pool*.
2. The <u>Exhibition</u> was visited yesterday by *the King of France*.

(1) and (2) are judged to be false because of the non-existence of the local swimming pool and the present King of France respectively. Strawson notes that in each of these cases, there is both an 'innocent' (underlined) and a 'guilty' (italicized) referring expression (Strawson 1964, 111).[7] He says that one explanation for why we judge (1) and (2) to be false is that the guilty referring expression has been absorbed into the predicate. For instance, (1) is a perfectly fine assertion about Jones but it is false because the predicate fails to apply to Jones. However else Jones spent his morning, he certainly didn't spend it at a non-existent local pool (Strawson 1964, 112).

Strawson goes on immediately to note that this appeal to the idea of absorbing a guilty referring expression into the predicate is not general enough. We want an account that can apply even in cases where there are not two referring expressions, one innocent and one guilty. As a first step he introduces the notion of a question which represents an 'antecedent centre of interest' (Strawson 1964, 113). This seems to be very similar to the notion of a question-under-discussion (QUD) that has been popularized by Roberts (2012). For instance, in some context we might be interested in the question 'What contemporary bald notables are there?' If someone replies 'The King of France is bald', we can say this is a false answer to a legitimate question. Yet, here we have a sentence with a single referring expression and a question that contains no referring expressions (unless one counts 'contemporary' as an indexical expression). Looking back at sentences (1) and (2), we can say that they too involve a centre of interest that can be formulated as a question: e.g. 'How did Jones spend his morning?' and 'What notables have visited the Exhibition?' respectively.

Strawson then attempts to make the point even more general by decoupling the notion of a centre of interest from the notion of a question. He writes: 'I used the hypothesis of a *question* to bring out, with some unnatural sharpness, the idea of a topic or centre of interest of a statement, the idea of what a statement could be said to be about' (Strawson 1964, 114, his emphasis.) In order to flesh out this concept of aboutness that he is interested in, he introduces a third principle (alongside the already mentioned PPI and PPK discussed in Section 2 above):

PR: The Principle of Relevance

This principle captures the 'platitude' that 'we do not, except in social desperation, direct isolated and unconnected pieces of information at each other, but on the

---

[7] There are also other referring expressions, namely 'the morning' and 'yesterday', but Strawson is ignoring them as they are not immediately relevant to the point he is making.

contrary intend in general to give or add information about what is a matter of standing or current interest or concern' (Strawson 1964, 115). It is not exactly clear how this moves much beyond Strawson's question formulation of topic/aboutness. One way in which it might be a generalization is that it can capture the notion of a discourse topic rather than confining ourselves to the topic of a single statement. This might help Strawson to avoid one sort of objection that has been raised against him.

Horn (1996), Atlas (2004), and Von Fintel (2004) all construe Strawson as arguing that all and only topical expressions carry presuppositions. This entails that if an expression is non-topical it lacks presuppositions. Hence, the assertive enterprise will not be wrecked if these non-topical expressions fail to refer. By the question test, 'the local swimming pool' and 'the King of France' in (1) and (2) above are non-topical and that is why (1) and (2) are false rather than neither true nor false. The objection to this account is that we can come up with examples in which an expression is topical and yet the assertive enterprise is not wrecked. An example along the lines of one given by Von Fintel (2004, 324) is as follows:

3. I had breakfast with the King of France yesterday. The king had eggs and toast.

By Strawson's question test applied at the sentence-level, the first sentence of (3) would be false, as the speaker would be the topic. However, Von Fintel thinks that by the time we get to the second sentence, 'the King' will have become the topic and hence the radical reference failure of this expression should wreck the assertive enterprise. Von Fintel's intuitions are that the second sentence is just as false as the first one and for the same reason (namely, the non-existence of the King of France).

If we appeal to PR instead of the question test, there may be a way of avoiding this alleged counterexample. Suppose that it is a matter of current or standing interest to us whether there are any current notables who have modest lifestyles. If you utter (3) in an attempt to address this interest of ours, we will say the whole conversational contribution is false. By this discourse-level test, the first sentence of (3) would not be about the speaker but rather would be more on the order of the speaker purporting to be in a position to give a first-hand account of a notable with modest tastes.[8]

---

[8] One could also argue that the assertive enterprise will indeed be wrecked by the time one reaches the second sentence of (3) because if one judged the first part to be false on the grounds of the non-existence of the King of France, there will be no individual who can be identified as the eater of the eggs and toast. See Bezuidenhout (2016) for an extended defence of Strawson and a discussion and critique of the alternative views of so-called non-catastrophic presupposition failure by Horn (2002), Lasersohn (1993), Atlas (2004), and Von Fintel (2004).

Further evidence that Strawson intends his notion of topic to apply at the discourse level comes from his discussion of an example he gives in Strawson (1954). In reference to the sentence 'My friend went for a drive with the King of France', he writes: 'the existence of a king of France is not, in this example, a presupposition *of the whole discussion*, as is the existence of the friend whose exploits I am recounting' (Strawson 1954, 230, my emphases).

Strawson complicates matters somewhat by distinguishing two ways of specifying a statement's topic that he labels Type 1 and Type 2 cases. A Type 1 case is one in which the topic of a statement containing a referring expression is specified by using that very referring expression. A Type 2 case is one in which the topic of a statement containing a referring expression is specified without purporting to refer to the entity (if any) that is picked out by that referring expression. An example of Type 1 would be to say that Jones is the topic of (1). Here we would be using the referring expression 'Jones' to specify the topic of a sentence containing that very expression. An example of Type 2 would be to say that the topic of 'The King of France is bald' concerns which bald notables there are. We have not used the term 'the King of France' to specify the topic.

The complication concerns what happens when we have a Type 1 case in which we try to specify the topic using a 'guilty' or 'peccant' referring term (Strawson 1964, 117). Strawson says that the reference failure 'affects the topic itself'. Hence, the statement 'cannot really have the topic it is intended to have' (Strawson 1964, 116). He thinks this may seem contradictory. We want to use this term to specify what seems to be the topic, but in so doing we are forced to say that there is no such topic. Strawson thinks the way out of this is to admit that there are two sorts of aboutness or topic-hood, a weaker and a stronger sort. A Type 1 case with a peccant referring expression is about something in the weak sense but not in the strong sense. For example, because it is not about anything in the strong sense, an out-of-the-blue utterance of 'The King of France is bald' will not make a truth-evaluable assertion. This is a case 'favourable to the truth-value gap theory' (Strawson 1964, 117).

Strawson's weak sense of aboutness can be construed as fictional aboutness. Strawson (1950) discusses fictional cases and writes: 'it is perfectly natural and correct to say that some of the statements in *Pickwick Papers* are *about* Mr Pickwick' (Strawson 1950, 13, his emphasis). He originally called such uses of referring expressions 'spurious', although a note added later indicates that he thinks it better to call such uses 'secondary'. At any rate, he thinks we are not confused about such cases. If someone uttered the sentence 'The King of France is wise and he lives in a golden castle and has a hundred wives' we would understand that the speaker is not talking about a particular individual in the strong sense nor making a false statement to the effect that such an individual exists (Strawson 1950, 13).

Strawson (1964) ends by providing a 'recipe' for deciding what a statement is about in both the weak and strong senses. The recipe requires us to describe the speech situation in which the statement was produced (Strawson 1964, 117). This will yield a description of what the statement is about in at least the weak sense and if the description contains no peccant referring expressions, it will also yield a description of what it is about in the strong sense. For example, we might describe the speech situation in which (1) is produced as follows:

4. The speaker was describing how Jones spent his morning.

Since 'Jones' refers to an existing individual, (4) tells us what (1) is about in the strong sense. Similarly, one might describe the speech situation I imagined for (3) as in (5) below, and hence (3) would count as being strongly about a notable with modest tastes, since this description contains no peccant referring expression. On the other hand, an out of the blue utterance of (6) below will yield a description of the speech situation in (7) and since this contains a peccant referring expression, (7) merely tells us what (6) is about in a weak sense:

5. The speaker was giving an instance of a notable with modest tastes.
6. The King of France is wise.
7. The speaker was saying what the King of France is like.

I have tried to argue that Strawson's interests lie in characterizing the 'assertive enterprise'. He thinks it is governed by principles such as PPI, PPK, and PR. Interlocutors share knowledge about centres of interest and this shapes their conversational contributions, determining what will be treated as the topic of their discourse about which knowledge can be presumed and what will count as the 'new' information that is asserted. In the following section I give a brief account of the notion of identificatory force that Strawson introduces in his 1974 book *Subject and Predicate in Logic and Grammar*. I will argue this this too shows that Strawson has an interest in information structuring in language use.

6. Degrees of Identificatory Force

Strawson (1974, chap. 4) introduces the notion of identificatory force. Strawson's overall project in the book is to argue that sentences of the types of languages whose grammars he takes himself to be laying bare 'involve the combination of substantiation in some mode with complementary predication of some kind' (Strawson 1974, 120). He connects the notion of the grammatical subject of a sentence to the substantiating part of a sentence. A special case of substantiation is *individually identifying* (i.i.) substantiation (Strawson 1974, 100). Typically, so-called 'i-words' are used for this purpose. This class of words includes proper names, demonstratives (including complex ones such as 'that fat cat'), and definite descriptions.

However, there are also cases of *non*-individually identifying (non-i.i.) substantiation. To mark the fact that the hearer is not supposed to have identifying knowledge of any particular object, we use indefinite expressions, such as 'a man' and 'some students'. In cases where the speaker herself lacks identifying knowledge of a particular, an expression such as 'a thing' or 'a person or persons unknown' can be used. Non-i.i. substantiation does not always use sortal expressions such as 'man' or 'student'. We might use an indefinite determiner together with an adjectival expression, as in 'a heavy round thing' or 'something red', to characterize the entity of concern.

Strawson's view is that we have here a gradation in identificatory force from strongest to weakest, as illustrated in Figure 1.1.

i-words have the greatest identificatory force, indefinites using sortals have less identificatory force than i-words, indefinites with non-sortals even less force again, and bare indefinites the least force. The reason that [indefinite determiner + sortal] has more identificatory force than [indefinite determiner + adjectival] is that sortals (count nouns) are terms of divided reference (unlike mass nouns, e.g.) and hence are useful for facilitating the listener's identificatory task. Adjectivals have some identificatory force, Strawson thinks, because they express features or characteristics or dispositions of objects that endure beyond the situation being talked about. These enduring features can be helpful to the listener in accessing the identifying knowledge required to interpret the speaker's utterance.[9]

Strawson believes that the properties of things that they have in passing are not good candidates for invoking identifying knowledge. Thus, if I become aware of something round flying past my head, I am likely to report this by saying:

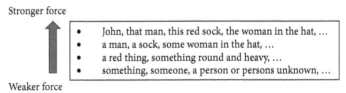

Figure 1.1 Strawson's Identificatory Force Hierarchy

---

[9] Strawson (1974, 135–8) discusses the mass-count distinction. He argues that terms referring to stuff, such as 'water', 'milk', and 'rice', 'present no very strong resistance to assimilation in our substantiating grammar' (Strawson 1974, 136). They have a role in 'feature-placing' sentences such as 'There is gold here', which Strawson proposes to handle much in the way he handles sentences with plural sortal expressions, such as 'Some men are here'. He also thinks we can easily accommodate uses such as 'This water is brackish' and uses of such terms to name *types* of stuff, as in 'Water is thirst-quenching' and 'Rice is grown in South Carolina'. These last two examples are cases of what Strawson calls 'generalized subjection' and are no different in function from sentences such as 'Humans will colonize Mars' or 'Students are poor'. It is not clear where on the Identificatory Force hierarchy these feature placing expressions are located, nor where the cases of generalized subjection would fall. I would assume they fall somewhere in the middle of the range.

'A round thing sped by me' rather than by saying 'A thing that sped by me was round', even if these two sentences have the same truth-conditions. The expression 'thing that sped by me' is what Strawson would call an 'undergoing-specifying term' (Strawson 1974, 136). However, if you were a witness to the event, I might say to you: 'That thing that sped by me was a gun pellet.' In other words, in a situation of shared visual awareness, these passing features can play an identificatory role, presumably because we are mutually aware of them.

What Strawson seems to be concerned with here is the idea of information packaging. We package our messages in a way that helps our interlocutors to access the identifying knowledge required to discern what it is we are talking about and what new information we are trying to impart. This is not simply a matter of presenting given information before new, a trend in English information structure that Strawson (1964, 118) was aware of. The substantiating part of the sentence could contain information new to the interlocutor. Still, it will be understood to have identificatory force and hence to be playing a different role from any information introduced by the predicative part.[10]

Let us work through an illustrative example, inspired by some examples Strawson (1974, 106) gives of how we might describe the disorder of a room. He says we are likely to use sentences such as 'A chair was overturned', 'A bottle was lying on the floor', and 'A picture was broken', rather than saying 'An overturned thing was a chair', 'A thing lying on the floor was a bottle', and 'A broken thing was a picture'.

Suppose you are a witness for the prosecution in the trial of someone accused of murdering your boss, although the lawyer for the accused claims her client is innocent and that the deceased died of natural causes. The prosecutor is trying to make a case that the scene of the alleged crime showed signs of a physical struggle between the deceased and the alleged murderer. You are called as a witness and asked to describe the scene you confronted when you arrived at the office and discovered your boss's body. You say: 'The boss's name plate was upside down and pens and pencils were mixed up in the pencil holder.' Your boss was a neat freak

---

[10] An interesting further question that I will not pursue here is whether or not the identifying information needs to be true of the referent. Regarding the special case of definite descriptions, Bezuidenhout (2016, 26–7) argues that this identificatory information could be mistaken but that so long as it serves its identificatory role, it does not wreck the assertive enterprise. See Stalnaker (1999, 43) for a similar claim. Strawson (1974, 61–6) discusses several possible stances we might take in cases of mis-description. One view is that the referent is the one the speaker intended. A second view is that no proposition is expressed unless the speaker's intended referent actually fits the description. A third view is that if there is an object satisfying the description that it would be 'reasonable and natural' according to the conventions of language to take the speaker to be referring to in the context, that is the referent even if it was not the speaker's intended referent. The first view gives most weight to the speaker's referential intentions, while the third gives the most weight to the conventions of the language, with the second view falling somewhere in between. Strawson thinks it is a mistake to insist that one of these is the correct view, since it is a mistake 'to think that there must always be one correct way of fitting the facts of discourse into the framework of logic' (Strawson 1974, 65).

and would never have allowed things on his desk to be in disarray. Pens and pencils were always strictly separated into the two compartments of the pencil holder. So, maybe things were knocked off the desk in a struggle and the killer put them back hastily before fleeing the scene. This way of presenting your testimony makes sense of the scene and feeds into your justification for bringing up these things you observed.

A much less perspicuous way of describing the scene would be to say: 'An upside-down thing was the boss's nameplate and some mixed up things were pens and pencils.' Why? This is because you want the jurors to focus on the boss's nameplate and the pens and pencils on his desk, which they will probably assume have some rightful place, and then you disclose that in fact they were out of place, a sign that the killer may have tried to cover his tracks. If instead you focus on upside down and mixed-up things, this presupposes that the jurors already knew things were out of place but just didn't know which things had got displaced. This would not be a good way of presenting your testimony and would be likely to leave the jurors confused about the point you are trying to make.

This illustrates Strawson's notion of degrees of identificatory force. You are not expecting that the jurors will have antecedent identifying knowledge of the boss's nameplate or the pens and pencils on the boss's desk. That there was a nameplate and a pencil holder on the boss's desk will be discourse-new information to the jurors, just as will the information that these things were misplaced. Still, the identificatory force of the nameplate and the pens and pencils is greater than the identificatory force of their displacement. The jurors already know the boss's body was discovered in the boss's office and they will likely already have conjured up an image of an office with a stereotypical desk with a nameplate and pens and pencils and other such things arranged in some stereotypical way. So, the boss's nameplate and the pens and pencils on the boss's desk are already 'given' in the sense of being inferable (see Section 4). The significant new information to the jurors will be that these things were in fact not in their proper places. Mentioning the disarray first will be less effective. For one thing, it could invoke an image of a stereotypical office crime scene—furniture knocked over, papers strewn all over the floor, desk drawers hanging open, etc. The subsequent mention of pens and pencils and nameplates in the wrong place will seem rather deflationary.

The fact that the nameplate and pens and pencils have a degree of identificatory force greater than their being in disarray isn't simply a matter of concrete *things* being more identifiable than concrete *situations*. For one thing, if I am right, the courtroom narrative will bring an office scenario to the minds of the jurors, with images of a desk and things like nameplates and pens and pencils arranged on its top. So, the mention of objects already invokes a situation.

Moreover, there may be other contexts in which these things have the opposite degrees of identificatory force. Suppose you are a criminology student and your professor is discussing a famous murder case which was cracked because some things at the murder scene were out of place and mixed up. She asks whether anyone in the class remembers what these out-of-place and mixed-up things were. You put up your hand and say: 'An out-of-place thing was the boss's nameplate and some mixed up things were the pens and pencils.'

The main take-away from this extended example is that we craft our conversational contributions in such a way as to make the audience's identificatory task easier and help them to discern the main point of our conversational contributions. The notion of identificatory force discussed in this section shows that Strawson (1974) was interested in generalizing the account of identifying reference that he had introduced in earlier writings, where his focus had been on i-words.

7. Connections to Contemporary Discussions of Discourse Structure

I have already mentioned some of the ways in which Strawson's views are connected to contemporary debates, especially debates about information structure and the organization of discourse. Contemporary debates about information structure go well beyond Strawson's ideas about sentences being structured into an identificatory part that presumes knowledge on the part of the audience and a predicative part that supplies new information. For one thing, there has been a great deal of work done on non-canonical sentence structures, such as ones involving left- or right-dislocation or clefting. See Birner (2013) and Birner and Ward (1998). The literature on focus structures is also large. For a sampling, see Rooth (1992), Lambrecht (1994), and Kadmon (2001). Others have investigated the role of prosody in marking information structure, including in non-Indo-European languages. See, e.g. Mithun (2014). Strawson was not able to see the full range of possibilities here because he relied solely on a priori methods and a rather impoverished diet of constructed examples.

In Section 4, I mentioned the connection between Strawson's work and some older work on the contrast between given and new information, such as the work of Halliday (1967), Clark and Haviland (1977), and Clark (1992). Strawson's ideas also resonate with the views of those interested in cognitive accounts of reference resolution. I mentioned Gundel et al.'s (1993) Givenness Hierarchy in this regard, since Strawson thinks that notions such as focus of attention in a visual field can play a role in getting an audience to identify the speaker's intended referent. Strawson's Identificatory Force hierarchy illustrated in Figure 1.1 is also reminiscent of the Givenness Hierarchy.

Strawson's ideas about centres of interest in discourse and their connection to the notion of topic-hood or aboutness can be connected to ideas in computational linguistics that attempt to model the way in which topics are identified and shift over the course of an evolving conversation. I have in mind the work of Grosz et al. (1995) on Centring Theory.

Strawson (1950) is often credited with introducing the notion of presupposition into late twentieth-century debates. As I mentioned in the introduction, Strawson's discussion of presupposition is largely confined to the case of the existence presuppositions associated with uses of definite descriptions, proper names, and other referring expressions whose function is to provide identifying reference. He does not discuss the host of other expressions that other scholars have argued are presupposition triggers (e.g. factive verbs such as 'know', aspectual verbs such as 'stop', adverbs such as 'even' and 'too', it-cleft constructions). And he does not engage with the debate about presupposition projection that has been at the heart of discussions of presupposition for decades. See Beaver and Geurts (2014) for a summary of the contemporary debate.

As we have seen, Strawson's enduring interest was in the subject-predicate distinction (and in subjection and predication in their most general forms). Many of his writings (e.g. the essays collected in *Logico-Linguistic Papers*) focus on basic sentences containing singular referring expressions. He regards the function of such referring expressions to be the making of an identifying reference to an entity that the predicate will then go on to say something about. Thus, it is natural that he would focus on the preconditions for the use of basic subject expressions, such as definite descriptions, demonstratives, and proper names. Many contemporary writings contain discussions and defences of a Strawsonian presuppositional approach to definite descriptions. See Elbourne (2013) and Coppock and Beaver (2015).

Strawson's idea that topics can be revealed by framing them as questions is connected to current discussions of the notion of a question-under-discussion (QUD). This literature in turn is connected to discussions of at-issue versus backgrounded content and to views that connect presuppositions to background information. See Abbott (2000), Roberts (2012), and Tonhauser et al. (2013).

In Section 2, I also mentioned the work by Grice (1981, 1989) and Schlenker (2008) on conversational tailoring. Grice's Conversational Tailoring principle (Grice 1989, 273, 276) constrains speakers to choose a form of expression that focuses their audience on those aspects of their claims that they deem the most likely to be challenged. Those aspects that are deemed to have common ground status will not be emphasized. For information to have common ground status in Grice's sense is just for it to be non-controversial, i.e. to be information that the listener will accept on the speaker's say-so, without challenge. It needn't be information that the hearer already possesses. Thus, when speakers choose the contracted form 'The F is not G' as opposed to the full Russellian expansion 'There is a unique F and it is G', they implicate that there is a unique F, since the contracted form in effect treats the implication of unique existence as having common ground status. This implication thus escapes the scope of operators such as negation.

My aim in connecting Strawson's ideas to these contemporary debates is to show that Strawson's ideas in the philosophy of language went well beyond the ideas introduced in 'On Referring' that he is most well-known for. His ideas ramify in many directions and thus it pays dividends to read some of Strawson's lesser-known works, such as his book *Subject and Predicate in Logic and Grammar*.

8. Conclusions

I hope to have shown a side of Strawson's work that goes beyond what most people will know about Strawson's contributions to the philosophy of language based on the essay 'On Referring'. I also hope to have made a case for Strawson's continuing relevance to many contemporary debates in the philosophy of language, as well as to current debates in linguistics (especially in semantics and pragmatics) and even to work in psychology and cognitive science on language processing (especially work on referential processing).

Strawson was disappointed with the reception his book *Subject and Predicate in Logic and Grammar* received when it was first published in 1974. There are probably several reasons for the lack of impact this work had. One gets the impression that Strawson saw himself in dialogue primarily with Quine and (early) Chomsky. However, it isn't clear that his arguments really engaged with either of their views.

Against Quine, Strawson suggests that first-order logic is inadequate to the task of representing the grammars of natural languages. He argues for an asymmetry between subject and predicate expressions, which mirrors an asymmetry between particulars and the concepts they fall under.[11] As we have already seen, along with the asymmetry between subjects and predicates, Strawson also makes a distinction in their roles in structuring assertive discourse. For example, if I say to you 'A man with a long grey ponytail dropped off this bag of tangerines for you', the information associated with the subject expression is intended to help you identify the man in question and has a different discourse status than the information associated with the predicate. In first-order logic, on the other hand, this distinction is erased and we have simply a statement that there is a thing that is simultaneously a man, has a

---

[11] Concepts come in incompatibility ranges with respect to the particulars that fall under them, whereas particulars do not come in incompatibility groups with respect to concepts. If something is red at time t_1 then it is not green at that time. However, it does not follow that if object a is red at t_1 that object b is not green at that time. Moreover, concepts stand in one-way entailment relations with respect to any particulars falling under them. Anything scarlet is red but not vice versa and anything that is red is coloured but not vice versa. On the other hand, individuals do not stand is such one-way relations to each other with respect to all the concepts they fall under. For instance, it is not the case that if object a is red, object b is coloured but not vice versa. See Strawson (1974, 18–20) and Strawson (1970).

long grey ponytail, and dropped off a bag of tangerines for you. However, this critique is unlikely to get much traction with Quine and his followers, who were interested in regimenting language for scientific purposes and not interested in the pragmatic principles governing the assertive enterprise.

Strawson (1974) takes it as part of his task to explore the grammars of natural languages. He indicates that he is following Chomsky's ideas about phrase structure rules. To this end he sketches a formalism that involves what he calls major and minor linkages and a system of bracketing to indicate these linkages that is vaguely reminiscent of the system of labelled bracketing that syntacticians use as an alternative to syntax trees to represent syntactic structure. However, his system will not have seemed to linguists at that time to yield a robust enough grammar formalism. Moreover, for those more interested in semantic and pragmatic questions, other formal approaches would have seemed more promising, such as Montague Grammar or File Change Semantics or Discourse Representation Theory (DRT). See Janssen and Zimmermann (2021) for an introduction to Montague Semantics, Heim (1983) for an account of File Change Semantics, and Kamp and Reyle (1993) for information about DRT.

Even though Strawson (1974) may not have directly shaped subsequent work on information structure and discourse organization, his book contains ideas related to these subsequent discussions that it is fruitful to explore. For me it was Strawson's idea of degrees of identificatory force that struck a chord. Many of Strawson's writings have this feature. For instance, 'On Referring' contains many nuggets that Strawson did not elaborate on but were subsequently explored in depth by others (such as the notions of incomplete definite descriptions and of referential uses of indefinites). That is what makes it such a pleasure to read his work, as one is sure to come away with valuable nuggets.

References

Abbott, Barbara (2000), 'Presuppositions as Non-Assertions', *Journal of Pragmatics* 32: 1419–37.

Akmajian, Adrian (1973), 'The Role of Focus in the Interpretation of Anaphoric Expressions', in Stephen R. Anderson and Paul Kiparsky (eds.), *A Festschrift for Morris Halle* (New York: Holt, Reinhart & Winston), 215–26.

Asher, Nicholas (2004), 'Discourse Topic', *Theoretical Linguistics* 30: 163–201.

Atlas, Jay (2004), 'Descriptions, Linguistic Topic/Comment and Negative Existentials', in Marga Reimer and Anne Bezuidenhout (eds.), *Descriptions and Beyond* (Oxford: Oxford University Press), 342–60.

Beaver, David, and Bart Geurts (2014), 'Presupposition', in *The Stanford Encyclopedia of Philosophy* (Winter 2021 Edition), Edward N. Zalta (ed.), https://plato.stanford.edu/archives/win2021/entries/presupposition/

Bezuidenhout, Anne (2010), 'Grice on Presupposition', in Klaus Petrus (ed.), *Meaning and Analysis: Themes from H. Paul Grice* (Basingstoke: Palgrave Macmillan), 75–102.

Bezuidenhout, Anne (2016), 'Presupposition Failure and the Assertive Enterprise', *Topoi* 35(1): 23–35.

Birner, Betty (2013), *Introduction to Pragmatics* (Oxford: Wiley-Blackwell).

Birner, Betty, and Gregory Ward (1998), *Information Status and Noncanonical Word Order in English* (Amsterdam: John Benjamins).

Chafe, Wallace (1970), *Meaning and the Structure of Language* (Chicago, IL: University of Chicago Press).

Clark, Herbert (1992), *Arenas of Language Use* (Chicago, IL: University of Chicago Press).

Clark, Herbert, and Susan Haviland (1977), 'Comprehension and the Given-New Contract', in Roy Freedle (ed.), *Discourse Production and Comprehension* (Norwood, NJ: Ablex), 1–40.

Clark, Herbert, and Catherine Marshall (1978), 'Reference Diaries', in David Waltz (ed.), *Theoretical Issues in Natural Language Processing 2* (New York: Association for Computing Machinery), 57–63.

Coppock, Elizabeth, and David Beaver (2015), 'Definiteness and Determinacy', *Linguistics & Philosophy* 38: 377–435.

Donnellan, Keith (1966), 'Reference and Definite Descriptions', *The Philosophical Review* 75(3): 281–304.

Elbourne, Paul (2013), *Definite Descriptions* (Oxford: Oxford University Press).

Frege, Gottlob (1892), 'Uber Sinn und Bedeutung', *Zeitschrift für Philosophie und philosophische Kritik* 100: 25–50.

Grice, Paul (1981), 'Presupposition and Conversational Implicature', in Peter Cole (ed.), *Radical Pragmatics* (New York: Academic Press), 183–98. Reprinted in *Studies in the Way of Words*, 269–82.

Grice, Paul (1989), *Studies in the Way of Words* (Cambridge, MA: Harvard University Press).

Grosz, Barbara, Aravind Joshi, and Scott Weinstein (1995), 'Centering: A Framework for Modeling the Local Coherence of Discourse', *Computational Linguistics* 21(2): 203–25.

Gundel, Jeanette, Nancy Hedberg, and Ron Zacharski (1993), 'Cognitive Status and the Form of Referring Expressions in Discourse', *Language* 69(2): 274–307.

Halliday, Michael Alexander Kirkwood (1967), 'Notes on Transitivity and Theme in English: II', *Journal of Linguistics* 3: 199–244.

Heim, Irene (1983), 'File Change Semantics and the Familiarity Theory of Definiteness', in Rainer Bäuerle, Christoph Schwarze, and Amim von Stechow (eds.), *Meaning, Use, and Interpretation of Language* (Berlin: De Gruyter), 164–89.

Horn, Laurence (1996), 'Presupposition and Implicature', in Shalom Lappin (ed.), *Handbook of Contemporary Semantic Theory* (Oxford: Blackwell), 299–319.

Horn, Laurence (2002), 'Assertoric Inertia and NPI Licensing', *Proceedings of the Chicago Linguistic Society* 38: 55–82.

Jackendoff, Ray (1972), *Semantic Interpretation in Generative Grammar* (Cambridge, MA: MIT Press).

Janssen, Theo, and Thomas Ede Zimmermann (2021), 'Montague Semantics', in *The Stanford Encyclopedia of Philosophy* (Summer 2021 Edition), Edward N. Zalta (ed.), https://plato.stanford.edu/archives/sum2021/entries/montague-semantics/

Kadmon, Nirit (2001), *Formal Pragmatics: Semantics, Pragmatics, Presupposition and Focus* (Oxford: Blackwell).

Kamp, Hans, and Uwe Reyle (1993), *From Discourse to Logic: Introduction to Model Theoretic Semantics of Natural Language, Formal Logic and Discourse Representation Theory* (Dordrecht: Springer).

Kripke, Saul (1977), 'Speaker's Reference and Semantic Reference', *Midwest Studies in Philosophy* 2: 255–76.

Kuno, Susumo (1972), 'Functional Sentence Perspective: A Case Study from Japanese and English', *Linguistic Inquiry* 3: 269–320.

Lambrecht, Knud (1994), *Information Structure and Sentence Form: Topic, Focus and the Mental Representations of Discourse Referents* (Cambridge: Cambridge University Press).

Lasersohn, Peter (1993), 'Existence Presuppositions and Background Knowledge', *Journal of Semantics* 10: 113–22.

McGinn, Colin (1978), 'Review of Strawson's *Subject and Predicate in Logic and Grammar*', *Mind* 87(345): 139–43.

Meinong, Alexius (1904), 'Über Gegenstandstheorie', in Alexius Meinong (ed.), *Untersuchungen zur Gegenstandstheorie und Psychologie* (Leipzig: J.A. Barth), 1–51. Translated (1960) as 'The Theory of Objects' in Roderick M. Chisholm (ed.), *Realism and the Background of Phenomenology* (Glencoe, IL: Free Press), 76–117.

Mithun, Marianne (2014), *Prosody and Information Structure: Segmentation, Integration, and in Between* (Amsterdam: John Benjamins).

Moravcsik, Julius M.E. (1976), 'Strawson on Predication', *Journal of Philosophy* 73(12): 329–48.

Moravcsik, Julius M.E. (1981), 'Universals and Particulars', *Philosophia* 10: 151–67.

Reinhart, Tanya (1981), 'Pragmatics and Linguistics: An Analysis of Sentence Topics', *Philosophica* 27: 53–94.

Roberts, Craige (2012), 'Information Structure in Discourse: Towards an Integrated Formal Theory of Pragmatics', *Semantics and Pragmatics* 5, Article 6: 1–69.

Rooth, Mats (1992), 'A Theory of Focus Interpretation', *Natural Language Semantics* 1(1): 75–116.

Russell, Bertrand (1905), 'On Denoting', *Mind* 14: 479–93.

Russell, Bertrand (1957), 'Mr. Strawson on Referring', *Mind* 66(263): 385–9.

Schlenker, Philippe (2008), '*Be Articulate*: A Pragmatic Theory of Presupposition Projection', *Theoretical Linguistics* 34: 157–212.

Snowdon, Paul, and Anil Gomes (2021), 'Peter Frederick Strawson', in *The Stanford Encyclopedia of Philosophy* (Summer 2021 Edition), Edward N. Zalta (ed.), https://plato.stanford.edu/entries/strawson

Soames, Scott (1989), 'Presupposition', in Dov Gabbay and Franz Guenthner (eds.), *Handbook of Philosophical Logic* (Dordrecht: Springer), 553–616.

Sperber, Dan and Deirdre Wilson (1986/1995), *Relevance: Communication and Cognition* (Oxford: Blackwell).

Stalnaker, Robert (1999), *Context and Content: Essays on Intentionality in Speech and Thought* (Oxford: Oxford University Press).

Strawson, Peter F. (1950), 'On Referring', *Mind* 59: 320–44. Reprinted in *Logico-Linguistic Papers*, 1–27.

Strawson, Peter F. (1954), 'A Reply to Mr. Sellars', *Philosophical Review* 63: 216–31.

Strawson, Peter F. (1964), 'Identifying Reference and Truth-Values', *Theoria* 30: 96–118. Reprinted in *Logico-Linguistic Papers*, 75–95.

Strawson, Peter F. (1970), 'The Asymmetry of Subjects and Predicates', in Howard E. Kiefer and Milton K. Munitz (eds.), *Language, Belief and Metaphysics* (Albany, NY: SUNY Press). Reprinted in *Logico-Linguistic Papers*, 96–115.

Strawson, Peter F. (1971), *Logico-Linguistic Papers* (London: Methuen).

Strawson, Peter F. (1974), *Subject and Predicate in Logic and Grammar* (London: Methuen).

Strawson, Peter F. (1981), 'Comments and Replies', *Philosophia* 10: 315–28.

Strawson, Peter F. (1998), 'Intellectual Autobiography', in Lewis Edwin Hahn (ed.), *The Philosophy of P. F. Strawson* (Chicago, IL: Open Court), 1–21.

Tonhauser, Judith, David Beaver, Craige Roberts, and Mandy Simons (2013), 'Toward a Taxonomy of Projective Content', *Language* 89(1): 66–109.

Von Fintel, Kai (2004), 'Would You Believe It? The King of France Is Back! (Presuppositions and Truth-Value Intuitions)', in Marga Reimer and Anne Bezuidenhout (eds.), *Descriptions and Beyond* (Oxford: Oxford University Press), 315–41.

Zemach, Eddy M. (1981), 'Names and Predicates', *Philosophia* 10: 217–23.

2
Meaning and Speech Acts

Ian Rumfitt

1. Introduction

On 5 November 1969, Peter Strawson delivered 'Meaning and Truth', his Inaugural Lecture at Oxford. Although more than fifty years have since elapsed, we are only beginning to come to terms with the approach to the theoretical study of language which Strawson then proposed. In this chapter,[*] I try to make some progress along the lines he indicated.

Strawson begins 'Meaning and Truth' by raising three constitutive questions about meaning. 'What is it for anything to have a meaning at all, in the way, or in the sense, in which words or sentences or signals have meaning? What is it for a particular sentence to have the meaning or meanings it does have? What is it for a particular phrase, or a particular word, to have the meaning or meanings it does have?' (Strawson 1970, 171). These are foundational questions which any adequate philosophy of language must address, but in his lecture Strawson only sketches his preferred answers to them. His chief concern, rather, is with a conflict, or apparent conflict, between two schools which take rival approaches to the questions. On one side in this 'Homeric struggle' we have the 'theorists of communication-intention', who seek to elucidate the concept of meaning by reference to speakers' 'audience-directed intentions of a certain complex kind' (Strawson 1970, 171). On the other side are the 'theorists of formal semantics', who explicate meaning by reference to syntactic and semantic rules. More specifically, their 'general idea... is that the syntactic and semantic rules together determine the meanings of all the sentences of a language and do this [in the case of declarative sentences] by means, precisely, of determining their truth-conditions' (Strawson 1970, 177).[1]

---

[*] Delivered as the Evert Willem Beth Memorial Lecture at the University of Amsterdam, 19 December 2019.

[1] According to Strawson, the only version of 'formal semantics' that 'has ever been seriously advanced or developed, or needs to be seriously considered,... rests on the notion of truth-conditions' (Strawson 1970, 176). One might wonder about semantic theories based on assertibility-conditions, which were being developed just up the Oxford High Street in All Souls College while Strawson was writing his lecture in Magdalen. However, I agree with Strawson that assertibility semantics—whatever its merits when applied to the languages of pure mathematics—does not in the end provide an adequate treatment of natural languages. See Rumfitt (2015, §5.4).

Ian Rumfitt, *Meaning and Speech Acts* In: *P. F. Strawson and his Philosophical Legacy*. Edited by: Sybren Heyndels, Audun Bengtson, and Benjamin De Mesel, Oxford University Press. © Oxford University Press 2024.
DOI: 10.1093/oso/9780192858474.003.0003

Strawson's choice of the term 'Homeric struggle' may have been partly ironic. Rather as the eventual destruction of a civilization—'the broken wall, the burning roof and tower'—was a disproportionate reaction to a woman's leaving her husband for another man, it is far from clear that Strawson's warring parties had a proper *casus belli*. One might, after all, seek to elucidate the concept of meaning by reference *both* to audience-directed intentions *and* to semantic and syntactic rules.[2] For all that, Strawson comes down on the side of the first school. 'It is a generally harmless and salutary thing to say that to know the meaning of a [declarative] sentence is to know under what conditions one who utters it says something true. But if we wish for a philosophical elucidation of the concept of meaning, then the dictum represents, not the end, but the beginning of our task' (Strawson 1970, 188–9). This is because 'when we come to try to explain in general what it is to say something true, to express a true proposition, reference to belief or to assertion (and thereby to belief) is inescapable.... Someone propounds, in some mode or other, a true proposition if things are as anyone who believes what he propounds would thereby believe them to be. And here the reference to belief is explicit' (Strawson 1970, 189). Any adequate theory of meaning, then, must assign a central role to the notion of expressing a belief. Moreover, Strawson contends, in unfolding that notion we will have to bring in communicative linguistic acts. An account on which speech was primarily and essentially the expression of one's beliefs, but only secondarily and contingently a matter of communicating those beliefs to others, would be 'too perverse and arbitrary to satisfy the requirements of an acceptable theory' (Strawson 1970, 188). An account of meaning, then, ineluctably takes us to the communicative intentions on which theorists of the first school focus.

One of my goals in this chapter is to evaluate this argument—which, to anticipate, I think is far too quick. I begin, though, with a point on which Strawson seems to me to be correct. He concludes his lecture by warning his audience that, when we inquire into the nature of meaning, we are liable to 'forget what sentences are *for*. We connect meaning with truth, and truth, too simply, with sentences; and sentences belong to language. But, as theorists, we know nothing of human *language* unless we understand human *speech*' (Strawson 1970, 189). What I take from this is that words and sentences are *au fond* no more than tools which may be used to perform various speech acts, and that an account of their meanings must yield an explanation—in tandem, no doubt, with more general conversational principles, such as those of Grice—of how they assist in the performance of those acts. To accept so much is not to beg the question in favour of Strawson's theorist of communication-intention. Even if an account

---

[2] Thus Simon Blackburn: 'although there is much more to say about particular proposals for filling out each analysis, there is no reason to see them as essentially in opposition' (Blackburn 1984, 134). See also Rumfitt (1995).

of some of the diverse speech acts we perform needs to invoke speakers' audience-directed intentions, it does not follow that a description of how words and sentences contribute to the acts' performance must itself invoke such intentions. All the same, a theory which does not eventually connect the meanings of words and sentences to the speech acts they are used to perform is sterile. To quote Strawson again, it would be 'too perverse and arbitrary' to be of serious interest.

2. Acts of Telling and Their Centrality

Strawson focuses on *communicative* speech actions, utterances or inscriptions which are directed at particular audiences or readers. I follow him in this too, in part to give his thesis the fairest possible wind before criticizing it, but mainly because communicative actions do occupy a central place in our speech and writing.

This is especially clear with interrogative and imperatival sentences. When I utter an interrogative sentence, I am almost always asking *someone* something; when I utter an imperative, I am almost always telling *someone* to do something. The range of acts that may be performed by uttering a declarative sentence is wider: such utterances may convey thanks, advice, warnings, encouragement, legal verdicts, etc. Most acts in this wide range, though, are directed towards particular hearers. In fact, instances of speech or writing which are entirely free from any communicative purpose are rarer than one might at first suppose. There are, to be sure, expostulations where it is a matter of indifference to the speaker whether anyone hears him or not. However, those who keep private diaries write, in part, for the benefit of their future selves, and authors who treat of theoretical matters still do well to keep an intended reader in mind. Setting aside its status as a dramatic device, even Macbeth's soliloquy, 'If it were done when 'tis done', is an attempt by the moral, or at least prudent, parts of his soul to communicate with his ego, and hence to restrain its 'vaulting ambition'.

More relevantly for a theorist of meaning, there are words whose meanings can be explained only by reference to communicative speech acts; second person pronouns are examples. *Per contra*, I know of no expression which may only be used in uncommunicative speech. (Frege postulated an 'I' of soliloquy (Frege 1918, 66), but even sympathetic commentators have struggled to give a coherent account of its purported sense.[3]) As Strawson says, our words and sentences are

---

[3] 'This reinforces our previous conclusion, that there is no distinction such as Frege supposed between the "I" of soliloquy and the "I" of communication'. 'For Frege, the "I" of soliloquy, as used by Dr Lauben, must be associated with the unique manner in which Dr Lauben is given to himself... It is dubious whether such a conception is even coherent' (Dummett 1981, 126, 490).

tools. A tool shaped for communicative purposes may be used in private soliloquy, but it is the shaping purpose which determines its meaning.

A theory of meaning must, in the end, say how sentences and words contribute to the performance of the entire gamut of speech acts. However, to quote Strawson once more, 'that is not a task for one lecture; or for one man' (Strawson 1970, 171). To limit the field to something manageable, I shall focus here on what I call *tellings*—utterances and inscriptions in which the speaker or writer, S, tells or informs an audience or reader, H, that such-and-such is the case.

Why take tellings to be a paradigm case of communicative speech? The best reason rests on two premises. The first is that communicative acts are of value to us primarily—not exclusively, but primarily—because they enable us to share knowledge with others. The second is that the speech act of telling is the main vehicle for this sort of sharing of knowledge. If a speaker S knows that p, and tells an audience H that p, then, if H understands what she has been told, she is, in the normal course, in a position herself to come to know that p. To be sure, there are many cases in which a telling that p does not result in H's knowing that p: S may not himself know that p; H may misunderstand the telling; H may be unable to bring herself to believe that p. On the other side, it must also be conceded that an audience can come to know things which the speaker is not telling her. An interrogator who already knows that not p will not credit a speaker who tells her that p, but she may still gain valuable knowledge (e.g. about what the speaker is most anxious to conceal) from the fact that he chooses to tell her that. These caveats are important, for an account of telling must distinguish cases in which someone is told that p from others in which they come to learn that p as a result of hearing something a speaker says. The caveats do not, though, compromise the claim that acts of telling are central to the sharing of knowledge.

3. Strawson's Account of Telling

What is it for S to tell H that p?

While Strawson does not directly answer this question in 'Meaning and Truth', we can reconstruct his preferred account. A speaker engaged in an attempt to communicate, he says,

> might have, as one of his intentions in executing his utterance, that of bringing his audience to think that he, the utterer, believes some proposition, say the proposition that p; and he might intend this intention to be wholly overt, to be clearly recognized by the audience. Or again, he might have the intention of bringing his audience to think that he, the utterer, wants his audience to perform some action, say a; and he might intend this intention to be wholly overt, to be clearly recognized by the audience. Then, provided certain other conditions on

utterer's intentions are fulfilled, the utterer may be said, in the relevant sense, to mean something by his utterance: specifically, to mean that *p*, in the declarative mode, in the first case and to mean, in the imperative mode, that the audience is to perform action *a* in the second case. Grice, for one, has given us reason to think that, with sufficient care, and far greater refinement than I have indicated, it is possible to expound such a concept of communication-intention or, as he calls it, utterer's meaning, which is proof against objection and which does not presuppose the notion of linguistic meaning. (Strawson 1970, 172–3)

In his first paper on 'Meaning', Grice contrasted Herod's presenting Salome with the head of John the Baptist on a charger with the sort of meaningful act he was concerned with, and wrote that 'what we want to find is the difference between "deliberately and openly letting someone know" and "telling" and between "getting someone to think" and "telling"' (Grice 1957, 382). In the case of declarative utterances, then, there is good reason to equate Grice's official target notion of 'non-natural meaning' with 'telling'. At any rate, in a paper of 1964 in which he proposed a refinement to Grice's analysis, Strawson expressly presented the *analysandum* as 'telling him "something"' (Strawson 1964, 156). We may, then, read Strawson as proposing an analysis of '*S* tells *H* that *p*' whereby it means:

S intends *H*

(1) to come to believe that he, *S*, believes that *p*;

(2) to recognize intention (1);

(3) to come to believe that he, *S*, believes that *p* in part because *H* recognizes intention (1); and

(4) to recognize his intention to get *H* to recognize intention (1).

(Condition (4) is not to be found in Grice's original paper but was added by Strawson (1964, 157) in an attempt to capture an aspect of the 'overtness' of communicative utterance which he thought Grice had missed.) In the terms of the Inaugural Lecture, then, '*S* tells *H* that *p*' is to be analysed as a species of 'Audience Directed Belief Expression' (ADBE; Strawson 1970, 185).

Strawson is well aware that many speech acts—indeed, many communicative speech acts which are performed by uttering declarative sentences—do not even purport to express the speaker's beliefs. He mentions (Strawson 1970, 180–1) *expressly supposing*, which I take to be the act of putting forward some proposition for consideration or investigation, as when a mathematician proposes a hypothesis for either proof or refutation, but not necessarily as something he believes. For Strawson, though, even this sort of case depends on the assertoric mode of speech and thereby involves the notion of belief. For an express supposition must have a *content*—it must be a supposition *that p*—and, when a philosopher comes to elucidate the notion of content, 'it is reasonable to regard [the acts] of statement or assertion as having an especially central position' (Strawson 1970, 181). A merely suppositional use of a declarative sentence, Strawson thinks, inherits its content from the corresponding assertion, which in turn gets its content from the belief thereby expressed. In the 'fundamental case of stating or asserting', the 'rules determining the conventional meaning of the sentence join with the contextual conditions of its utterance to determine what the belief in question *is*... And in determining what the belief in question is in such a case, the rules determine what statement is made in such a case. To determine the former *is* to determine the latter' (Strawson 1970, 181). We can now see why, in the master argument against the truth-conditional semantic theorist which I sketched at the outset, Strawson maintains that 'when we come to try to explain in general what it is to say something true, to express a true proposition, reference to belief or to assertion (and thereby to belief) is inescapable' (Strawson 1970, 189). One can begin the task of explaining truth as it applies to a supposition by saying: 'one who expresses a supposition expresses a true supposition if and only if things are as, in expressing that supposition, the way he expressly supposes them to be' (Strawson 1970, 180). But this can only be a beginning. For when we further ask—as ask we must—what is the way the speaker expressly supposes things to be, we shall be referred first to the way a speaker who made the corresponding assertion would thereby *state* things to be, and then to the belief that such a statement would be understood to express.

The idea that a declarative sentence's meaning derives from its assertive uses has been oddly popular in the philosophy of language. (For all his differences with Strawson, Michael Dummett accepted a version of the same idea.[4]) I say 'oddly' because there are many declarative sentences whose meaning we can readily grasp but assertive uses of which make no sense: examples include variants of Moore's Paradox such as 'It is raining but no one is asserting that it is raining'. I shall return to this (in §8), but first I want to challenge Strawson's key claim about telling—namely that it is to be analysed as a species of ADBE.

We need not trouble ourselves over the niceties of the various attempts to capture the relevant form of 'overtness', for Strawson's claim falls at the first

---

[4] (1) From the 1970s onwards—although perhaps not earlier—Dummett held that 'under any theory of meaning whatever—at least, any theory of meaning which admits a distinction like that Frege drew between *sense* and *force*—we can represent the meaning (sense) of a sentence as given by the condition for it to be true, on some appropriate way of construing "true": the problem is not whether meaning is to be explained in terms of truth-conditions, but of what notion of truth is admissible' (Dummett 1978, xxii). It was on this basis that Dummett argued against realist notions of truth: if truth were to transcend what we can verify, he contended, then stating the conditions under which a sentence is true could not specify its sense. The requirement that truth-conditions should specify senses, then, imposes substantial and unexpected constraints on the notion of truth itself. (2) Dummett also held, though, that the notion of truth was itself a refinement of a concept which is applicable only to assertions: 'Any workable account of assertion must recognize that an assertion is judged by objective standards of correctness... It is from these primitive conceptions of the correctness or incorrectness of an assertion that the notions of truth and falsity take their origin' (Dummett 1976, 83). For Dummett too, then, albeit less directly, the notion (sc. of a truth-condition) which is needed to specify a declarative sentence's content derives from a concept (sc. of correctness) which applies only to assertive uses of such sentences.

hurdle. Condition (1) in his analysis implies that a necessary condition for S to tell H that p is that S should intend H to come to believe that he, S, believes that p. However, S can tell H that p when this condition is not met. I cited a case of this kind more than twenty-five years ago, as part of my first published attempt to come to terms with Strawson's Inaugural Lecture (Rumfitt 1995). The 'Birmingham Six' were Irishmen who were arrested on suspicion of murder, and later convicted, following the bombing of two public houses in Birmingham in November 1974. Two of the Six had tested positive on the Griess Test, which the West Midlands Police then took to show conclusively that they had handled explosives. (It was later established that the positive result was due to their having touched laminated playing cards.) Consider, then, an utterance by one of the suspects, S, during his interrogation by the police: 'I played no part in planting the bombs.' In the circumstances, it would soon have become clear to S that there was absolutely no chance of bringing it about that the audience, H, would come to believe that he, S, believed that he had played no part in planting the bombs. However, a plausible principle about intention says that one cannot intend to do something unless one sees some chance of success. If that is right, then S could not, at the time of his interrogation, have intended that H should come to believe that he, S, believed that he had played no part in planting the bombs. That is, condition (1) of Strawson's analysis was not, and could not have been, fulfilled. For all that, it seems clear that in making his utterance, S told H that he had played no part in planting the bombs. Although he failed to *persuade* H of his sincerity, S succeeded in telling him. S could truly say at the subsequent trial that he had protested his innocence when interviewed by the police.

The principle about intention on which this argument rests is due to Grice: 'it is in general true that one cannot have intentions to achieve results which one sees no chance of achieving' (Grice 1969, 158). I still find this principle compelling: it is part of what distinguishes intending that p from merely wishing that p. The force of the counterexample to Strawson's analysis of telling, though, does not depend upon it. The key point is simply this. On Strawson's account, the primary intention of someone who tells H that p is to get H to believe that he, the speaker, believes that p. It follows from this that the speaker cannot succeed in telling H that p unless that intention is fulfilled. The case shows, though, that a speaker can succeed in telling H that p even when H is not brought to believe that the speaker believes that p. So Strawson's analysis of telling is wrong.

4. McDowell's Account of Telling

What might a correct account be?

In 'Meaning, Communication, and Knowledge', his commentary on Strawson's Inaugural Lecture, John McDowell objects that 'the primary point of making assertions is not to instil into others beliefs about one's own beliefs, but to inform others—to let them know—about the subject matter of one's assertions (which need not be, though of course it may be, the asserter's beliefs)' (McDowell 1980, 127). McDowell's observation is correct so far as it goes, and it suggests an emendation to Strawson's analysis whereby condition (1) is replaced by the following:

S intends H
(1′) to come to believe that p.

This alteration, however, would not really help, for the emended analysis is vulnerable to the same objection as the original. In the Birmingham Six example, there was also no chance of S's bringing H to believe that S had played no part in planting the bombs.

McDowell does not himself propose the emendation. He makes the remark just quoted en route to an account of telling which differs more radically from Strawson's. Earlier, I justified focusing on telling by pointing out that instances of that speech act are the main way people gain knowledge from hearing others speak. McDowell goes much further. For him, communication, in the most basic sense of the word, simply *is* 'the transmission of knowledge', or 'the instilling of information' (McDowell 1980, 128, 133).[5] 'When the communicative process functions properly', he elaborates,

> sensory confrontation with a piece of communicative behaviour has the same impact on the cognitive state of a perceiver as sensory confrontation with the state of affairs which the behaviour, as we may say, represents; elements of the communicative repertoire serve as epistemic surrogates for represented states of affairs. (McDowell 1980, 134)

McDowell argues for this view by way of an extended comparison between human acts of telling and the instinctive sounds made by unselfconscious creatures. When a bird instinctively emits a characteristic sort of squawk on seeing a predator,

> other birds might acquire, on hearing such a squawk, a propensity towards behaviour appropriate to the proximity of a predator (flight, increased caution in feeding, or whatever). This propensity might match a propensity they would

---

[5] McDowell recognizes that we count people as having communicated even when no knowledge is transferred (for example, because the hearer does not believe the speaker). He insists, though, that this application of the concept occupies a 'second level' which has to be understood by reference to an underlying level at which 'communication takes place ... only when information is actually transmitted about the topic of discourse' (McDowell 1980, 131).

> have acquired if they had seen the predator themselves. In such a case we can regard the squawk as a further mode of sensitivity to the presence of predators, over and above more direct kinds of perception. (McDowell 1980, 129)

He goes on to suggest that this sort of atavistic propensity provides the best explanation of how it is that we can gain knowledge by being told. 'It seems unpromising to suppose', he writes,

> that knowledge by <testimony> owes its status as knowledge, quite generally, to the knower's possessing a cogent argument to the truth of what he knows from the supposed reliability of the speaker. A more attractive line of thought is that the linguistic repertoire retains, through the alteration in nature involved in the onset of self-consciousness, a form of the characteristic which was essential to its pre-linguistic ancestor: in suitable circumstances (to be spelled out in any fuller elaboration of this idea) its exercises are cognitive stand-ins for the states of affairs which they represent. (McDowell 1980, 135)

I want to argue, though, that this cannot be the best explanation of how we humans can acquire knowledge by being told. It cannot be that because it is not a good explanation.

My objection is not to McDowell's treatment of animal communication. His 'line of thought' may look like armchair speculation, but in fact closely related ideas have been found fruitful by those engaged in investigating communication between non-linguistic animals. A well-known case, involving creatures further up the evolutionary scale than birds, is the alarm calls of vervet monkeys. Vervets have three kinds of call for different kinds of predator, calls which prompt very different kinds of responsive behaviour. On spotting a leopard, a vervet makes a 'bark' and monkeys who hear this call run up a tree. On spotting a python, a vervet makes a 'chutter' call; monkeys who hear this stand on tiptoe and look closely at the ground. On seeing a martial eagle, a vervet makes a 'cough' and monkeys who hear this call dive under bushes. What is particularly significant is that this last call is, in part, learned. Baby vervets are innately disposed to 'cough' on seeing anything in the sky, including falling leaves, but during infancy they learn to narrow down the class of things on sight of which they give the cough. When fully mature, they give the call only when they see an eagle. Even when the responses are not purely instinctual, then, we can still conceptualize their contents in the way McDowell suggests, namely, as an additional mode of sensitivity to various kinds of predator (see Hurford 2014, 41 and 43).

Contra McDowell, some people may still doubt if the alarm calls of lower animals have any representational content. The vervet's 'cough' call is, in part, a learned response. All the same, the reaction to it—that of diving under a bush—may yet be a reflex; and if it is simply a reflex, there is no warrant for the thesis that hearing the call provides information about the monkey's environment. There is, though, evidence that tells against the hypothesis that responses of this kind are always reflexes. The relevant observations this time concern Diana monkeys, which, like vervets, have different alarm calls for leopards and eagles. Experimenters recorded four different sounds: a leopard alarm call, the growl of an actual leopard, an eagle alarm call, and the screech of an actual eagle. They then played back these sounds, in different orders, to group of monkeys in their natural habitat (an African tropical forest). In the first scenario, the leopard alarm call was followed five minutes later by the leopard's growl and (after a long pause) the eagle alarm call was followed five minutes later by the eagle's screech. In the second scenario, the leopard alarm call was followed five minutes later by the eagle's screech, and (after a long pause) the eagle alarm call was followed five minutes later by the leopard's growl. In both phases of the second scenario, the monkeys showed considerably more alarm than in any phase of the first scenario. This suggests that the responses to calls are not purely reflexive, but that the monkeys form expectations about their environment as a result of hearing them. If that is right, then it is reasonable to ascribe to the calls some primitive representational content (Hurford 2014, 69–70).

For these reasons, I accept McDowell's account as an outline of a theory of animal communication. We may also accept, for the sake of argument, his speculative suggestion that human language evolved from calls of this kind. I deny, though, that McDowell provides a remotely plausible account of telling as a form of communication between mature human beings. The kernel of his account is the claim that 'sensory confrontation with a piece of communicative behaviour has the same impact on the cognitive state of a perceiver as sensory confrontation with the state of affairs which the behaviour...represents'. However, while human communicative behaviour can always be 'confronted' in experience, many of the states of affairs which such behaviour represents cannot. Someone may tell me that π is a transcendental number, and what they tell me is the case. Yet it makes no sense to speak of a 'sensory confrontation' with the state of affairs of π's being transcendental. As a general description of acts of telling, then, McDowell's account will not do.

What is worse, his account fails even when applied to tellings whose contents consist in the obtaining of perceptible states of affairs. Suppose John tells me that Sarah is in the Wharton Room. In this case, it at least makes sense to speak of a 'sensory confrontation' with the relevant state of affairs. An example of such a confrontation, I take it, would be my seeing Sarah in the Wharton Room. It is, though, extremely implausible to claim that hearing John say that Sarah is in the Wharton Room has 'the same impact on my cognitive state' as seeing her there. In both cases, we may grant, the end result may be my learning—my coming to know—where Sarah is, but there is a crucial difference in how that result is attained. If I see Sarah in the Wharton Room, an account of how I know that she is there will not involve John at all. That, however, cannot possibly be the case when I hear John say that she is there. My trusting him on this matter—my believing him, as we say—is clearly crucial to any explanation of how I come to know where Sarah is as a result of being told. McDowell may be correct when he writes that my acquiring knowledge in such a case cannot be due, 'quite generally, to [my] possessing a cogent argument to the truth of what [I] know from the supposed reliability of the speaker'. However, my learning something by being told must in *some* way involve my relationship with the speaker. Describing that relationship precisely is a difficult task to which we must soon turn. It cannot be right, though, to delete the audience's belief or trust in the speaker from the description of the epistemic situation, which is what McDowell's account does.

5. A Better Account of Telling

Our question, then, remains: what is it for S to tell H that p?

According to C.S. Peirce, 'to assert a proposition is to make oneself responsible for its truth' (Peirce 1934, 384). Even in a situation where S is addressing H, S can assert that p without telling H that p. When I lead H, a student, through a formal proof that p, I am addressing her, and in concluding the proof I shall assert that p. However, although I have performed communicative speech acts which have brought her to know that p, I have not *told* her that p. Why not?

Whatever its merits as an analysis of assertion—a notion which is, in any case, something of a philosopher's term of art—Peirce's proposal suggests a cognate account of telling which provides an answer to this question. For S to tell H that p is for S to make himself responsible *to* H for the truth of the claim that p. It is, moreover, to do that precisely by offering H his *assurance* or *guarantee* of the truth of p. I take this formulation from the illuminating discussion of telling in Richard Moran's *The Exchange of Words*: 'the speaker, in presenting her utterance as an *assertion*, one with the force of *telling* the audience something, presents herself as *accountable* for the truth of what she says, and in doing so offers a kind of guarantee for this truth' (Moran 2018, 51; see also Hinchman 2014, from where I take the term 'assurance'). This account explains why leading H through a proof of p is not a case of telling her that p. In leading H through the proof, I am not offering her *my* assurance of the truth of p. To the contrary, I am trying to bring her to a point where she does not need my guarantee of that, or indeed anyone else's. For, once she apprehends the proof, she will have her own reason for believing that p.

This Peirce-inspired account of telling also deals well with the example which caused trouble for Strawson's analysis. In speaking as he did, the suspect in Birmingham knew there was no chance of persuading his audience that he had not planted the bombs, nor of persuading the audience that he believed that he had not planted the bombs. All the same, in speaking as he did, the suspect could, and did, offer his assurance of the truth of that claim. The audience rebuffed the offer, but it was still made. By making the offer, the suspect made himself responsible to the police for the truth of his claim. Making himself so responsible, or so accountable, was crucial to his protestation of innocence.

On this conception, telling is a social act whose performance creates a particular relationship between speaker and audience. The relationship in question has a number of features. First and most obviously, it puts H in a position to complain to S in the event that the claim turns out to be untrue. I can protest to John 'You told me that Sarah is in the Wharton Room, but she isn't there.' It is an important feature of the relationship that I may still make this complaint even if I never believed what I was told. The act of telling will have been successfully performed if the audience receives the *offer* of an assurance that such-and-such is the case. Moreover, the audience can take up the offer without believing what he is told. One may respond to a far-fetched claim by saying 'I'll hold you to that, even though I suspect it's baloney.' In taking up the offer, the audience acquires the right to complain if it turns out to be defective, regardless of whether he believes it.

Another important feature of the relationship created between speaker and audience is that a third party cannot complain in the same terms. If Fred overhears John telling me that Sarah is in the Wharton Room, comes thereby to believe as much, but later discovers that what John said is false, he will think less of John as a potential informant, and he will be entitled to tell others that John is an unreliable source of information about people's whereabouts. He cannot, though, complain to John in the way that I did. He cannot protest 'What you told me is false', for John did not tell him anything. The conception of telling as offering an assurance explains this. The speaker will have made the offer *to* a particular audience (which may of course include more than one person). If the offer turns out to be defective, anyone who discovers as much will take that into account in assessing the trustworthiness of the speaker. Only the members of the intended audience, though, have standing to complain *to* the speaker rather than complain *about* him, for it was only to them that the offer was made.

It is helpful, up to a point, to compare the guarantee of truth offered by a speaker in telling someone something with a financial guarantee. If I guarantee my son's debts, I become liable to repay his creditors in the event that he is unable to do so. Similarly, if I tell you that p, I may be asked to answer sceptics about p in the event that you cannot do so. If I tell you that π is a transcendental number without giving you a proof, you can fairly refer a sceptic about that proposition to me: 'It was Rumfitt who told me this; you had best take it up with him.'

A deep problem in epistemology is to say how, if at all, the creation of these social relationships provides an epistemic reason for a hearer to believe what he has been told. I write here of 'hearers' and of 'what has been told', for an adequate account of the matter needs to explain why it is not only the intended audience who may acquire such a reason. Eavesdropping Fred may have just as much reason as I do to believe that Sarah is in the Wharton Room. I shall not try to address this problem here.[6] I note, though, that a natural approach to it—one which accords a central place to the notion of *believing the speaker*—is in no way incommoded by the fact just cited. For even though Fred was not the intended audience, he can still be said to have *believed John* just as readily as I (the addressee) can.

6. The Role of Truth-Conditions in Telling

Rather than pursue this discussion into the epistemology of testimony, I want to return to my main theme and consider whether the proposed analysis of telling casts any light on the Homeric struggle between the theorists of communication-intention and the theorists of formal semantics. I think it does, initially by exposing the fallacy in Strawson's argument in favour of the first party to the dispute.

That argument, it will be recalled, ran as follows. The theorist of formal semantics is right to say: 'To know the meaning of a declarative sentence is to know under what conditions one who utters it says something true.' By itself, though, that claim does not take us very far, for the notion of saying something true demands explanation. An adequate explanation, Strawson contends, will have to involve such notions as 'expresses such-and-such a proposition' or 'expresses the thought that p', and these notions can themselves be explained only by reference to acts of telling and cognate ADBEs. That is why he holds the theorist of communication-intention's account of meaning to be fundamental. On the conception of telling recommended here, however, this explanatory story unravels. Telling cannot satisfactorily be analysed as a form of ADBE. Instead, it is a speech act in which the speaker offers an audience his assurance that the sentence uttered expresses a truth. It is here that the theorist of formal semantics sees *his* chance. On the recommended conception, the notion of truth is internal to that of telling. Might not the cognate notion of a truth-condition also be involved in an adequate account of that act?

There is a simple and powerful argument for an affirmative answer. For let us reflect on the situation of a speaker who wants to tell someone something. Suppose, for example, that I want to tell my monoglot German friend Kurt that dogs bark. Given our analysis of telling, what this means is that I want to offer Kurt my assurance that dogs bark. That account of my goal sounds right, but how am I to achieve it? I shall have to say something, but how shall I choose what to say? I shall need to find a sentence, A, such that Kurt will take my utterance of A (in that context) *as* offering him my assurance that dogs bark. But what has to obtain for me to have any reason to expect that Kurt will take my utterance of A in that way?

---

[6] For illuminating discussions, see Hinchman (2014) and Moran (2018, chap. 2).

Two factors must be in place for this expectation to be reasonable. First, there has to be some general practice, to which both Kurt and I are parties, of using sentences of a certain sort so as to offer assurances of this kind. Second, a particular sentence must have a particular property—a property related to that general practice—which make it reasonable to expect Kurt to hear an utterance of that sentence as offering the specific assurance that dogs bark. Now when we try to articulate what this general practice is, and what the related properties of sentences are, the notion of truth, and a certain conception of a truth-condition, force their way in as indispensable parts of the story. For the general practice which makes any act of telling possible is surely this: when a speaker S directs a declarative sentence A to an audience H, H will take S to have offered H his assurance that A expresses a truth, in the context in which it was uttered. To be sure, the practice is general, not universal. There will be many occasions on which the speaker is speaking flippantly, or ironically, or manifestly joking, etc., and on these occasions the audience will not take the speaker to have assured anyone of anything. Such occasions apart, though, the audience will take the speaker to have offered his assurance of the truth of the declarative sentence uttered, and the speaker will know as much.

As regards the second factor, assuming that this is the right account of the general practice of telling, the relevant property of the particular sentence uttered is pretty well determined. I want to offer Kurt my assurance that dogs bark. I know that if I utter sentence A in a context where my utterance will be taken seriously, Kurt will take me to have offered him my assurance that A expresses a truth (as uttered in that context). So I shall select an A which I know Kurt will take to express a truth (in the context of utterance) *only if* dogs bark. For in that case, Kurt will move from taking me to have offered him my assurance that A expresses a truth, to taking me to have offered him my assurance that dogs bark. Generally, if a speaker S has reason to tell H that p, S also has reason to utter a sentence A which he knows H will take to express a truth (in the context of utterance) *only if p*.

In fact, further reflection shows that the relationship between Kurt and A needs to satisfy an additional requirement. One sentence that meets the condition stated at the end of the last paragraph is 'Hunde bellen und England wird die nächste Weltmeisterschaft gewinnen.' For I know that Kurt will take that sentence to express a truth only if dogs bark and England will win the next World Cup, from which I may reasonably expect him to infer that it expresses a truth only if dogs bark. It is clear, though, that this would be a poor choice of sentence to utter if *all* I want to tell Kurt is that dogs bark. For in uttering the sentence I would also be offering Kurt my assurance that England will win the next World Cup, and this is something I may not want to do. Certainly, if my aim is simply to tell Kurt that dogs bark, making that choice would leave me unnecessarily liable to complaint. In telling Kurt that dogs bark, I unavoidably risk complaint should it turn out that they do not. However, uttering the conjunctive sentence under consideration would also leave me at risk in the event that England does not win the next

World Cup. The suggested choice of sentence, then, would be poor because, in making it, I would unnecessarily jeopardize my reputation as a reliable and trustworthy interlocutor. Generalizing this consideration, we see that there is a further condition which must obtain between Kurt and a well-chosen sentence. It is not enough that Kurt should take the sentence I utter to express a truth (as uttered in the relevant context) *only if* dogs bark. He must also take it to express a truth (as uttered in that context) *if* dogs bark. Putting the two conditions together, we conclude that a well-chosen sentence must be such that Kurt will take an utterance of it to express a truth (in the relevant context) *if and only if* dogs bark. Moreover, for my choice to be fully reasonable I shall need to *know* that Kurt will take the sentence I utter to express a truth if and only if dogs bark.

7. Knowledge of Truth-Conditions: The Fourfold Inferential Disposition

The knowledge I am counting on Kurt's having, then, is knowledge that '*Hunde bellen*' (as uttered in the relevant context) expresses a truth *if and only if* dogs bark. That may look like ordinary propositional knowledge. When we analyse the situation more closely, though, we see that it is not.

I aim to offer Kurt my assurance that dogs bark. I fulfil this goal by uttering a sentence, *A*, whose truth Kurt will take me to have guaranteed. If my goal is to be fulfilled, what is required of the relationship between Kurt and *A*? What is essential is that Kurt should be disposed to *infer* from the premise that *A* expresses a truth to the conclusion that dogs bark. His being so disposed is not equivalent to his knowing, or believing, any single proposition. In particular, it is not equivalent to his knowing the conditional proposition that dogs bark if '*Hunde bellen*' expresses a truth. It is certainly not equivalent to his knowing the pertinent material conditional, i.e. to his knowing that either '*Hunde bellen*' does not express a truth or dogs bark. For Kurt could know *that* while failing to notice that it combines with the premise that '*Hunde bellen*' expresses a truth to entail that dogs bark, and hence not being disposed to infer from that premise to the conclusion that dogs bark. Yet it is Kurt's having that inferential disposition which is vital to the achievement of my communicative goal. Finally, I need to know, at least implicitly, that Kurt has that disposition if I am to have good reason to direct the words '*Hunde bellen*' towards him. It may be granted that I shall have succeeded in telling Kurt that dogs bark if, on the basis of some half-remembered German lessons, I utter the words '*Hunde bellen*', even though those half memories do not amount to present knowledge. Success of that kind is fluky, though. If I am reliably to find sentences which Kurt will take to have certain truth-conditions, that will be because I possess the linguistic capability called 'knowing German'.

The like goes for the disposition to make the converse inference. If I want to tell Kurt that dogs bark but no more than that, I shall choose to utter a sentence, A, for which I know that Kurt will take my guarantee that A expresses a truth to have been fulfilled in any circumstance where dogs bark. So, when I choose to utter 'Hunde bellen', I am relying on Kurt's being disposed to infer from the premise that dogs bark to the conclusion that 'Hunde bellen' (as uttered by me in the relevant context) expresses a truth. This inferential disposition, too, is not equivalent to knowledge of, or belief in, any single proposition. In particular, it is not equivalent to the knowledge that either 'Hunde bellen' expresses a truth or dogs do not bark. As before, Kurt could know that proposition without being disposed to infer from the premise that dogs bark to the conclusion that 'Hunde bellen' expresses a truth. What I need to select, then, is a sentence A for which Kurt is disposed to make a *two-way inference*: from the premise that A expresses a truth to the conclusion that dogs bark, and conversely.

Competent German speakers may be said to know that the sentence 'Hunde bellen' (when uttered in a context where it will be heard *as* a German sentence) expresses a truth *if and only if* dogs bark. The knowledge thereby attributed to them, though, is a certain inferential disposition and not ordinary propositional knowledge. The force of 'knows' in this context is that the disposition in question is grounded in a process of *learning*—in the present case, the process of having learned German. It was this use of 'knows' plus a conditional which Ryle noticed when he wrote that 'knowing "*if p, then q*" is...having a license or warrant to make a journey'—viz., the intellectual journey from the antecedent 'p' to the consequent 'q' (Ryle 1950, 250). Pace Ryle, I do not imagine that this dictum provides an adequate general account of the meaning of the English conditional; it may even be that this use of the conditional is somewhat sloppy. In the analysis of telling, though, we can always find a less sloppy formulation by specifying the inferences which the speaker relies on the audience's being disposed to make.

Further reflection on the relationship which must obtain between speaker and audience in successful acts of telling shows, indeed, that S must take H to have two additional inferential dispositions. As we saw, any speaker who tells someone something puts some of his own credibility on the line. When John tells me 'Sarah is in the Wharton Room', he offers me his assurance of the truth of the sentence he utters; he will lose credit if what he assures me of turns out not to be the case. We mark this loss of credit by saying: 'John has spoken falsely' or 'John's statement is false', and the loss will accrue in any circumstance where Sarah is not in the Wharton Room. A sentence A which is selected in order to tell H that p, then, will have a third property: H will be disposed to infer from the premise that not p to the conclusion that A (as uttered in the relevant context) expresses a falsehood.[7]

---

[7] By 'the premise that not p', I mean a premise whose content is the negation of the proposition that p (and similarly for 'the conclusion that not p' in the next paragraph). How best to explicate the notion

Finally, consideration of another sort of situation shows that a teller will take an audience to have a fourth disposition. Suppose I am part of an audience listening to a politician who tells us 'Widget exports to the EU have rebounded above their pre-Brexit level.' Suppose also that I am sitting beside a statistician in the Department of Trade who responds to this claim by whispering in my ear, 'That's false'. Suppose, finally, that I accept the statistician's counter-claim. Then I shall conclude that widget exports to the EU have *not* rebounded above their pre-Brexit level. In telling us what he did, the politician knew that an audience who came to think that he had spoken falsely would reach precisely my conclusion. Generally, a speaker who uses A to tell H that p will take H to be disposed to infer from the premise that A expresses a falsehood to the conclusion that not p. A teller, then, will expect an audience to have a *fourfold inferential disposition*.

A Homeric struggle, Strawson wrote, calls for 'living captains and benevolent shades' (Strawson 1970, 172). The only then-living officer in the army of formal semanticists whose work he quoted was Donald Davidson (see Strawson 1970, 176–7). It should be clear that the account of truth-conditions which has emerged from our analysis of telling differs radically from Davidson's. For Davidson, knowing that '*Hunde bellen*' expresses a truth if and only if dogs bark precisely *is* a piece of propositional knowledge. Specifically, it is the knowledge that both (1) either '*Hunde bellen*' does not express a truth or dogs bark and (2) either dogs do not bark or '*Hunde bellen*' expresses a truth.[8] For the reasons explained above, this account will not do.

In fact, there is no single proposition, knowledge of which will serve. Suppose we had said (overcoming Davidson's taboo on intensional notions) that the crucial condition on A is that Kurt should know that A *means* that dogs bark. Again, we would have a problem, for Kurt might know that '*Hunde bellen*' means that dogs bark while not being disposed to infer from the premise that '*Hunde bellen*' expresses a truth to the conclusion that dogs bark. The premises that '*Hunde bellen*' means that dogs bark, and that '*Hunde bellen*' expresses a truth, jointly entail that dogs bark; that is, they necessarily imply that conclusion.[9] There is,

---

of negation is a difficult problem in philosophical logic. When A says that p, it cannot be assumed that the result of prefacing A with the words 'It is not the case that' expresses the negation of p. 'It is not the case that Napoleon, who recognized the danger to his right flank, himself led his guards against the enemy position' does not express the negation of 'Napoleon, who recognized the danger to his right flank, himself led his guards against the enemy position', for neither sentence is true if Napoleon was unaware of the danger.

[8] Davidson was led to focus on *T*-sentences in the form '*s* is true if and only if p' because he proposed to 'sweep away the obscure "means that" [in the intensional locution "*s* means that p"], provide the sentence that replaces "p" with a proper sentential connective, and supply the description that replaces "*s*" with its own predicate' (Davidson 1967, 23). The context makes it clear that 'proper' here means 'extensional'. This is confirmed by the discussion of the rogue but nevertheless true *T*-sentence '"Snow is white" is true if and only if grass is green' at Davidson (1967, 25–6). For an introduction to Davidsonian truth-conditional semantics, see Lepore and Ludwig (2007).

[9] The entailment is not formally valid, but that is true of many necessary implications. Compare the old chestnut 'It is red all over; so it is not green all over.'

however, no general requirement that a rational thinker must be disposed to infer from any premises which he accepts to any conclusion which those premises entail. To the contrary, it is clear that our inferential dispositions barely begin to cover the range of entailments of things which we accept (see Harman 1986). I accept that cats do not bark, and this proposition entails that the moon is made of cheese if and only if either cats bark or the moon is made of cheese. All the same, I am not disposed to move from accepting that cats do not bark to accepting that conclusion. What matters for successful telling is that the audience is reliably disposed to make (and is known to be disposed to make) the relevant fourfold inference: from 'A expresses a truth' to 'p'; from 'p' to 'A expresses a truth'; from 'not p' to 'A expresses a falsehood'; and from 'A expresses a falsehood' to 'not p'. Being so disposed is not equivalent to knowledge of any single proposition.

8. The Homeric Struggle Resolved

Where does this leave Strawson's Homeric struggle between the theorists of communication-intention and the theorists of formal semantics?

As I explained in §6, our analysis of telling exposes the fallacy in Strawson's argument in favour of the theorists of communication-intention. That argument requires telling to be an ADBE; it is not. But what about his conclusion? Was he wrong to give the palm to the theorists of communication-intention? He allowed that the *dictum* 'to know the meaning of a declarative sentence is to know under what conditions one who utters it says something true' was itself true. Has our discussion shown anything more than that this *dictum* is, indeed, true?

I think our analysis does refute Strawson's conclusion. On Strawson's view, a telling's content *ipso facto* determines the conditions under which it is true, but the telling's content is determined first, as that of the belief the telling expresses. On our account, beliefs do not enter the picture, and truth-conditions are not inherited from their contents. Rather, a sentence's truth-conditions are determined by the syntactic and semantic rules of the language to which it belongs, alongside relevant contextual factors. This account of what determines linguistic content is fundamentally at odds with Strawson's.

To say so much, though, is not to claim that the theorists of formal semantics are the victors in the Homeric struggle. The proper conclusion is that an adequate philosophical account of meaning—and of the content of speech acts—will have to do what has been attempted here for the case of telling, and analyse those acts so as to reveal how syntactic and semantic rules contribute to their successful performance. 'There is no hope', Strawson says, 'of elucidating the notion of the content of such speech acts <as stating, expressly supposing, and so on> without paying some attention to the notions of those speech acts themselves' (Strawson 1970, 181). I agree. Where I differ is in denying that these acts are adequately described as ADBEs. A satisfactory account of them will bring in the rules and conventions which determine truth-conditions, or the corresponding semantic features of non-declarative sentences. It need not bring in *beliefs* or their contents.

This approach has benefits when we return to the problem of saying how speech acts of different sorts can share a content. For Strawson, a non-assertive utterance such as an express supposition inherits its contents from related assertions, for assertive acts express, or purport to express, beliefs. As remarked in §3, such a view faces problems, for there are express suppositions whose contents cannot be asserted. The present account suggests a different picture of the relationship between (for example) the acts of expressly supposing that p and of telling someone that p. When a speaker expressly supposes that p, he does not offer his audience his assurance of the truth of the sentence he utters. The act he performs, though, may still be characterized in terms of truth and truth-conditions. For the speaker puts a sentence forward as something whose truth might fruitfully be investigated or inquired into. Moreover, in order to ensure that that investigation is one into the question *whether p*, he needs to choose a sentence, A, which his audience will take to express a truth (in the relevant context of utterance) *if and only if p*. As before, analysis shows that this amounts to the audience's being disposed to make a particular fourfold inference. For the speaker needs to choose an A for which, if the audience discovers that p, it will infer that A is true; and for which, if it discovers that not p, it will infer that A is false. It is these inferential dispositions which ensure that an inquiry into the truth of A is an inquiry into whether p.

On this conception of the matter, an express supposition that p does not inherit its content from a telling that p. The conception, then, is not embarrassed by express suppositions which are unassertible, such as 'Suppose it is raining but no one is asserting that it is raining.' Rather, the rules which determine under what conditions the uttered sentence expresses a truth determine the contents of both kinds of speech act. They do this because, different as the acts are, both involve uttering a sentence which has truth-conditions. The rules which determine those truth-conditions are the crucial common factor in determining the contents of the various speech acts which may be performed by uttering declarative sentences.

9. Conclusion

In this way, Strawson's Homeric struggle can be brought to a peaceful conclusion. Our analysis also offers hope for the irenic resolution of another long-lasting battle. It is common for philosophers of language to write as though 'inferentialist' accounts of the meanings of declarative sentences are fundamentally opposed to 'truth-conditional' theories. It is, of course, possible to fill out those labels in such a way that the results are incompatible. Our account of sentential meaning, though, combines elements of both. Knowledge of truth-conditions is vital to communicative success; yet knowledge of truth-conditions turns out to be the possession of a suitably grounded, and suitably reliable, set of inferential dispositions.

The shift from propositional knowledge to possession of inferential dispositions is liberating for truth-conditional semantics. In particular, it helps in dealing with certain modal constructions which have been the source of difficulties for traditional truth-theories. We shall expect an adequate semantics for German to license the inference from the premise that 'Zwei ist eine Primzahl' expresses a truth to the conclusion that two is a prime number, and also to license the converse inference. We can then handle the modal operator '*es ist notwendig daß*' by way of the following semantical *rule of proof*: given licences for the inference from the premise that *A* expresses a truth to the conclusion that *p*, and for the converse of this inference, the following inferences are also licensed: from the premise that '*Es ist notwendig daß A*' expresses a truth to the conclusion that it is necessarily the case that *p*, and *its* converse. This rule of proof licenses the inference from '*Es ist notwendig, daß Zwei eine Primzahl ist*' expresses a truth to it is necessarily the case that two is a prime number, and conversely. The licence holds good even if the German language is so conceived that it is a contingent matter what its constituent words mean. (For the importance of such semantical rules of proof, see Rumfitt 2001.)

It remains to be seen how far this approach assists the construction of semantic theories for natural languages. Reaching a judgement on that issue would take a book, at least. I am confident that the rule-based approach will prove fruitful and, while that approach diverges from Strawson's in several respects, there remains a fundamental affinity. 'As theorists', he remarked, 'we know nothing of human *language* unless we understand human *speech*' (Strawson 1970, 189). The chief aim of this chapter has been to show how an attractive and fecund conception of truth-conditions may be rooted in an analysis of the speech act of telling.

References

Blackburn, Simon (1984), *Spreading the Word: Groundings in the Philosophy of Language* (Oxford: Clarendon Press).

Davidson, Donald (1967), 'Truth and Meaning', *Synthese* 17: 304–23. Page references are to the reprint in Davidson, *Inquiries into Truth and Interpretation* (Oxford: Clarendon Press, 1984), 17–36.

Dummett, Michael (1976), 'What Is a Theory of Meaning? (II)', in Gareth Evans and John McDowell (eds.), *Truth and Meaning: Essays in Semantics* (Oxford: Clarendon Press), 67–137.

Dummett, Michael (1978), *Truth and Other Enigmas* (London: Duckworth).

Dummett, Michael (1981), *The Interpretation of Frege's Philosophy* (London: Duckworth).

Frege, Gottlob (1918), 'Der Gedanke', *Beiträge zur Philosophie des deutschen Idealismus* I: 58–77.

Grice, Paul (1957), 'Meaning', *The Philosophical Review* 66: 377–88.

Grice, Paul (1969), 'Utterer's Meaning and Intentions', *The Philosophical Review* 78: 147–77.

Harman, Gilbert (1986), *Change in View: Principles of Reasoning* (Cambridge, MA: MIT Press).

Hinchman, Edward (2014), 'Assurance and Warrant', *Philosophers' Imprint* 14 (7): 1–58.

Hurford, James (2014), *The Origins of Language: A Slim Guide* (Oxford: Oxford University Press).

Lepore, Ernest, and Kirk Ludwig (2007), *Donald Davidson's Truth-Theoretic Semantics* (Oxford: Clarendon Press).

McDowell, John (1980), 'Meaning, Communication, and Knowledge', in Zak van Straaten (ed.), *Philosophical Subjects: Essays Presented to P. F. Strawson* (Oxford: Clarendon Press), 117–39.

Moran, Richard (2018), *The Exchange of Words: Speech, Testimony, and Intersubjectivity* (Oxford: Oxford University Press).

Peirce, Charles Sanders (1934), *Belief and Judgment* (Cambridge, MA: Harvard University Press).

Rumfitt, Ian (1995), 'Truth Conditions and Communication', *Mind* 104: 827–62.

Rumfitt, Ian (2001), 'Semantic Theory and Necessary Truth', *Synthèse* 126: 283–324.

Rumfitt, Ian (2015), *The Boundary Stones of Thought: An Essay in the Philosophy of Logic* (Oxford: Clarendon Press).

Ryle, Gilbert (1950), '"If", "So", and "Because"', in Max Black (ed.), *Philosophical Analysis: A Collection of Essays* (Englewood Cliffs, NJ: Prentice Hall), 302–18. Page references are to the reprint in Ryle 2009, 244–60.

Ryle, Gilbert (2009), *Collected Essays, 1929–1968* (London: Routledge).

Strawson, Peter F. (1964), 'Intention and Convention in Speech Acts', *The Philosophical Review* 73: 439–60. Page references are to the reprint in Strawson 1971, 149–69.

Strawson, Peter F. (1970), *Meaning and Truth: An Inaugural Lecture Delivered Before the University of Oxford on 5 November 1969* (Oxford: Clarendon Press). Page references are to the reprint in Strawson 1971, 170–89.

Strawson, Peter F. (1971), *Logico-Linguistic Papers* (London: Methuen).

3
Strawson's Basic Particulars

Paul Snowdon

1. Introduction

Individuals is the work by Strawson that established him as one of the leading philosophers in the world. It is a work which was immediately regarded as a must-read book. In its ambition and generality of conclusion it represented a change of direction in philosophy, especially in Oxford. In this chapter I want to engage with some aspects of the arguments he presents in chapter 1 of that book. Strawson's work was, and remains, highly influential, and it is both very interesting in itself, but also engaging with it enables us to gain insights, even if they are not, in all cases, exactly the ones that Strawson intended us to gain—or at least, so I shall suggest. I want to say right at the beginning that Strawson's chapter is long, complicated, and deep, and my exposition of it and responses to it are partial and nowhere near adequate. I have no doubt overlooked many points about it that others have made and which deserve serious attention. The response to Strawson that I have primarily in mind in saying this is Evans's *Varieties of Reference*.

2. Chapter 1 of *Individuals*

Chapter 1 of *Individuals* is divided into three main parts. The first part (Strawson 1959, 15–30), is called 'The Identification of Particulars'. In it Strawson does three main things. The first is that he more or less immediately analyses reference to particulars taking the notion of *identification* as central. He starts, that is, in a place that had been central to his philosophical concerns since his earliest days—the reference to objects in speech and the understanding of that reference by audiences. *Individuals* (Strawson 1959) starts from where Strawson had got to by then in thinking about this topic. His account is set out very rapidly at the beginning of the chapter. The second thing that Strawson does is to introduce the general notion of a certain type of particular being basic to such reference, a type which would then merit being called basic to our conceptual scheme. Ultimately, but not yet, Strawson will suggest a type which does merit being so counted. The third move that Strawson then makes is to argue that the identificatory conditions involved in speaker and hearer identification in reference require that the spatio-temporal framework is, in some sense, *the* framework in terms of which the required identifications are made. As he says, 'By means of identifying reference we fit other people's reports and stories, along with our own, into a single story about empirical reality; and this fitting together, this connexion, rests ultimately on relating particulars which figure in the stories in the single spatio-temporal system which we ourselves occupy' (Strawson 1959, 19). As we might put it, those two great things, space and time, enter Strawson's story by the end of this first part.

The second part, entitled simply 'Reidentification' (Strawson 1959, 31–8), starts with Strawson isolating a new 'sense, or application' of the word 'identify' (Strawson 1959, 31), and arguing, first, that a condition for having the spatio-temporal conceptual scheme unearthed as central in the previous part, is that we have 'criteria or methods' (Strawson 1959, 31) for *reidentifying* some particulars, by which he means something like encountering the particular on one occasion and identifying it with something encountered on another occasion. Strawson means by 'criteria' a way of *knowing* that some such judgements are true. Second, he also argues that we must be capable of reidentifying *places* as well as particulars. In this part, for the first time in the book, Strawson explicitly engages with scepticism and seems to think of himself as revealing it, in relation to its application to reidentificatory judgements, as incoherent or self-refuting. Urging such an attitude to scepticism is one recurring theme in *Individuals*, and the argument he gives is, perhaps, the first example in *Individuals* of a so-called transcendental argument.

In the final part, entitled 'Basic Particulars' (Strawson 1959, 38–58), Strawson argues that it is a requirement on operating this spatio-temporal system that *material bodies are the basic particulars*. That is the major conclusion towards which the whole argument in this chapter is meant to lead us. Strawson argues for this in two ways. He offers an abstract argument that our spatio-temporal framework is *constituted* by material objects. But he also argues in a careful way by considering different candidates for being basic and offering reasons against the others, the most serious alternative candidates to material bodies being events and processes.

3. Our Conceptual Scheme

Now, when Strawson speaks of basicness he talks of being basic to or in 'our scheme'. Thus, at the very beginning of chapter 1 he says, 'Part of my aim is to exhibit some general and structural features of the conceptual scheme in terms of which we think about particular things' (Strawson 1959, 15).

There are perhaps different ways to understand the transition that Strawson is making in this bold argument. But one way to see it is as an attempt to move from certain claims in the philosophy or theory of reference—that is certain claims that we would naturally describe as belonging to the philosophy of language—to a general characterization of some fundamental aspect of what Strawson calls 'our conceptual scheme'. But what does talk of 'our conceptual scheme' mean?

There are two elements to clarify. The first is what is meant by 'our' or 'us'. Strawson does not say, but if he had been asked I think that he would have had to say that by 'we' is meant at least all normal human beings (maybe, with language). Two things stand out once we explain it that way. The first is that the scope of Strawson's conclusion is very broad. The broadness of the conclusion is *one* reason that *Individuals* definitely represented a real shift in philosophical ambition in the late 1950s, at least in Oxford. Someone might say that in the 1950s people in Oxford were interested in general questions—and of course they were. Thus, they were certainly prepared to generalize about the nature of moral thinking, or about the notion of knowledge, say, but they did so without insisting that the concepts they were focusing on were in fact totally universal. Maybe not everyone operates with the concept of knowledge, and maybe not everyone engages in moral thinking. What is striking about Strawson is that he is advancing a positive universal hypothesis.

The second consequence of this universalism is that in supporting his claim we cannot rely on what are obvious aspects of how *we* (in another reading), by which I mean people reading this, twenty-first century, *educated city-dwellers*, think about things. The generalization is supposed to apply far more broadly than that. Although this may not be a politically correct way to put it, Strawson's conclusion is supposed to apply to humans whose environments are quite unlike ours and whose understanding is far more primitive than ours is, and whose communicative purposes and knowledge are very different to ours.

Those are two things to note, but a further question still remains. Is there really any good reason to generalize *solely* across humans? Should we extend the conclusion to types of pre-human creatures who employed language to communicate? If not, why? All I can say is that when this question is brought into contact with Strawson's programme it is completely unclear how Strawson would, or should, have answered it.

So much by way of reflecting on 'our'—but what of 'conceptual scheme'? Well, we can pretend for present purposes that we know what concepts are, or, perhaps better, that we understand talk about concepts. Now, one way to take talk of someone's conceptual scheme is to talk about what *notions* they *have*. Relative to this someone who believes in ghosts and someone who believes there are no ghosts share the same conceptual scheme in a certain respect, namely they share the concept of a ghost, but their beliefs involving that concept are quite different. When Strawson talks about conceptual schemes he clearly does not mean it in this sense. For Strawson, talk of conceptual schemes obviously picks out what one might call the beliefs, or cognitive states, of an individual. So, in his second step when Strawson brings in space and time he is talking about believing in space and time, having spatio-temporal concepts, and *applying* them. We can say that Strawson's conclusion amounts to the ascription to everyone of certain psychological states, which in the seventeenth century they might have called our understanding, or more recently what Quine and Quineans might call our theory. Now, this characterization is not totally precise, but I think that it is obvious that we have to understand Strawson's talk of conceptual schemes this way.

I have tried to offer a very broad characterization of Strawson's argument in chapter 1, and to say how in some ways it represented a revolutionary development in the philosophical environment from which it emerged. But I think that viewing it this way should also make one wonder whether we are really in a position to be confident about such an ambitious project. Or perhaps it might be better to say, it is a type of conclusion about which we need to be very careful in scrutinizing its basis.

4. Some Aspects of the Broader Context

Before analysing the arguments in chapter 1 I want to mention, and comment on, where Strawson goes next. By the end of the first chapter Strawson concludes that material bodies are basic to particular-identification in 'our conceptual scheme'. The question that Strawson next pursues is whether there *could be* a conceptual scheme which involves reference to 'objective and identifiable particulars' but in which material bodies are not basic. As Strawson puts it: 'Could there exist a conceptual scheme which was like ours in that it provides for a system of objective and identifiable particulars, but was unlike ours in that material bodies were not the basic particulars of the system?' (Strawson 1959, 60). Now, as I read it, Strawson's answer to his own question is that there could be such a scheme, an example being the conceptual scheme that a subject could operate within the sound world that he describes.[1] Since the example that Strawson constructs, the sound world, is one which is deemed to be non-spatial, in an important sense, he not only thinks that there can be a system of objective reference in which material bodies are not basic but also there can be objective reference in a system which is *non-spatial*. In a slogan—objectivity does not *require* spatiality. When Evans responds to Strawson he reads him differently, regarding him as arguing for the idea that objectivity requires spatiality, though in Evans's view arguing the case badly, but it is, I think, reasonable to interpret Strawson as supporting the opposite.[2] What Strawson would say, I think, is that in so far as

---

[1] This is how, so it seems, Strawson leaves the question on page 81.
[2] See Evans (1982, 77). Evans labels the claim that space is a necessary condition for objective experience the 'Kantian thesis'. This is, it seems to me, a not entirely happy name. We should recall that Kant is an idealist who thinks that space is ideal, and that the genuinely objective world is not spatial.

the sound world subject can make objective judgements there must be some element in its experience which functions for that subject in an analogous way that spatial experience functions for us (whatever that is exactly), and that can be said to be *close* to how Evans reads it. Strawson is not, however, prepared to allow that a subject in the sound world which he envisages could have a conception of him- or herself as opposed to other particulars. Such a creature could not have what Strawson calls a 'non-solipsistic consciousness' (Strawson 1959, 84). His reflections on this at the end of the chapter provide the link with the famous third chapter on persons, where he explores, as it might be put, the conditions for having a non-solipsistic consciousness.

I want to make a few remarks about some aspects of this broader context.

(1) In chapter 1 Strawson is focusing on the character of referential communication between people. Basicness is, therefore, as the elucidation to be quoted later shows, an interpersonal matter, relating to communication between subjects. In chapter 2 the subject that Strawson is focusing on cannot give or receive communications. The question of structure within conceptual schemes becomes totally individualistic and nothing to do with interpersonal reference. Noticing this contrast leads to the following question: Why not start at the beginning from an individualistic understanding of conceptual schemes and of basicness? But there is another question to be suggested in relation to this idea. What would the appropriate notion of basic be? It would need to be two-sided. The objects that the subject first starts to think about, that is, has concepts for, would count as basic. And it may be that the earliest categories cover more than one sort. But if there should be categories that the subject acquires later but which are not dependent on the earlier categories, they should also count as among the most basic ones. How dependence is to be defined and applied is a further and difficult matter.

(2) It should strike us that Strawson's engagement with the sound world is a very extreme case to focus on if the aim is to consider whether there are possible cases where material bodies are not basic in a communicative scheme. Strawson clearly holds that material bodies are not the only particulars in space. Other cases are events and processes. So, a simpler case to consider would be whether creatures with spatial experience but who live in an environment where the things they can perceive are mainly events could communicate with each other without referring to material bodies. And, of course, in considering this, since it is simply a question about possibility, the character of the surrounding events can be imagined to be as conducive as possible to what is being envisaged. There is, therefore, I believe a real puzzle why Strawson chose to explore such an extreme

---

Further he seems to allow the possibility of non-spatial intuition. See Kant, *Critique of Pure Reason*, A 27. If so, Kant did not believe the Kantian thesis in its full generality, indeed it might be called an un-Kantian thesis.

case. Of course, this choice, even if extreme, led to some very ingenious philosophical discussion on his part, for which we should be grateful.

(3) Not only is the sound world an extreme case, but what exactly is it? It is described as a no-space world. But as we think of sounds they are *in their nature* things that are in space. Thus, there was a noise in the garden, we say. So, strictly sounds are not non-spatial things. What might be correct is that limiting a creature's perceptual experience to hearing sounds is to strip it of experience with a spatial character. Strawson also claims that a creature of the kind he is envisaging cannot have self-consciousness.[3] But why? Thus, nothing is said as to what the creature is, what nature it actually has, nor indeed what other experiences he or she has. If Strawson were to reply that as envisaged the creature has no other experiences than its auditory perception, and on that basis alone it could not develop self-consciousness, we could respond by asking quite why that is, but also even if that is true it would not establish any link between self-consciousness and perception of environmental material bodies, since the impossibility of self-consciousness might derive from the stipulation of extreme experiential poverty on behalf of the creature, (or something else) rather than its limited *perceptual* experience.

I now want to turn to the argument of chapter 1 and to express some reservations about each step in the argument.

5. The Identification of Particulars (pp. 15–17)

Strawson introduces his conception of referential communication in these words:

> The application of the phrase "identification of particulars" which I shall first be concerned with is this. Very often, when two people are talking, one of them, the speaker, refers to or mentions some particular or other. Very often, the other, the hearer, knows what, or which, particular the speaker is talking about; but sometimes he does not. I shall express this alternative by saying that the hearer either is, or is not, able to *identify* the particular referred to by the speaker.... Expressions of these kinds [viz., which are used to do this by speakers] include some proper names, some pronouns, some descriptive phrases beginning with the definite article, and expressions compounded of these. When a speaker uses such an expression to refer to a particular, I shall say that he makes an *identifying reference* to a particular. It does not follow, of course, from the fact that a speaker, on a given occasion, makes an identifying reference to a particular that his hearer does in fact identify that particular. I may mention someone to you by name and

---

[3] This is what Strawson is arguing for on pages 81–4.

you may not know who it is. But when a speaker makes an identifying reference to a particular, and his hearer does, on the strength of it, identify the particular referred to, then I shall say the speaker not only makes an identifying reference to, but also *identifies*, that particular. So, we have a hearer's sense, and a speaker's sense of "identify". (Strawson 1959, 15–16)

Strawson then poses the following question: 'What are the tests for hearer's identification? When shall we say that a hearer knows what particular is being referred to by a speaker?' (Strawson 1959, 17).

What I want to ask is whether the invocation of the notion of identification in this way is appropriate. Now, Strawson's use of identification can be divided into three cases. The first is (a) that speakers make what he calls identifying reference to particulars. The second is (b) that hearers identify the particulars referred to. The third is (c) that when both happen the speaker identifies the particular in question.

Let us focus on case (a) first. It is important that the talk of identifying here does not depend in any way on the uptake of the hearer. On the face of it adding 'identifying' to the term 'reference' adds nothing to simply saying that the speaker refers to or makes reference to an object. Do we think there are two kinds of reference—identifying and non-identifying? What though is 'identification'? Here is a joke to shed light on that issue. I am assaulted and go to the police to report it. I say: 'I have been assaulted and I want you to catch the person who assaulted me.' The policeman says: 'Can you identify your assailant?' I reply by saying: 'Yes, he was the person who assaulted me. As Strawson has revealed I have already identified him for you twice already.' At which point the policeman says, with a sigh, 'I see—you can't identify him.' Now, surely, the policeman is right. I have not done and cannot do what would be described as identifying my assailant. But that seems to be because to identify X, say my assailant, requires me to provide a true identity which applies to X, e.g. that X is identical to Y. Now, this story leads to the following proposal: to talk of identifying X is shorthand for talking of endorsing an identity claim of the form X = Y (for some suitable Y). Holding on to that elucidation it follows that it is quite wrong to describe someone who refers to an object which is X as X as identifying X, or indeed as identifying anything at all.

Let us now look at case (b). Suppose someone says to me 'Fa', in so doing referring to a. I hear the remark and understand it as saying that a is F. Now, in understanding it I do not, or need not, know an identity for a—say that it is b. So, it seems misleading to describe the hearer who understands the message in a normal sense as *identifying* a.

One possible response to this simple point is to say that in understanding I do know an identity—namely that the referent of 'a' is (identical to) a. So, in understanding I do pass the test of accepting an identity judgement.

This is indeed an identity judgement, but it is a strange one. Thus, even in the assault case the policeman is in a position to know that 'the referent of "the man who assaulted me" is the man who assaulted me'. But in knowing such an identity judgement he would not count as being able to identify the assailant. Further, when I hear someone say 'Fa' and understand it, need I register the particular expression 'a'? It seems to me that I gain from hearing it the message or information that a is F, but if someone asked what expression precisely 'a' was I might not be sure. It needs to be remembered that 'a' might be syntactically complex. So, maybe I needn't be in a position to know the proposed identity, even though I count as understanding the utterance. Finally, if we want the hearer to register some linguistic information we can suggest that he or she will know that 'a' refers to a. That is, the information need not be viewed as *identificatory* information, but is rather linguistic information. So, I suggest that this attempt to rescue the presence of identification in hearer understanding is not cogent.

One final comment about *identification*. We have seen how Strawson in chapter 2 on the sound world drops focus on communication and reference in speech with others. In thinking in that chapter about the necessary structure of objective thought he focuses on an individual's picking out objective particulars in thought. Now, it is on the face of it obvious that when someone simply picks out an object that does not amount to an identification. Rather, to make an identification of it one must already have picked it out. This should make us wonder, I suggest, why Strawson did not start his investigation of the basic structure of our conceptual scheme by focusing on an individual thinker picking out objects, in which case one need not start from joint identification between speaker and hearer.

My conclusion at this point is that Strawson's invocation of identification in his starting point is problematic, and I have tried to present some evidence for that. However, two alternative starting points suggest themselves. The first is the one just hinted at, in which the focus is immediately on picking out by an individual of particulars and what its conditions are. But the second would be to retain the focus on communication and its conditions but to modify the characterization of that, and rather than talk of identification, talk instead of reference and hearer understanding of reference. These are vague hints of alternative routes that a Strawsonian might explore.

6. The Spatio-Temporal Framework (pp. 17–30)

I want next to engage with the second stage of argument that is present in this part of Strawson's chapter.

Strawson starts by demarcating what he calls 'story-relative' identification, which he takes to be an inferior sort of identification. He says:

> Consider first the following case. A speaker tells a story which he claims to be factual. It begins: "A man and a boy were standing by a fountain", and it continues: "The man had a drink". Shall we say that the hearer knows which or what particular is being referred to in the second sentence? We might say so. For, of a certain range of two particulars, the words "the man" serve to distinguish the one being referred to, by means of the description which applies only to him. But though this is, in a weak sense, a case of identification I shall call it only a *story-relative* or for short, a *relative* identification. For it is identified only relative to a range of particulars (a range of two members) which is itself identified only as the range of particulars being talked about by the speaker.
>
> (Strawson 1959, 18)

Now, what Strawson says here is not outrageous but it is less clear than Strawson implies or assumes. Consider this example. On entering the grounds of an hotel you are told by A that Leo will meet you when you get to reception. Do you know who will meet you? If you were asked whether you know you would say that you did, namely Leo. But your link to the individual Leo depends on taking it that the Leo in question is the one that person A was talking about, and not another Leo. So, we can say that it is relative to a communication by A that you understand the reference. If so, it is hard to see why in Strawson's example something similar is not also true—namely, that 'he' refers to the man about whom the storyteller was speaking.[4]

Strawson's own attempt to answer this question is this: 'But he [the hearer] cannot place the figures, without the frame, of the speaker's picture in his own general picture of the world. For this reason, the full requirement for hearer's identification is not satisfied' (Strawson 1959, 18). To which, I think, we should respond by asking—'Why does this dependence mean that the understanding of reference is inferior?'

To this can be added a second point. Our picture of the world which we rely on in understanding speech and reference is built, in part, on what we might call stories—things that people tell us—where the story is really all we have to go on. We can then relate the first story to another story, and if asked who the second speaker was referring to we can answer that it was the person the first teller was talking about. In this way we build up our picture of the world and draw on that in understanding reference. Understanding reference on the basis of stories is not really an inferior mode of understanding.

---

[4] Maybe Strawson was influenced by the fact that in his little narrative the first sentence does not *refer* to a man and a boy but simply says there were such individuals—and so there is no reference that the expression 'the man' could be latching onto or picking up on. If so, in uttering the first sentence the speaker can be described as *talking about a man and boy*—if not referring to them—and that is a link that is drawn on in understanding the reference in the second sentence of 'the man'.

What Strawson next brings in is a type of case of knowing what is being referred to which is certainly not an inferior sort—namely, where the hearer 'can pick out by sight or hearing or touch, or can otherwise sensibly discriminate, the particular being referred to, knowing that it is that particular' (Strawson 1959, 18). Strawson describes this type of case as one where the hearer is 'able directly to locate the particular referred to' (Strawson 1959, 19).

There is a parallel here with Russell. Strawson is taking a good case to be understanding demonstrative reference, just as Russell takes singling out items we are acquainted with as a central case of referential thought. There are three differences, at least. Strawson takes the items of this kind of reference to be public particulars, whereas for Russell they are not public things, but rather private things. And along with this Strawson's demonstrated particulars are in space—are locatable—whereas for Russell they are not. One could say that Strawson is an externalist—our perceptual experiences enable us to stand in the sort of relation to external objects that allows us to single them out in this way. Strawson's externalist perspective here is surely one we should all share. Along with this, Strawson is taking demonstratives to be elements in public interpersonal discourse, whereas in Russell's model they are ways an individual targets his or her own private thought onto private elements.

Now, let's allow that demonstrative reference is certainly a good case of reference, as Strawson thinks. Strawson's explanation is that it is reference allowing the hearer to 'directly locate' the referent. This brings in the idea of locating an item *in space*. So, one of the two big things that Strawson is wanting to centre-stage, namely space, is brought in in the way he speaks here. In fact, although there are complications which I don't want to engage with, one might say that demonstrative reference normally involves *an ability to locate the referent in space and time*—that thing over there NOW. So, it is not just a spatial locating, but rather a spatio-temporal locating.

I think, though, that we should ask whether understanding demonstratives *must* involve the ability to spatially locate the referent. What does Strawson mean by that ability? The most obvious interpretation is that the understander *knows where the referent is*. Now, the question here is not whether in normal circumstances someone who picks out a sensibly presented particular demonstratively indicated by a speaker counts as knowing where it is but whether that knowledge must be present simply in virtue of that sort of picking out. I want to concentrate on the visual case, which is presumably the main case. One point is that simply in virtue of picking out an object its distance away need not be known. How far away is a certain discriminated light? There need be no way to tell. But must the direction of the object be known? Ways of capturing direction would be in terms of notions like straight ahead, or to the right, or up, say. However, it seems clear that the generation of such spatial knowledge depends on the subject's knowledge of his or her bodily layout and its link to the perception. Thus, the subject might know that the object is to the right if he or she knows that the eyes are looking to the right, say because the subject's head is turned to the right and the eyes are looking forward in the head. I'm not here appealing to any advanced theory about how humans can tell matters of direction but just to obvious dependencies. In the absence of such extra information the subject might count as knowing that the presented particular is *there*—but 'there' just means 'where that thing is'. So spatial locatability is not essential to grasping demonstrative reference.

Strawson next quite correctly points out that much reference is not demonstrative reference. As he says, we use 'descriptions or names or both' (Strawson 1959, 20). He evidently thinks that names are secondary to descriptions, a view which was the dominant one at the time. But in relation to descriptions he voices the worry that we cannot really know that there is a unique satisfier of a description. Strawson's suggested response is that 'non-demonstrative identification may rest securely upon demonstrative identification' (Strawson 1959, 20). How does it so rest, according to Strawson? The answer seems to be conveyed in these words:

> ... by demonstrative identification we can determine a common reference point and common axes of spatial direction; and with these at our disposal we have also the theoretical possibility of a description of every other particular in space and time as uniquely related to our reference point. (Strawson 1959, 22)

Strawson raises the query as to why the framework of uniqueness must be spatio-temporal (see Strawson 1959, 25). His reply is that 'the system of spatio-temporal relations has a peculiar comprehensiveness and pervasiveness, which qualify it uniquely to serve as the framework within which we can organize our individuating thought...' (Strawson 1959, 25).

Now, I have in sketching Strawson's direction of thought bypassed much of the detail of what he says. On the very general analysis of the direction of his approach that I am working with here, there are two main moves. The first is to make demonstrative reference the fundamental case, because in the situation uniqueness of reference is guaranteed. The second move is the claim that the descriptions that ultimately build on this case and allow reference outside that range are spatio-temporal descriptions.

One point I wish to make is that the second move seems exaggerated, or perhaps arbitrary. We can pick out objects via a description linked to a demonstrative in all sorts of ways that are not explicitly spatio-temporal. I might say 'the man who mended that car...' and you understand the reference, but not in virtue of knowing where he was or is or when he was around. You are ignorant of his spatio-temporal properties. The causal feature cited is enough. And so it is in many cases, or at least might be, for all we know. Again, someone might say to me

'Where is the mop?' and I might have no idea where it is or where it has been, but I understand what item is being looked for—as one might put it—the favoured mop!

I am suggesting that there is no obvious reason to favour spatio-temporal descriptions or categories at this point. However, what is true is that we all have a conception of the world we inhabit and knock around in as spatio-temporal. The actual things around us and which we talk and think about have their unique position in space and time. And thinking of the world this way is as clear a universal feature of human thought as anything. It certainly forms a central part of our shared conceptual scheme. This leads to the following somewhat depressing conjecture—if Strawson has good reasons to claim that material bodies are the most basic building blocks for spatio-temporal thought, as he is about to suggest, he did not really need to get to the centrality of space and time from claims about interpersonal reference. Or rather, he does not need to do it the way he did if he has a notion of being basic which does not tie the issue to interpersonal reference, which as it happens, he does not.

7. Reidentification

Strawson then turns to what he calls 'reidentification', developing an anti-sceptical argument of great interest, which I want briefly to analyse.

Strawson starts from our conviction about objects in space and time that they are all spatio-temporally related. We do not assume that we know what the relations are, but we do assume there is always a fact of the matter. Thus, a star far away in the Milky Way is now a certain distance in a certain direction away from my computer. He aims to articulate 'some conditions and then some consequences' (Strawson 1959, 31) of this conception.

First, though, Strawson contrasts the use of 'identify' he has already made when talking about reference with the use of 'identify' he is about to make. He characterizes the new use as 'identifying a particular encountered on one occasion or described in respect of one occasion, as the same individual as a particular encountered on another occasion, or described in respect of another occasion' (Strawson 1959, 31). The kind of identity judgements he seems to have in mind are ones where the identity sign is flanked by two descriptions which relate to what applied to the object at different times. For example, 'the man who opened that door now is the man who opened the door yesterday'. Encountering can drop out since the descriptions need have nothing to do with encountering. Further, calling this 'reidentification' is odd, since it is simply what we would call identifying— there not being a previous identification. And if we can formulate what understanding ordinary reference is in terms of identity judgements some of them would count as what Strawson is here calling 'reidentifications'. Thus, if someone says to me 'The man who gave Fred the book yesterday is generous' then the identity I supposedly grasp is 'the referent of "the man who gave Fred the book yesterday" is the man who gave Fred the book yesterday', which describes the item in respect of different occasions. Let us just take it that we know what identity judgements Strawson is talking about.

Now, Strawson's claim is that it is a condition for us 'operating with the scheme of a single, unified spatio-temporal system' that we have 'criteria or methods' which enable us to know, for some of these types of identity judgements that they are true. Standing back from this we can regard it as a transcendental argument in which certain requirements, in this case an epistemological requirement, supposedly must obtain for certain ways of thinking, or sets of concepts, to exist. The resulting problem for the sceptic who claims we do not know what we might call identities over time is that they express the claims we are supposed not to know in judgements which can make sense only if we do know some are true.

We can agree, surely, that our attitude is the one that Strawson is saying we *have to have* as a condition for thinking the way we do. If I fall asleep in a room and then wake up in a qualitatively very similar room I do unhesitatingly take it that I know where I am and that the surrounding objects are the ones there were before. This is not to say, however, that viewing things that way is a *condition* for having the beliefs and concepts as Strawson claims.

So, if the characterization of the end point here is accurate two questions immediately arise. The first is: What exactly is the starting point for which conditions are being sought? The second is: What reason is there to suppose the specified condition is a condition for that starting point? Now, the starting point as already specified is the conviction that everything in the spatial world, the universe, is spatio-temporally related. So we should characterize the starting point as the presence of a conviction that our environment has a certain spatio-temporal structure. How then does Strawson get out his epistemological condition for this? As I read it, he, with typical ingenuity, has two routes, of which he seems to think the second is clearer. So I shall focus on it.

This is what Strawson says:

> I say that a condition of our having this conceptual scheme is the unquestioning acceptance of particular identity in at least some cases of non-continuous observation. Let us suppose for a moment that we were never willing to ascribe particular identity in such cases. Then we should...have the idea of a new, different, spatial system for each new continuous stretch of observation...Each new system would be wholly independent of every other. There would be no doubt about the identity of an item in one system with an item in another. For such a doubt makes sense only if the two systems are not independent, if they are parts, in some way, related, of a single system which includes them both.
>
> (Strawson 1959, 35)

There are a number of steps in this derivation which might be questioned, but I want to raise two simple queries. First, what Strawson needs to show is that we could not arrive at the view we have as described in the starting point unless we have *genuine knowledge-generating methods* for some identities where it is not based on continuous observation. But what Strawson actually considers is what would happen to our thinking if we are not even *willing to* make such judgements. It seems to me there is no reason to claim that consequences, if there are any, of our having no inclination to judge must also be consequences if our inclinations to judge do not amount to knowledge. Second, there seems to me no reason to agree with Strawson's description of what there being no inclination would actually mean. Why could not the subject form the concept or idea of identity over time without continuous observation? We are offered no reason to suppose they could not. Once the concept is available what suspicions and opinions might then emerge? We cannot really say.

I think that the suspicion has to be that this *transcendental argument* does not work.

8. Material Objects as Basic

Let us now scrutinize Strawson's understanding of basicness *in a conceptual scheme*. Strawson's focus, as we have seen, is on the different things we refer to when communicating with others. Relative to this context Strawson introduces the idea of there being a basic class of particulars in the following words:

> First, is there a class or category of particulars such that, as things are, it would not be possible to make all the identifying references which we do make to particulars of other classes, unless we made identifying references to particulars of that class, whereas it would be possible to make all the identifying references we do make to particulars of that class without making identifying reference to particulars of other classes? (Strawson 1959, 38–9)

The condition in this question is the condition for *being basic*. I want to add one further detail which will facilitate our elucidation. Strawson's proposal is that what he calls 'material bodies' are, in fact, basic in this sense.

First, let us assume, as Strawson evidently does, that sounds do not belong to the class of material bodies (see Strawson 1959, chapter 2). It seems that we can refer to something which is (or counts as being) a material body via reference to a sound, e.g. 'The person making that grating sound'.[5] Now, on the face of it I could

---

[5] I am assuming for purposes of this example that a person counts as being a material body. Strawson would not, perhaps, count a person *as* a material body, but he speaks of a person as 'associated with a material body'.

not make that reference to a material body without referring to a non-material item. Does this count against the idea that we can make *all* the identifying references we do to material bodies without making identifying reference to particulars of other classes? If we understand 'all the identifying references we do make' to range over actual cases in speech then this seems to discredit material bodies as basic *strictly speaking*.

Strawson might respond by proposing a weaker interpretation of 'all', so that it means rather identifying reference to the same object at the same time, even if the referring expression itself is different. But there is no guarantee, given the cognitive position of the speaker at the time of making the reference, that he or she has to have available a way of picking out the material body which does not rely on reference to the sound. Maybe all that the speaker remembers of, or can tell about, the person is that they made the grating sound. This problem makes it look rather unlikely that any category will be *strictly* speaking basic as Strawson defines it.

Second, there is another oddity in Strawson's elucidation of basicness. Taking what he says strictly a category of things to which we do refer is not basic if there is another set of things that we must refer to in order to refer to *all* of the items of the former sort we do refer to. But that is consistent with there being some references to items in that category which do not depend on there being reference to the supposedly more basic things. If so, it would seem that a better way to put this would be that there are two categories of things that are basic, only within one general category some of the references to its members are dependent on reference to the other basic category. Implicit in this observation is a recipe for guaranteeing that there would be two basic categories in the stronger sense (if we ignore the first problem set out above). Namely, let it be the case that the speaker only speaks about items in the non-material-body category that they can do without referring to a material body.[6]

Taken together these points suggest that Strawson's definition of being basic requires too much and does not categorize things in a totally illuminating way.

Next, we need to consider Strawson's understanding of material bodies. When developing his argument for the basicness of 'material bodies' Strawson indicates that if the idea of material bodies as space occupiers required that they occupy space in the sense of being resistant to touch then his general argument for the basicness of material bodies would not go through. So, he allows the term 'material bodies' to cover what he describes as 'purely visual occupiers of space' (Strawson 1959, 40), as well as other more standard occupiers of space. Strawson's idea in saying this is that his requirement for identification would be fulfilled if the space

---

[6] This criticism and suggestion skates around an aspect of Strawson's use of 'basic'. His definition requires that a single category be basic if any is. In the way to use 'basic' in the proposal above that aspect is abandoned. Roughly it means—objects of reference not dependent on objects in other categories.

looked to be filled as it does, even if the 'objects' seen were not solid in a strong sense. The subsequent discussion of his argument should be read with this interpretation in mind.

However, there is something strange here. When discussing the possible role of events or processes as alternatives to material bodies in identification Strawson remarks that there simply aren't the sequences of events to do the necessary job. He does not seem to regard it as a drawback to his argument that this absence is in some sense clearly *contingent*. But if so, his response in the case of the idea of purely visual indicators of position and place could, or perhaps, should have been that there aren't enough of these to do the job. In fact, what examples are there at all? Strawson did not really need to offer a rather restricted definition of material body to save his argument, if that is, his points against processes etc., are sound relative to his argumentative purpose.

Leaving these comments aside, the main question to be faced in the complex argument developed in chapter 2 is, as we have seen, whether it *has* to be the case that material bodies are basic in any conceptual scheme enabling objective reference to particulars. Now, one thing to note about this question is that there are two ways the answer might be 'no'. The first is if there is a conceptual scheme in which some *other* category of referent is basic but communication can occur. The second is if there need be no basic category for communication to proceed.

However, in order to test this the most obvious case to consider initially would surely be that of a world, not in any way non-spatial, but which does not contain any material bodies perceptible by speakers, who will not, therefore, refer directly to material bodies nor develop concepts of material bodies, and to ask whether in a such a world there can be communication with others about the particulars that there are in their shared environment. (Or perhaps what should be considered is a world in which there are *far fewer* material bodies than there are in the actual world, which might result in a downgrading of their role.) This is to say the sound world of chapter 2 is a very extreme case to consider. Of course, a second element for the discussion to focus on, which I shall take up shortly, is whether Strawson has so much as a prima facie plausible argument for thinking that material bodies are basic.

I want now, though, to return to an issue raised earlier but not properly discussed. Does Strawson really have a deduction of the basicness of material objects from the idea that we think of the world as having three spatial dimensions and one temporal dimension? If he does not have a good argument for that he has no reason to introduce the so-called no space world. This is, of course, a major question and I can only sketch a case for doubting that Strawson has such an argument.

In fact, Strawson offers two different arguments for his claim that material objects are basic.

The first argument, which is very abstract and general, is presented on page 39. Strawson says that it moves from the idea that identification, and here we can think that he means by an audience as to what a speaker is referring to, rests ultimately on the audience locating the referred to object in a unitary spatio-temporal framework, to the final conclusion that certain objects, namely material bodies, are basic in the specified sense.

Strawson's first move is to suggest that the so-called spatio-temporal framework is, or has to be, constituted by something. Further these constituting elements must be among the objects of which we speak, to which we refer. Moreover, to be the right constituents, they must be spatial three-dimensional objects that endure through time and be observable by us. Finally, he claims that only material bodies satisfy these requirements. The conclusion is, then, that they are basic in the sense under consideration.

Now, about this line of thought many questions, of different degrees of difficulty and interest, can be raised. I shall here restrict myself to one query.

Suppose we allow that identification of referents requires locating them in a spatio-temporal framework of three spatial and one temporal dimension. Why must the framework for thinking of space and time be based on material bodies? It is quite unclear that thinking of *time* depends on material bodies. What is required for time is a way of picking out times, and a simple way to do that is in terms of days, weeks, years, etc. Thus, if I talk about twenty years ago, I would not explain that in terms of material bodies. In the ordinary human case this framework is, as Strawson himself points out, available to us given the recurring rhythm of such environmental changes as day following night, season following season, etc., plus the cognitive capacity to count and remember when things happened within that presented framework. Thus, when I refer to a day as 'two days ago' that reference does not rest on referring to a material body. Strawson's idea is, I think, that it is thinking *about space* that is done in terms of material bodies. Now, one might say that given the world as we (in the restricted sense of 'we') know it we do plot space in terms of material bodies often. But is there any reason to think that is necessary for all human creatures? Thus imagine two aboriginals in the central Australian desert thinking about space and talking about it. For them the spatial world is not divided into enduring streets lined by houses, or squares formed by buildings. They do not inhabit a world of enduring buildings and cities, etc. Rather, at a time they perhaps need to talk in terms of directions—over there (say)—and distance—two hours' walk (say). Their thinking and speech about space and about elsewhere would get by with indications along these lines perfectly happily. So, I suggest, it is quite unclear that the spatio-temporal framework does or has to rely in the way Strawson suggests on material bodies.[7]

---

[7] If we categorize what Strawson is doing as descriptive metaphysics we should acknowledge James Gibson as a superb descriptive metaphysician, and compare what he says in Gibson (1986, Part 1) about the nature of the environment with what Strawson says about the spatio-temporal framework. It would be a very complex matter to develop this comparison properly, but my remark about aboriginal ways of thinking is meant as a crude illustration of what it seems to me Gibson's reflections reveal.

Now, a possible reply to this suggestion is that bodies are still central to these ways of indicating spatial factors. They depend on using our bodies to indicate direction, and on the speed of our bodily movements to indicate distance. So, material bodies are still central to this mode of spatial reference. Given the material nature of human beings this is surely a universal truth—a plausible point somewhat different from both of Strawson's arguments.

What needs adding though is that there is a difference between the ability to speak about space depending on certain material bodies, and the idea that those material bodies are themselves what we basically refer to. This second idea of basicness is what Strawson's notion of basicness requires and rests on, but it is not derivable from the sense of dependence that the argument reveals. So, this defence of Strawson throws up a further problem for his notion of basicness.

Strawson develops a second argument, about which I also wish to express some scepticism. Strawson himself says of the first argument we looked at: 'To rest any philosophical position on argument so general and so vague would be undesirable. But there is no need to do so' (Strawson 1959, 40). He says that he will 'inquire more directly and in greater detail' into referential dependencies. Strawson's lengthy and subtle discussion deserves a very full analysis, but here I wish to make just two suggestions. In considering which category of referent is basic he operates with what is basically a twofold division, into material bodies, his favoured category, on the one hand, and on the other, events and processes (or happenings).[8] Now, if Strawson is thinking that his detailed case-by-case analysis will yield a conclusion that supports something like the idea that material bodies have to be basic given certain very general and hard to think away aspects of our world and thought, then he cannot really rest the conclusions of his survey on manifestly contingent features of our speech and thought and the world. But what we find seems to be that he does precisely that. Thus, he imagines a speaker referring to flashes which form a perceptible regular sequence which both speaker and the audience can hear. In this case the audience can identify the one referred to simply by relating it to the current sequence. No material bodies need to be picked out. Strawson points out that not all flashes belong in such sequences. He then adds 'perhaps this is merely a contingent limitation of the human condition. If so, it is a limitation which determines the nature of our identifying reference to flashes...' (Strawson 1959, 47). But this seems to make it obvious that the restriction which shapes our referential practice is one that need not obtain. In effect Strawson seems to allow that if the world were different our referential practices could be different. Strawson also points out a further limitation of the

---

[8] See Strawson (1959, 46–7). Prior to drawing this distinction Strawson has scrutinized what he thinks of as private particulars, such as pains, etc., and the unobservable micro-entities postulated by science.

flash case when he says, 'But the bang made by an exploding tyre in London is not audible in Edinburgh' (Strawson 1959, 48). That is, of course, true, but it invites the following question: Why must the speaker in London be able to refer in conversation to the London bang when speaking to the Edinburgh audience? It seems wrong to assume that communication about such things between differently situated subjects has itself to be possible. Why must they share a framework even if they happen to do so? Strawson should not assume either that the world has to run as it in fact does, or that communicative capacities and cognitive capacities have to be what they in fact are. It appears that evidently contingent features are being appealed to here.

There is a second aspect of the argument that I wish to focus on. When Strawson makes his twofold division between material bodies and happenings, he remarks that 'a field or a river will count as material bodies or things possessing material bodies' (Strawson 1959, 46). Now it is clear that such things are not processes or happenings, but are they actually material bodies? Take the example of the Grand Canyon. No one would say that it possesses a material body, so is it a material body? The problem is that the canyon seems not to occupy space, but rather to be an empty space, into which we can descend, within an environment. When we talk of the Grand Canyon it seems we are talking rather of a *feature* of the earth's surface, a feature amounting to there being a spectacular gap across it. Equally, Everest is not a material body, but rather the feature of having a certain peak-like shape that the earth's surface has, up which we, or some of us, can ascend. I am suggesting that such geographical elements are neither happenings nor material bodies, but are, rather, features of a surface.[9] Without bodies, e.g. the rocks and particles of sand, there would not be such a surface with its features, but those features themselves are not further bodies in the environment. If this is right, the whole picture of spatial reference as material body based begins to look highly dubious.[10] Speakers in a desert landscape can pick out spatial locations in terms of such features, e.g. 'at the bottom of the Grand Canyon'. This means that Strawson's twofold division is problematic.[11]

It begins to appear that the fuller line of thought that Strawson develops is evidently based on contingencies, and that the basic division in the argument, between bodies and events, is too simple.

---

[9] I owe to a remark of John Campbell that if we should count such things as features, then features are among the nameables. 'Everest' and 'The Grand Canyon' are simply examples of such names.

[10] One test for something being an object is that it can be transported or brought somewhere. One can say of what Gibson calls attached objects, say a tree with its roots in the ground, 'Bring me that tree'. But one cannot say 'Bring me the Grand Canyon'. How could one do that? We might call that the *'bring-me-test' for objecthood.*

[11] In the first part of Gibson (1986) the idea of the surface, and the contrasting idea of objects, is presented with real insight, and it should be read by anyone thinking about our thought about space.

9. Conclusion

It is a measure of the depth and originality of Strawson's discussion that it stimulates so many questions and alternative speculations. It also stimulated what might be called a Strawsonian tradition of philosophical discussion, in which his ideas were reacted to in different ways, although Strawson did not encourage in any way the existence of a Strawsonian school. In this tradition we can place, to name but three, Wiggins, Campbell, and especially Evans.[12] Each of these writers focuses, as Strawson does, on what might be called singling out objects in thought and speech, and the conditions and consequences of doing that. They share, too, a deep interest in the notion of identity. They all tend to replace the centrality in Strawson's discussion of conversation with the more individualistic notion of picking out things in thought. Strawson himself had moved to that in chapter 2, though in his case in a quite unrealistic context. In Campbell and Evans, though not in Wiggins, another move away from Strawson is an illuminating engagement with empirical psychological research about, e.g. memory and perception and sense of direction. We can say that Strawson's thought grabbed the interest of many of the most able philosophers of the subsequent generations, and it has remained a goal of philosophers to get into focus the questions about our thought about the world that he was aiming with great ingenuity to answer.[13]

References

Campbell, John (1994), *Past, Space, and Self* (Cambridge, MA: MIT Press).

Evans, Gareth (1982), *The Varieties of Reference* (Oxford: Clarendon Press).

Gibson, James J. (1986), *The Ecological Approach to Visual Perception* (London: Lawrence Erlbaum Associates).

Strawson, Peter F. (1959), *Individuals: An Essay in Descriptive Metaphysics* (London: Methuen).

Wiggins, David (1980), *Sameness and Substance* (Cambridge, MA: Harvard University Press).

---

[12] See Campbell (1994), Evans (1982), and Wiggins (1980).

[13] I wish to thank John Campbell, David Charles, Tony Cheng, Stefaan Cuypers, Anil Gomes, Naomi Eilan, Al Martinich, Mike Martin, Benjamin De Mesel, Arthur Schipper, and Sebastian Sanhueza for comments and discussions which have helped me, though not perhaps as much as they should have, and also for their encouragement at different stages in the writing of this chapter.

4
Strawson on Other Minds

Quassim Cassam

1. Strawson's Contribution

Philosophical discussions of the so-called 'problem of other minds' standardly distinguish two versions of the problem, a conceptual and an epistemological version.[1] The conceptual version concerns our ability to *conceive* of minds other than our own. How does it make sense to me that other people have thoughts, feelings, and experiences in exactly the same sense that I have thoughts, feelings, and experiences? The epistemological challenge is to account for *knowledge* of other minds. Here the question is: How is it possible for an individual to know anything at all about the thoughts, feelings, experiences, and other mental states of others? Answering this question is usually understood as requiring a response to scepticism about other minds. Since the sceptic denies that knowledge of other minds is possible, a response to the epistemological problem may be expected to show that the sceptic is mistaken about that. This is the *sceptical problem* of other minds. Even if scepticism is not the issue, there is still an explanatory question that needs answering: Given that we know about the mental states of other people, *how* do we know?[2] This is the *explanatory problem* of other minds.

The conceptual version of the problem is one that Strawson takes seriously in chapter 3 of *Individuals* (Strawson 1959). He attempts what might be described as a 'solution' to the problem, and much of his discussion is taken up with elucidating his solution and the problem to which it is a solution. His attitude to the epistemological version of the problem of other minds is quite different. He argues that the 'the sceptical problem does not arise' (Strawson 1959, 106), since the sceptic lacks the resources even to formulate it. In effect, therefore, what Strawson offers is not a solution to the sceptical problem but a *dis*solution. However, the explanatory problem is not one that he dismisses. With respect to the various states of consciousness that one ascribes to oneself, he asks: 'how is it that one can ascribe them to others?' (Strawson 1959, 100).[3] Strawson argues that one ascribes

---

[1] For an account of this distinction, see Avramides (2001), Gomes (2011), and Parrott (2019).
[2] As Snowdon notes, it is taken by many 'to be a condition on the existence of knowledge that there is a way the knowledge was received or generated' (Snowdon 2019, 26).
[3] Notice, however, that asking how one can *ascribe* states of consciousness is not equivalent to asking how one can *know* of others' states of consciousness. Ascriptions need not constitute knowledge.

Quassim Cassam, *Strawson on Other Minds* In: *P. F. Strawson and his Philosophical Legacy.* Edited by: Sybren Heyndels, Audun Bengtson, and Benjamin De Mesel, Oxford University Press. © Oxford University Press 2024.
DOI: 10.1093/oso/9780192858474.003.0005

states of consciousness to others 'on the strength of observation of their behaviour' and that 'behaviour-criteria' are 'criteria of a logically adequate kind' (Strawson 1959, 106) for the other-ascription of states of consciousness. Logically adequate behavioural criteria settle the question whether a person who satisfies them is actually in the state of consciousness for which a particular type of behaviour is criterial. That is how behavioural criteria put us in a position to *know* (in at least some cases) the mind of another person.

In *Scepticism and Naturalism: Some Varieties*, first published in 1985, Strawson sees things somewhat differently. The emphasis is on belief rather than knowledge: in order for self-conscious thought and experience to be possible, we must *believe* that we have knowledge of other minds.[4] If one were looking for an argument against scepticism about other minds, the best that can be done is something along the following lines:

> Given the non-uniqueness of one's physical constitution and the general uniformity of nature in the biological sphere as in others, it is in the highest degree improbable that one is unique among members of one's species in being the enjoyer of subjective states, and of the kind of subjective states one does enjoy in the kind of circumstances in which one enjoys them. (Strawson 2008, 16)

However, Strawson insists, this is no one's reason for believing in the existence of other minds. Rather, 'we simply react to others as to other people' (Strawson 2008, 16). Since we can't help believing in the existence of minds other than our own, both sceptical and scepticism-rebutting arguments are equally idle.

The following discussion is in three parts. Part 2 will focus on Strawson's approach to the conceptual problem of other minds. The two key questions here are: How and why does the conceptual problem arise, and does Strawson have a satisfactory solution? A satisfactory solution will either be one that solves the problem on Strawson's own terms or, if his terms are rejected, one that solves the problem on a better account of how and why it arises. Part 3 will address Strawson's attempted dissolution of the sceptical problem. The issue here is whether he succeeds in showing that the sceptical problem does not arise. A further question concerns the evolution of Strawson's thought between the publication of *Individuals* and the publication a quarter of a century later of *Scepticism and Naturalism*. Part 4 will address the explanatory problem. What is the problem, and how satisfactory is Strawson's quasi-behaviourist response to it?

Regarding the conceptual issue, there are reasons to be sceptical about Strawson's account of the problem and his solution. Regarding the sceptical problem, Strawson's attempted dissolution is problematic but remains of

---

[4] See Strawson (2008, 17). This is a reprint, with additional material, of the 1985 edition of *Scepticism and Naturalism*.

considerable interest. The same cannot be said of his response to the explanatory challenge, which is both dated and unsatisfactory. The emphasis on logically adequate behavioural criteria for the ascription of states of consciousness to others gives Strawson's account a strong Wittgensteinian flavour, which is not necessarily to its advantage. Furthermore, even if states of consciousness are ascribed to others on the strength of observation of their behaviour, it should be acknowledged that there are also significant non-behavioural routes to knowledge of other minds.[5]

The deeper point here is that, as Paul Snowdon points out, 'there is no reason in advance for supposing that all our knowledge of other minds in its great variety must receive the same answer to the relevant "how" question' (Snowdon 2019, 27), the question: How do we know about other minds? Just as there are multiple pathways to knowledge of the external world, so there are multiple pathways to knowledge of other minds. Strawson was, of course, well aware of this. He would not have supposed that 'diarists, novelists, biographers, historians, journalists, and gossips' (Strawson 2008, 46) ascribe mental states to others *solely* on the strength of observation of their behaviour. A popular proposal today is that empathy is a fundamental source of our knowledge or understanding of other people.[6] Something along these lines was also proposed by R. G. Collingwood, who was one of Strawson's predecessors as Oxford's Waynflete Professor of Metaphysics.[7] Strawson would have been quite familiar with Collingwood's views, and it is an interesting question whether there is room in Strawson's framework for Collingwood's insights about the nature of human understanding.

2. The Conceptual Problem

The solipsist is someone who believes, or pretends to believe, not merely that he is at the centre of the mental universe but that he *is* the mental universe. The solipsist claims (to himself, presumably) that while he has the conception of himself and his mental states, he has no conception of mental states that are not his and, correlatively, no conception of other selves. The conception of other minds and their mental states is one that, he insists, makes no sense. Strawson's response to solipsism in *Individuals* is both straightforward and profound: a person who does not have the conception of mental states that are not his could not have the conception of his own mental states. He would lack the distinction between self and other, and this means that he could have no conception of self. A true solipsist

---

[5] The notion of a person's 'behaviour' is also less straightforward than Strawson's discussion assumes.
[6] See, e.g. Matravers (2011) and Campbell (2020).
[7] The classic text here is Robin G. Collingwood, *The Idea of History* (1946). Collingwood occupied the Waynflete Chair from 1936 to 1941. Strawson's tenure lasted from 1968 to 1987.

would be incapable of thinking about himself or his states of mind and so would not be in a position to give expression to his bizarre view.

This is not exactly how Strawson puts it. Instead of talking about mental states, he talks about 'states of consciousness' or 'experiences', which are a sub-class of mental states. Rather than formulating his own view as a view about the necessary conditions for *conceiving* of one's own states, or thinking about them, he formulates it as a view about the necessary conditions for *ascribing* experiences or states of consciousness to himself. He claims that 'it is a necessary condition of one's ascribing states of consciousness, experiences, to oneself, in the way one does, that one should also ascribe them, or be prepared to ascribe them, to others who are not oneself' (Strawson 1959, 99). He interprets the solipsist as someone who wants to hang on to his mental self-ascriptions while denying the possibility of ascribing states of consciousness to anyone other than himself. This, Strawson argues, is incoherent.

Why does the self-ascription of states of consciousness require a willingness to ascribe states of consciousness to others? The point, Strawson argues, is a 'purely logical one: the idea of a predicate is correlative with that of a *range* of individuals of which the predicate can be significantly, though not necessarily truly, affirmed' (Strawson 1959, 99 n.1). This is the case even if the predicate happens to be a psychological predicate, such as 'is in pain' or 'is depressed'. To *ascribe* a predicate F to an individual a is to think or judge that a is F. If it makes sense to judge that a is F, then it must make sense to judge that b is F, c is F, and so on. In other words, if it makes sense to think that I am depressed then it must make sense to me that someone other than me is depressed. At this stage in the argument, there is no mention of knowledge. Thinking that a is F is one thing, knowing that a is F is another.

Even if it is true that in order to ascribe states of consciousness to oneself one must be prepared to ascribe them to others, this is not yet an explanation of how the ascription of states of consciousness to others is possible or even intelligible. Showing that something is necessary is one thing. Explaining how it is possible is another.[8] We ask how x is possible when there appears to be an obstacle to the existence of x.[9] The challenge, therefore, is to identify the apparent obstacle or obstacles to x and show how they can be overcome. Strawson's discussion implies that to have the conception of other minds is to have the idea that the mental states one ascribes to oneself can be ascribed in *exactly the same sense* to others. There is no difference in the meaning of a psychological predicate such as 'is depressed', regardless of whether the predicate is ascribed to oneself or to someone other than oneself. Call this the *univocity* requirement. Anything that prevents a

---

[8] The importance of this distinction is highlighted in chapter 2 of Cassam (2007).
[9] See Cassam (2007) for this conception of the 'how-possible' framework. Anil Gomes uses this framework in his illuminating account of Strawson's version of the conceptual problem. See, especially, Gomes (2011, 356–61).

person's use of psychological predicates from meeting this requirement is an obstacle to their genuinely being able to conceive of other minds.

What might this obstacle be? Strawson distinguishes between two kinds of predicates. M-predicates, like 'weighs 10 stone', 'are those which are also properly applied to material bodies to which we would not dream of applying predicates ascribing states of consciousness' (Strawson 1959, 104). P-predicates, like 'is depressed' and 'is going for a walk', are predicates that we apply to persons. What P-predicates have in common is that 'they imply the possession of consciousness on the part of that to which they are ascribed' (Strawson 1959, 105). One ascribes P-predicates to others on the strength of observation of their behaviour. This is also the basis on which one ascribes some P-predicates to oneself, namely, those P-predicates which 'carry assessments of character or capability' (Strawson 1959, 107). However, there are also P-predicates such that 'when one ascribes them *to oneself*, one does not do so on the strength of observation of those behaviour criteria on the strength of which one ascribes them to others' (Strawson 1959, 107). I ascribe depression to other people on the strength of their behaviour, but I do not usually ascribe depression to myself on the basis of observation of my own behaviour.

Suppose, next, that the meaning of a statement is its method of verification.[10] To say that P-predicates are ascribed to others on the strength of observation of their behaviour is to imply that we rely on other people's behaviour to verify (or falsify) our ascription to them of such predicates. The epistemology of mental self-ascriptions is quite different. Observation of one's own behaviour is not one's method for verifying the ascription of P-predicates to oneself. One might go further and argue that in this case there is no method of verification. This brings the univocity requirement into focus. If the meaning of a statement is its method of verification, then how can the P-predicates that figure in mental self-ascriptions and other-ascriptions meet the univocity requirement? As Strawson asks, how could the sense of P-predicates be the same 'when the method of verification was so different in the two cases—or, rather, when there *was* a method of verification in the one case (the case of others) and not, properly speaking, in the other case (the case of oneself)?' (Strawson 1959, 99–100).[11]

Here, then, is an obstacle to conceiving of minds other than one's own: *if* the meaning of a statement is its method of verification, then how is it possible to think of minds other than one's own in a way that meets the univocity requirement? One option would simply be to drop the univocity requirement and accept that predicates like 'is depressed' do *not* mean the same in 'I am depressed' and

---

[10] This implausible supposition is only worth mentioning here because it, or something like it, plays a significant role in Strawson's discussion.

[11] As Anil Gomes puts it, the suggestion here is that 'the generality of our mental concepts is threatened by the fact that we have different ways of coming to know whether they apply' (Gomes 2011, 357).

'She is depressed'. However, this violates the requirement that the idea of a predicate is correlative with that of a range of individuals of which the predicate can be significantly affirmed. It must be the *same predicate* that can be ascribed to a range of different individuals, and it is not the same predicate if 'depressed' is not univocal in 'I am depressed' and 'She is depressed'. Indeed, if an other-ascription can only be verified on the strength of observation of the ascribee's behaviour, then it is open to question whether 'She is depressed' ascribes a genuine state of consciousness rather than a certain pattern of behaviour.

A different response to the 'how possible' question is to reject the verificationist theory of meaning that puts pressure on the univocity of mental self-ascriptions and other-ascriptions. There are good independent reasons for rejecting this approach to meaning. Furthermore, if 'depressed' has the same meaning in self-ascriptions and other-ascriptions of depression, even though self-ascriptions and other-ascriptions have different methods of verification, then this is in itself a reason for detaching the meaning of a statement from its method of verification. The conceptual problem of other minds, if indeed there is such a problem, will need to be explained in some other way, and there are many non-verificationist accounts of why there is a question about one's ability to conceive of minds other than one's own.[12]

The problem that Strawson faces is that, unlike most philosophers today, he is by no means hostile to verificationism. However, the issues here are complex because he does not say that the meaning of a statement is its method of verification. Instead, he explains his version of verificationism in the following terms in his later paper 'Entity and Identity':

> You do not know what you mean by 'telepathy' unless you know how to identify it, i.e. how you would tell that you have a case of it. You do not know what souls are unless you know how to tell one from another and to say when you have the same one again. And if someone should say that this is just old verificationism writ small, or loose, then I am quite content with that. (Strawson 1997, 50–1)

The implication is that I do not know what I mean by 'depression', or what depression is, unless I can tell when I or someone else has a case of it. However, this leaves it open whether my way of telling must be the same in both cases and, if not, whether this puts pressure on the notion that 'depressed' means the same in the self-ascription and the other-ascription. The challenge for Strawson is to say enough to make it *appear* difficult to reconcile sameness of meaning with the existence of different ways of telling in the two cases, but without thereby making it impossible to secure sameness of meaning.

---

[12] Gomes (2011) also expresses concern about the role in Strawson's argument of 'a controversial claim linking meaning and verification' (Gomes 2011, 357) but makes the point that verificationism is not the only potential source of the conceptual problem of other minds.

Having raised the question how sameness of meaning can be reconciled with different methods of verification, Strawson responds as follows:

> We might say: in order for there to be such a concept as that of X's depression, the depression which X has, the concept must cover both what is felt, but not observed, by X, and what may be observed, but not felt, by others than X (for all values of X). But it is perhaps better to say: X's depression *is* something, one and the same thing, which is felt, but not observed, by X, and observed, but not felt, by others than X... To refuse to accept this is to refuse to accept the *structure* of the language in which we talk about depression.   (Strawson 1959, 108–9)

While what Strawson says here is plausible, it is hard not to suspect that all he has done is to restate the desired result rather than explain how it can be achieved. What has yet to be explained is *how* the language in which we talk about depression makes it possible for the concept of X's depression to be univocal in self-ascriptions and other-ascriptions.

Recall that the question that Strawson is supposed to be answering is: How, given the factors that make such a thing difficult to achieve, can there be 'a kind of predicate which is unambiguously and adequately ascribable *both* on the basis of observation of the subject of the predicate *and* not on this basis' (Strawson 1959, 108)? Strawson's reply at this stage is that the existence of predicates of this type is built into the structure of the language in which we talk about states of consciousness like depression. However, he does not leave the matter there. Instead, he begins the penultimate section of chapter 3 of *Individuals* with the following:

> Now our perplexities may take a different form, the form of the question: 'But how can one ascribe to oneself, not on the basis of observation, the very same thing that others may have, on the basis of observation, reasons of a logically adequate kind for ascribing to one?' This question may be absorbed in a wider one, which might be phrased: 'How are P-predicates possible?'.
> (Strawson 1959, 110)

This passage comes as a surprise. Up to this point, Strawson gives every impression of being content to say that the existence of univocal P-predicates is built into the structure of our language and leave it at that. Now he feels the need to say more and offer a richer explanation of how it can be that the P-predicates meet the univocity requirement. The question to which he now seeks an answer is: What are 'the natural facts' (Strawson 1959, 111) that make it intelligible that such predicates are available to us?[13]

---

[13] Strawson does not explain the notion of a 'natural fact'.

Strawson's answer to this far from self-explanatory question consists in 'moving a certain class of P-predicates to a central position in the picture' (Strawson 1959, 111). This is the class of predicates which 'involve doing something, which clearly imply intention or a state of mind or at least consciousness in general, and which indicate a characteristic pattern, or range of patterns, of bodily movement, while not indicating at all precisely any very definite sensation or experience' (Strawson 1959, 111). Examples include 'going for a walk', 'coiling a rope', and 'writing a letter'. These are P-predicates that one ascribes to others, but not to oneself, on the strength of observation. However, 'in the case of these predicates, one feels minimal reluctance to concede that what is ascribed in these two different ways is the same' because of 'the marked dominance of a fairly definite pattern of bodily movement in what they ascribe, and the marked absence of any distinctive experience' (Strawson 1959, 111).

Take the example of writing a letter. Suppose that my knowledge that I am writing a letter is non-observational, whereas my knowledge that you are writing a letter is observational. However, there is little inclination to suppose that 'writing a letter' means something different in 'I am writing a letter' and 'you are writing a letter'. Since writing a letter is an action, Strawson's suggestion is that our ability to think of ourselves and others as acting in the same way, despite the obvious differences in how we know about our own actions and those of other people, is the 'natural fact' that makes available to us the idea that P-predicates mean the same thing in self-ascriptions and other-ascriptions. We see the movements of some other bodies as *actions*, and 'we see others as self-ascribers, not on the basis of observation, of what we ascribe to them on this basis' (Strawson 1959, 112).

There are several things to be said about this argument. The first is that Strawson makes no attempt to defend the idea that knowledge of our own actions is non-observational. This approach to the epistemology of action is associated above all with Anscombe, whose *Intention* (1957) was published two years before *Individuals*. Perhaps influenced by Anscombe, Strawson takes it for granted that we have non-observational knowledge of our own actions, and he expects his readers to do the same. The second is that while Strawson's 'argument from action' is helpful in weakening objections to the possibility of univocal P-predicates that are known in quite different ways to apply to oneself and to others, it is unclear whether we are any further forward when it comes to explaining how P-predicates that do *not* ascribe actions can be univocal in self-ascriptions and other-ascriptions. In the case of P-predicates like 'is thinking of writing a letter', it is the marked *absence* of a definite pattern of bodily movement in what they ascribe that stands out, and this means that the argument from action does not identify the 'natural facts' that make *these* P-predicates available. A third comment is that the argument from action finally puts paid to any idea that the meaning of a term is tied to our way of knowing whether or not it applies. Since Strawson cannot be a verificationist in *this* sense, he cannot rely on this form of verificationism to motivate his concern with the conceptual problem of other minds. The non-verificationist view of meaning required to solve the problem does not allow the problem to arise in the first place, at least as Strawson understands it. This gives his position a distinct air of instability: he *relies on* but is ultimately committed to *rejecting* verificationism. He relies on it to generate his concerns about how it is possible to conceive of other minds, but his solution to the conceptual problem commits him to rejecting it.

Before turning to the epistemological problem of other minds, there is one more thing to say about Strawson's struggle with the conceptual problem. It is striking how much of the heavy lifting in his discussion is done by the principle that the idea of a predicate is correlative with that of a range of individuals of which the predicate can be significantly, though not necessarily truly, affirmed. The incoherence of solipsism follows from this principle, and this makes it all the more surprising that Strawson offers no defence of his principle and only states it in a footnote. Perhaps he regarded the principle as a conceptual truth about the idea of a predicate. In any event, more can be and has been said in defence of Strawson's idea of a predicate. In *The Varieties of Reference*, Gareth Evans, a former pupil of Strawson's, sees the thought that a is F as 'lying at the intersection of two series of thoughts: on the one hand, the series of thoughts that a is F, that b is F, that c is F,... and, on the other hand, the series of thoughts that a is F, a is G, that a is H,...' (Evans 1982, 104 n.21). Evans calls this the Generality Constraint on our conceivings. He adds that even readers not persuaded that *any* system of thought must conform to this constraint may be prepared to admit that *our* system of thought—the system that underlies our use of language—does conform to it.

In these terms, what Strawson says about the idea of a predicate is, in effect, a statement of one dimension of the Generality Constraint, and the fundamental objection to solipsism is that it fails to respect this constraint. Where 'F' is a psychological predicate, the solipsist is precisely someone who fails to see the thought that 'I am F' as lying at the intersection of two series of thoughts in Evans's sense. The solipsist has a problem with the Generality Constraint because he sees an insuperable obstacle to the intelligible other-ascription of psychological predicates. Among the many accounts of the alleged obstacle, verificationism is the least compelling but it is the only one that Strawson considers. For this reason, philosophers who take solipsism more seriously may feel short-changed by Strawson's discussion. Nevertheless, it is a major insight of Strawson's that reflection on the idea of a predicate can be used to raise questions about the coherence of solipsism.

3. The Sceptical Problem

The epistemological problem of other minds can be expressed in the form of a question: How is it possible for one to know anything at all about the thoughts, feelings, experiences, and other mental states of others? The sceptic thinks that knowledge of one's own states of mind is easy, whereas knowledge of the mental states of others is impossible. In formulating his view, the sceptic relies on a commitment to what Snowdon calls the 'interiority of the mental'. That is:

> When we observe those around us in normal circumstances we observe them by observing their surfaces, the movements of those surfaces, and also what we might call emissions from their surfaces (say, the sounds they make). However, although the surface and its behaviour (and products) are observed by us, it is a very basic part of our conception of mental states and occurrences that they require things to be a certain way behind or within that presented surface.
>
> (Snowdon 2019, 35)

This means that 'my ascriptions of mental states to others goes beyond anything on the surface' (Snowdon 2019, 37) and 'there is no way to explore the interiors to confirm there is mentality behind the encountered surface' (Snowdon 2019, 38). We might regard what we encounter when we observe the surfaces of those around us as *signs* of the presence of mentality behind those surfaces, but the sceptic argues that any inference to mentality is distinctly shaky since it needs to cross a logical and ontological gap between what is visible on the outside and what is actually there on the inside. Thus, we are left in a position of never really knowing whether there any minds other than our own, and this is the essence of the sceptical problem.

Taken in this way, scepticism implies the epistemological priority of self-knowledge over knowledge of other minds: I can know my own states of mind without knowing whether there are any minds other than my own, and it is only because I am aware of how my own states of mind correlate with *my* behaviour or bodily movements that I ascribe mental states to others on the strength of *their* behaviour or bodily movements. I interpret the latter as *signs* of mentality because of what I know to be true in my own case, but the ascription of mentality to others is the conclusion of an inference from premises that include statements about my own mind. This is the 'argument from analogy' for other minds. As Ayer puts it, an essential feature of this argument is that 'the justification, as distinct from the cause, of my ascribing experiences to others must issue from the premise that I have experience myself' (Ayer 1963, 104). However, this argument does not rule out the possibility that 'one might be able to ascribe experiences to oneself, while being invariably mistaken in ascribing them to others' (Ayer 1963, 108).

If one could show that knowledge of other minds is necessary for knowledge of one's own mind, then the argument from analogy could never get off the ground and the sceptical problem would not arise. If knowledge of other minds is presupposed by knowledge of one's own mind, then self-knowledge would *not* be epistemologically prior to knowledge of other minds, and the considerations we rely on in ascribing states of mind to others would have to be conceived of as more than mere signs of mentality in others. Instead, the behavioural and other outward signs that ground our other-ascriptions would need to be viewed as ways of *knowing* the mind of another person. However, this assumes that self-knowledge would not be possible without knowledge of other minds, but why should one believe that?

It might seem that Strawson has already answered this question. Hasn't he already argued that it is a necessary condition of one's ascribing states of consciousness to oneself that one should also ascribe them, or be prepared to ascribe them, to others who are not oneself? Is this not just another way of denying the epistemological priority of self-knowledge over our knowledge of other minds, and thereby dissolving the sceptical problem? As Strawson puts it in *Scepticism and Naturalism*:

> [T]he sceptic could not even raise his doubt unless he knew it to be unfounded; i.e. he could have no use for the concepts in terms of which he expresses his doubt unless he were able to know to be true at least some of the propositions belonging to the class all members of which fall within the scope of the sceptical doubt. (Strawson 2008, 7)

However, *if* this is Strawson's reply to the argument from analogy then it is unsuccessful for a fairly obvious reason: being able to other-ascribe states of consciousness is not the same as knowing whether one's ascriptions of mental states to others are actually correct.[14] It is one thing to say that my ascribing states of consciousness to others is a necessary condition of my being able to ascribe them to myself. It is another to say that my *correctly* or *knowledgeably* ascribing states of consciousness to others is a necessary condition of my being able to self-ascribe them. The most that Strawson is entitled to is the former claim. What he needs is the latter claim. As he recognizes in *Scepticism and Naturalism*, his anti-sceptical argument in *Individuals* turns on the idea that in order to have self-conscious experience one must have 'knowledge...of the states of mind of other beings' (Strawson 2008, 7).

Strawson's diagnosis of sceptical problems generally, including scepticism about other minds, is that 'their statement involves the pretended acceptance of a conceptual scheme and at the same time the silent repudiation of one of the conditions of its existence' (Strawson 1959, 106). The conceptual scheme that the sceptic about other minds pretends to accept is one that allows for a grasp of P-predicates and their self-ascription other than on the basis of observation. The condition for the existence of this scheme that the sceptic allegedly repudiates is

---

[14] As Ayer points out. See Ayer (1963, 105).

that the P-predicates that one ascribes to oneself are ones that one is also willing to ascribe to others, albeit on a different basis. On the face of it, however, the sceptic has no difficulty accepting this condition since he is not a solipsist. He *is* willing to ascribe P-predicates to others, and so is *not* in the position of trying to self-ascribe P-predicates while at the same time insisting that he has no conception of other minds. What he is unsure of is whether his other-ascriptions are ever *correct*.

Strawson's response to this line of reasoning is to argue, in effect, that it is built into the conceptual scheme in terms of which the sceptical problem is stated that the behavioural criteria one relies on in ascribing P-predicates to others 'are not just signs of the presence of what is meant by the P-predicate, but are criteria of a logically adequate kind for the ascription of the P-predicate' (Strawson 1959, 106). For example, if one ascribes a P-predicate like 'is depressed' to someone other than oneself because they satisfy the behavioural criteria for depression, then it is no longer an open question whether they really are depressed. In Strawson's terminology, the relevant criteria are 'ways of telling' (Strawson 1959, 105). It is because they put one in a position to *know* the other's state of mind that the sceptical problem does not arise. The sceptic is in the incoherent position of denying knowledge of other minds while simultaneously applying to himself P-predicates that are ascribable to others on the basis of behavioural criteria that, of necessity, provide us with knowledge of other minds.

It has to be said that this is a remarkably weak argument. It is just a roundabout way of insisting, once again, that the *knowledgeable* ascription of P-predicates to others is a necessary condition for ascribing these same predicates to oneself. The question to which Strawson fails to provide a satisfactory answer is: Why isn't it enough for the self-ascription of P-predicates that the self-ascriber can conceive of ascribing these same predicates to others on the basis of behavioural evidence without ever *knowing* that there are other minds? There is a quick but unsatisfactory answer to this question by which Strawson may well have been tempted. According to this answer, one cannot even *think* of other minds unless one can *know* whether or not there are other minds. These ways of knowing are precisely the logically adequate criteria that Strawson posits. If the sceptic is right that there really is no way of telling anyone else's state of mind, then one would lack the conception of other minds and therefore lack the conception of one's own mind.

The problem with this argument is that it does not just rely on old verificationism writ small, or loose. It relies on old-fashioned verificationism writ large and strict.[15] One would have to suppose that the only meaningful statements are ones that can be empirically verified. This would instantly knock out scepticism about other minds since the sceptic is precisely someone who thinks that statements

---

[15] See Ayer (1963, 110) and Stroud (2000) on the role of verificationism in Strawson's argument.

about other minds are meaningful but cannot be verified. However, this argument against scepticism comes at a high price. Apart from objections to old-fashioned verificationism, relying on this principle to deal with scepticism makes much of the complex theoretical machinery of chapter 3 of *Individuals* redundant for anti-sceptical purposes. Why bother with this machinery if the self-defeating character of scepticism is a direct consequence of verificationism? As Barry Stroud notes, there is 'nothing special or unique' (Stroud 2000, 24) about this way of attacking scepticism, and it would be disappointing if the supposedly self-defeating character of scepticism 'amounts to nothing more and nothing less than an application of some version of the verification principle' (Stroud 2000, 24).

The only reasonable conclusion is that in chapter 3 of *Individuals* Strawson fails to deliver a convincing refutation of scepticism. This is how Strawson himself came to see things in *Scepticism and Naturalism*. He accepts Stroud's criticisms of his earlier argument but still maintains that he got something right in *Individuals*. What he got right is that 'self-ascription implies the capacity for other-ascription' (2008, 18). This looks like a notational variant of his claim that it is a necessary condition of one's ascribing states of consciousness, experiences, to oneself that one should also be willing to ascribe them to others who are not oneself. To ascribe states of consciousness to others is to judge that those others are in, or have, the relevant states of consciousness. To judge that another person is F, where F is a P-predicate, is to *believe* that he is F. Hence, 'we must take it, or believe, that we have knowledge of... other minds' (2008, 17).

If philosophical sceptics are among those who must believe that they have knowledge of other minds, then they are in the incoherent position of believing that they have knowledge of other minds while at the same time denying that knowledge of other minds is possible. The sceptic might respond that since he can self-ascribe experiences while denying that knowledge of other minds is possible, he is living proof that the self-ascription of experiences does *not* require belief in knowledge of other minds. Strawson's reply to someone who argues in this way is that they are deluding themselves. They think that they believe that they lack knowledge of other minds, but this is not, and cannot be, what they actually believe. In practice, they believe, like the rest of us, that they have knowledge of other minds. One startling consequence of this argument is that philosophical sceptics do not know what they believe. What they think they believe about knowledge of other minds is not what they actually believe.[16]

Suppose that Strawson is right, and that the sceptic must believe that he has knowledge of other minds, and so must believe that there are states of mind that are not his own. However, if one is to believe that there are other minds, one needs

---

[16] As argued in Cassam (1996), this is a general problem with 'transcendental' arguments that try to establish claims about what we must believe to be the case. The sceptic claims not to believe what these arguments say he must believe.

adequate reasons to believe this.[17] It cannot be Strawson's view that a self-ascriber of states of consciousness must believe that there are other minds regardless of whether he has any reason to believe this. The required reasons must be *epistemic*, and evidence for P is the most basic type of epistemic reason for believing that P. But is there any guarantee of the availability of such evidence of other minds? What if one never encounters any other minds, or any other being that behaves in ways that would warrant the ascription to them of states of consciousness?[18] In reply, Strawson could retreat to the position that in order to self-ascribe P-predicates one must be *prepared* to ascribe them to others, even if one never actually does so because one is alone in the world. On this view, the self-ascriber is like a juror who is prepared to believe that the defendant is guilty but only if presented with adequate evidence of the defendant's guilt. Even though there is no guarantee that such evidence will be forthcoming, and therefore no guarantee that the juror will *actually* believe that the defendant is guilty, it is essential that this is something that the juror is prepared to believe.

In the case of other minds, the worry that we lack evidence or reasons for believing that there are other minds is not serious. Evidence of other minds is not lacking, and what Strawson says about the behavioural criteria for ascribing states of consciousness to others can be read in this light. To describe these criteria as 'logically adequate' is not to suppose that their being satisfied in a given case logically entails that the individual in question is in the mental state for which the criteria are criterial. Going by a person's behaviour, it can look for all the world as if she is depressed and yet she is not depressed. It is sometimes suggested that what Strawson wishes to rule out is that our other-ascriptions are *always* mistaken but even this might be going too far. Strawson's point is that the logically adequate criteria for, say, depression are criterial for the *belief* that some other person is depressed: the concept of depression is such that a person's satisfying the associated behavioural criteria is an adequate reason for *believing* that he or she is depressed in the case in which the person is not oneself.

It is a perfectly familiar point that even justified beliefs can be false. Even if one has good behavioural reasons for other-ascribing depression, these reasons do not logically entail that the person to whom depression is ascribed is depressed. There is still room for the sceptic to stick in his knife, so it cannot be said that 'the sceptical problem does not arise' (Strawson 1959, 106). However, Strawson might reasonably claim to have emasculated scepticism about other minds. For once it is agreed that self-conscious beings, including sceptics, must be prepared to other-ascribe states of consciousness and so must believe and have adequate reasons to believe in the existence of other minds, the residual sceptical worry is that there is

---

[17] This claim assumes the truth of some version of evidentialism about belief. For a defence of this view, see Adler (2002, 5).
[18] See Ayer (1963, 106–9).

no absolute guarantee that this belief is correct. Perhaps not, but does that matter? Strawson thinks not, and it is arguable that he is right about that.

Where does this leave his suggestion that the best argument against scepticism about other minds is that the non-uniqueness of one's physical constitution and the general uniformity of nature make it highly improbable that one is unique among members of one's species in having subjective states? Strawson maintains that 'this is no one's reason for believing in the existence of other minds' (Strawson 2008, 16) because it over-intellectualizes this belief. The existence of other minds is something that we take for granted, but Strawson cannot have it both ways. If we must *believe* that there are other minds, and this is an example of a genuine belief, then we must have reasons for the belief, that is, reasons for which we believe that there are other minds. There are, no doubt, many such reasons, and they could include the non-uniqueness of one's physical constitution.

This brings into focus another aspect of Strawson's discussion. When he asks how it is that one can ascribe states of consciousness to others, his answer is strikingly one-dimensional: one ascribes states of consciousness to others on the strength of observation of their behaviour. However, there is no reason to suppose that this is the sole basis on which we ascribe states of consciousness to others, even if a person's 'behaviour' includes their utterances about their own states of consciousness; that is, if even their behaviour includes what Strawson calls their 'first-person P-utterances' (1959, 108). As Strawson knew quite well, many other-ascriptions are based on something other than a person's behaviour. Furthermore, the biological justification for general belief in the existence of other minds is of little help in resolving what *specific* state of mind another person is in. A realistic account of the basis on which mental states are ascribed to others needs to be thoroughly multi-dimensional. Indeed, it is rather surprising that a thinker as subtle as Strawson should have said so little about non-behavioural sources of knowledge or justified belief about other minds, and the next task is to correct this troubling limitation in his account.

4. The Explanatory Problem

In a discussion of physicalism in *Scepticism and Naturalism*, Strawson distinguishes between the physical and the personal history of a person. In recounting a person's history in purely physical terms, in terms of bodily movements and electrochemical events, we would 'leave out almost everything that was humanly interesting' (Strawson 2008, 46). It is a person's personal history that is humanly interesting; that is, the history of their actions, thoughts, desires, beliefs, intentions, and so on. Personal histories, told in mentalistic terms, are the main concern of diarists, novelists, biographers, historians, journalists, and gossips. These histories are exercises in folk psychology, a type of psychological explanation favoured by 'such simple folk as Shakespeare, Tolstoy, Proust, and Henry James' (Strawson 2008, 46).

How do biographers and historians go about their business? They ascribe P-predicates to the human subjects of their enquiries, but what is the basis on which they do that? Historians and biographers are not in a position to ascribe P-predicates to Julius Caesar on the strength of observation of his behaviour, since it is no longer observable. They might rely, instead, on the historical record of his actions and utterances, but that is hardly sufficient. The distinguished biographer Richard Holmes describes *empathy* as 'the biographer's most valuable and perilous weapon' (Holmes 2017, 6). Empathy in some form is also seen by some philosophers of history as the key to historical explanation. Of particular interest in this regard are the views of Collingwood. He defends the radical thesis that what he calls the 'historical method' is 'the only one by which I can know the mind of another' (Collingwood 1946, 219). The historian 'does not know the past by simply believing a witness who saw the events in question and has left his evidence on record' (Collingwood 1946, 282). History is the re-enactment of past thoughts and experiences in the historian's own mind. This is Collingwood's version of empathy, which he sees as delivering imaginative knowledge or understanding of other minds.[19]

This is far removed from the Strawsonian reliance on behavioural criteria in ascribing mental states to other minds. Indeed, for Collingwood, the historical method also provides one with knowledge of one's *own* mind since 'it is only by historical thinking that I can discover what I thought ten years ago' (Collingwood 1946, 219). In this sense, *all* knowledge of mind is historical. If Strawson's conception of our knowledge of other minds is too behaviouristic for some tastes, Collingwood's account is the perfect antidote, but only if it is successful. Even if it is not, this does not invalidate the concern that Strawson's theory is too narrow. Our picture of the mental states of others is shaped by a variety of factors apart from their behaviour. It is an argument in favour of treating empathy as one such factor that it accords with the practice of biographers and, if Collingwood is to be believed, historians.

In what sense must historians or biographers re-enact the thoughts and experiences of those they seek to understand? Suppose that an historian is trying to ascertain Caesar's thoughts when he decided to cross the Rubicon.

> But how does the historian discern the thoughts which he is trying to discover? ... [T]he historian of politics or warfare, presented with an account of certain actions done by Julius Caesar, tries to understand these actions, that is, to discover what thoughts in Caesar's mind determined him to do them. This implies

---

[19] Dray (1995) provides an illuminating account of Collingwood's view.

envisaging for himself the situation in which Caesar stood, and thinking for himself what Caesar thought about the situation and the possible ways of dealing with it. The history of thought, and therefore all history, is the re-enactment of past thought in the historian's own mind. (Collingwood 1946, 215)

However, this is to be understood as 'a labour of active and therefore critical thinking' rather than 'a passive surrender to the spell of another's mind' (Collingwood 1946, 215). The historian criticizes past thoughts in re-enacting them: 'nothing could be a completer error concerning the history of thought than to suppose that the historian...merely ascertains "what so-and-so" thought, leaving it to some one else to decide "whether it was true"' (Collingwood 1946, 215–16).

What is going on here? On a purely epistemological reading, what re-enactment offers the historian or biographer is a way of *knowing* the mind of another. This fits with the repeated references to the task of *discerning* or *ascertaining* the thoughts of one's subject. Yet there is an obvious difficulty with the idea that it is possible to discover Julius Caesar's thoughts by re-enacting them: one cannot re-enact his thoughts if one does not know what they are. However, the appearance of circularity is only superficial. The sense in which one might re-enact Caesar's thoughts about crossing the Rubicon is that one can imagine oneself in Caesar's place and ask what one would have thought or done in his place. By engaging in this imaginative exercise, one can ascertain Caesar's thoughts.

On the face of it, there is little justification for supposing that the thoughts that *I* would have had in Caesar's place are thoughts that *he* had, even if I do my best to take on board his context and background assumptions. In defence of Collingwood, John Campbell argues that what needs to be acknowledged is what he calls the *dynamic* role of imagination in providing knowledge of the mind, that is, the role that imagination plays in 'an understanding of how one mental state generates or produces another' (Campbell 2020, 71). For example, did Brutus assassinate Caesar because he was jealous or because he loved the republic? When Brutus's countrymen found him to be acting from one motive rather than another, 'they used their imaginative understanding of him to get a sense of how the action was generated. It was their empathetic understanding of Brutus that provided knowledge of which mental process was operative here' (Campbell 2020, 11). Far from regarding our imaginative understanding of one another as speculative, we see our ordinary knowledge of which motive someone acted from as 'meeting the highest possible epistemic standard' (Campbell 2020, 12), that is, as beyond reasonable doubt.

This is far-fetched. Knowledge of other people's motives is notoriously elusive, and the most we can say about Brutus is that it is plausible or likely that he acted from a given motive. However, hypotheses about other people's motives are just that: hypotheses that are far from being beyond reasonable doubt. Findings in this domain are provisional even if Campbell and Collingwood are correct to draw attention to 'the use of imagination to track the ballistics of people's thoughts and feelings' (Campbell 2020, 9). However, the fact that imagination is used in this way is something that Strawson ought to acknowledge. Even if there are questions about the extent to which the procedures described by Campbell and Collingwood yield *knowledge* of other minds, it is beyond question that empathy is one basis on which we *ascribe* states of mind to other people, that is, form *beliefs* about their thoughts and feelings. Observation of Brutus's behaviour might leave one none the wiser as to his true motives unless supplemented by imaginative understanding.

There is also another lesson in for Strawson in Collingwood's account. In discussing whether we have knowledge of other minds or only the belief that there are minds other than our own, Strawson does not take due account of another fundamental aspect of our interest in minds other than our own: an interest in *understanding* them. From this perspective, the challenge is not so much to work out what another person thinks but rather to make sense of their thinking what they think. The question in this context is: Why would someone think that? In the same way, other people's actions lead us to wonder: Why would they do that? The focus of such questions is *Verstehen*, the attempt to understand beliefs and actions from within, that is, from the standpoint of the thinker or agent. What we are after is not so much *knowledge* but *intelligibility*. We want to make what other people think and do intelligible to ourselves, and thereby not only to see them as minded but as minded in a sense that makes sense to us. In these terms, Collingwood was what Michael Martin calls a 'radical Verstehenist', someone who held that 'historical events must be understood from the inside, and that in order to understand the action of historical agents, historians must rethink the agents' thoughts' (Martin 2000, 7). When it is a matter of Verstehen, talk of logically adequate behavioural criteria for the other-ascription of P-predicates is beside the point.

Consider, in this light, the example of Caesar and the Rubicon. In the words of the eminent Collingwood scholar William Dray, what would make Caesar's action understandable is the thought that 'given the situation as he conceived his to be, and goals like the ones he wanted to pursue, faced by a barrier like the Rubicon, the thing to do would be to cross it' (Dray 1995, 55). The only way to establish whether this is in fact the case would be to try out Caesar's practical argument for crossing the Rubicon, to re-enact it and see whether it can really be thought. Thus, 'to understand an action in a properly historical way is in some degree to see it as having been appropriate to the circumstances as the agent saw them' (Dray 1995, 56). This is a form of normative assessment that explains Collingwood's insistence that re-enactment is a labour of active and therefore critical thinking.

Since Strawson rather than Collingwood is our main concern here, what is most helpful about this account is the way that it highlights a lacuna in Strawson's theory of other minds in *Individuals*. Not only does Strawson not make enough of our desire for Verstehen, but his emphasis on behavioural criteria also leaves out the normative dimension of our engagement with other minds, the subjecting of other minds to what Davidson calls 'the constitutive ideal of rationality' (Davidson 1980, 223). When we attempt to make sense of other people, we attribute to them mental states that it makes sense for them to have in the circumstances in which they find themselves. We have their behaviour to go on, including their utterances, but their utterances are not self-interpreting. We can talk about logically adequate behavioural criteria for the other-ascription of P-predicates, but such criteria are only of any use to us if we haven't misunderstood the relevant behaviour. In *Individuals*, Strawson says remarkably little about the extent to which our interest in behavioural criteria for the other-ascription of P-predicates is shaped by our desire for Verstehen.

These gaps in Strawson's account are, no doubt, a reflection of when *Individuals* was written. Philosophical writing is always influenced by contextual factors, and *Individuals* is no exception. Its arguments suggest that Strawson was heavily influenced by Wittgenstein and the crude behaviourism of some of his followers. Strawson was far too subtle a thinker to fall for this and he saw himself as avoiding the extremes of behaviourism and Cartesianism. However, just as the residual influence of Cartesianism is evident from his insistence in *Individuals* on intelligibility of life after death, his epistemology of other minds fails fully to shake off the influence of behaviourism. As a result, we have less to learn from *Individuals* about the epistemological problem of other minds than about the conceptual problem. As far as the latter is concerned, however, Strawson's discussion remains essential reading.

References

Adler, Jonathan (2002), *Belief's Own Ethics* (Cambridge, MA: MIT Press).

Anscombe, Gertrude E. M. (1957), *Intention* (Oxford: Basil Blackwell).

Avramides, Anita (2001), *Other Minds* (London and New York: Routledge).

Ayer, Alfred J. (1963), 'The Concept of a Person', in *The Concept of a Person and Other Essays* (London: Macmillan), 82–128.

Campbell, John (2020), *Causation in Psychology* (Cambridge, MA: Harvard University Press).

Cassam, Quassim (1996), 'Self-Reference, Self-Knowledge and the Problem of Misconception', *European Journal of Philosophy* 4: 276–95.

Cassam, Quassim (2007), *The Possibility of Knowledge* (Oxford: Oxford University Press).

Collingwood, Robin George (1946), *The Idea of History* (Oxford: Oxford University Press).

Davidson, Donald (1980), 'Mental Events', in *Essays on Actions and Events* (Oxford: Oxford University Press), 207–25.

Dray, William H. (1995), *History as Re-Enactment: R. G. Collingwood's Idea of History* (Oxford: Oxford University Press).

Evans, Gareth (1982), *The Varieties of Reference* (Oxford: Clarendon Press).

Gomes, Anil (2011), 'Is There a Problem of Other Minds?', *Proceedings of the Aristotelian Society* 111: 353–73.

Holmes, Richard (2017), *This Long Pursuit: Reflections of a Romantic Biographer* (London: HarperCollins).

Martin, Michael (2000), *Verstehen: The Uses of Understanding in Social Science* (Abingdon: Routledge).

Matravers, Derek (2011), 'Empathy as a Route to Knowledge', in Amy Coplan and Peter Goldie (eds.), *Empathy: Philosophical and Psychological Perspectives* (Oxford: Oxford University Press), 19–30.

Parrott, Matthew (2019), 'Enquiries Concerning the Minds of Others', in Anita Avramides and Matthew Parrott (eds.), *Knowing Other Minds* (Oxford: Oxford University Press), 1–19.

Snowdon, Peter F. (2019), 'The Problem of Other Minds; Some Preliminaries', in Anita Avramides and Matthew Parrott (eds.), *Knowing Other Minds* (Oxford: Oxford University Press), 20–40.

Strawson, Peter F. (1959), *Individuals: An Essay in Descriptive Metaphysics* (London: Methuen).

Strawson, Peter F. (1997), 'Entity and Identity', in *Entity and Identity and Other Essays* (Oxford: Oxford University Press), 21–51.

Strawson, Peter F. (2008), *Scepticism and Naturalism: Some Varieties* (Abingdon: Routledge).

Stroud, Barry (2000), 'Transcendental Arguments', in *Understanding Human Knowledge* (Oxford: Oxford University Press), 9–25.

5
P. F. Strawson and the 'Pseudo-Material Shadows'

Michelle Montague

1. Introduction

In section IV of 'On Referring' (1950), P. F. Strawson writes as follows:

One of the main purposes for which we use language is the purpose of stating facts about things and persons and events. If we want to fulfil this purpose, we must have some way of forestalling the question, 'What (who, which one) are you talking about?' as well as the question, 'What are you saying about it (him, her)?'. The task of forestalling the first question is the referring (or identifying) task. The task of forestalling the second is the attributive (or descriptive or classificatory or ascriptive) task. In the conventional English sentence which is used to state, or claim to state, a fact about an individual thing or person or event, the performance of these two tasks can be roughly and approximately assigned to separable expressions. And in such a sentence, this assigning of expressions to their separate roles corresponds to the conventional grammatical classification of subject and predicate. There is nothing sacrosanct about the employment of separable expressions for these two tasks. Other methods could, and are, employed. There is, for instance, the method of uttering a single word or attributive phrase in the conspicuous presence of the object referred to; or that analogous method exemplified by, for example, the painting of the words 'unsafe for lorries' on a bridge, or the tying of a label reading 'first prize' on a vegetable marrow... Two points require emphasis. The first is that the necessity of performing these two tasks in order to state particular facts requires no transcendental explanation: to call attention to it is partly to elucidate the meaning of the phrase, 'stating a fact'. The second is that even this elucidation is made in terms derivative from the grammar of the conventional singular sentence; that even the overtly functional, linguistic distinction between the identifying and attributive roles that words may play in language is prompted by the fact that ordinary speech offers us separable expressions to which the different functions may be plausibly and approximately assigned. And this functional distinction has cast long philosophical shadows. The distinctions between particular and universal, between substance and quality, are such pseudo-material shadows, cast by the grammar of the conventional sentence in which separable expressions play distinguishable roles.   (Strawson 1950)

The last two sentences have a dramatic, Ramseyan-Whiteheadian sweep. For Ramsey, 'the whole theory of particulars and universals is due to mistaking for a fundamental characteristic of reality what is merely a characteristic of language' (Ramsey 1925, 405). Whitehead, criticizing the direction of philosophy, complains that 'all modern philosophy hinges round the difficulty of describing the world in terms of subject and predicate, substance and quality, particular and universal' (Whitehead 1929, 49).

When Strawson republished 'On Referring' in *Logico-Linguistic Papers* in 1971, he added the following footnote: 'What is said or implied in the last two sentences of this paragraph no longer seems to me true, unless considerably qualified'.

What I want to do in this chapter is assemble some reflections on the recurrence of this theme in Strawson's work, with a particular focus on how the claim about pseudo-material shadows is qualified—'considerably' or not—in his book *Individuals*, published in 1959.

2. 'Objective Particulars'

In *Individuals*, Strawson defines 'objective particulars' as 'those particulars which are not experiences or states of consciousness of one's own, or of anyone else's either, though they may be objects of experience' (Strawson 1959, 61).[1] Examples include paradigmatically, ordinarily perceptible material bodies, but also their shadows, together with processes, events, etc. Strawson also allows that 'particularized qualities', often now known as 'tropes', may count as objective particulars (Strawson 1959, 168n.). All such things are distinguished, as objective particulars, from general properties, species, qualities, and also from things like numbers.

What makes thought about objective particulars possible? This is a central question in *Individuals*, and it is in answering this question that Strawson articulates the fundamental place of the subject-predicate distinction in our thought, and more generally in our overall conception of the nature of reality, in which the distinction between object (particular) and property (universal) plays such a central role. I want to consider the way in which, taking full account of the qualifications he signalled in 1971, Strawson still places the subject-predicate distinction (formal mode) or particular-universal distinction (material mode) under the wing of the Ramseyan–Whiteheadian sweep in 1959.

Individuals has two parts, 'Particulars' (Part I) and 'Logical Subjects' (Part II), each of which makes a distinctive and significant contribution to Strawson's

---

[1] From now on I shall refer to *Individuals* with year and page numbers in parentheses.

overall picture of our thought about objective particulars. Strawson himself says of the two parts, 'I doubt if it is possible for us to fully understand the main topics of either part without consideration of the main topics of the other' (Strawson 1959, 12). Chapters 1 and 2 of Part I have been much discussed, and I shall keep my exposition of them short. It is the much less explored Part II that will be my focus, particularly chapter 6, the core chapter of Part II. It is only with a careful reading of chapter 6 that we get to see Strawson's full picture of what is involved in thinking about objective particulars.[2]

3. Descriptive Metaphysics and Thinking of 'Basic' Particulars

Strawson's approach to thought about objective particulars in *Individuals* is embedded in his methodology of 'descriptive metaphysics', which he describes as follows:

> ...there is a massive central core of human thinking which has no history—or none recorded in the histories of thought; there are categories and concepts which, in their most fundamental character, change not at all... It is with these, their interconnexions, and the structure that they form, that a descriptive metaphysics will be primarily concerned. (Strawson 1959, 10)

The core concepts and categories that we use to think about and perceive the world form part of Strawson calls 'our conceptual scheme'. I do not want to get bogged down in debates about the merits and demerits of descriptive metaphysics, or about whether or how we can give an exact definition of a conceptual scheme.[3] Even if we disagree about the value of descriptive metaphysics or the existence of *a* (single) human conceptual scheme, *Individuals* contains many insights concerning thought about objective particulars, which I shall examine in their own right. Part I reaches two central conclusions about how such particulars feature in our conceptual scheme. The first is that

(1) material bodies and persons are 'basic' particulars.

For the purposes of this chapter I shall focus on ordinarily perceptible material bodies.

---

[2] Some of the themes of Part II of *Individuals* are discussed in Strawson's earlier article 'Particular and General' (1953–4). He returns to them in *Subject and Predicate in Logic and Grammar* (1974), in which his Ramseyan torch is very much in the background; but nothing he says in this book requires him to extinguish it.

[3] See e.g. Haack (1979) and Snowdon (2006) for a discussion of descriptive versus revisionary metaphysics.

Strawson defines 'basicness' in terms of priority or fundamentality with respect to *identifiability*. If identifying particulars of kind A, for example, does not require identifying any other kind of particulars, then As are basic particulars. If identifying particulars of kind B requires identifying particulars of some other kind, then particulars of kind B are non-basic.

With this notion in hand, Strawson argues that such basic particulars play a fundamental role in our general conceptual scheme, and that one takes a large step in grasping the nature of this conceptual scheme in seeing why and how this is so. So too, understanding what it takes to think of a basic particular reveals further fundamental structural features of our thought.[4]

This leads to the second central conclusion from Part I—that

> (2) thinking of material bodies, having the idea of an objective particular, requires the concept of spatiality—or at least something very like it.

But although (2) has received a great deal of attention,[5] it is only part of Strawson's account of what makes thought about objective particulars possible. In Part II of *Individuals* Strawson argues that

> (3) there is a fundamental level of thought that does not involve particulars,

and that

> (4) this fundamental level of thought is what makes thought about objective particulars possible *at all*.

What emerges, then, is a picture of our conceptual scheme as comprising different levels of thought, some more fundamental than others. Strawson is explicit about the explanatory role of this fundamental level when he says 'what is in question is not an order of temporal development, but an order of explanation' (Strawson 1959, 209).[6]

Strawson's claim—which may be surprising to many—that the fundamental level of thought does not involve thought about particulars is intimately linked to

---

[4] In what follows I shall take 'identifying a particular' and 'thinking about a particular' to be roughly synonymous. Strawson explicitly endorses such a move when discussing the basicness of material bodies: '...for it is not to be supposed that the general structure of such thinking is different when we are concerned to communicate with others in speech and when we are not. The assertion that material bodies are basic particulars in our actual conceptual scheme, then, is now to be understood as the assertion that, as things are, identifying *thought* about particulars other than material bodies rests in general on identifying *thought* about material bodies, but not vice versa' (Strawson 1959, 60).

[5] See especially Evans (1980/1985), Cassam (2005), and Snowdon (2006).

[6] The notion of 'of an order of explanation' is not explicitly defined by Strawson, but I take it to have both epistemological, conceptual, and metaphysical import.

his claim that the fundamental level of thought does not have a subject-predicate structure. This latter claim comes on the heels of a detailed discussion of the traditional view that the subject-predicate distinction is intimately related to the particular-universal distinction. Strawson argues that this traditional view can be supported, and although this discussion is of independent interest, the main curiosity is the way in which it leads Strawson to postulate a fundamental level of thought that does not involve subject-predicate structure.

Plainly, if we think of particulars as the paradigm 'logical subjects', and if the fundamental level of thought does not proceed in terms of particulars, then it will not involve deployment of the subject-predicate structure. What then is its character? In order to characterize it, Strawson introduces what he calls 'feature-concepts' or 'feature-universals'. Feature-universals indicate *kinds of stuff*, like snow and water, and the feature-placing sentences or statements or utterances that express thoughts at the fundamental level do not have subject-predicate form but rather demonstratively indicate 'the incidence of a general feature', such that 'in feature-placing propositions, in propositions demonstratively indicating the incidence of a general feature which is not, or not yet, a sortal universal, we can find the ultimate propositional level we are seeking' (Strawson 1959, 209).

I find this an incredibly intriguing picture of the overall structure of our thought and many questions arise. I shall consider three.

First: what led Strawson to think that he needed to identify this fundamental level of thought in order to account for how we come to have thoughts about particulars? His stated reason is that an account of the conditions of thought about particulars *in general* must not appeal to particulars in order to avoid circularity (Strawson 1959, 199). I shall consider the strength of this motivation.

Second: the concept of spatiality plays a central role in Strawson's account of the possibility of thinking about material bodies, but what is its role in theorizing about the fundamental level of thought? The answer I shall explore is that different kinds of feature-universals, with their associated distinctive spatial peculiarities, constitute alternative routes to particular-identity.

Third: if we accept this proposal about the fundamental level of thought, what lessons should we take it to offer about the ontology implied by—implicit in—our conceptual scheme? At one level of thought we think about (ordinarily perceptible) particulars, tables, chairs, flashes, bangs, and battles. With Strawson we can say that at this level of thought 'our ontology comprises objective particulars' (Strawson 1959, 15). The fundamental level of thought, by contrast, seems to carry in itself a different basic ontology, which we might perhaps call a 'stuff ontology'. And just as the fundamental level of thought is said *to make possible* the level of thought that naturally comprises material bodies as we ordinarily conceive of them, the stuff ontology of the fundamental level of thought is more fundamental than the ontology of material bodies. So, why are material bodies introduced at all? I shall consider Strawson's suggestion that the concept of a material body as a kind of particular plays the role of a simplifying device in our conceptual scheme.

What is of particular interest is that Strawson remained true to the sweeping and seemingly revisionary Ramseyan–Whiteheadian claim that he endorsed in 1950, even while dedicating himself to descriptive metaphysics in 1959. In other words, what looked like a piece of revisionary metaphysics in 1950 fell out of his descriptive metaphysics in 1959.

So far, I have painted Strawson's overall picture of our conceptual scheme with a broad brush. In what follows, I shall first briefly consider the main conclusions of chapters 1 and 2 of Part I of *Individuals* in a bit more detail. However, the bulk of the rest of the chapter focuses on chapter 6 of Part II, which introduces the fundamental level of thought and considers its implications for the subject-predicate form and the particular-universal form.

4. *Individuals*: Part I, Chapters 1 and 2

A general feature of our conceptual scheme is that we take our experience to be experience of a single, unified, objective, ordered world, a world whose order is independent—this is the principal force of 'objective'—of the order of our subjective experience of it. More specifically, we take ourselves to inhabit a single 'common spatiotemporal framework' (Strawson 1959, 22). 'Objective experience' is experience that has this general character. In our case it is centrally constituted by experiences of objective particulars. The question is then this: 'what are the necessary or constitutive features of any experience of objective particulars?' It is this question that sets Strawson's agenda.

As is well known, Strawson argues that material bodies like tables, chairs, cats, and mountains are the basic objective particulars in our conceptual scheme.[7] The identification of all other particulars such as theoretical entities, events, and processes depend on the identification of such spatially located material bodies. He then asks whether this is a special feature of our conceptual scheme or whether it must hold for any conceptual scheme with the resources to identify objective particulars. This leads to the famous non-spatial 'sound-world' thought-experiment, and the conclusion that the possibility of being able to identify objective particulars requires at least some very close analogue of our actual concept of spatiality.

We can group actual spatiality and its sufficiently close analogues together under the name 'spatiality*'. Strawson's argument for the necessity of possessing the concept of spatiality* for thinking about objective particulars proceeds in two steps. The first step in the argument is that the idea of an objective particular is deeply bound up with the idea of the possibility of coming across it again,

---

[7] I am using 'material bodies' to refer to ordinarily perceptible items and not, say, PM2.5 particles, which are invisible to the naked eye.

i.e. *reidentifying* it. The second step is that the possibility of reidentifying objective particulars requires that they exist in a spatial* dimension. I shall briefly consider each of these steps in turn.

Part of what is included in the very idea of an objective particular is that it can exist independently of the thinking subject and her experiences. It follows that an objective particular can possibly exist when it is not being observed. Strawson next links (i) grasp of the idea of a particular existing unobserved to (ii) the idea of an already observed particular *continuing to exist* unobserved, an idea whose possession essentially involves (iii) being able to make sense of the idea of coming upon it again, reidentifying it, after a period of not observing it (or thinking about it).

The step from (ii) to (iii) is crucial,[8] because reidentification requires more than a temporal dimension. This is because the temporal dimension does not in itself provide what one might call a *realm of existence* for particulars (and oneself) of a sort that provides for the possibility that one can take oneself to be encountering the same one again. Even if there is some difficult—to me puzzling—sense in which the past, present, and future exist 'all at once', we cannot 'move' freely between past, present, and future time in such a way that we can re-encounter particulars.

The claim, then, is that spatiality* provides the needed non-temporal dimension necessary for the possibility of reidentification. Spatiality* gives particulars places to be, and the subject can conceive of them as being at those places while they are unobserved and so being in those places (or being in a place related to those places) to be observed again. The particular has a place in the system, a place where the subject may not now be, but can (ultimately) relate to her own current position.

5. *Individuals*: Part II, Chapter 6

Although Part I of *Individuals* provides a substantive account of what it takes to think of or talk about objective particulars, Strawson expands it considerably in Part II. In chapter 6, he distinguishes between two types of accounts, which I shall call I-accounts and G-accounts:

I-account: an account of the conditions of the introduction of a particular into a *particular piece* of discourse, or into a *particular train* of thought.

G-account: an account of the conditions of the introduction of particulars into discourse or thought *in general*.

Strawson offers accounts of both kinds. Much of his discussion turns around logico-linguistic topics such as the subject-predicate distinction, and the conditions of introducing a particular term into a sentence or statement by means of a definitely identifying expression. But since he is also clearly concerned with

---

[8] The step from (i) to (ii) might possibly be questioned.

thought, and with what it is to have a particular in mind, I shall move freely between talking about introducing a particular into discourse and introducing a particular into thought.

What is the difference between the two types of account? A first, short answer is that giving an I-account can involve reference to particulars and ultimately quantification over particulars without a worry about circularity, while giving a G-account must not appeal to particulars at all, on pain of circularity. Strawson claims that an I-account is better off if supplemented by a G-account.

In giving an I-account Strawson takes himself to find support for the traditional association between the subject-predicate distinction and the particular-universal distinction. Once we see what it takes to introduce a particular into a specific train of thought, he argues, we shall see that the traditional association holds. His discussion of a G-account, by contrast, involves the introduction of the notion of a 'fundamental level of thought', a level of thought that involves no thought of objective particulars, and which provides the *basis* for thought about objective particulars. At the fundamental level of thought there is nothing corresponding to the subject-predicate distinction: 'at this limit, we say, the antithesis, subject-predicate, disappears' (Strawson 1959, 212).

To see how Strawson eliminates the subject-predicate form from the fundamental level of thought, we shall begin with his I-account and its relation to the subject-predicate distinction.

6. The Subject-Predicate Distinction and the Particular-Universal Distinction

The traditional doctrine, according to which there is a fundamental connection between the subject-predicate distinction and the particular-universal distinction, has a distinguished history. It is in Strawson's words:

> the doctrine that particulars can appear in discourse as subjects only, never as predicates; whereas universals, or non-particulars generally, can appear either as subjects or as predicates... There is an asymmetry between particulars and universals in respect of their relations to the subject-predicate distinction.
> (Strawson 1959, 137–8)

Others have cast the doctrine slightly differently. Frege (1891), for example, introduced the idea of 'saturated' and 'unsaturated' entities based on considerations about mathematical expressions:

> people... recognize the same function again in '$2.1^3 + 1$', '$2.4^3 + 4$', [and] '$2.5^3 + 5$', only with different arguments, viz. 1, 4, and 5. From this we may discern that it is

the common element of these expressions that contains the essential peculiarity of a function, i.e., what is present in

'$2.x^3 + x$'

over and above the letter 'x'. We could write this somewhat as follows:

'$2.(\ )^3 + (\ )$'.

I am concerned to show that the argument does not belong with a function, but goes together with the function to make up a complete whole; for a function by itself must be called incomplete, in need of supplementation, or 'unsaturated'. And in this sense functions differ fundamentally from numbers. Since such is the essence of functions, we can explain why, on the one hand, we recognize the same function in '$2.1^3 + 1$' and '$2.2^3 + 2$', even though the numbers these expressions mean are different, whereas on the other hand, we do not find one and the same function in '$2.1^3 + 1$' and '$4 - 1$' in spite of their equal numerical values... We recognize the function in the expression by imagining the latter as split up, and the possibility of splitting it up is suggested by its structure.

The two parts into which a mathematical expression is thus split up, the sign of the argument and the expression of the function, are dissimilar; for the argument is a number, a whole complete in itself, as the function is not... An object is anything that is not a function, so that an expression for it does not contain any empty place. (Frege 1891, 36–7, 43)

According to Frege, we recognize or discover different kinds of entities by observing the structure of linguistic expressions, not only in mathematics but also in logic and natural language. He defined what he called 'concepts' in logic as functions with one argument place whose value is always a truth-value.[9] Similarly for ordinary language: an expression like 'x is wise', now called a 'logical predicate', is an incomplete expression that designates an unsaturated constituent. Complete expressions such as 'logical subjects' and sentences designate complete objects.[10]

Russell embraced this Fregean idea, claiming similarly that there is something incomplete about universals, and that this tells us something fundamental about the form of the proposition (Russell 1918/1986, §6). A universal can never stand alone or be the subject of a proposition; it must always be completed into a proposition. The symbol for redness is not 'red' but rather the argument-place-including functional symbol 'x is red'. According to Russell, an occurrence of a universal as a grammatical subject as in 'wisdom is a virtue' can be paraphrased to

---

[9] Functions with two or more argument-places whose values are always truth-values are called relations.

[10] I am putting aside the complication of Frege's claim that sentences designate truth-values construed as objects.

show how it is actually occurring as a predicate: 'for all x, if x is wise, then x is virtuous'.[11]

Strawson takes a different approach. He attempts to support the traditional doctrine by giving an I-account of the essential difference between how particulars and universals get introduced into a particular train of thought or into a particular piece of discourse. In order for a subject to *refer* to or *think* about a particular in its absence, he says, there must be a description that the subject has in mind such that there is at most one thing that satisfies that description:

> For him to be referring to just one particular, it is not enough that there should be at least one particular which his description fits. There must be at most one such particular *which he has in mind*. But he cannot, for himself, distinguish the particular *which he has in mind* by the fact that it is the one he has in mind. So there must be some description he could give, though it need not be the description he does give, which applies uniquely to the one he has in mind and does not include the phrase, 'the one I have in mind'. (Strawson 1959, 182)

So, for example, in order to refer to or think about a particular object o by using a description, say 'the Queen of England', I have to know an empirical proposition that (a) grounds the claim that there is only one particular satisfying this description, and (b) does not include reference to the particular meant to be introduced:[12]

> ... in order for an identifying reference to a particular to be made, there must be some true empirical proposition known, in some not too exacting sense of this word, to the speaker, to the effect that there is just one particular which answers to a certain description. (Strawson 1959, 183)

In contrast, introducing a universal into thought or discourse does not require knowledge of an empirical proposition. All one needs to know is the meaning of the terms that introduce universals. Strawson considers and rejects a few attempts to argue that knowledge of empirical propositions is also necessary for the introduction of universals. One might suggest that to introduce a universal, using the symbol 'φ', say, one must at least presuppose the empirical proposition '"something is φ" is true or false'. But although this is an empirical proposition, it is utterly different from the substantive kind of empirical propositions that must be known to introduce particulars. Empirical propositions of the former kind are facts about language, whereas the latter are facts about the non-linguistic world.

---

[11] See MacBride (2005) and (2018) for detailed discussion of the traditional doctrine.
[12] I am putting aside the well-worn debate concerning how names and definite descriptions refer since my main goal is to explicate Strawson's views.

Strawson marks the distinction between expressions introducing particulars and expressions introducing universals into thought with the Fregean–Russellian terms of 'completeness' and 'incompleteness', but he means something entirely different by them. Both kinds of expressions are of course incomplete in the sense that neither one on its own is a complete assertion, while both can be parts of an assertion. However, expressions introducing particulars into thought have a *kind* of intrinsic completeness that expressions introducing universals into thought lack; a completeness deriving, according to Strawson, from the fact that a particular has in itself a 'completeness for thought', and in that sense 'a logical complexity' (Strawson 1959, 210), that a universal lacks. Strawson proposes to express the complexity by saying that the particular 'unfolds into a fact' (Strawson 1959, 212): the introduction of a particular into thought necessarily carries the weight of an empirical fact for its backing. Terms for particulars 'perform their role only because they present or represent facts, only because they presuppose, or embody, or covertly carry, propositions which they do not explicitly affirm' (Strawson 1959, 187). And this is not so in the case of terms for universals.

Strawson admits that the 'backing' propositions—the empirical propositions necessary for introducing particulars into individual trains of thought—will often themselves contain reference to other particulars. But this admission need not lead to an infinite regress:

> For we can always count on arriving, in the end, at some existential proposition, which may indeed contain demonstrative elements, but no *part* of which introduces, or definitely identifies, a particular term, though the proposition as a whole may be said to *present* a particular term. (The simple form of such a proposition is: 'There is just one so-and-so there'.) (Strawson 1959, 193)

Strawson goes on to acknowledge that it is plausible that:

> sentences involving quantification over particulars (e.g., 'There is just one so-and-so there') could have no place in language unless definitely identifying expressions for particulars ('That so-and-so') also had a place in language.
> (Strawson 1959, 194)

But there is no difficulty in this—in the fact that one must ultimately appeal to particulars in some fashion or other so long as one's aim is to give an I-account. All that is required for such an account is that:

> expressions introducing particulars, unlike expressions introducing universals, should *always* be complete in a certain sense; and that sense is explained when it is shown how those expressions must always carry an empirical proposition.
> (Strawson 1959, 193)

If, however, one is attempting to give a G-account, an account of the conditions of the introduction of particulars into discourse or thought in general, particulars cannot be appealed to without circularity.[13]

7. The Fundamental Level of Thought

What then is the correct *general* account of the conditions of the introduction of particulars into discourse or thought, i.e. the correct account of what is required in order for one to be able to think or talk about particulars at all? What—connectedly—is required for the subject to be able to think about *kinds* of particulars—about cats in general, or spruce trees in general?

Although these two questions may appear distinct, for Strawson, they are ways of asking the same question and so can be answered in one fell swoop. This approach is plausible on the assumption that if one is to think about *basic* particulars *at all*, they must be brought under some *kind* or other, whether it's the kind *cat*, or *tree*, or *mountain*, or, perhaps, the very general kind *physical object*. The qualification of 'basic' is also important because we are, as Strawson says, 'looking for the classes of facts which supply a basis for the introduction of those particulars upon which the introduction of all others directly or indirectly rests' (Strawson 1959, 201).

In order to distinguish this 'general' sense of introducing a particular into thought from the sense discussed in the last section, Strawson distinguishes between introduction$_1$ and introduction$_2$. *Individual particulars* are introduced$_1$ into discourse; *kinds of particulars* are introduced$_2$ into discourse.

Parallel to the two uses of 'introduction' Strawson distinguishes two senses of 'presupposition':

> The truth of some presupposed$_1$ proposition is a condition of the successful introduction$_1$ of a certain particular, and hence a condition of the presupposing statement's having a truth-value. The existence of facts of a presupposed$_2$ kind is a condition of the introduction$_2$ of a certain *kind* of particulars, i.e. is a condition of there being any propositions at all into which particulars of that *kind* are introduced$_1$. (Strawson 1959, 199, my emphasis)

---

[13] Strawson (1959, 194–7) considers and rejects Quine's (1950) attempt at giving a G-account according to which subject-expressions or other referring expressions for particulars do not occur either in the analysis of propositions containing expressions that introduce particulars or in an ideal language which *replaces* them with variables of existential quantification. I cannot go into the details of his criticism here, but Strawson claims that 'the linguistic terms in which [Quine's] analysis is couched are terms which, if we are to understand them in the way we are invited to, presuppose the existence of subject-expressions, of linguistic singular terms' (Strawson 1959, 196). That is, Quine's account is guilty of the circularity Strawson is trying to avoid in giving a G-account.

Strawson argues that there is a non-circular account for explaining how *kinds* of particulars, or particulars in general, get introduced into thought. I shall call it (R1), in order to contrast it with another possible response to this issue that Strawson does not consider.

(R1)   There is a fundamental level of thought involving no particulars, which provides the basis for thinking about any kinds of particulars at all.

The other response I have in mind is

(R2)   There is, built into our innate cognitive equipment from the start, a primitive 'object-concept', or a small set of such concepts, which is soon activated by experience, and which ultimately undergirds all other identification of particulars.[14]

Part of my reason for mentioning (R2) is that it casts doubt on whether Strawson's worry about circularity is a genuine one. Why should we think we need to give an account of the 'conditions of the introduction of particulars into discourse or thought *in general*'? Why can't it be particulars all the way down, so to speak?

The defence of (R2) would presumably require an account of how any such primitive object-concept or set of primitive object-concepts came to exist, and would presumably be an evolutionary account of a sort that lies outside the scope of Strawson's analytical investigation. I think nevertheless that it would fit very well with some of his central themes. For, first, it would surely be an account of how the primitive object-concept evolved over time out of a more fundamental level of thought involving no particulars. In this respect it would be in line with (R1); it would simply shift the scope of (R1) from the individual to the species considered over time, and find no need to attribute the fundamental particular-free level of thought to each one of us individually.

An (R2) account would also be highly likely to include reference to the notion of *reidentification*: an account of the enormous adaptive value of the capacity and tendency to think 'same *x* again'. I am, however, going to put (R2) aside, and try to show that (R1) is plausible. Even if one could show that there was no theoretical *need* to attribute a fundamental particular-free level of thought to each one of us individually, in order to explain how we come to be able to think about particulars, there might well *be* such a fundamental level in each of us. Certainly, Quine seems to have thought so.[15]

---

[14] See e.g. Spelke (1990, 1994), Spelke and Hermer (1996). I have also argued that something like an 'object-concept' is a fundamental structuring feature of our perception; see Montague (2011, 2016). Of course, Strawson might question the felicity of a general 'object-concept'.

[15] Quine (1960, §19, 89–94). Here it is worth considering the contrast between *phylogenetic* as opposed to *ontogenetic* empiricism; see G. Strawson (2021, §11).

8. Feature-Universals, Feature-Concepts, and Feature-Placing Sentences

Strawson begins his defence of (R1) by distinguishing three kinds of universals: *characterizing* universals, *sortal* universals, and what he calls '*feature*-universals'.

Characterizing universals, such as being funny or tall, characterize particulars.

Sortal universals, such as *man, cat,* and *tree*, provide principles for distinguishing, enumerating, and reidentifying particulars.[16] With the sortal universal *cat*, I can distinguish cats from non-cats and one cat from another, I can count the number of cats around, and I can reidentify particular cats.

Since Strawson's project requires a level of thought in which no particulars feature, characterizing and sortal universals cannot be what constitute such thought, for their deployment in thought presupposes thought of particulars. Strawson therefore introduces 'feature-universals' or 'feature-concepts' as a third kind of universal, thought about which requires no appeal to particulars. Strawson offers the following examples of 'feature-universals' occurring in what he calls 'feature-placing' sentences:

> Now it is raining.
> Snow is falling.
> There is coal here.
> There is water here.

Snow, coal, rain, and *water* are not functioning as characterizing universals. They indicate general kinds of stuff, not characteristics of particulars, though *being made of snow* or *being made of gold* are characteristics of particulars. Nor are they sortal universals. None of them in itself provides a principle for distinguishing, enumerating, and reidentifying particulars of a sort, although each can be modified to yield such principles: *lumps of coal, flakes of snow, pools of water*. According to Strawson 'these feature-placing sentences...neither contain any part that introduces a particular, nor any expression used in such a way that its use presupposes the use of expressions to introduce particulars' (Strawson 1959, 203).

Strawson argues that the occurrence of 'here' in a feature-placing sentence such as 'there is water here' does not pick out a particular, because it in no way bounds a spatial area. Similarly, 'now' does not pick out a temporally bounded area. 'Now' and 'here' 'merely act as pointers to some extent of space and time which they do not, by themselves, delimit' (Strawson 1959, 216). This point plays a pivotal role in his argument that feature-placing sentences cannot be construed as having subject-predicate form by taking 'here' and 'now' as subjects and the general

---

[16] I am using italics for concepts of sortal universals and feature-universals.

feature as predicate. The only way for 'here' and 'now' to become bounded in such a way as to function as the subjects of a singular sentence would be to use the general feature to mark off the relevant area of space. This, however, would be using the predicate, the general feature, to obtain a proper subject.

The feature-placing sentences so far considered deliver what is needed for Strawson's analysis:

> though feature-placing sentences do not introduce particulars into our discourse, they provide a basis for this introduction. The facts they state are presupposed, in the required sense, by the introduction of certain kinds of particular. That there should be facts statable by means of such sentences as 'There is water here', 'It is snowing', is a condition of there being propositions into which particulars are introduced₁ by means of such expressions as 'This pool of water', 'This fall of snow'.   (Strawson 1959, 203)

Water can be divided in various ways to produce sortals such as *pool of water* or *puddle of water* of which this pool of water and this puddle of water are instances. Similarly, snow can be divided in various ways to produce sortals such as *fall of snow* or *drift of snow*. The key idea here is that water, gold, snow, and rain are kinds of stuff that do not in themselves have a characteristic shape, but can be spatially divided in such a way that we can move from the feature-universal to sortal universals, e.g. *pools, drifts, falls,* and *lumps*.

Part of what is unique about these feature-universals is that the names of the sortal universals derived from them (*'pool of water', 'lump of gold'*) incorporate the names of kinds of stuff (*'gold', 'water'*). Since names of kinds of stuff are well adapted to be part of feature-placing sentences, it is easy to find examples in ordinary language where we operate not with a particular instance of gold or water, but only with the feature-universal itself and the notion of placing.

So far so good, but we have not yet got very far. Although *pools of water* and *lumps of gold* have basic particulars as instances, such instances are a special class. How will this strategy work for basic particulars in general? We need an account that covers sortal universals like *cat, mountain,* and *tree*.

There are two immediate challenges when we turn to these more typical sortals, one linguistic, one metaphysical. First, the linguistic challenge. Whereas ordinary language does contain names for stuffs like water and snow, there is no ordinary language term for the corresponding general feature for cats or trees, what Strawson calls 'cat-feature' (Strawson 1959, 219) or 'tree-feature'. Ordinary language contains names only for the sortal *cat* and the sortal *tree*.

But even though there is no ordinary-language evidence for a level of thought at which *cat-feature* is present without thinking about particular cats, such a level of thought still seems coherent. Strawson asserts:

> [It] is not logically absurd to suppose that there might be a level of thought at which we recognize the presence of cat, or signs of the past or future presence of cat, yet do not think identifyingly of particular cats. (Strawson 1959, 205)

If we have enough reason for thinking that such a level of thought exists, the lack of ordinary-language evidence becomes less pressing. As Strawson points out: 'We can readily acknowledge that the introduction of particulars is so fundamental a conceptual step as to leave the primitive pre-particular level of thought as, at most, no more than vestigial in language' (Strawson 1959, 206).

Strawson introduces something called 'the naming-game', where we explicitly introduce names such as 'cat-feature' to show it is logically coherent that 'one should recognize the features without possessing the conceptual resources for identifying reference to the corresponding particulars' (Strawson 1959, 206).

The second challenge for dealing with our more ordinary sortals is metaphysical. Explicating how *cat-feature* is the basis for the sortal *cat* cannot be totally analogous to how *water* and *coal* provide the basis for the sortals *pool of water* and *lump of coal* for the simple reason that a big lump of cat can't be spatially divided in various ways to produce an individual cat. Conversely, although heaps of snow could be physically lumped together to yield a big mass of snow, we cannot lump particular cats together to yield one big cat.

This metaphysical difference makes it difficult to think of situations in which, instead of operating with the notion of the sortal universal *cat* or *tree*, and hence with the notion of particular cats or trees, we operate with the notion of a corresponding feature and of feature-placing. As mentioned, ordinary language contains no names for what Strawson is calling 'cat-feature' or 'tree-feature'.

Should we conclude from this difference between water and cats that *cat-feature* simply does not exist and that we always only operate with a *cat* sortal? If the only way of moving from feature-universals to sortal universals were in terms of the general stuff being divided in different ways to yield different sortals, then it seems that there could be no idea of a *cat-feature* that would be distinct from, yet yield a basis for, the sortal universal *cat*.

Strawson argues that what this difference between cats and water shows is that the cat-feature concept, unlike *water*, must include *in itself* the basis for the criteria of distinctness and reidentification that we apply to cats. We can move from the cat-feature concept to the sortal *cat* because the cat-feature concept includes the idea of a characteristic shape, a characteristic pattern of occupation of space. This idea gives us a basis for the criteria of distinctness that we apply to particular cats. This is of course the crucial difference between water and cat-feature; water in itself has no *characteristic* occupation of space. Only once we have something like the concept of pool of water do we conceive of water as having a characteristic occupation of space.

The idea of a characteristic occupation of space also gives us a hint about how *cat-feature* includes a basis for the criteria of reidentification of cats. The idea of a characteristic occupation of space leads naturally to the idea of a continuous path traced through space and time by such a characteristic pattern. The reasoning seems to be that if this feature has a characteristic shape, then it makes sense to think that it will continue to have that shape through space and time. Strawson adds, 'and this idea in turn provides the core of the idea of particular-identity for basic particulars' (Strawson 1959, 207).

It is important to note that claiming that the cat-feature concept already contains the basis for a criterion of distinctness and reidentification does not mean that it entails the possession of these ideas. Strawson elucidates this point:

> Operating with the idea of reidentifiable particular cats, we distinguish between the case in which a particular cat appears, departs and reappears, and the case in which a particular cat appears and departs and a different cat appears. But one could play the naming-game without making this distinction. Someone playing the naming-game can correctly say 'more cat' or 'cat again' in both cases; but someone operating with the idea of particular cats would be in error if he said 'Another cat' in the first case, or 'The same cat again' in the second. The decisive conceptual step to cat-particular is taken when the case of 'more cat' or 'cat again' is subdivided into the case of 'another cat' and the case of 'the same cat again'.
> (Strawson 1959, 207)[17]

9. Ontology for the Fundamental Level of Thought

Our ordinary talk and thought about the world commits us to an ontology of particulars such as cats, mountains, pools of water, and so on, and the characterization of this level of thought involves the subject-predicate structure. But this level of thought and its accompanying ontology are not fundamental. According to Strawson, our thought and talk about particulars are ultimately made possible by a level of thought that does not contain particulars at all, and accordingly does not have a subject-predicate form. Since particulars do not appear at the fundamental level of thought, and since the antithesis between completeness and incompleteness that characterizes the subject-predicate distinction is grounded in the particular-universal distinction, the subject-predicate form is absent from this level of thought.

The fundamental level of thought consists of feature-concepts or feature-universals, and it is clear that these feature-universals indicate kinds of stuff, i.e. a feature-universal indicates matter of a certain sort, e.g. water or gold, rather than

---

[17] Here it is worth comparing Quine's discussion of 'divided reference' (Quine 1960, §19).

indicating material individuals of a certain sort, e.g. cats or cows. So Strawson's fundamental level of thought is committed to a stuff ontology.

What is the ontological relationship between what is indicated by feature-universals, stuff, and what is indicated by the sortal universals that are based on them? If we assume that there is a layering of fundamentality in reality that mirrors the layering of fundamentality of thought in our conceptual scheme, then the stuff ontology that accords with feature-universals would be more fundamental than the particular-endorsing ontology that sortals invoke.

One way of thinking about this is that water is intrinsically a stuff, and the fact that it can be divided in various ways to yield sortals does not change its metaphysical character. Even when water is occurring as an instance of a sortal as in this pool of water it is still a stuff. The sortal just picks out the way some water-stuff happens to be accidentally spatially shaped. The sortal doesn't introduce something (fundamentally) new into reality.

Unless we have a reason for thinking otherwise, the same kind of reasoning should apply to *cat-feature*. The fact that the feature-universal *cat-feature* provides the basis for the sortal universal *cat* does not change the metaphysical nature of the cat-feature, and hence does not change the metaphysical nature of particular cats. On this view, *cat-feature* indicates a kind of stuff that is spread out, and there can be more or less of it.[18] The sortal *cat* does not introduce something (fundamentally) new into reality.

If something like this is right, then it seems that we may say that language and much of our thought obscures the fundamental *nature* of reality. Strawson certainly gives reason for thinking he has something metaphysical (and also Wittgenstein's *Tractatus*!) in mind when he says:

> If any facts deserve, in terms of this picture, to be called ultimate or atomic facts, it is the facts stated by those propositions which demonstratively indicate the incidence of a general feature. These ultimate facts do not contain particulars as constituents but they provide the basis for the conceptual step to particulars. The propositions stating them are not subject-predicate propositions, but they provide the basis for the step to subject-predicate propositions.
>
> (Strawson 1959, 212)

This passage, in combination with Strawson's claim that particulars 'have logical complexity we are trying to get below' (Strawson 1959, 203) and that 'we try to get at the complexity of the particular by resolving it' (Strawson 1959, 210) seems to support the metaphysical interpretation of our conceptual scheme I have suggested.

---

[18] One might argue that 'a characteristic shape' somehow pushes cathood into a different ontological category from water. The idea might be that the nature of spatial binding somehow makes a difference to something's metaphysical kind.

10. Ordinary Basic Particulars Are a Simplifying Device

If the considerations of the last section are correct, then even if our ordinary basic particulars are central to our conceptual scheme, they do not involve a metaphysical addition to the fundamental level, given that stuffs occupy this level. Why, then, are our ordinary basic particulars introduced? Strawson's answer is that 'the premium on the introduction of ordinary concrete particulars is enormous, the gains in simplicity overwhelming' (Strawson 1959, 225).

To illustrate the simplifying 'conceptual effect' of the introduction of ordinary particulars, in chapter 7 of *Individuals* Strawson imagines 'a language without particulars—or, at least, without any such particulars as are instances of ordinary sortal universals' (Strawson 1959, 217). If the imagined language is to be successful, it should provide the resources to say what we would like to say, especially at the level of discourse about our ordinary basic particulars, but without actually introducing such particulars.

In the end, Strawson imagines a conceptual scheme where 'place-particulars' based on feature-placing replace the ordinary particulars of our conceptual scheme. Although 'the language of places' does not succeed in being a completely 'particular-free' language, it does succeed at being a language free of our ordinary sortal universals.

On this imagined scheme, particular places are marked off by general features, and these marked-off places are meant to do the work of the particulars of our ordinary conceptual scheme.

Taking 'It φs' as an expression for introducing a feature-concept, and using 'p' and 't' as place and time variables, Strawson defines *places* as follows:

> 'It φs p, t' holds for any point or area or volume of, p, and for any instant or stretch of time, t, such that the spatial boundaries of p are co-extensive with the set of spatial boundaries traced out by φ-feature during the whole of t.
>
> (Strawson 1959, 219)

A simple example of a description of a place would be 'the place here at which it snows now'. And also 'the place here at which it cats now'.

Of course, these would be very different kinds of particulars from our ordinary particulars:

> ...they would not be instances of sortal universals. One and the same place could be very differently occupied at different times; no feature could ever be named of which a given place was an instance; the fact that a certain place was a certain time occupied in a certain way would be an accidental fact about it in just the sense in which it is not an accidental fact about Socrates that he is a man.
>
> (Strawson 1959, 222)

Strawson considers a block of granite which maintains its position and boundaries. So long as things remain stable, any difference between the language of places and the language of our ordinary particulars would be inoperative. However, once movement and alteration of shape and size are introduced, the language of ordinary particulars is far simpler. The ordinary particulars of our conceptual scheme offer a great—necessary—expedient for navigating an environment with movement and change. The lesson seems to be that the scheme of particulars that we do in fact operate within our conceptual scheme is a practical, simplifying matter.

The *final* lessons to draw from Strawson's overall metaphysical and conceptual picture are potentially far-reaching and require much more investigation. I shall finish by summarizing the movement of Strawson's thought over this crucial period. In 'On Referring' in 1950, Strawson endorses a piece of revisionary metaphysics in banishing the particular-universal distinction to the philosophical shadows. Although the 1971 Strawson feels he might have spoken too rashly twenty years prior, his 1959 self finds a place for these revisionary claims in his descriptive metaphysics. In fact, we reach similar revisionary claims by way of doing descriptive metaphysics. On the final analysis of descriptive metaphysics, thought does not fundamentally have the subject-predicate form and reality does not fundamentally have the particular-universal form. Although particulars such as material bodies are certainly part of reality, they are not what is fundamental to reality; stuff is.[19] And although thinking about particulars involves the subject-predicate structure, thoughts reflecting the fundamental level, the level of stuff, lack the subject-predicate structure.[20]

References

Cassam, Quassim (2005), 'Space and Objective Experience', in José Luis Bermudez (ed.), *Thought, Reference and Experience: Themes from the Philosophy of Gareth Evans* (Oxford: Oxford University Press), 258–89.

Evans, Gareth (1980), 'Things Without the Mind', in Zak Van Straaten (ed.), *Philosophical Subjects* (Oxford: Oxford University Press). Reprinted in Gareth Evans (1985), *Collected Papers* (Oxford: Clarendon Press).

Frege, Gottlob (1891/1997), 'Function and Concept', in David Hugh Mellor and Alex Oliver (eds.), *Properties* (Oxford: Oxford University Press), 130–49.

---

[19] What this amounts to exactly requires a careful consideration of the notion of fundamentality.

[20] I would like to thank the editors of this volume, Audin Bengtson, Benjamin De Mesel, and Sybren Heyndels, for putting it together and for their insightful comments on earlier drafts of my chapter. I would also like to thank the audience at Rice University's 'Workshop in Philosophy of Mind' (March 2022) and the students in two of my graduate seminars at the University of Texas at Austin. Finally, a special thanks to Galen Strawson for many discussions about *Individuals*.

Haack, Susan (1979), 'Descriptive and Revisionary Metaphysics', *Philosophical Studies* 35(4): 361–71.

MacBride, Fraser (2005), 'The Particular-Universal Distinction: A Dogma of Metaphysics?', *Mind* 114: 565–614.

MacBride, Fraser (2018), *On the Genealogy of Universals: The Metaphysical Origins of Analytic Philosophy* (Oxford: Oxford University Press).

Montague, Michelle (2011), 'The Phenomenology of Particularity', in Tim Bayne and Michelle Montague (eds.), *Cognitive Phenomenology* (Oxford: Oxford University Press), 121–40.

Montague, Michelle (2016), *The Given: Experience and Its Content* (Oxford: Oxford University Press).

Quine, Willard Van Orman (1950), *Methods of Logic* (New York: Holt, Rinehart & Winston).

Quine, Willard Van Orman (1960), *Word and Object* (Boston, MA: MIT Press).

Ramsey, Frank (1925), 'Universals', *Mind* 34(136): 401–17.

Russell, Bertrand (1918/1986), 'The Philosophy of Logical Atomism', in *The Philosophy of Logical Atomism and Other Essays 1914–19* (London: Allen & Unwin).

Snowdon, Paul (2006), 'P. F. Strawson: *Individuals*', in John Shand (ed.), *Central Works of Philosophy, Volume 5: The Twentieth Century: Quine and After* (London: Routledge), 40–64.

Spelke, Elizabeth (1990), 'Principles of Object Perception', *Cognitive Science* 14: 29–56.

Spelke, Elizabeth (1994), 'Initial Knowledge: Six Suggestions', *Cognition* 50: 431–45.

Spelke, Elizabeth, and Linda Hermer (1996), 'Early Cognitive Development: Objects and Space', in Rochel Gelman and Terry Kit-Fong Au (eds.), *Perceptual and Cognitive Development* (San Diego, CA: Academic Press), 72–116.

Strawson, Galen (2021), 'The Mechanism—the Secret—of the Given', *Synthese* 199. https://doi.org/10.1007/s11229-021-03273-7

Strawson, Peter F. (1950), 'On Referring', *Mind* 59 (235): 320–44. Reprinted in Peter F. Strawson (1971/2004), *Logico-Linguistic Papers* (London: Ashgate).

Strawson, Peter F. (1953–4), 'Particular and General', *Proceedings of the Aristotelian Society* 54: 233–60.

Strawson, Peter F. (1959), *Individuals: An Essay in Descriptive Metaphysics* (London: Methuen).

Strawson, Peter F. (1974), *Subject and Predicate in Logic and Grammar* (London: Methuen).

Whitehead, Alfred (1929/1978), *Process and Reality: An Essay in Cosmology*, corrected edition, ed. David Griffin and Donald Sherburne (New York: Free Press).

Wittgenstein, Ludwig (1922), *Tractatus Logico-Philosophicus*, trans. Charles Kay Ogden (London and New York: Routledge).

6
Concepts and Experience in *Bounds of Sense* and Beyond

Hans-Johann Glock

1. Introduction

From its beginnings, two themes played a pivotal role in Strawson's work. The first one, not pertinent to this chapter, is the scope and limitations of formal logic as a tool of analytic philosophy. The second one is the character of two fundamental features of human thought and speech—the distinct yet complementary operations of reference and predication. This theme was deepened in his masterwork, *Individuals* (1959). In it Strawson shifted his focus from ordinary language to what he eponymously called 'descriptive metaphysics'. The Kantian inspiration behind that project was directly explored in *The Bounds of Sense*. That book is not a straightforward commentary on *The Critique of Pure Reason*, yet it provides a brilliant reconstruction of its central ideas.[1] As Strawson later put it, it was a 'somewhat ahistorical attempt to recruit Kant to the ranks of the analytical metaphysicians, while discarding those metaphysical elements which refused any such absorption' (Strawson 2003, 9). The basic interpretative idea of *Bounds of Sense* is ingeniously epitomized by the title. There are three strands to the *Critique*: on the one hand, against empiricism Kant maintains that 'a certain minimal structure is essential to any conception of experience which we can make truly intelligible to ourselves' (Strawson 1966, 11, see 24, 44). On the other hand, against rationalism he insists that concepts—including the categorial concepts that define this minimal structure—cannot be applied beyond the limit of possible experience. In these two regards, Kant seeks to draw, respectively, the lower and the upper bounds of sense. But he does so from within a framework that itself transgresses the bounds of sense, a framework that consists of the untenable metaphysics of transcendental idealism and the 'imaginary subject of transcendental psychology' (Strawson 1966, 32). The first two strands constitute the fruitful side of the *Critique*, the third constitutes its 'dark side', which is 'no longer

---

[1] Unspecified references are to Peter F. Strawson, *Bounds of Sense* (1966), those using the familiar A/B notation to the first and second editions, respectively, of Immanuel Kant, *Critique of Pure Reason* (1998).

acceptable, or even promising'. The central task of the interpreter is that of 'disentangling' an 'analytical argument' which 'proceeds by analysis of the concept of experience in general' from its idealist and psychologistic surroundings (Strawson 1966, 16, 31).

Strawson did more than anyone else to rehabilitate Kant among analytic philosophers. He was not just the most important source of analytic Kantianism in a *wide* sense of that label. He also pursues an analytic Kantianism in a *narrower* sense: it maintains that the central insight of the *Critique* is an analysis of complex connections between concepts such as experience, self-consciousness, objectivity, space, time, and causation. This narrow analytic Kantianism is shared by some other commentators, notably Bennett (1966, 1974), yet repudiated by many analytic admirers of Kant. Strawson's interpretation and appropriation of Kantian ideas have provoked a heated controversy which lasts to this day.

My chapter explores a central theme of both descriptive metaphysics and analytic Kantianism (in both narrower and wider sense). The Western philosophical tradition has given rise to three paradigms concerning the relation between concepts and experience: contrast, hierarchy, and complementation. The first one is readily associated with rationalism: sensory perception must be sharply distinguished from intellect and reason, which alone afford genuine insight. The second, related one, is pivotal to Aristotelianism: both sensation and perception on the one hand and intellect and rational will on the other are part of the *psyche* of animals; yet only the latter, 'higher' faculties are genuinely mental, and they are the prerogative of rational animals, i.e. human beings. The third paradigm was famously epitomized by Kant: 'thoughts without content are empty, intuitions without concepts are blind' (Kant 1988, B 75). Judgements require both the experiential input of intuitions and the structure imposed by concepts. Simplifying grossly: intuitions + concepts = judgement.

Strawson's approach revolves around the Kantian model of an interplay between the 'conceptualizability of experience' and the applicability of concepts to experience (Strawson 2003, 11). Kant's 'duality of intuitions and concepts' turns into 'the necessary cooperation of sensibility and understanding' in experience (Strawson 2003, 72). The resulting picture is immensely powerful, though currently underappreciated. Among other things, it is right in conceiving concepts as principles of classification (Section 5), the way it distinguishes universals like concepts from particulars, and in resisting their nominalist-cum-extensionalist elimination (Glock 2012, 402–7). At the same time it is problematic in making the possession of experiences dependent on that of concepts, as well as on the capacity for self-consciousness. Put bluntly: Strawson is *right* in diagnosing limits to the concept of a possible experience, yet *wrong* in suggesting that those limits imply that any conceivable experience must be conceptual and can be enjoyed only by subjects that can ascribe experiences to themselves. Furthermore, these limits are not of a *sui generis* kind specific to a Kantian metaphysics of experience. They have to do with the role that certain concepts and propositions play within our overall conceptual scheme.

To substantiate these verdicts, I start out by sketching the connection between conceptual analysis, descriptive metaphysics, and transcendental philosophy in Strawson (Sections 2–4). Next I take a look at the two key notions of my title (Section 5). In the sequel I extract from *Individuals* and *Bounds of Sense* two transcendental arguments revolving around the preconditions of experience. The first one (Section 6) invokes the fact that I can ascribe experiences to myself to conclude both that I can ascribe experiences to others and that experience is 'objective' in the sense of there being a contrast between my experiences and their mind-independent objects. I shall defend both conclusions, while insisting that they are vindicated not by general principles governing self-consciousness or predication, but by specific conceptual truths concerning, respectively, personal pronouns and the seems/is contrast. The second transcendental argument (Sections 7–8) derives the self-ascribability of experiences from the idea that experience consists of recognizing particulars as falling under general concepts; it concludes that experience must possess 'unity of consciousness', i.e. be self-ascribable and hence propositional. Again I shall champion a deflationary gloss: the self-ascribability of experience rests on a logico-grammatical point rather than a metaphysics of experience. I shall also criticize the argument for implying that experiences can be enjoyed only by subjects with self-consciousness. Section 9 turns to Strawson's insistence that in all experiences general concepts are applied to specific instances. This conceptualism leads to a dilemma: either a subject possesses concepts, or it lacks bona fide experiences. Kant and Pittsburgh philosophers like McDowell have embraced the second horn. But that option is not supported by the kernel of truth in conceptualism, and it is incompatible with the kind of perception higher animals enjoy (Section 10). Section 11 takes issue with a related development of Strawson's Kantianism, McDowell's claim that genuine experience requires a kind of epistemic autonomy, accusing it of evincing a 'myth of spontaneity'. I end on a positive note by defending Strawson's analytic Kantianism in the narrower sense (Section 12). The insights descriptive metaphysics has to offer are best conceived neither as synthetic a priori (contrary to orthodox Kantianism), nor as straightforwardly analytic or 'grammatical' (contrary to Wittgensteinian commentators), but as conceptual truths of a special, mediated, kind.

2. Descriptive Metaphysics and Connective Analysis

Descriptive metaphysics is often explained (and criticized) exclusively through its contrast with revisionary metaphysics (e.g. Haack 1979). But Strawson himself characterized the project through a *fourfold* contrast, namely with revisionary metaphysics, conceptual analysis, a historicist conception of metaphysics, and explanatory metaphysics.[2]

For present purposes we can confine ourselves to the first two. Revisionary metaphysicians like Descartes, Leibniz, or Berkeley seek to *correct* our world-picture, not just by altering our empirical beliefs, in the manner of empirical scientists. Instead, they repudiate our entire conceptual framework and ordinary way of thinking, on the grounds that it is delusive and fails to mirror the nature or essence of reality. Descriptive metaphysics, on the other hand, 'is content to describe the actual structure of our thought about the world', rather than attempting 'to produce a better structure' (Strawson 1959, 9; 1995, 5). Strawson's role-models here are Aristotle and Kant.

Descriptive metaphysics differs from the 'conceptual analysis' of previous Oxford philosophy not in 'kind of intention', but in its greater 'scope and generality'. It seeks to 'lay bare the most general features of our conceptual structure'. The 'close examination of the actual use of words' may be the only 'sure way in philosophy'; yet it is insufficient to reveal these 'general elements' and 'structural connections'. For these are not visible in the motley of ordinary use, but lie 'submerged' beneath 'the surface of language' at 'a deeper level' (Strawson 1959, 9–10; 1995, 15).

The contention that descriptive metaphysics 'lays bare' structures beneath the surface of language suggests a programme similar to those of early logical and conceptual analysis (Moore, logical atomism, logical positivism). But the phrase is misleading. Strawson later distinguished between 'atomistic', 'reductive', and 'connective analysis' (Strawson 1992, chap. 2). He rejects the former two, thereby abandoning the idea that philosophical analysis decomposes or dismantles a complex phenomenon, displaying its simple elements and their mode of composition (Strawson 1992, 17–19; 1995, 15–17). Instead he promotes connective analysis, the elucidation of concepts by way of explicating their connections of implication, presupposition, and exclusion, without harbouring the ambition to define all of them in terms of ultimate (atomistic analysis) or at any rate simpler (reductive analysis) semantic components. Any conceptual explication or explanation of meaning will eventually move in a circle. But this does not entail that they are inevitably trivial or pointless. For there are more or less illuminating circles.

The same connectivist aspiration guides descriptive metaphysics, namely 'to establish the connections between the major structural features or elements of our conceptual scheme—to exhibit it, not as a rigorous deductive system, but as a coherent whole whose parts are mutually supportive and mutually dependent, interlocking in an intelligible way' (Strawson 1985, 22–3). In view of these statements, the 'surface of language' mentioned in *Individuals* should be

---

[2] These are distinct enterprises, but not all of them are mutually exclusive. Thus Strawson endorses both descriptive and explanatory metaphysics. See Glock (2012, 393–7).

understood as the *form* of expressions; what needs to be revealed is the *way expressions operate* in linguistic practice and their *role* within the scheme.

Connective analysis and descriptive metaphysics also share an interest in concepts, and thereby in patterns of classification and inference that straddle different natural languages. What separates them is more subtle. Whereas connective analysis describes linguistic patterns with a view to clarifying *specific* concepts—those giving rise to philosophical puzzles—descriptive metaphysics *ab initio* describes them in terms suitable to identifying those concepts that form the stable 'core of human thinking' (Strawson 1959, 10)—roughly speaking categories in the sense of Aristotle and Kant.

These concepts are *general* in subordinating numerous more specific concepts. Thus the concepts *material object* and *event* are general for more specific concepts such as, respectively, *chair, lump of sugar, river* and *explosion, birth*. They are *irreducible*, not in being simple and unanalysable (as Moore held *good* to be), but rather in resisting reduction without circularity. They are *basic* in as much as they are both pervasive and central to the framework of our actual mode of thought (Strawson 1992, 24).

Finally, they are *necessary* in the sense of constituting 'limiting features in any conception of experience which we can make intelligible to ourselves' (Strawson 1966, 24, 44, 68; 1992, 26), i.e. essential to our conception of experience.

3. Descriptive Metaphysics and Transcendental Philosophy

The first characteristic of its target concepts links descriptive metaphysics to traditional metaphysics, the second to anti-reductionism. The last two forge its distinctive ties to transcendental philosophy. The most striking feature of descriptive metaphysics is its Kantian provision that metaphysics is a *second-order discipline*. Instead of scrutinizing the essence of reality it reflects on our conceptual scheme, the fundamental structure of thought and discourse. In particular, it delineates the conceptual preconditions of our experience of objects, which Strawson takes to be a kind of thought.[3]

---

[3] This common ground needs to be handled with care (Glock 2003, 21–6). The chief task of the *Critique* is to vindicate the possibility of *metaphysics* and hence of synthetic knowledge a priori, rather than the possibility of empirical knowledge. Furthermore, contrary to many commentators, Strawson included (18), transcendental philosophy is originally explained not as an investigation into experience, or into representation and knowledge in general, but exclusively into *synthetic* ('of objects') *knowledge* a priori (B 25). Nevertheless, in showing how synthetic knowledge a priori is possible, transcendental philosophy turns into a theory of experience. Metaphysical judgements hold true of the objects of experience (i.e. are synthetic) independently of experience (i.e. are a priori), because they express necessary preconditions for the possibility of *experiencing* objects (A 158/B 196).

Strawson parallels this move from metaphysics to epistemology. The prime project of *Individuals* is to establish a distinctive type of metaphysics. The sceptic features primarily not as someone who doubts the possibility of knowledge, but as someone who distorts our conceptual scheme. And that certain forms of scepticism are self-refuting is a corollary of delineating the structure of our conceptual scheme. By

A second connection to Kant's transcendental philosophy concerns Strawson's ambition to vindicate our extant conceptual framework for thought and experience. The label notwithstanding, descriptive metaphysics is *not just* a descriptive inventory of our actual conceptual scheme. It also adopts a *validatory* stance. Admittedly, Strawson later contrasted 'validatory or revisionary' with descriptive metaphysics (Strawson 1985, 23). But the former two are *not* equivalent. For validatory metaphysics can also seek to show that our conceptual scheme is legitimate and hence need not be modified. More importantly, while Strawson later scaled down his validatory ambitions, he clearly harboured them in *Individuals* and *Bounds of Sense*. Thus he writes of commonsense beliefs in the primacy of material bodies and persons:

> It is difficult to see how such beliefs could be argued for except by showing their consonance with the conceptual scheme which we operate, by showing how they reflect the structure of that scheme. So if metaphysics is the finding of reasons, good, bad or indifferent, for what we believe on instinct, then this has been metaphysics. (Strawson 1959, 247)

Why can Strawson argue for these beliefs in this fashion? Because, according to him, certain features of our conceptual scheme are indispensable, and hence immune to the doubts of sceptics and the reforms of revisionary metaphysicians.[4] Some concepts and conceptual connections do not just in fact play a central role in our conceptual scheme, they *must* play such a role in any conceptual scheme we are capable of understanding.

4. Transcendental Arguments

Individuals is predominantly Aristotelian in content, yet Kantian as regards method. It investigates not purported *de re* essences, but the conceptual framework of our thinking and speaking. Furthermore, Strawson seeks to establish that certain aspects of this framework are indispensable. Finally, to this end he employs transcendental arguments, arguments to the effect that these features are *preconditions* or *presuppositions* of the possibility of things we *know to be possible*. They

---

contrast, in *Bounds of Sense* the emphasis is on delineating the essential structure of experience. Even here, however, the prime target is not the sceptical denial of the possibility of knowledge, but rather the contrasting excesses of rationalists on the one hand, sense-data empiricists on the other, excesses that distort epistemic concepts like *experience* and *self-consciousness* (Strawson 1966, 12). A further complication arises from the fact that some passages reverse the order of priority between discourse (language, thought) and reality. According to them, the logico-grammatical subject/predicate distinction does not provide the 'foundation' of the ontological particular-universal distinction, but the other way around (Strawson 1959, 161; 1995, 9; 1998, 383). Glock (2012, 412–13) attempts to reconcile these passages with Strawson's characterizations of descriptive metaphysics by appealing to the idea of ontological commitment.

[4] On the relation between anti-scepticism and anti-revisionism in Strawson's descriptive metaphysics see Glock (2022).

are preconditions of types of knowledge, experience, abilities, or concepts which we *in fact* possess or *could not fail to possess*.

Among the transcendental arguments discussed in the wake of Strawson, one can distinguish two different types. Both of them employ the idea of a necessary precondition. But they differ at least in their manner of presentation. The first type is *deductive* in that it proceeds along the following scheme:

P_1 We have experience (knowledge) of type K/the ability to Φ

P_2 It is a necessary condition for experience (knowledge) of type K/the ability to Φ that p

C   Therefore p.

This is a valid deductive inference. Its special force is supposed to be that P_1 is a premise which the sceptic grants or could not even coherently deny, and that P_2 states a necessary condition of this uncontentious starting-point.

The second type of transcendental argument is *elenctic*. It aims to show that sceptical doubts are incoherent or self-refuting, since they question the conceptual scheme in terms of which the sceptical problem is stated. The sceptic himself employs concepts which make sense only on the tacit assumption of conceptual connections he explicitly rejects. Therefore the sceptical position is self–refuting or self-stultifying: it could not be stated unless it were unfounded. In expressing his doubts, the sceptic quietly presupposes our conceptual framework, while at the same time explicitly rejecting that framework.

> He pretends to accept a conceptual scheme, but at the same time quietly rejects one of the conditions of its employment. Thus his doubts are unreal, not simply because they are logically irresoluble doubts, but because they amount to the rejection of the whole conceptual scheme within which alone such doubts make sense. (Strawson 1959, 35, see 106, 109)

This line of reasoning accuses sceptical doubts about the possibility of various kinds of knowledge not of leading to false conclusions or resting on unsound arguments, but of failing in an even more fundamental way, namely by being *incoherent* and nonsensical.[5]

Deductive transcendental arguments are prominent in *Bounds of Sense*, while *Individuals* tends to advance elenctic arguments. However, there are various connections between these two types of arguments. On the one hand, elenctic arguments trade on the kind of conceptual connections claimed by premises of

---

[5] For a partial rebuttal of Stroud's well-known objections to the very idea of transcendental arguments see Glock (2003, 37–9).

form P_2, namely between the commonsense beliefs sceptics impugn and the concepts they themselves rely on. On the other hand, elenctic arguments can be employed to show that premises of form P_1 are indeed unassailable, because their sceptical denial is self-defeating.

Whether this is an auspicious ploy depends, of course, on the knowledge, abilities, or concepts invoked by such premises. In this respect, there is a further difference between *Individuals* and *Bounds of Sense*. The former starts out by considering preconditions of the possibility of linguistic communication between speaker and hearer. In the latter, by contrast, we encounter a 'metaphysics of experience' (see chap. I.1 and Part II) which is not just transcendental in its structure but genuinely Kantian in its materials.

5. 'Concept' and 'Experience': Preliminary Clarifications

Before turning to this metaphysics of experience, it behoves us to take a propaedeutic look at our two key notions. In the spirit of connective analysis, we should look at both the established use of these terms and their employment in Strawson's writings.

The term 'experience' is employed in at least three capacities. For

- *what is experienced* by the subject S—X, that *p*, the 'content of experience'
- the episode or state of *S experiencing X*, that *p*.
- *S*'s *capacity* to experience X, that *p*.

Next, the term is sometimes applied very widely, to encompass any mental episode or capacity. Thus one might speak of the 'experience that π resists paraphrase in terms of a quotient of natural numbers'. In a somewhat more restricted sense, the term denotes sentience in general, including sensations like pains or tickles. Thus qualia-merchants are fond of musing about 'what it is like to experience a toothache'. Finally, in its narrower denotation experience equates to sense perception.

In Strawson we encounter all these employments. He often speaks of 'experiences or states of consciousness' and seems to regard 'experience' and 'state of consciousness' as interchangeable (e.g. Strawson 1959, 61, 90–3). But he recognizes the difference between bodily sensations and cognitive experiential states (Strawson 1959, 89), albeit without elaborating on it. Moreover, the metaphysics of experience is mostly concerned with sensory perception—'outer sense' in Kant's taxonomy. Next, animadversions to transcendental psychology notwithstanding, under various terminological guises the capacities for states of consciousness, sentience, perception, and self-consciousness play an important role. Finally, while the initial focus of *Bounds of Sense* is on episodes or states of perceiving, the *content* of particular experiences-qua-perceptions also plays a central role since it must display a certain unity to be self-ascribable (see 25 and Section 8 below).

The concept of a concept would require more elaborate treatment. Elsewhere (2011) I have argued for a non-representationalist, 'cognitivist' account. Concepts are neither mental representations in the minds of individuals; nor are they abilities, even though concept-possession is tantamount to the possession of a set of abilities, and it is constitutive of concepts that they play a role in the exercise of cognitive capacities. Concepts are best conceived as *rules* or *principles* governing higher cognitive, i.e. intellectual operations, especially classification and inference. In conceptual thought—'judgement'—we *classify* things into those that do and those that do not possess a certain property, or we *draw inferences* leading from one proposition to another (exploiting material or logical concepts).

A cognitivist approach chimes well with Strawson's explicit discussions of the nature of concepts.[6] But these are deplorably brief, especially in *Individuals* and *Bounds of Sense*. Fortunately, *Subject and Predicate in Logic and Grammar* is more forthcoming. From chapter 1 one can garner three points. The first is that the concepts at issue, 'general concepts', are capable, at least in principle, of being 'exemplified' by 'different particular cases', and especially by different 'spatio-temporal particulars' (Strawson 1974, 14–15). As such, concepts are universals to be contrasted with particulars (e.g. Strawson 1959, 126). The second point is that concepts are 'principles of collection' (Strawson 1974, 17; see also 1959, 228). Thirdly, concepts are essentially tied to judgements in which they are exercised: it is constitutive of the concept F that it is exercised in judgements of the form x is F.

From my perspective, four further lessons must be drawn. First, 'collection' here amounts to *classification*, sorting candidate objects into those that do and those that do not exemplify the concept. Secondly, a concept is neither the activity of collecting nor the ability exercised by that activity. It is rather a principle or rule *guiding* that exercise. Thirdly, a concept is not a bona fide representation. It does not refer to or denote the things that the judgements or propositions in which it occurs are about. Fourthly, a universal can enter a proposition not just in the

---

[6] It contrasts with Kant's official explanations, which are representationalist *au pied de la lettre*. Concepts are 'predicates of a possible judgement' (B 94). The modal modification leaves room for the idea that concepts have an existence independent of particular mental episodes of judging. But even then they remain components of (type) representations. Furthermore, like intuitions, concepts are explicitly classified as a type of representations—*Vorstellungen* (A 320/B 376–7). As such they are 'in us'. Concepts have 'subjective reality, as modifications' of our minds; and they may have objective reality by representing an 'object' (A 197/B 242). On the other hand, a cognitivist approach is congenial to Kant's doctrine of the collaboration between the powers of sensibility, understanding, imagination, and judgement. In that context concepts emerge not as representations in the minds of individuals, but as rules of cognitive operations that can be shared between different subjects (see A 106, 40–1/B 179–80; Bennett 1966, chap. 10). Finally, this *intersubjectivity of concepts* must be held apart from two Kantian ideas discussed below, the *objectivity of experience*—its relation to mind-independent experienced objects (Section 6)—and the *unity of experiences*—their propositional status and conceptual structure (Section 8).

direct sense that the sentence expressing the proposition contains a word or phrase *referring* to the property of being *F*, but also in the indirect sense that the sentence contains a word or phrase signifying it (Strawson 1959, Pt. II). This idea can fruitfully be extended from properties to concepts (Glock 2011, 145–9). A sentence can contain a predicate *expressing* the concept *F*, *without* referring to or denoting the concept *F*.

6. Self-Conscious Experience and Objective Particulars

With these clarifications in mind, let us turn to Strawson's transcendental line of reasoning concerning the connection between concepts and experience. The key to one transcendental argument is the possibility of self-conscious experience, of experiences that each subject can ascribe to herself. Its main thesis runs: a necessary precondition for ascribing experiences to oneself is the possibility of distinguishing between one's own experiences and an objective (mind-independent, non-chaotic, and unified) world that they are experiences of. Some of our experiences are of *mind-independent* things, 'objects in the weighty sense' (Strawson 1966, 73, 88). These 'objective particulars', in the terminology of *Individuals*, exist independently of being spoken or thought about by anybody; they include material objects, persons, and spatio-temporal goings-on (events and processes). Objective particulars must be situated in a spatio-temporal framework, and material bodies are ontologically prior because they alone can sustain this framework.

With some support from other writings, the first steps of this argument in *Bounds of Sense* (see Pt. II chap. II) can be reconstructed as follows:

(I) I have a series of experiences (this is common ground between Strawson and his opponents—sceptics and revisionists).
(II) Any experience must be ascribable to a subject. There is no such thing as an experience without someone whose experience it is, contrary to the 'no ownership theory', associated with Lichtenberg, Schlick, and middle Wittgenstein (Strawson 1959, chap. 3.3).
(III) The experiences *I* have according to (I) are of necessity ascribable to *me*.
(IV) It makes sense to ascribe experiences to myself, as of (III) only if it is possible to distinguish these experiences from *something else*. This follows from a semantic principle: a predicate like '*x* has the experience that *p*' presupposes a range of cases of which it can significantly be asserted, but can also significantly be negated.[7]

---

[7] The principle is implicit in Strawson (1974, chap. 1).

At this juncture, two contrasts come into play—between self-ascriptions of experience and *other-ascriptions* of experience, and between self-ascriptions of experience and the objective particulars that *they are experiences of*.

- (IVa) To speak meaningfully of *my* experience it must also be possible to speak about the experiences of *others*. If experiences were *ipso facto* unascribable to subjects other than myself, then ascribing them to me would be vacuous, and the no ownership theory would be rehabilitated (Strawson 1959, 94–100).
- (IVb) To speak meaningfully of my *experiences* it must also be possible to speak of the mind-independent particulars that they are experiences of. More generally, the idea of a 'subjective order and arrangement of a series of... experiences' makes sense only in contrast to the idea of 'the objective order and arrangement of the items of which they are experiences' (Strawson 1959, 101).
- (Va) From (IVa) it follows that it must be possible for me to ascribe experiences to subjects other than myself. It is a necessary precondition of one's ascribing experiences to oneself that one should also be prepared to ascribe them to others.
- (Vb) From (IVb) it follows that it must be possible for me to apply concepts of mind-independent objects to some of the things I experience.

It is a moot point whether (Va) and (Vb) have the potency of refuting scepticism about, respectively, other minds or the objective world (either on their own or in conjunction with other ideas). That would require a transition from the contention that we must be able to apply concepts for the experiences of other subjects or for mind-independent particulars *meaningfully* to the contention that we at least sometimes apply such concepts *correctly*, in true judgements (see Glock 2003, 36–42). Even leaving aside epistemological implications, the claims that make up this line of reasoning stand in need of clarification and defence. We have reason to endorse (II). The no ownership theory is untenable since it makes no sense to call something an experience unless it is the (potential) experience of a subject. Let us also grant the semantic 'principle of contrast' mentioned in (IV). To be sure, barring complications arising from vagueness, it does not hold for 'x is identical with x' or predicates like 'x is either a misogynist or not a misogynist'. But even if these are bona fide predicates—something Wittgenstein denied (Glock 1996, 164–9)—they are not prerequisites for the experiential judgements we are dealing with.

Now consider the kinds of self-ascriptions Strawson has in mind.

(1) The experience that a is F belongs to me.

Or, scaling down the misleading connotation of genuine ownership

(2) I have the experience that *a* is *F*.

Or, finally, an even less misleading wording close to one employed by Strawson in his defence of the causal theory of perception

(3) It (sensibly) seems to me just as if *a* is *F*.

Applied to (3), the principle of contrast demands that it must make sense to draw *one* of the following distinctions. Between

- it seeming to *me* just as if *a* is *F* and it seeming to *someone else* just as if *a* is *F*
- it seeming to me that *a* is *F* with *a* being *F* (it actually being the case that *a* is *F*).[8]

Alas, it does not entail that I must be able to draw *both* of these contrasts.

Fortunately, there are independent reasons to insist on the meaningfulness of both contrasts. Concerning the first (IVa), the first-person pronoun 'I' makes sense only by contrast to other personal pronouns. Concerning the second (IVb), it is constitutive of the predicate 'seems to *x* just as if *a* is *F*' that it contrasts with '*a* is in fact *F*'. This means that 'seeming' statements presuppose the possibility of referring to mind-independent objects and to ascribe to them properties that they possess or fail to possess objectively (respectively, *a* and being *F* in (3)).

So far so good as regards supporting the conclusions (Va) and (Vb). However, in this reconstruction of the argument neither (IVa) nor (IVb) emerge in the way Strawson envisages, namely from a general metaphysical contrast between universals and particulars—something one might claim for the general principle of contrast. Instead, (IVa) and (IVb) are non-trivial consequences of logico-semantic features of a loosely speaking *analytic* kind. Furthermore, both concern specific expressions like personal pronouns or epistemic verbs like 'seem'. The next two sections extend this deflationary perspective to Strawson's second transcendental argument which links the self-ascribability of experience to the unity—propositional nature and conceptual articulation—of the contents of experience.

7. Particulars, Concepts, and Judgements

Strawson accords primordial status to the distinction between particular and universal. This explains a rarely noted aspect of *Bounds of Sense*. Some passages

---

[8] Of course, the possibility of drawing the first contrast does not rule out that both I *and* someone else actually have the experience that *a* is *F*. And the possibility of drawing the second contrast does not rule out that it is the case that it both seems to me that *a* is *F and* that *a* is in fact *F*.

base the Kantian argument in favour of objective particulars on the self-ascribability of experiences (Strawson 1966, 28–9). This corresponds to statement (III) in the previous section. However, instead of treating (III) as a conceptual point about the senselessness of speaking of 'unowned experiences', other passages attempt to deduce the self-ascribability of experiences from a more basic fact, namely the 'conceptualizability of experience'. It is part of the 'standard-setting definition' of 'experience' that it involves a 'duality of general concepts...and particular instances of general concepts' (Strawson 1966, 25, 20, see 47, 97, 271–2). Echoing Kant, Strawson declares: '*Thought* about the World requires general concepts; and thought about the *world* requires their application in particular instances' (Strawson 1975, 6). The 'primary use' of concepts is in 'thought about the world', of which we are 'made aware' in experience.

While Strawson pays handsome tribute to Kant in acknowledging the interplay between 'judgement, concept and experience' (Strawson 1974, 14), there are important differences. For Kant, concepts are applied to intuitions or appearances, and hence to things which may be 'empirically real' but which, according to Kant's explicit statements, are representations in the minds of individuals (see fn 4 above). Strawson avoids this baneful legacy of the seventeenth- and eighteenth-century 'way of ideas'. In experiential judgements concepts are applied to the *objects* of experience, namely particulars that are mind-independent, *punkt*!

Furthermore, Strawson's account of thought and talk is built on two dichotomies: one between two *operations*—reference and predication, the other between *two types of entities*—particulars and universals (including concepts). Treating them as at least extensionally equivalent would be congenial to Kant's dualism of particular intuitions and general concepts; yet it is incompatible with Strawson's edifice. For one thing, Strawson rightly insists that one can refer to universals (Strawson 1959, Pt. II). For another, although he denies that singular, identifying reference to objective particulars can ultimately be *secured* by description alone, such reference proceeds through description in countless common-and-garden respectable speech acts. Furthermore, following Strawson, the ultimate identification of particulars, which locates them in 'a single unified spatio-temporal system' (Strawson 1959, 38), requires concepts. It cannot be secured by purely indexical thought like '*This* Φ'; instead it requires demonstrative concepts like 'The *so-and-so* over there Φ'. Reference to particulars as well as predication involves concepts and thereby universals.

8. Recognition and the Self-Ascribability of Experience

Strawson regards conceptualizability as a precondition not just of talk and intellectual thought, but of perceptual experience as well. 'There can be no experience at all which does not involve the recognition of particular items *as* being of such and such a general kind'. Furthermore, it is a necessary precondition of this 'recognitional component' that different experiences should be capable of being ascribed to a single subject. This in turn is supposed to imply that experience cannot have the chaotic character of the 'purely sense-datum "experience"' like a melange of after-images (Strawson 1959, 100–1). Sense-data experience is the kind of experience to which empiricists would reduce human perception. It is also the only type of experience William James granted to babies, and presumably to non-human animals, the registration of a 'blooming, buzzing, confusion' (James 1890, 488).

Strawson's second transcendental argument also starts out from

(I) I have a series of experiences.

From there it proceeds as follows:

a. It is part of the 'standard-setting definition' of 'experience' that it involves a 'duality of general concepts... and particular instances of general concepts' (Strawson 1959, 25, 20).
b. Accordingly, 'there can be no experience at all which does not involve the recognition of particular items *as* being of such and such a general kind'.
c. It is a necessary precondition of this 'recognitional component' that different experiences should be capable of being ascribed to a single subject.
d. Consequently, the experiences I enjoy cannot have the chaotic character of a 'purely sense-datum "experience"' a 'blooming, buzzing confusion' like a melange of after-images (Strawson 1959, 100–101).

The first point to note about this transcendental argument is that (d.) is right to question the idea of an experience that is nothing but blooming, buzzing confusion. But the rationale is not accurately pinpointed by (a.)–(c.). Assume that I am knocked over the head; as a result I suffer a concussion and momentarily see after-images. I might then exclaim

(4) I see stars.

This episode has the character of a blooming, buzzing confusion; it registers a sequence of fleeting coloured shapes. Its content lacks the reference/predication or particular/universal structure of perceptual judgements on display in

(5) I see that there are stars in the night sky above.

The comparison of cases (4) and (5) shows that the problem with experiencing a blooming, buzzing confusion is *not* that it would defy the self-ascription (c.) insists on. In (4) I ascribe seeing stars (i.e. after-images) to myself. Moreover, the question of *who* undergoes the mental episode no more arises for (4) than it does for (5). Both self-ascriptions are criterionless.

What rules out sense-datum experience, then, is *not* lack of self-ascribablity. It is rather that such episodes lack the kind of content which is *truth-apt*. (4) is not an experiential *judgement*, a judgement to the effect *that* such-and-such is the case. I cannot experience, judge, or think *that @#*%^!!!* or that stars, or for that matter, that *ouch* or even that *red, round, cool, tasty*. By contrast, I can experience, judge, or think that *this (apple) is red, round, cool, and tasty*.

This is the crux of what Kant calls the 'unity of apperception' (Kant 1998, B 132–4) and Strawson the 'necessary unity of consciousness' (Strawson 1966, 93–111): the 'I think' must be capable of accompanying all my judgements. But it does not reflect a metaphysical fact about self-consciousness. Instead, it is a point of *logical grammar*: the string 'I judge/think/experience that…' requires completion by a *well-formed sentence in the indicative*.[9] Belief in a propositional content expressed by such a sentence can be self-ascribed in sentences like (5). Yet this is a fallout from what Wittgenstein called 'the general propositional form'. We judge that things are thus-and-so. In Strawson's own words: 'The fundamental form of affirmative judgement…is that in which we judge that some *general* concept has application in some *particular* case' (Strawson 1992, 54). Once more we are dealing with a logico-semantic feature that is captured by conceptual truths of a non-trivial kind.

My second comment does not just concern the characterization of Strawson's argument, but is directly critical of it. The move from (b.) to (c.) is based on the idea that recognition requires thoughts of the kind

(6) *I* have encountered a thing of this kind *before*.

Yet the recognition in (b) is not *re*-cognition. It is merely subsumption of *a* particular *a* under a concept *F*, an experience of *a* as being of a certain universal kind. For a subject *S* can recognize that a particular *a* is *F* without ever having encountered an *F* before. Recognition implies at most subsumption of a particular under a concept, an experience of the particular as being of a certain universal kind. Now, re-cognition may require the capacity for I-thoughts like (6), and hence for relating distinct experiences to a single subject referred to by the first-person pronoun singular. But why should any such capacity for self-reference be required for mere recognition?

As mentioned just now, contents involving recognition are self-ascribable, by subjects capable of self-consciousness. Yet Strawson provides no rationale for

---

[9] In spirit, though not in detail, my point is in line with Rorty (1970). It leads on to the hairy problem of explaining 'the unity of the proposition', which, fortunately, need not be solved in this context.

ruling out that experiences with such contents can be *enjoyed* by creatures *incapable* of such self-ascription. The capacity for having experiences with a certain type of content must be kept apart from the capacity to ascribe experiences with such contents to oneself.

Strawson might protest that the mental episodes of such creatures would not meet his specification of experience as 'the conscious framing or holding of beliefs' (Strawson 1974, 14), since the latter requires at least a capacity for consciously framing beliefs. However, that specification is more demanding than the established concept of experience in both everyday parlance and science (see also Section 11 below). That concept may imply that experience is conscious. But to infer from this that experiences can be had only by subjects with self-consciousness would trade on an equivocation of 'conscious'. We must distinguish

- mental states being in which makes a subject *conscious of something*
- mental states the subject is 'conscious of', actually or potentially.

To enjoy experiences, a subject must possess the former; it needs to be conscious of something. Yet it need not possess the latter, since what it is even potentially conscious of need not include its own mental states. That is good news for animals and infants: we can credit them with experiences, even though it is contentious whether they can do so themselves.

9. Animals and Conceptualism About Experience

Strawson concedes that animals are 'perhaps' capable of enjoying experiences (Strawson 1959, 41). But he does so parenthetically and, it would appear, grudgingly.[10] More seriously, we have seen that his second transcendental argument ties the possession of experiences to the capacity of self-ascription. This commits him *either* to accepting that some animals, namely those with experiences, must also possess self-consciousness, *or* to denying that any animals enjoy experiences.

A related quandary arises from Strawson's claim that experience is per se *conceptual*, ostentatiously enshrined in the standard-setting definition. In the same vein he states that 'we are concerned with the temporally extended experience of conceptualizing or thinking beings' (Strawson 1966, 271–2). He also tends to treat experience as a kind of thought; and he explicitly contends that it is a 'platitude' that 'thought about the world involves general concepts' (Strawson 1974, 14). It is legitimate to tie the notion of thought to judgement and thence to

---

[10] Note that his celebrated discussion of the category of a person lumps animals and infants together with inanimate objects, since it does not provide for creatures that can satisfy some yet not all mental predicates (Glock and Hyman 1994).

concepts. In that case, however, it is far from obvious that *all experience* must qualify as thought. Indeed, Strawson here faces a second dilemma: *either* some animals, namely those with experiences, also possess concepts, their lack of language notwithstanding; *or* no animals enjoy experiences.

In the current setting I remain agnostic on whether animals can possess either self-consciousness or concepts. My contention here is that the second horn is intolerable. The conceptualist theory of perceptual experience that gives rise to the dilemma has been repudiated by philosophers and cognitive scientists who maintain that the perceptual experiences enjoyed by animals, infants, and pre-reflectively by adults have a special kind of non-conceptual content (see Schmidt 2015). It can also be rejected on the grounds that talk of the 'content of experience'—whether conceptual or not—is a reification, and that one can ascribe perceptions to a subject S without imputing to S possession of the concepts expressed by the predicates used in our ascriptions (Glock 2013).

By contrast, Kant is committed to endorsing the second horn of the dilemma.[11] And Pittsburgh philosophers like Sellars, Brandom, and McDowell have done so emphatically. They detect a sharp contrast between the ways in which humans and animals cognitively relate to the world. Only we enjoy 'experience of objective reality'. Animals simply cannot perceive the world in a sense of 'perception' that applies univocally to humans as well (Brandom 1994, Pt. I; McDowell 1996, 108–26, 181–7). All three luminaries draw inspiration from Kant. McDowell is also indebted to Strawson in particular.

According to Kantian conceptualism, genuine experience is conceptual and propositional. Therefore it is beyond the capacities of non-conceptual animals. This stance is liable to induce exasperation about 'unscientific' anthropocentrism among ethologists and paroxysms of righteous indignation among pet-owners. Nonetheless we need to consider potential defences of it.

10. Second-Class Perception?!

One line of argument might be based on McDowell's contention that every object humans can identify perceptually can somehow be described conceptually *by us*, if only with the additional aid of demonstratives. It does not follow, however, that there is a list of *propositions* which captures precisely and completely what S perceives—the content of S's visual field.[12] And even if a propositional description

---

[11] This alights from two claims of his. First, unlike 'judgements of perception', 'judgements of experience' about how things are objectively (*Prolegomena* §18) presuppose 'pure concepts of understanding'. Secondly, unlike the faculty of intuition, that of understanding is the prerogative of humans.

[12] Kant and Strawson would agree. Both accept that visual experience is governed by principles that differ from those governing propositional thought, non-conceptual forms of intuition in Kant, rules of a phenomenological geometry in Strawson (Pt. V).

of S's visual field were available, it would outstrip what humans endowed with language are capable of verbalizing.

Nor does it follow that creatures without concepts cannot perceive what creatures with concepts can perceive. It only follows that they cannot *understand* or *characterize* what they perceive in conceptual terms. It is a privation of thinking rather than of perceiving.

Furthermore, even if there *were* a sharp difference in type between propositional and non-propositional perception, neither of the following two claims would follow:

- animals only perceive in an attenuated, 'second-class' (Brandom 1994, 150) sense rather than literally speaking.
- 'perception' is equivocal.

One might defend Strawson and the Pittsburghers by appealing to a distinction between two types of perception, merely perceiving 'things' (including organisms and events) as in (4) above, and perceiving 'facts' as in (5) (see Dretske 2004). Animal perception, the story goes, falls short of genuine experience because it is confined to perceiving things. However, this ploy fails. The behavioural capacities of at least some animals cannot be explained by reference to perception of the form

(a) S perceives X (the snake, the explosion, etc.).

It must also make reference to perception of the form

(b) S perceives that p (there is a snake ahead, there is an explosion, etc.).

Consider a dog that has learnt not to grab anything when it is lying on the table but only when it is lying in his bowl. At t_1 this dog sees a bone on the table, but refrains from grabbing it and instead looks on, panting. Yet as soon as the bone is placed in the bowl at t_2, the dog goes for it. This mundane sequence is not explained by the dog simply perceiving discrete objects—the bone, the table, and the bowl. It can only be explained in terms of the following opposition:

- the dog sees at t_1 that the bone is on the table
- the dog sees at t_2 that the bone is in the bowl.

Why? Because at both t_1 and t_2 the dog can see bone, table, and bowl. So perception of the conglomeration formed by these three objects cannot explain the difference in its reactions at t_1 and t_2. One might respond that the problem vanishes if spatial relations like x *being on* y are among the objects that the dog can perceive. However, simply perceiving three distinct objects—bone, table, x

being on y—does not explain the dog's behaviour. Such an explanation is only in the offing if it can also perceive *that* the bone stands in the relation of *being on* to the table at one moment, to the floor at the next. And in that case we are back with perceiving that *p*.

It might be objected that the dog's performance can be explained behaviouristically. We only posit

- stimulus at t_1: 'bone on table' – reaction: 'do not take'.
- stimulus at t_2: 'bone in bowl' – reaction: 'take'.

But what sort of perceptual stimulus is this supposed to be? Is it purely proximal and physiological, like the pain stimuli to which even oysters react? This behaviourist fairy tale ignores that the vision of mammals is much closer to human vision than to that of molluscs, as regards both physiological vehicles (sense organs and corresponding centres in the brain) and performance. Dogs satisfy standard tests for object permanence and identification (Miller et al. 2009), and primates do so comfortably (Seed and Tomasello 2010, 409).

The alternative is to concede that the dog reacts not just to a proximal stimulus but to perceived information. Yet how can this information be specified if not as a perceiving that such-and-such? A tempting response runs as follows: what the dog perceives is not *that* the bone is on the table or in the bowl; what he perceives is '*bone on table*' or '*bone in bowl*'. However, if the determinants 'on table' and 'in bowl' are used *restrictively*, to indicate *which* bone the dog perceives, this does not explain the change in behaviour. For the dog perceives the *same* bone at t_1 and t_2. Alternatively, if they are used as ellipses for 'lying on the table' and 'lying in the bowl', this explains the divergent behaviour alright. Yet to perceive the bone *as* lying in the bowl is to perceive—albeit by another name—*that* the bone is lying in the bowl. One way or another, the dog's behaviour can only be explained on the assumption of *that-ish* perception.[13]

There is a case for maintaining that even such that-ish perception 'means'—i.e. *amounts to*—something different in conceptual and non-conceptual subjects. It has different preconditions and implications. But that does not imply that 'perception' *linguistically means* something different in the two cases. In both it means roughly something like the following: a subject's capacity to gather information which can be correct or incorrect with the aid of dedicated sense organs. Irrespective of whether this explanation hits the mark precisely, it is difficult to see on what grounds one could deny the univocality of 'perception'.

One possible rationale is an extreme holism, according to which *any* significant difference in the context of a phenomenon per se constitutes a distinct

---

[13] I have deliberately avoided the idiom of perceiving facts. As Strawson argued, facts are not located in space and time; consequently explaining what it is to perceive facts is a delicate matter in the case of humans as well as animals (see Glock 2019, 150–7).

phenomenon or concept. But such holism reduces to absurdity, at least in the case of animal perception. That, at any rate, was suggested by Plutarch in his criticism of the Stoics:

> As for those who foolishly say of animals that they do not feel pleasure, nor anger, nor fear, nor do they make preparations, nor remember, but the bee only 'as-if' remembers, and the swallow 'as-if' makes preparations, and the lion is 'as-if' angry, and the deer 'as-if' afraid:—I do not know how they will treat someone who says that they do not see nor hear either, but 'as-if' see and 'as-if' hear, and do not give voice, but 'as-if' give voice, and, in general, do not live, but 'as-if' live. For these last statements, I believe, are no more contrary to plain evidence than their own. (Plutarch 1957, 961 E–F)

Why should holistic as-ifness about perception or emotion imply as-ifness about forms of behaviour like acoustic signalling or about life? Because, by the holist's own lights, it is *partly constitutive* of perception that the information it provides can guide activities like signalling, running, swimming, etc. Similarly, it is partly constitutive of that concept that such information can be put in the service of biological functions, and hence, roughly speaking, of life. By the same holistic token, however, the *converse* conceptual dependencies also hold: it is partly constitutive of those behavioural and biological concepts that the activities and functions they express are capable of being guided by perception. But now, if what is partly constitutive, e.g. of running, namely perception, differs between humans and animals, then what is constituted must *differ as well*. The moral is manifest. At least from a holistic perspective, all capacities interact, in the behavioural repertoire of a subject that possesses them, not just in causal but also in conceptual ways. Therefore, *if* lack of rational powers barred animals from anything exceeding as-if perception, it would *also* bar them from anything exceeding as-if movement, as-if digestion, as-if life, etc. Anyone willing to bite that bullet incurs the consequence of intellectual lead-poisoning.

11. The Myth of Spontaneity

In considering the legacy of Strawson's conceptualism, one should mention another intriguing development of it, which harks back to the idea that all experience is potentially self-conscious (Section 8). According to McDowell, experience of objective reality requires concepts and thereby a 'faculty of spontaneity'. The subject must have the power of actively and 'autonomously' adjusting not just action and intentions but also beliefs to the 'deliverances of experience'. Such autonomous subjects are 'in charge of their thinking', which means that they are capable of 'taking charge of [their] own beliefs' (McDowell 1996, 29, 114).

This reaction to the empiricist 'myth of the given' is genuinely Kantian, yet it is also excessive. It amounts to an equally unwarranted 'myth of spontaneity'. The capacity for conceptual judgement—classification—is not tied to freedom or autonomy. It requires neither freedom of indifference (S could have done otherwise) nor freedom of spontaneity (S is capable of acting according to S's wants).

Just like the exercise of linguistic understanding, the exercise of conceptual abilities is not normally subject to the will. I might be able to decide not to employ certain concepts actively in a complex train of thought. And I can refrain from exercising my linguistic understanding actively, by performing or responding to certain utterances. By contrast, passive understanding is not subject to the will: 'Looking up at the flashing lights of the advertisements in Piccadilly Circus, one cannot prevent oneself from understanding their message. (How much more beautiful they would be, G. K. Chesterton once remarked, if only one could not read!)' (Kenny 1989, 22).

Similarly, while we can decide whether or not to take a look, once we do look, we cannot decide whether or not to see something within our field of vision. By the same token, a conceptually gifted subject S cannot decide whether or not to conceptualize what they see, in the sense of recognizing it as being of a certain kind. At most, S can try to reconceptualize what they see by thinking of less obvious categories that also apply to it. Nor can S decide not to recognize the immediate logical implications of her beliefs, much as she may occasionally wish to.

In later contributions McDowell tried to accommodate such qualms. He distinguishes the passive 'actualization' from the active 'exercise' of conceptual capacities (McDowell 2009, 12). But in that case he is confronted with a dilemma. If conceptual capacities require only actualization, they are no longer tied to spontaneity. And if they require exercise, he owes us an explanation of what kind of spontaneity is involved and why it should be prerequisite for experiencing an objective world.

12. An Analytic Take on Transcendental Arguments

From his general views concerning the relation between concepts and experience, Strawson derives not just the objectivity and propositional unity of experience, but also more specific consequences: objective particulars must be located in a spatio-temporal framework; bodies are ontologically prior because of their unique capacity to sustain that framework and thereby referential identification and reidentification; persons are embodied; experiential episodes are identifiability-dependent on the identity of their subjects; self-ascription of experience presupposes other-ascription of experience, and so on. What is the status of such claims? They are neither empirical truths, nor do they fit the standard conception of analytic truths. Nor can Strawson appeal to the category of the synthetic a priori.

According to Kant's transcendental idealism, 'we can know a priori of things only what we ourselves have put into them' (Kant 1998, B xviii). Synthetic a priori propositions state features to which the objects of experience have to conform because they are imposed on them by our cognitive apparatus in the course of processing 'sensations', the material component of our experience. Strawson condemns transcendental idealism as the model of 'the mind producing Nature as we know it out of the unknowable reality of things as they are in themselves' (Strawson 1966, 16). Furthermore, transcendental idealism cannot sustain a metaphysical enterprise of the Kant-Strawson variety. For in that capacity it depends on a genetic theory—transcendental psychology. The latter at best boils down to a highly theoretical yet empirical psychological theory; at worst, it is simply a fairy tale (Glock 2003, 26–33).

Once transcendental idealism is relinquished, Strawson contends, synthetic a priori propositions are merely a residuum of propositions that are neither analytic nor empirical, even though they 'have a distinctive character or status' (Strawson 1966, 44). For instance, 'it does not seem to be a contingent matter about empirical reality that it forms a single spatio-temporal system'. Consider someone who tells us of a material object undergoing changes, while insisting that this object was not located at any distance from here, and that its changes stood in no temporal relation to now, since they did not belong to our spatio-temporal system. We should probably take her to be saying that the events had not really occurred and that the object in question did not really exist. In this reaction we would show how we operate with the *concept* of reality. 'We are dealing here', Strawson maintains, 'with something that conditions our whole way of talking and thinking, and it is for this reason that we feel it to be non-contingent' (Strawson 1959, 29, also 24).

As Hacker has pointed out, however, this does not explain the peculiar status of descriptive metaphysics. 'The fact that something conditions our whole way of talking does not obviously suffice to explain why we should think of it as non-contingent. Our size conditions at least much of our way of talking and thinking too, but there is nothing non-contingent about it' (Hacker 2003, 56–7). Hacker's own solution is to treat the propositions of descriptive metaphysics as expressions of 'norms of representation' in Wittgenstein's sense, of rules determining the meaning of words by governing their correct use. Thus the propositions

(7) Every event is spatio-temporally related to every other event

and

(8) Every event has a cause
are rules for the use of the word 'event'. (8), the principle of causation, licenses us 'to infer from any event-identification that there is a cause of that event, which may or may not be known (and may or may not be discovered)' (Hacker 2003, 58).

This treatment of (8) is unsatisfactory. Our conceptual scheme does not simply rule out as nonsensical the expression 'uncaused event', even at a macroscopic level. Let's assume that one morning we find dinosaur footprints on the ceiling. Let's further assume that we have a reason to abandon the search for an explanation of the footprints, e.g. because the laws of nature not only fail to provide one, but suggest that none is to be had—the example of quantum mechanics shows that this is at any rate a possibility. Even in that case, we would *not* cease to call the appearance of the footprints an event. A physical change counts as an event, even if a causal explanation of it could be ruled out *ab initio*. Consequently, being caused is not part of our explanation of the term 'event', or of the linguistic rules governing its use. *Mutatis mutandis* for (7). Even if the rules for fictional discourse in general precluded calling Humpty-Dumpty's fall an event, a very substantial *if*, the rules for the term 'event' as such do not, even though Humpty-Dumpty's mishap is not spatio-temporally related to *either* the American invasion of Iraq *or* to another fictional event like Gretel's rescue of Hänsel.

Kant is right, therefore, to deny that propositions like (7) or (8) are *simply analytic*, analytic in the standard sense of being true by virtue of the meaning of their constituent terms alone. On the other hand, he has not made out a case for the idea that there is a kind of necessity which is not *conceptual* or analytic in a wider sense. We can know a priori of things not 'what we ourselves have put into them', as Kant's genetic story had it, but only what we ourselves have put into the *concept* of a thing, or of an *object of experience*. Unlike most material objects, concepts are creatures of human thought and action. The best path for descriptive metaphysics, accordingly, is to start out from a minimalist idea, also found in *Individuals*, according to which its propositions are 'conceptual truth[s]' (Strawson 1959, 58), i.e. articulations of our concepts and the connections between them.

Strawson claims, plausibly, that propositions like (7) and (8) can have an a priori status only if they occupy a constitutive role in our conceptual scheme. Kant claims, plausibly, that they do not simply explicate the concept of an event. More generally, not all a priori propositions can be treated as definitions or explanations of at least one of their *constituent terms*. My resolution of this quandary runs as follows. Among the pronouncements that have been lodged by descriptive metaphysicians we should distinguish at least two kinds. Some are 'hinge-propositions', commonsense certainties à la Moore and Wittgenstein. They have a special status in that their revision may have unacceptable and perhaps self-defeating consequences for our whole web of belief.[14] The epistemic coherence in play here is connected to and shades off into a conceptual coherence. And some statements of descriptive metaphysics are indeed conceptual since they are abandoned only at

---

[14] This category includes Strawson's claim that only an objective framework constituted by spatio-temporal relations between material bodies but not one of causal relations between events is 'humanly constructible' (Strawson 1959, 46–56).

the price of making (parts of) our conceptual scheme unintelligible. To appreciate this point we need to acknowledge, against Kant, that not all conceptual or analytic truths are obvious or trivial. But we further need to recognize that some conceptual truths are non-trivial because they are *not definitional* in even a catholic sense of that label. The connection between the constituent concepts of such propositions is provided by a *third* concept, one which does *not itself* occur in the proposition. Take (7). As Strawson suggests, what connects the concept of an event with that of a unified spatio-temporal framework is the notion of *reality*. Nevertheless, (7) is not simply a consequence of a more general principle, namely that everything which is real is part of a unified of spatio-temporal framework. Facts are real, yet, as Strawson (1971, 195–9) points out, they are not located in space or time.

Similarly for (8) and Strawson's mitigated version of the principle of causality.

(9) Most (macroscopic) events have a cause.

If anything can sustain a bona fide a priori connection between the concept of an event and the concept of causation, it is a *third* concept, one which does *not itself* occur in the judgement, namely that of experience. Events must be caused not because random and chaotic changes do not qualify as events, but because *persistently* chaotic events are not *possible objects of self-conscious experience*. Whether this claim can actually be sustained is contentious. But Strawson has shown that descriptive metaphysics holds the promise of establishing this kind of connection. The transcendental preconditions of experience are conceptual rather than psychological or *sui generis* metaphysical. At the same time, metaphysically important conceptual connections are mediated by a whole network of psychological and epistemic concepts, the *concept of experience* prominent among them.[15]

References

Bennett, Jonathan (1966), *Kant's Analytic* (Cambridge: Cambridge University Press).

Bennett, Jonathan (1974), *Kant's Dialectic* (Cambridge: Cambridge University Press).

Brandom, Robert B. (1994), *Making It Explicit* (Cambridge, MA: Harvard University Press).

Dretske, Fred I. (2004), 'Seeing, Believing and Knowing', in Robert Schwartz (ed.), *Perception* (Malden, MA: Blackwell), 268–86.

Glock, Hans-Johann (1996), *A Wittgenstein Dictionary* (Oxford: Blackwell).

---

[15] For comments I am grateful to an anonymous referee, the editors, and to audiences at Leuven and Zurich. I should also like to thank Christoph Wagner for assistance and proof-reading.

Glock, Hans-Johann (2003), 'Strawson and Analytic Kantianism', in Hans-Johann Glock (ed.), *Strawson and Kant* (Oxford: Clarendon Press), 15–42.

Glock, Hans-Johann (2011), 'A Cognitivist Approach to Concepts', *Grazer Philosophische Studien* 82: 111–43.

Glock, Hans-Johann (2012), 'Strawson's Descriptive Metaphysics', in Leila Haaparanta and Heidi Koskinen (eds.), *Categories of Being* (New York: Oxford University Press), 391–419.

Glock, Hans-Johann (2013), 'Animal Minds: A Non-Representationalist Approach', *American Philosophical Quarterly* 50: 213–32.

Glock, Hans-Johann (2019), 'Aristotle on the Anthropological Difference and Animal Minds', in Geert Keil and Nora Kreft (eds.), *Aristotle's Anthropology* (Cambridge: Cambridge University Press), 140–60.

Glock, Hans-Johann (2022), 'Strawson and Non-Revisionary Naturalism', in Mario De Caro and David Macarthur (eds.), *Routledge Handbook of Liberal Naturalism* (Abingdon: Routledge), 441–54.

Glock, Hans Johann, and John Hyman (1994), 'Persons and their Bodies', *Philosophical Investigations* 17: 365–79.

Haack, Susan (1979), 'Descriptive and Revisionary Metaphysics', *Philosophical Studies* 35(4): 361–71.

Hacker, P.M.S. (2003), 'On Strawson's Rehabilitation of Metaphysics', in Hans-Johann Glock (ed.), *Strawson and Kant* (Oxford: Clarendon Press), 43–66.

James, William (1890), *The Principles of Psychology*, vol. I (New York: Holt).

Kant, Immanuel (1963), *Prolegomena zu einer jeden künftigen Metaphysik die als Wissenschaft wird auftreten können*, in *Kants gesammelte Schriften*, vol. IV, ed. Preußische Akademie der Wissenschaften (Berlin: De Gruyter).

Kant, Immanuel (1998), *Kritik der reinen Vernunft* (Hamburg: Meiner).

Kenny, Anthony J.P. (1989), *The Metaphysics of Mind* (Oxford: Oxford University Press).

McDowell, John (1996), *Mind and World* (Cambridge, MA: Harvard University Press).

McDowell, John (2009), *Having the World in View* (Cambridge, MA: Harvard University Press).

Miller, Holly C., Rebecca Rayburn-Reeves, and Thomas R. Zentall (2009), 'What Do Dogs Know About Hidden Objects?', *Behavioural Processes* 81(3): 439–46.

Plutarch (1957), 'De sollertia animalium', in *Plutarch's Moralia*, vol. XII, ed. and trans. Harold Cherniss and William Helmbold (Cambridge, MA and London: Loeb).

Rorty, Richard (1970), 'Strawson's Objectivity Argument', *The Review of Metaphysics* 24: 207–44.

Seed, Amanda, and Michael Tomasello (2010), 'Primate Cognition', *Topics in Cognitive Science* 2: 407–19.

Schmidt, Eva (2015), *Modest Nonconceptualism* (Cham: Springer).

Strawson, Peter F. (1959), *Individuals: An Essay in Descriptive Metaphysics* (London: Methuen).

Strawson, Peter F. (1966), *The Bounds of Sense: An Essay on Kant's Critique of Pure Reason* (London: Methuen).

Strawson, Peter F. (1971), *Logico-Linguistic Papers* (London: Methuen).

Strawson, Peter F. (1974), *Subject and Predicate in Logic and Grammar* (London: Methuen).

Strawson, Peter F. (1975), 'Semantics, Logic and Ontology', *Neue Hefte für Philosophie* 8: 1–13.

Strawson, Peter F. (1985), *Scepticism and Naturalism: Some Varieties* (London: Methuen).

Strawson, Peter F. (1992), *Analysis and Metaphysics: An Introduction to Philosophy* (Oxford: Oxford University Press).

Strawson, Peter F. (1995), 'My Philosophy', in Pranab Kumar Sen and Roop Rekha Verma (eds.), *The Philosophy of P. F. Strawson* (New Delhi: Indian Council of Philosophical Research), 1–18.

Strawson, Peter F. (1998), 'Reply to Chung M. Tse', in Lewis Edwin Hahn (ed.), *The Philosophy of P. F. Strawson* (Chicago: Open Court), 383–4.

Strawson, Peter F. (2003), 'A Bit of Intellectual Autobiography', in Hans-Johann Glock (ed.), *Strawson and Kant* (Oxford: Clarendon Press), 7–14.

7
Strawson's Metacritique

Anil Gomes

1. Introduction

Strawson's Kant occupies an equivocal place in the philosophical study of Kant. On the one hand it is charged with revitalizing interest in Kant, opening 'the way to a reception of Kant's philosophy by analytic philosophers' in the words of Hilary Putnam (1998, 273). On the other, it is criticized by Kant scholars for its less than comprehensive engagement with Kant's works and its less than charitable interpretation of his theses. 'I have not been assiduous in studying the writings of Kant's lesser predecessors, his own minor works or the very numerous commentaries which two succeeding centuries have produced', Strawson warns us at the start of *The Bounds of Sense* (Strawson 1966, 11). This, says Lucy Allais, 'seems an enormous understatement' (Allais 2016, 893). And yet there is no denying the power and creative verve of Strawson's philosophical interrogation of Kant's text.

Strawson's interest in Kant arose from the peculiarities of Oxford's degree in Philosophy, Politics, and Economics. At the time he was a student, there were two subjects which those who wished to specialize in philosophy were obliged to take: Logic and Kant. The latter involved the study of two of Kant's texts: the *Critique of Pure Reason* and the *Groundwork of the Metaphysics of Morals*. Strawson found the *Groundwork* 'deeply impressive' but thought it conceived its subject altogether too narrowly. In the *Critique of Pure Reason*, on the other hand, he found 'a depth, a range, a boldness, and a power unlike anything I had previously encountered' (Strawson 2003, 8). Kant's influence threads through Strawson's writings, not least in both the conception and conclusions of *Individuals* (Strawson 1959), a work 'subtly and in part consciously influenced by [the first *Critique*]' (Strawson, 2003, 8). But it is in the book which grew out of his lectures on the first *Critique—The Bounds of Sense*—that Strawson takes on Kant explicitly.[1]

Strawson's central approach to the first *Critique* is captured by the threefold pun which constitutes his title. It is an echo of a title that Kant considered for the

---

[1] Strawson continued to publish on Kant's theoretical philosophy, most notably the four essays collected together in his *Entity and Identity* (1997). These are important for tracing the development of his views.

Anil Gomes, *Strawson's Metacritique* In: *P. F. Strawson and his Philosophical Legacy*. Edited by: Sybren Heyndels, Audun Bengtson, and Benjamin De Mesel,Oxford University Press. © Oxford University Press 2024.
DOI: 10.1093/oso/9780192858474.003.0008

first *Critique*.[2] And it plays on the ambiguity of the word 'sense' which can denote both sense-experience and sense-meaning. It thus, Strawson tells us in his Preface, 'alludes compendiously to the three main strands in [Kant's] thought' (Strawson 1966, 11). First, that there is a lower limit on sense, 'a certain minimum structure is essential to any conception of experience which we can make truly intelligible to ourselves' (Strawson 1966, 11). Second, that there is an upper limit on sense, for 'the attempt to extend beyond the limits of experience the use of structural concepts, or of any other concepts, leads only to claims empty of meaning' (Strawson 1966, 11–12). Finally, that Kant draws these limits from 'a point outside [the bounds of sense], a point which, if they are rightly drawn, cannot exist' (Strawson 1966, 12). Strawson's project is to extract what is valuable in the first two strands from what is supposed to be the incoherence of the last.

Strawson's negative assessment of this final strand drew immediate discussion. It includes his rejection of Kant's metaphysics of transcendental idealism and his rejection of the 'imaginary subject of transcendental psychology' (Strawson 1966, 32). The response to the rejection of transcendental idealism was not to defend the doctrine so understood against Strawson's attack. It was rather to deny the attribution of that doctrine to Kant. Graham Bird had already offered an alternative in his *Kant's Theory of Knowledge* (Bird 1962) and Henry Allison's *Kant's Transcendental Idealism* (Allison 1983) explicitly used Strawson as a foil for his own supposedly more sympathetic interpretation. The response of these defenders was that Strawson's account of transcendental idealism was exegetically unsound but philosophically on point.

The response to Strawson's rejection of transcendental psychology made a contrasting case. It did not deny that Kant engaged in such a subject. It rather denied that it was problematic for him to do so. This is most clear in Patricia Kitcher's *Kant's Transcendental Psychology* (Kitcher 1990) which defended transcendental psychology as neither imaginary nor excisable from Kant's text. Here the thought was that Strawson is right to understand Kant as engaged in transcendental psychology but wrong to think there is anything improper in being so.

Strawson's discussion of transcendental idealism has provoked reams of commentary. My focus in this chapter is his criticism of the 'imaginary subject of transcendental psychology' (Strawson 1966, 32). It is a quotable and oft-quoted line, characteristic of Strawson's ear for the right phrase. But what exactly is the nature of Strawson's criticism? That is the topic of this chapter. It is a small exegetical issue which turns out to have important implications for understanding

---

[2] In a letter to Marcus Herz from 1771, Kant writes 'I am therefore now busy on a work which I call "The Bounds of Sensibility and of Reason"' (1999, 10, 123); he repeats the title in a letter to Herz from 1772, writing of a work 'which might perhaps have the title, *The [Bounds] of Sensibility and Reason*' (1999, 10, 129)—both references to the volume and page number of Kant (1900). Zweig's translation renders the second title as *The Limits of Sensibility and Reason*, but both titles use the same German term, '*Grenzen*'.

what Strawson thought he was doing when he was doing philosophy. And perhaps also for what Kant thought he was doing as well.

Here is the structure of what follows. In §2 I'll reconstruct Strawson's criticism of transcendental psychology and suggest that it instantiates a challenge which stretches back to the very first readers of the *Critique of Pure Reason*—a challenge about Kant's grounds for the claims which make up the argument of the Transcendental Deduction. Does Strawson's own reconstruction of the Deduction avoid this problem? Answering this question requires us to understand how Strawson understood the grounds for the claims which make up his own version of the Deduction. In §3 I shall argue, against what I take to be the general consensus, that Strawson did not and should not have understood the claims which make up his own argument to be analytic. Rather he is puzzlingly committed to our possessing non-analytic but still a priori knowledge of the claims which constitute his own argument. But what could such knowledge consist in?

In the second part of the chapter, I'll sketch an answer to this question, starting in §4 with a discussion of G.E. Moore's early writings on Kant and a consideration of Moore's own methodology. Moore too was committed, I'll suggest, to our possessing non-analytic but still a priori knowledge of the claims which constitute his own arguments. Consideration of Moore's methodology will offer a model in §5 for understanding what Strawson is up to in his version of the Transcendental Deduction. And it will allow us in §6 to better appreciate the way in which Strawson's methodology dovetails with Kant's own.

2. Kant (I)

Why does Strawson think that transcendental psychology is an imaginary subject? His use of that phrase occurs in his overview of Kant's Transcendental Deduction of the Categories. It is worth quoting the passage in full:

> [The Transcendental Deduction] is also an essay in the imaginary subject of transcendental psychology. Since Kant regards the necessary unity and connectedness of experience as being, like all transcendental necessities, the product of the mind's operations, he feels himself obliged to give some account of those operations. Such an account is obtained by thinking of the necessary unity of experience as produced by our faculties (specifically by memory and imagination controlled by understanding) out of impressions or data of sense themselves unconnected and separate; and this process of producing unity is called by Kant "synthesis". The theory of synthesis, like any essay in transcendental psychology, is exposed to the *ad hominem* objection that we can claim no empirical knowledge of its truth; for this would be to claim empirical knowledge of the occurrence of that which is held to be the antecedent condition of empirical knowledge. (Strawson 1966, 32)

The Transcendental Deduction aims to show that we are entitled to use a set of pure concepts: the categories. It does this by arguing that these concepts are a priori conditions on the possibility of experience and that this suffices to show how they can relate to objects a priori and why we are entitled to use them. Strawson's gloss on this argument reads Kant as showing that the categories are conditions on the possibility of experience by identifying features of experience—its necessary unity and connectedness—which are imposed by our faculties through a process of synthesis. The imposition of this unity through synthesis is supposed to explain why the categories are conditions on the possibility of experience.

Strawson claims that this aspect of Kant's argument—the claim that the mind imposes unity through the operation of synthesis—is exposed to 'the *ad hominem* objection that we can claim no empirical knowledge of its truth' (Strawson 1966, 32). It is not clear what makes this objection *ad hominem* but it at least seems true. Indeed, its truth looks overdetermined so far as Kant is concerned. Kant holds that empirical knowledge is established by experience and that experience can only tell us what is, never that it must be so (B 3).[3] It follows that experience cannot be a source of knowledge, of necessary truths, that they are necessary. So, if it is known to be a necessary truth that the mind imposes unity in experience through the operation of a process of synthesis, then experience is not in a position to support the claim and it cannot be an object of empirical knowledge.[4]

In fact, we do not even need to assume that the claim is a necessary truth. For Kant also holds that experience can only tell us about how things appear. So, if the claim that the mind imposes unity through synthesis were an item of empirical knowledge, it would be a claim only about how things appear. But a truth about how things appear cannot itself be a condition on the *possibility* of appearances. So the mere fact that this claim is supposed to be a necessary condition on experience shows that we cannot have empirical knowledge of its truth.

Note that Strawson's charge here is independent of his characterization of the cognitive faculty as *producing* some aspects of our experience. This terminology reflects Strawson's reading of Kant as endorsing 'a relatively familiar kind of phenomenalistic idealism' (Strawson 1966, 240) on which the objects of experience are constructed out of sense-impressions. Some have thus thought that the objection he raises to transcendental psychology is inseparable from his interpretation of transcendental idealism more widely such that the rejection of transcendental psychology stands or falls with the rejection of transcendental idealism.[5] But this is not the case. Say one thought only that synthesis is one of the 'epistemic conditions' under which objects can be known by us (Allison 1983, 10). Strawson

---

[3] All references of this form are to Kant (1998) and use the standard A/B pagination.
[4] On the question of whether it is a necessary truth, see Gomes et al. (2022) for relevant discussion.
[5] E.g. Guyer (2017, 368).

can still hold that this claim is exposed to the objection that we can claim no empirical knowledge of its truth.

If this is right, then the claims which make up Kant's transcendental psychology cannot be empirical truths. How do we get from there to the claim that transcendental psychology is an imaginary subject? Strawson offers us no more in this initial discussion but further considerations are forthcoming in the discussion of synthesis in §6 of the discussion of Objectivity and Unity in Part II of the book. This is the part in which Strawson lays out his own version of the Transcendental Deduction of the Categories. Strawson there repeats the charge that the doctrine of synthesis cannot be a matter of empirical knowledge, this time emphasizing the reason that it is not and cannot be an object of empirical self-consciousness.

Strawson then goes further and considers whether there is some *other* way in which we might know that the mind imposes unity through synthesis. He considers those passages in the Deduction in which Kant seems to suggest that we are conscious of the activity of synthesis.[6] And Strawson thinks they are to be interpreted away:

> Kant does not, after all, think that we have a special kind of experience or awareness of the self or its activity, distinct from that empirical self-consciousness in which, as he holds, we are aware only of appearances of ourselves.
> (Strawson 1966, 95)

If right, this rules out an alternative way of our coming to know that the mind imposes its unity through synthesis—through some special non-empirical awareness of the activity of synthesis. But it does not yet show that there is *no* way of coming to know the claim. And that is what we need if Strawson is to show that the subject is imaginary.

I think there are two assumptions lying behind Strawson's discussion here and once we make them explicit we can see both why the challenge which he presents to Kant is a good one and how it instantiates a schema of objection which has been raised since the earliest engagements with the first *Critique*. Note, first, a curious omission. Strawson does not here consider whether the doctrine of synthesis might be an analytic truth, knowable in whatever way we know analytic truths more generally. Perhaps Strawson thinks it obvious that it is not an analytic truth or that Kant could not have thought it such. This is the first assumption. One might support it by noting that it does not seem built into the concept of experience that its unity is the result of a process of synthesis. Or alternatively, that Kant's aim in the Transcendental Deduction of the Categories is to show the objective validity of the categories and that this requires showing that their objects

---

[6] Strawson cites B 133 and A 108; he might further have appealed to the footnote at B 157 and its suggestive comments about the relation of the 'I think' to activity.

are *really* possible. But analytic truths determine only *logical* possibilities. So if the doctrine of synthesis were an analytic truth, it would need supplementation with non-analytic considerations to show the real possibility of the categories. Strawson must be assuming that this cannot be done.[7]

Given this assumption, Strawson may conclude that the doctrine of synthesis is not an item of empirical knowledge nor an item of analytic knowledge. In order to complete the argument, he needs further to show that we cannot have non-analytic a priori knowledge of the doctrine of synthesis. This, I suggest, is how we should understand his rejection of 'a special kind of experience or awareness of the self or its activity, distinct from...empirical self-consciousness' (Strawson 1966, 95). Knowledge based on such special experience or awareness would be non-analytic, in virtue of its basis in experience or awareness. But it would also be a priori, in virtue of being distinct from empirical self-consciousness. This is Strawson's second assumption: that such special experience is the only way in which Kant could claim non-analytic a priori knowledge of the doctrine of synthesis.

We can now see the shape of Strawson's challenge to the subject of transcendental psychology. First, he claims that we cannot have empirical knowledge of the doctrine of synthesis. Second, he assumes that we cannot have analytic knowledge of the doctrine of synthesis. Finally, he claims that we cannot have a special kind of awareness of synthesis and assumes that this would be the only way to have non-analytic a priori knowledge of the doctrine of synthesis. Since these exhaust our ways of knowing, the doctrine of synthesis cannot be known: it is part of the imaginary subject of transcendental psychology.

Once set out in this way, Strawson's challenge instantiates a more general form of objection to the first *Critique*, one which traces back to its very first interlocutors. The *Critique of Pure Reason* aims to explain the possibility of synthetic a priori judgement. Kant's explanation of this possibility involves certain claims about the structure of the mind. There are two faculties to the cognitive mind, a passive faculty of sensibility and an active faculty of the understanding. Neither faculty can be reduced to the other. But they are individually necessary and jointly sufficient in finite beings for knowledge [*Erkenntnis*].[8] Each of these faculties has its own representations by means of which it relates to objects. Objects are given to

---

[7] See Gomes et al. (2022, §6.1) for discussion relevant to the question of whether the doctrine of synthesis is an analytic truth.
[8] Kemp Smith's translation (1933)—used by Strawson—renders this term as 'knowledge'. But there are textual and philosophical grounds for disquiet. It elides Kant's distinction between *Erkenntnis* and *Wissen* if 'knowledge' is used to translate both terms. And it overemphasizes the connections between *Erkenntnis* and the kind of propositional knowledge which has been the subject of much contemporary epistemology. Recent translations prefer the term 'cognition'. I will continue to use the term 'knowledge' in order to remain connected to Strawson's discussion but will flag any occasions where the translation is relevant. See Gomes and Stephenson (2016); Watkins and Willaschek (2020); Schafer (2022) for discussion of the issue.

us in sensibility by means of intuitions but we think of objects through the understanding by means of concepts. And Kant's explanation of the possibility of synthetic a priori knowledge turns on the claim that each of these faculties has an a priori element. Sensibility has pure intuitions, space and time; the understanding has pure concepts, the categories. It is these a priori elements to sensibility and the understanding—their pure forms—which explain the possibility of synthetic a priori knowledge.

What is the status of these claims about the structure of our cognitive faculties and their role in producing experience? Strawson's version of the challenge focuses on the doctrine of synthesis specifically but the question ranges more widely. It is a question about the claims about the structure of our cognitive faculties which make up the first *Critique* rather than the claims which are established on their basis. That some account is owed of how we know these claims was recognized by Kant's contemporaries. His sometime friend and close interlocutor Johann Georg Hamann wrote in 1784 that they show the need for a *metacritique*: an examination of the foundations and fundamentals of philosophical critique itself.[9] Hamann sent his ideas to Herder who sent them on to Jacobi and through them they set the foundations for the way that the post-Kantian German idealists engaged with Kant's text.[10] In its most general form, the metacritical challenge to Kant is to explain how we know those claims which he appeals to in his explanation of the possibility of synthetic a priori knowledge.[11]

This gives us a framework for understanding Strawson's objection to the imaginary subject of transcendental psychology. Once extended in the way I have suggested, it becomes a recognizable objection from the history of engagement with Kant's first *Critique*. We will not consider here whether Kant succumbs to the challenge. Instead, I want to pursue a more *ad hominem* route. Does Strawson's own version of the Transcendental Deduction avoid the metacritical problem which (I have suggested) he thinks afflicts Kant's own? This is our concern in the rest of the chapter.

3. Strawson (I)

Strawson's challenge to Kant focuses on the doctrine of synthesis. And since Strawson makes no use of that doctrine in his reconstruction of the Deduction,

---

[9] In his *Metacritique of the Purism of Reason*, reprinted in Hamann (2007).
[10] See Beiser (1987, 37–43).
[11] There is a version of the metacritical trilemma in Bennett (1966, 16–17). Colin Marshall (2014) provides a comprehensive overview of the trilemma and the possible responses. Note that nothing here turns on the use of Kemp Smith's term 'knowledge' as a translation for '*Erkenntnis*'. The assumption is only that Kant's claims about the structure of our cognitive faculty must have some positive epistemic status in order to explain the possibility of synthetic a priori cognition.

the specifics of his objections get no purchase on the reconstructed argument. Our question then is whether the more general metacritical challenge applies to Strawson's reconstruction. How do we know the claims which make up Strawson's argument? This is the metacritical challenge to Strawson.

Answering that question requires a quick sketch of Strawson's reasoning in the section Objectivity and Unity in Part II of *The Bounds of Sense*. I have argued elsewhere that the argument can be represented as follows:

1. The self-ascription of experiences requires possession of the concept of experience.
2. Possession of the concept of experience requires possession of a conception of objectivity.
3. Possession of a conception of objectivity requires experience of objective things.[12]

This beguiling argument was influential on a generation of philosophers and has been the impetus to many fruitful discussions.[13] We can prescind from the details for our purposes. How does Strawson think we know the claims which make up his argument?

Many will think the answer obvious: through conceptual analysis. Strawson after all characterizes his argument as one 'which proceeds by *analysis* of the concept of experience in general' (Strawson 1966, 31), as one which establishes 'a direct *analytical* connexion between the unity of consciousness and the unified objectivity of the world of our experience' (Strawson 1966, 96, my emphases in both quotations). Hans-Johann Glock stands for many when he characterizes Strawson, in his editorial introduction to the collection *Strawson and Kant* (2003), as 'the leading proponent of analytic Kantianism' (Glock 2003a, 1), that view being one on which 'the central insight of the *Critique* is an analysis of complex connections between concepts such as experience, self-consciousness, objectivity, space, time and causation' (Glock 2003b, 30).[14] This much is unproblematic. The interesting question is whether it follows that Strawson thinks that the claims which make up his argument are instances of analytic knowledge. That is invariably assumed.[15] But there are reasons to be wary.

The first concerns Strawson's discussion of Jonathan Bennett's book, *Kant's Analytic* (1966). It is Bennett who most clearly identifies both the claims which make up Kant's arguments and their conclusions as analytic. '[T]he most

---

[12] See Gomes (2016) for elaboration and defence.
[13] These include Bennett (1968); Harrison (1970); Rorty (1970); Walker (1978, 116–21); Hurley (1994); Van Cleve (1999, 98–104). Its influence can be seen on Evans (1982); McDowell (1994); Cassam (1997); Campbell (2002).
[14] For similar characterization of Strawson, see Rorty (1970); Hacker (2003); Guyer (2017).
[15] E.g. by Marshall (2014, 557) and Guyer (2017, 368).

interesting truths which Kant calls synthetic and a priori', he writes, 'are unobvious analytic truths' (Bennett 1966, 42). These are, to a rough approximation, those which are established by a series of steps involving only obviously analytic truths, such that the resulting truth is both analytic, in virtue of being established solely on the basis of analytic truths, and yet unobviously so, in virtue of the length of reasoning involved in establishing it (Bennett 1966, 7–8). Others who have taken this line include Ralph Walker (1978, 18–19) and Richard Rorty who, in a posthumously published paper dating from the 1960s, writes 'The only possible conclusion is that all of Kant's remarks about human knowledge, must, on Kant's own grounds, be construed as analytic propositions' (Rorty 2020, 53). Bennett thinks the same is true of Strawson's claims in *Individuals* (Bennett 1966, 41–2).

Kant's Analytic and *The Bounds of Sense* were published in the same year. Both instantiate a distinctive approach to the engagement of Kant's texts. These genuine commonalities have allowed people to read into Strawson something like Bennett's notion of the unobviously analytic. But Strawson's review of *Kant's Analytic* (Strawson 1968) suggests that this is a mistake. (Is it mischievous to say that those who lump Strawson and Bennett together have not been assiduous in studying Strawson's own minor works?)

In that review, Strawson points out a series of problems with Bennett's account of the unobviously analytic. Most basically, the claims which Bennett takes to be unobviously analytic simply do not fit the model of being established by a series of steps involving obviously analytic truths (Strawson 1968, 334). Nor do the claims which make up Strawson's version of the Transcendental Deduction. Either, then, they are not unobviously analytic or we need some alternative way of characterizing the notion. But Strawson also expresses scepticism about 'the utility of invoking the notion [of analyticity] to preserve the respectability of our metaphysics' (Strawson 1968, 335). This suggests that he does not take the claims in his reconstruction to be analytic.

The second reason for hesitation in classifying Strawson's claims as analytic concerns his elusive remarks on the notion of the synthetic a priori. Say that the claims which make up Strawson's argument are analytic. Then the claims which they support will be analytic as well. And there will be no use for the notion of the synthetic a priori in characterizing such claims. This is the line that Bennett and Walker take (Bennett 1966, 42; Walker 1978, 18). Bennett, for instance, replaces the class of the synthetic a priori with the class of the unobviously analytic. Strawson is more cagey. For although he thinks that Kant 'has no clear and general conception of the synthetic *a priori* at all' (Strawson 1966, 43) he does think that the notion can be used to pick out a class of propositions that have a distinctive character or status: those which are descriptive of the 'fundamental general structure of any conception of experience such as we can make intelligible to ourselves' (Strawson 1966, 44). Strawson does not say that these propositions are a special class of analytic propositions. But this is what we should expect him to say if he thought the claims which constitute his argument were analytic.[16]

These considerations are not decisive. Many readers will struggle to hear a difference between those claims which are descriptive of the fundamental general structure of any conception of experience such as we can make intelligible to ourselves and those claims which are analytically obtained through articulation of the concept of experience. And given that Strawson talks freely and easily of analysis and analytical (but not *analytic*) connections, the position I am ascribing to Strawson seems to be one on which analysis need not result in analytic knowledge. I do think Strawson is committed to such a claim. And I'll give more evidence for this in a moment, if not quite from the horse's mouth, then at least from the mouth of a horse in the same stable. For now, let us examine which options are open to Strawson if he denies that the claims that make up his arguments are analytic truths.

There are two. Either Strawson rejects the terms in which the metacritical trilemma is posed and does not have to choose between options. Or the conceptual analysis which delivers knowledge of the main conditions in Strawson's argument is not supposed to result in analytic knowledge but one of either empirical knowledge or non-analytic a priori knowledge. Let us consider them in turn.

First, the rejection of the terms. There are a number of places where it looks like Strawson might reject the terms in which the metacritical trilemma has been phrased. In the review of Bennett, for instance, he does not forswear the notion of analyticity but instead expresses doubt about whether it is of any use in characterizing Kant's arguments (Strawson 1968, 335). More generally, he expresses scepticism about whether some more basic explanation can be given of those claims that are descriptive of the fundamental general structure of any conception of experience such as we can make intelligible to ourselves. Kant took his transcendental idealism to be the explanation for the possibility of synthetic a priori knowledge. Strawson 'see[s] no reason why any high doctrine should be necessary here' (Strawson 1966, 44). And that can suggest that far from offering an answer to the metacritical challenge, he denies the obligation of answering its question.

There are some problems with taking this route on Strawson's behalf. First, it is not clear how the metacritical challenge can be sidestepped. The challenge asks only what grounds one has to endorse the claims which make up one's philosophical arguments. Of course, arguments have to begin somewhere. ('What about the premises?', Cian Dorr once asked, 'Where did they come from? The premise factory?' (Dorr 2010).) But it would be an odd philosopher who thought their premises lacking in any positive epistemic status. Second, Strawson's remarks on the synthetic a priori do not themselves show that he resists the terms in which the

---

[16] See Stroud (2003) for an excellent discussion of Strawson's notion of the synthetic a priori.

metacritical challenge is put. He says only that an explanation of those fundamentally descriptive claims will not appeal to high theory. That is compatible with it appealing to something else. Finally, and most relevant dialectically, a defence of Strawson which has him resisting the terms of the metacritical challenge blunts his use of a version of that trilemma as an objection to Kant.

Turn instead to the second option. If Strawson does not reject the terms in which the trilemma is posed, and if he does not take the claims which constitute his own argument to be analytic, then that leaves him with two options: either the claims which constitute his own argument are known empirically or they are known in some non-analytic yet a priori way. The first of these options is unpromising. Strawson's use of the term 'analysis' to pick out the activity in which he engaged is partly aimed to dissociate it from the kind of empirical support gained through a study of the mechanisms of self-conscious thought and experience.[17] And, like Kant, Strawson is sceptical about whether experience alone could identify the kinds of necessary conditions which his version of the Transcendental Deduction sets out to establish.

What about the second disjunct? Could Strawson answer the metacritical challenge by holding that the claims which constitute his arguments are instances of non-analytic a priori knowledge? This option was supposed to be a problem for Kant because it seems to entail that Kant's explanation of synthetic a priori knowledge appeals, in part, to instances of synthetic a priori knowledge. And that circularity looks to undermine the cogency of Kant's explanation. Since Strawson does not share Kant's notion of the synthetic a priori and since his aim is not to explain the possibility of such knowledge, there is no obvious circularity in his appealing to non-analytic a priori claims in the identification of that general structure of any conception of experience such that we can make intelligible to ourselves. So, on the face of it, nothing precludes Strawson from taking this route.

In fact, we can go one better. Not only is Strawson not precluded from taking this option, we have testimony for his endorsing it. Quassim Cassam, on the fiftieth anniversary of the publication of *The Bounds of Sense*, writes:

> Strawson was absolutely clear in discussion that he never regarded experience of mind-independent objects as an analytically necessary condition for reflective experience and that many of his claims about necessary conditions of experience in *The Bounds of Sense* had a different status. He sometimes described them, somewhat mysteriously, as non-analytically but still conceptually necessary conditions. (Cassam 2016, 915)

Non-analytic but still conceptually necessary. This is our third option. It shows that Strawson's response to the metacritical challenge would be to hold that the

---

[17] See his remarks on the relation between Kant's doctrine of synthesis and scientific investigation in Strawson (1989).

claims which constitute his reconstruction of the Transcendental Deduction are not known empirically nor known analytically. They are non-analytic but still a priori truths.

Let us take stock. We are considering how Strawson would fare against his own metacritical challenge. I have suggested, conventional wisdom notwithstanding, that Strawson did not think of the claims which make up his arguments as analytic truths. Not only is this suggested by his review of Bennett and his account of the synthetic a priori, it is, according to Cassam, how Strawson himself described his claims. So despite the fact that *The Bounds of Sense* is involved in an *analysis* of any conception of experience that we can make intelligible to ourselves, the resulting claims are to be thought of as non-analytic but still conceptual, a priori truths. Cassam calls this mysterious. And so it is. My aim in the second part of this chapter is to see if we can make it less so.[18]

4. Moore

I noted above that the metacritical trilemma is as old as the first *Critique* itself. One striking place where it surfaces is at the very foundation of analytic philosophy. It is common, perhaps too common, to present analytic philosophy as arising from the rejection of neo-Hegelian idealism undertaken by Moore and Russell in Cambridge at the start of the twentieth century.[19] One of the key moments in that process is Moore's transition from idealism to realism, a transition charted in the 1897 and 1898 dissertations which Moore submitted for the Trinity College Prize Fellowship examinations.[20] At the start of the 1897 dissertation, Moore is an idealist of the McTaggart variety. By the end of the 1898 dissertation, he is the full-fledged realist that we know from the famous 1903 papers. Both dissertations are on Kant.

Moore's central objection to Kant, repeated in various ways across the dissertations, is that the necessary conditions which Kant sets out are either purely psychological conditions about the way we are conditioned to think and behave, or else purely logical truths which cannot explain the possibility of the states and activities in question.[21] We can think of this charge, in very broad terms, as challenging the claims about the cognitive faculties which constitute premises in

---

[18] Wittgenstein's appeal to grammar has sometimes been understood as allowing for a kind of non-analytic, conceptual truth. Hacker (1996, 177–8) offers this notion as a salve to Strawson but does not see that something similar might already be operative in Strawson's text.

[19] See Bell (1999); Kalderon and Travis (2013); Gomes (2017a) for discussion of the way that the traditional story obscures key parts of that history

[20] Recently published as *G. E. Moore: Early Philosophical Writings* (2011).

[21] See Moore (2011, 141ff.) for a version of the dilemma in the 1898 dissertation and Caird's examiner's report (2011, 103) for a discussion of the issue as it arises in the 1897 discussion. The pages which follow give Caird's defence of Kant. The editors' introductory material provides further discussion (2011, xlvi–lxvii).

Kant's arguments in the first *Critique*. Either these claims are analytic a priori truths, Moore says, in which case they cannot explain the possibility of synthetic a priori knowledge. Or they are empirical truths, in which case they concern only the psychological structure of how human beings actually operate and cannot be used to explain synthetic a priori knowledge. In 'Kant's Idealism', presented to the Aristotelian Society in 1903, Moore completes the trilemma by noting that if they are synthetic and a priori then 'Kant has not, in his own words, "explained the possibility of all synthetic propositions a priori"' (Moore 1903, 133).

Moore's challenge to Kant, then—a challenge which forms part of the foundational texts of analytic philosophy itself—is an instance of the metacritical trilemma. Does this trilemma have force against Moore himself? These early dissertations do not contain a detailed account of methodology but the notion of analysis is already central to how Moore understands his approach. '[A] thing becomes intelligible first', he tells us 'when it is *analysed* into its constituent concepts' (Moore 1898 dissertation 2011, 168, my emphasis). Yet this coexists with a dismissive stance on analytic truth (Moore 1898 dissertation 2011, 139–41). As his editors put it, 'Moore does not think that philosophical analysis brings with it a commitment to regarding a priori philosophical truth as "analytic"' (Moore 2011, lviii). This suggests the kind of distinction between analysis and analytic truths which I have proposed is found in Strawson.

How could analysis not result in analytic truths? The notion of analysis remains central in Moore's mature writings, coming to signify, as John Wisdom wrote in 1931, a method that 'Wittgenstein has lately preached and Moore long practised' (Wisdom 1931, 195 n.2).[22] But what does such a method involve? We can extract an answer from the influential 'A Defence of Common Sense' (Moore 1925). This was Moore's contribution to a series of invited essays by British philosophers which aimed 'to give the contributors an opportunity of stating authentically what they regard as the main problem of philosophy and what they have endeavoured to make central in their own speculation upon it' (Muirhead 1924, 10, quoted in Baldwin 2013). Moore focuses his essay on the importance of identifying the correct analysis of commonsense propositions. How does such analysis work?

We get an answer in the final part of this paper, where Moore analyses the proposition 'This is a hand'. He argues that analysis shows the existence of a *sense-datum* which is the subject of the proposition and thus that perception involves a relation to sense-data. How does analysis do this? Moore's answer is instructive:

[I]n order to point out to the reader what sort of things I mean by sense-data, I need only ask him to look at his own right hand. If he does this he will be able to pick out something (and, unless he is seeing double, *only* one thing)... Things *of*

---

[22] See Baldwin (2013) on 'the Cambridge School of Analysis'.

the sort (in a certain respect) of which this thing is, which he sees in looking at his hand, and with regard to which he can understand how some philosophers should have supposed it to be the part of the surface which he is seeing, while others have supposed that it can't be, are what I mean by 'sense-data'.

(Moore 1925, 54)

What should we say about Moore's philosophical method here? It offers us, in effect, a set of instructions to be followed by the reader. Similar instructions are found across Moore's writings on perception (e.g. Moore 1953, 29–30). The supposed result of following this method is the identification of a truth about the nature of perceptual experience, namely that it involves a relation to sense-data. Moore's philosophical argument involves asking the reader to engage in a certain kind of first-personal reflection, the result of which will be to disclose a philosophical truth about the nature of perception. And he presents this first-personal reflection as part of what is to be understood as involved in the method of analysis.

How should we understand the knowledge which results from this process? I noted that Moore's dissertations make a distinction between analysis and analytic truths such that not all instances of analysis result in knowledge of analytic truths. Moore's analysis of the proposition 'This is a hand' suggests one reason why this is so. For if one's first-personal perspective is exploited in recognition of the fact that perception is a relation to sense-data, then we can see why Moore might distinguish it from analytic knowledge: it does not involve mere explication of that which is involved in the *concept* of perception. This is a way of understanding Moorean analysis which makes clear why Moore denied its results the status of analytic knowledge.

Does analysis, then, result in empirical knowledge? This is a more delicate question. It is important to Moore that the knowledge delivered by first-personal reflection is not the kind of knowledge which requires investigations into the mechanics of the perceptual system. But a Kantian might claim that it is still the result of the deliverances of inner-sense and in this sense counts as empirical. This was one reaction of those working in early twentieth-century philosophy and psychology who took disputes about the knowledge delivered through first-personal reflection to motivate scientific study of the mechanisms of introspection and their reliability.[23]

An alternative is to think of first-personal reflection as delivering knowledge about the *nature* of perception in a way that precludes the characterization of such knowledge as empirical. Husserl, writing at a similar time to Moore and on a set of related issues, endorsed the idea that phenomenological reflection could identify the essential features of experience. This reflection is supposed to be both distinct from and more fundamental than any empirical psychological investigations

---

[23] See Spener (2018) for the details.

of experience.[24] If Moore also thinks that the involvement of the first-personal perspective in philosophical theorizing ensures that the knowledge gained is non-empirical, then we have an explanation for why he thinks his philosophical claims about the nature of perception are both non-analytic and yet in some sense a priori.[25]

I won't make the case that Moore endorses this claim here.[26] But even if it can be defended, there are deep and difficult issues about whether the resulting view is coherent. If the thought is that first-personal reflection does not deliver empirical knowledge on grounds of enabling knowledge of *natures*, then there needs to be a reckoning with Saul Kripke's identification of truths about essence which can be known through experience (Kripke 1980). If Husserl's model of phenomenological reflection is a model for how such first-personal reflection works, then there is a question about whether it can be detached from the idealism about the objects of first-personal reflection which Husserl seems to endorse in his later writings.[27] And independent of both of these issues, one might still want some story about how it is that the use of first-personal reflection in philosophical theorizing results in knowledge which is both non-analytic and a priori.[28]

Still, without pretending to address these issues, we have enough to return to Strawson. For the suggestive thought we have extracted from Moore is that one might take the involvement of first-personal reflection in analysis to explain why its deliverances should be classified as both non-analytic and yet a priori. This does not yet make the category unmysterious. But it opens up a route for understanding Strawson. For if Strawson shared this view—that first-personal reflection can deliver non-analytic but a priori knowledge of philosophical truths—then we can make sense of his puzzling claims about the methodology of *The Bounds of Sense* so long as that methodology involves essential use of first-personal reflection. Does it?

5. Strawson (II)

On the face of it, *The Bounds of Sense* does not contain any of the explicit instructions to attend to one's own perspective which characterize the writings of Moore and Husserl. Here is how Strawson opens the book:

---

[24] See especially Husserl (1917).
[25] These commonalities should serve as a reminder that the phenomenological and analytic traditions are but two stems of philosophy with a common (and known) root in Kant. See Martin (2003) for discussion of Moore and Husserl and Gomes (2017a) for discussion of the Kantian influence on early-analytic philosophy of perception.
[26] See Baldwin (2013); Martin (2003) for discussion. Gomes (2017b) compares the methods of Moore and Strawson in more detail.
[27] See Bell (1990, §III) for discussion.
[28] See Spener (2018) for discussion of the way in which this question shaped the development of early twentieth-century philosophy and psychology.

It is possible to imagine kinds of world very different from the world as we know it. It is possible to describe types of experience very different from the experience we actually have. But not any purported and grammatically permissible description of a possible kind of experience would be a truly intelligible description. There are limits to what we can conceive of, or make intelligible to ourselves, as a possible general structure of experience. The investigation of these limits, the investigation of the set of ideas which forms the limiting framework of all our thought about the world and experience of the world, is, evidently, an important and interesting philosophical undertaking. (Strawson 1966, 15)

There is nothing comparable here to Moore's instructions for revealing sense-data, no precept to the reader to examine their own perspective, and no indication from Strawson that he takes the truths he identifies to be established directly through simple reflection on the character of one's experience.

Nevertheless, once we look at the details of Strawson's arguments, we can see a way in which one's first-person perspective plays an essential role in establishing the conditions in his reconstructed Deduction. Consider the last of those claims: that possession of a conception of objectivity requires experience of objective things. How does Strawson establish this condition? He does not do so directly, drawing our attention to some manifest truth about the character of experience. Rather he argues for what he takes to be the contrapositive: that subjective experience is incompatible with the possession of a conception of objectivity (Strawson 1966, 98–100). Sense-datum experience, Strawson says, consists of 'impressions which neither require, nor permit of, being "united in the concept of an object" in the sense in which Kant understands this phrase' (Strawson 1966, 99). If subjects had nothing but this form of experience, they would not possess a conception of objectivity. So subjective experience entails lack of a conception of objectivity. Strawson takes this as equivalent to the claim that possession of a conception of objectivity requires objective experience.[29]

How does Strawson establish that purely subjective experience would lack a conception of objectivity? This is a counterfactual about what would be the case if perceptual experience lacked some feature which it actually has. A natural thought is that we determine its truth by engaging in imaginative reflection about how things would be were perceptual experience to be different. Imagine that you have a sense-datum experience. What would you be able to do in that scenario? Answering this question requires us to draw on the knowledge we possess of the character of our experience. We exploit that knowledge in determining the kinds of things which would be possible were experience to lack the character that it actually has. So in coming to know the counterfactual at the heart of Strawson's

---

[29] For some concerns about whether these claims are equivalent, see Gomes (2016, 957–60) and Gomes (2017b, 141–5).

argument, we have to exploit our first-person perspective on the world. The first-person perspective is thus central to an account of how we know the counterfactuals which make up Strawson's reconstruction of the Deduction.[30]

Indeed, it is central to the arguments of Strawson and his students more widely. In *Individuals*, Strawson argues that (the perception of) space is a necessary condition on the reidentification of particular bodies. And he does this by imagining a sound world in which we do not perceive spatial properties and asking whether we would be able to reidentify particulars in such a scenario (Strawson 1959, 59f.). In his commentary on this chapter, Gareth Evans imagines a world of purely sensory properties and asks whether we could extract the idea of an objective property from such a world (Evans 1980, 98f.). John Campbell, in defending a relational conception of experience, asks whether our conception of a mind-independent world could be made available by the experience of a conscious image, before concluding that it could not (Campbell 2002, 134–5). In each case, the main condition in some argument is supported by imaginative reflection on the kinds of things we would be able to do were experience otherwise. These exercises of imaginative reflection draw on our knowledge of the character of our experience. They exploit our first-person perspective on the world.

What are the implications for Strawson's response to the metacritical challenge? We noted above that Strawson disavows that his claims are instances of analytic knowledge. And if the above account of Strawson's methodology is along the right lines, then we have the shape of an explanation as to why this should be so. Both Moore and Strawson hold that analysis need not result in analytic truths. In the case of Moore, I suggested that this thought is underwritten by the way in which his use of analysis involves essential use of one's first-personal perspective. The same, we can now see, holds true of Strawson: it is because knowledge of the character of experience is exploited in our coming to know the truths of various counterfactuals that the claims which make up Strawson's arguments in the Deduction should not be characterized as analytic knowledge.

But Strawson also takes his claims to be non-empirical, in some broad sense. And one might worry that if they are supported by a process of imaginative reflection, then they should count as empirical. Perhaps this is because such reflection involves empirical mechanisms of introspection, as many in early twentieth-century psychology alleged.[31] Or perhaps this is because the only way such claims would fail to be empirical would be if some form of idealism were true, as some readers of Husserl have alleged.[32] Or perhaps one might simply claim that the distinction between the a priori and the empirical loses significance at exactly

---

[30] This interpretation of Strawson is defended more generally in Gomes (2017b).
[31] See Spener (2018) for discussion.   [32] See Zahavi (2007).

this point, once one recognizes the role that imagination plays in counterfactual reasoning more generally.[33]

These are important challenges to the coherence of Strawson's view. But they are not challenges to its attribution. Rather, they demonstrate the difficulty in deciding whether the involvement of one's first-person perspective in philosophical theorizing suffices to insulate philosophical reasoning from the methodologies of natural science. These issues were central to early twentieth-century debates in philosophy and psychology. They were less central, if present at all, in the debates occasioned by Strawson's use of transcendental arguments in *Individuals* and *The Bounds of Sense*. If what has been said here is along the right lines, that is a lacuna. Both Moore and Strawson want a philosophical method which is more than simply the unpacking of definitional truths but is yet distinct from the methodologies of natural science. My suggestion has been that if Moore and Strawson thought themselves to have such a method, it is because of the role that the first-person perspective plays in their philosophical theorizing. And it is a deep and difficult question whether such appeal to the first-person perspective is enough to underwrite philosophical autonomy.

Let me draw these threads together. I have suggested that Strawson's criticism of the imaginary subject of transcendental psychology is best understood as an instance of metacritique, challenging Kant to provide grounds for the claims which make up his argument in the Transcendental Deduction. Strawson's own reconstruction of the Deduction is open to such a challenge and he does not evade it by taking the claims which make up his own argument to be analytic. Rather he puzzlingly commits to our possessing non-analytic but still a priori knowledge of their truth. I've suggested that this may be a result of the role that our first-personal perspective plays in establishing those claims. And although this does not make the view any less mysterious, it at least situates him within a recognizable tradition in twentieth-century philosophical theorizing. For Strawson, we might say, it is the involvement of the first-person perspective in philosophical theorizing which distinguishes it from both analytic explication and empirical science.

6. Kant (II)

This would be an appropriate note on which to end a paper for a volume on Strawson. But chiasmus demands that we end with Kant. For one way to read Kant's own route out of the metacritical trilemma is to hold that he too thinks we

---

[33] See, especially, Williamson (2007, 2013). Williamson takes his account of the role imagination plays in our knowledge of modality to undermine the significance of the distinction between the a priori and the empirical.

have a source of non-analytic a priori knowledge which can be appealed to in explaining the possibility of synthetic a priori knowledge. It is Kant after all who asks us to imagine the kinds of things that a being without spatial representation could do (A 23–5/B 38–9), to imagine the representation of a body without impenetrability, hardness, colour etc. (A 20/B 35), and to imagine deviance in the appearance of cinnabar (A 100–1). And all of this in service of the identification of necessary conditions on our representation of objects. These processes look to involve the kind of imaginative reflection I have identified in Strawson. And one might take them to show that Kant allowed us to have synthetic a priori knowledge of the claims which underwrite the project of the *Critique of Pure Reason*.

Still, the metacritical challenge had force for Kant because it seemed that Kant was precluded from taking his claims about the structure of the cognitive faculty to be both synthetic and a priori on grounds of undermining his explanation of the possibility of synthetic a priori knowledge. So if the metacritical challenge is going to be answered in this way, we need a principled explanation for why some kinds of synthetic a priori knowledge do not need explanation and can thus be appealed to in the explanation of some others. Only so can the challenge be disarmed.

Strawson's version of the metacritical challenges focuses on the subject of transcendental psychology, that is, on Kant's claims about the structure of the cognitive faculty and its role in legislating experience. And if it is these claims that Kant thinks are known both synthetically and a priori, then one natural way to distinguish between the problematic and unproblematic synthetic a priori claims—which is to say, those which need and those which can be appealed to in explanation—is in terms of those which concern the structure of the mind and those which do not.[34] Kant sometimes uses the term *reflection* to pick out that 'state of mind in which we first prepare ourselves to find out the subjective conditions under which we can arrive at concepts' (A 260/B 316). And one answer to the metacritical challenge is to say that the structure of the cognitive mind is known, for Kant, through reflection. And that there is nothing problematic in appealing to such knowledge in an explanation of those synthetic a priori claims which cannot be established by reflection.[35]

It requires work to see if this suggestion can bear weight. But if it does, then there is a pleasing convergence in the methodologies of Kant and Strawson. It is Strawson, of course, who co-opts Kant into his methodology, classifying him with Aristotle in the Preface of *Individuals* as a purveyor of descriptive metaphysics (Strawson 1959, 9). This has always been a source of bafflement. How could Kant, that transcendental idealist who thought that spatio-temporal objects are nothing

---

[34] See Smit (1999); Marshall (2014) for versions of this response.
[35] See Smit (1999); Westphal (2004: 12–32); Marshall (2014: 564–7); Merritt (2018) for discussion of the role reflection plays in Kant's arguments and Gomes (2017b) for wider discussion.

but appearances (A 490-1/B 158-9), be a descriptive metaphysician? The suggestion sketched above suggests an answer. Kant must distinguish the grounds for his claims about the structure of the mind from the grounds for his claims about the structure of the world. Strawson is thus half-right: Kant has a *descriptive metaphysics of mind* but he combines it with a *revisionary metaphysics of nature*.[36]

References

Allais, Lucy (2016), 'Strawson and Transcendental Idealism', *European Journal of Philosophy* 24(4): 892–906.

Allison, Henry E. (1983), *Kant's Transcendental Idealism: An Interpretation and Defence* (London: Yale University Press).

Baldwin, Thomas (2013), 'G.E. Moore and the Cambridge School of Analysis', in Michael Beaney (ed.), *The Oxford Handbook of the History of Analytic Philosophy* (Oxford: Oxford University Press), 430–50.

Beiser, Frederick C. (1987), *The Fate of Reason: German Philosophy from Kant to Fichte* (Cambridge, MA: Harvard University Press).

Bell, David (1990), *Husserl* (London: Routledge).

Bell, David (1999), 'The Revolution of Moore and Russell: A Very British Coup?', *Royal Institute of Philosophy Supplement* 44: 193–209.

Bennett, Jonathan (1966), *Kant's Analytic* (Cambridge: Cambridge University Press).

Bennett, Jonathan (1968), 'Strawson on Kant', *The Philosophical Review* 77(3): 340–9.

Bird, Graham (1962), *Kant's Theory of Knowledge* (London: Routledge & Kegan Paul).

Campbell, John (2002), *Reference and Consciousness* (Oxford: Oxford University Press).

Cassam, Quassim (1997), *Self and World* (Oxford: Oxford University Press).

Cassam, Quassim (2016), 'Knowledge and its Objects: Revisiting the Bounds of Sense', *European Journal of Philosophy* 24(4): 907–19.

Dorr, Cian (2010), 'Review of James Ladyman and Don Ross, *Every Thing Must Go: Metaphysics Naturalized*', *Notre Dame Philosophical Reviews* 6.

Evans, Gareth (1980), 'Things Without the Mind: A Commentary Upon Chapter Two of Strawson's *Individuals*', in Zak Van Straaten (ed.), *Philosophical Subjects: Essays Presented to P. F. Strawson* (Oxford: Clarendon Press), 76–116.

Evans, Gareth (1982), *The Varieties of Reference* (Oxford: Clarendon Press).

Glock, Hans-Johann (2003a), 'Introduction', in Hans-Johann Glock (ed.), *Strawson and Kant* (Oxford: Clarendon Press), 1–6.

---

[36] Thanks, as always, to Andrew Stephenson for discussion and comments and to the editors of the volume for their comments.

Glock, Hans-Johann (2003b), 'Strawson and Analytic Kantianism', in Hans-Johann Glock (ed.), *Strawson and Kant* (Oxford: Clarendon Press), 15–42.

Gomes, Anil (2016), 'Unity, Objectivity, and the Passivity of Experience', *European Journal of Philosophy* 24(3): 946–69.

Gomes, Anil (2017a), 'Naïve Realism in Kantian Phrase', *Mind* 126(502): 529–78.

Gomes, Anil (2017b), 'Perception and Reflection', *Philosophical Perspectives* 31(1): 131–52.

Gomes, Anil, Adrian Moore, and Andrew Stephenson (2022), 'On the Necessity of the Categories', *The Philosophical Review* 131(2): 129–68.

Gomes, Anil, and Andrew Stephenson (2016), 'On the Relation of Intuition to Cognition', in Dennis Schulting (ed.), *Kantian Nonconceptualism* (London: Palgrave Macmillan), 53–80.

Guyer, Paul (2017), 'The Bounds of Sense and the Limits of Analysis', *Journal of the History of Philosophy* 55(3): 365–82.

Hacker, Peter M.S. (1996), *Wittgenstein's Place in Twentieth-Century Analytic Philosophy* (Oxford: Blackwell).

Hacker, Peter M.S. (2003), 'On Strawson's Rehabilitation of Metaphysics', in Hans-Johann Glock (ed.), *Strawson and Kant* (Oxford: Clarendon Press), 43–66.

Hamann, Johann Georg (2007), 'Metacritique on the Purism of Reason', in *Johann Georg Hamann: Writings on Philosophy and Language*, ed. Kenneth Haynes (Cambridge: Cambridge University Press), 205–18.

Harrison, Ross (1970), 'Strawson on Outer Objects', *Philosophical Quarterly* 20: 213–21.

Hurley, Susan L. (1994), 'Unity and Objectivity', in Christopher Peacocke (ed.), *Objectivity, Simulation, and the Unity of Consciousness* (Oxford: Oxford University Press), 49–77.

Husserl, Edmund (1917), 'Pure Phenomenology, its Method, and its Field of Investigation'. Reprinted in Dermot Moran and Tim Mooney (eds.), *The Phenomenology Reader* (London: Routledge, 2002).

Kalderon, Mark E., and Charles Travis (2013), 'Oxford Realism', in Michael Beaney (ed.), *The Oxford Handbook of the History of Analytic Philosophy* (Oxford: Oxford University Press), 489–517.

Kant, Immanuel (1900), *Kants Gesammelte Schriften* (Berlin: De Gruyter).

Kant, Immanuel (1933), *Critique of Pure Reason*, trans. Norman Kemp Smith (London: Macmillan).

Kant, Immanuel (1998), *Critique of Pure Reason*, ed. and trans. Paul Guyer and Allen W. Wood (Cambridge: Cambridge University Press).

Kant, Immanuel (1999), *Correspondence*, ed. and trans. Arnulf Zweig. The Cambridge Edition of the Works of Immanuel Kant (Cambridge: Cambridge University Press).

Kitcher, Patricia (1990), *Kant's Transcendental Psychology* (Oxford: Oxford University Press).

Kripke, Saul (1980), *Naming and Necessity* (Oxford: Basil Blackwell).

McDowell, John (1994), *Mind and World* (Cambridge, MA: Harvard University Press).

Marshall, Colin (2014), 'Does Kant Demand Explanations for All Synthetic A Priori Claims?', *Journal of the History of Philosophy* 52(3): 549-76.

Martin, Michael G.F. (2003), 'Sensible Appearances', in Thomas Baldwin (ed.), *The Cambridge History of Philosophy 1870-1945* (Cambridge: Cambridge University Press), 519-30.

Merritt, Melissa (2018), *Kant on Reflection and Virtue* (Cambridge: Cambridge University Press).

Moore, George Edward (1903), 'Kant's Idealism', *Proceedings of the Aristotelian Society* 4: 127-40.

Moore, George Edward (1925), 'A Defence of Common Sense'. Reprinted in *G.E. Moore: Philosophical Papers* (1959) (London: George Allen & Unwin).

Moore, George Edward (1953), *Some Main Problems of Philosophy* (London: George Allen & Unwin).

Moore, George Edward (2011), *G. E. Moore: Early Philosophical Writings*, ed. Thomas Baldwin and Consuelo Preti (Cambridge: Cambridge University Press).

Muirhead, John H. (1924), 'Editor's Preface', in John H. Muirhead (ed.), *Contemporary British Philosophy: Personal Statements* (London: George Allen & Unwin).

Putnam, Hilary (1998), 'Strawson and Skepticism', in Lewis Edwin Hahn (ed.), *The Philosophy of P. F. Strawson* (La Salle, IL: Open Court), 273-87.

Rorty, Richard (1970), 'Strawson's Objectivity Argument', *Review of Metaphysics* 24: 207-44.

Rorty, Richard (2020), 'Kant as a Critical Philosopher', in Richard Rorty, *On Philosophy and Philosophers: Unpublished Papers, 1960-2000* (Cambridge: Cambridge University Press), 38-64.

Schafer, Karl (2022), 'Kant's Conception of Cognition and Our Knowledge of Things in Themselves', in Nicholas Stang and Karl Schafer (eds.), *The Sensible and Intelligible Worlds: New Essays on Kant's Metaphysics and Epistemology* (Oxford: Oxford University Press), 248-78.

Smit, Houston (1999), 'The Role of Reflection in Kant's *Critique of Pure Reason*', *Pacific Philosophical Quarterly* 80(2): 203-23.

Spener, Maja (2018), 'Introspecting in the Twentieth Century', in Amy Kind (ed.), *Philosophy of Mind in the Twentieth and Twenty-First Centuries* (London: Routledge), 148-74.

Strawson, Peter F. (1959), *Individuals: An Essay in Descriptive Metaphysics* (London: Methuen).

Strawson, Peter F. (1966), *The Bounds of Sense: An Essay on Kant's Critique of Pure Reason* (London: Methuen).

Strawson, Peter F. (1968), 'Bennett on Kant's Analytic', *The Philosophical Review* 77(3): 332–9.

Strawson, Peter F. (1989), 'Sensibility, Understanding, and the Doctrine of Synthesis', in Eckart Förster (ed.), *Kant's Transcendental Deductions: The Three Critiques and the Opus postumum* (Stanford, CA: Stanford University Press), 69–78.

Strawson, Peter F. (1997), *Entity and Identity and Other Essays* (Oxford: Oxford University Press).

Strawson, Peter F. (2003), 'A Bit of Intellectual Autobiography', in Hans-Johann Glock (ed.), *Strawson and Kant* (Oxford: Clarendon Press), 7–14.

Stroud, Barry (2003), 'The Synthetic A Priori in Strawson's Kantianism', in Hans-Johann Glock (ed.), *Strawson and Kant* (Oxford: Clarendon Press), 109–26.

Van Cleve, James (1999), *Problems from Kant* (Oxford: Oxford University Press).

Walker, Ralph C.S. (1978), *Kant* (London: Routledge & Kegan Paul).

Watkins, Eric, and Marcus Willaschek (2020), 'Kant on Cognition and Knowledge', *Synthese* 197(8): 3195–213.

Westphal, Kenneth R. (2004), *Kant's Transcendental Proof of Realism* (Cambridge: Cambridge University Press).

Williamson, Timothy (2007), *The Philosophy of Philosophy* (Oxford: Blackwell).

Williamson, Timothy (2013), 'How Deep Is the Distinction between A Priori and A Posteriori Knowledge?', in Albert Casullo and Joshua Thurow (eds.), *The A Priori in Philosophy* (Oxford: Oxford University Press), 291–312.

Wisdom, John (1931), 'Logical Constructions', *Mind* 40(158): 188–216.

Zahavi, Dan (2007), 'Subjectivity and the First-Person Perspective', *The Southern Journal of Philosophy* 45: 66–84.

8
Seeing (More than) What Meets the Eye
A Critical Engagement with P. F. Strawson

Lilian Alweiss

1. Introduction

It has become a bit of truism that we do not perceive sensations. As Edmund Husserl observed tellingly more than a century ago, when we give an account of our perceptual experience, we refer to objects of experience and not sensations. 'We never see sense data but the object itself: "I see a thing, e.g., this box; I do not see my sensations"' (Husserl 1970, 2, 104). 'I do not see colour-sensations but coloured things, I do not hear tone-sensations but the singer's song' (Husserl 1970, 2, 99). Martin Heidegger reiterates the view when he observes: 'we never... originally and really perceive a throng of sensations, e.g., tones and noises, in the appearance of things... rather, we hear the storm whistling in the chimney, we hear the three-engine aeroplane, we hear the Mercedes in immediate distinction from the Volkswagen. Much closer to us than any sensations are the things themselves. We hear the door slam in the house, and never hear acoustic sensations or mere sounds' (Heidegger 1977, 156). Whether or not we are able to distinguish a Mercedes from a Volkswagen, there seems no doubt that our perceptual experience is rich and structured. Clearly, we see more (and less) than what sense-data theorists believe we see. The assumption is thus that we see more than what meets the eye.

Yet what may appear as a mere platitude is difficult to explain. How can we account for the fact that in normal perceptual experience, we see the 'things themselves', which seem much closer to us than a 'throng of sensations'? The problem is that what we report ourselves as seeing does not reflect what theory tells us we are *actually* seeing. We are inclined to think that sense-data theorists *must* be right, the most we see are patterns, shape, colour, and maybe extension, the rest is just inferred from, or added to experience. We certainly do not see a unified three-dimensional object. When Mark Rothko claims: 'We are for flat forms because they destroy illusion and reveal truth' (Rothko 1943), he seems to be onto something important: our everyday talk about perception may well dupe us into believing that we see a three-dimensional world, but what we report seeing resembles little what we actually see. What we report to be seeing is clearly more than what we believe meets the eye.

But is that correct? Do we merely perceive flat forms, patterns, and light? It seems that even when I concentrate on my experience and try to tease out what I 'actually' see, my descriptions cannot live up to what the sense-data theorists or Rothko want me to see. As P. F. Strawson observed so tellingly, I do not start talking about lights and colours, patches and patterns, I still see 'the red light of the setting sun filtering through the black and thickly clustered branches of the elms; I see the dappled deer grazing in groups on the vivid green grass...'; and so on (Strawson 2011, 43). Indeed, I see the actual elms and deer and no shadowy intermediary resemblances of physical things. I am in direct contact with the object in the world (Strawson 2011, 50). Theory makes us believe that we *must* be seeing something else, but surely as Henry James observed so tellingly: 'no theory is kind to us that cheats us of *seeing*' (James 1891, 242).

Strawson, particularly in his later work, gives a brilliant account for why this is so. He seems to be in agreement with James, insofar as if we wish to provide an adequate account of perceptual experience, we must acknowledge that we never 'see' what sense-data theories argue we must be seeing, because a faithful account of perceptual experience tells us otherwise: we see much more than what sense-data theorists tell us meets the eye. If this is correct, then the question arises *how* can we account for the fact that we see more, or for that matter less, than what sense-data theorists maintain meets the eye? Strawson's answer seems quite straightforward: As a 'natural and unforced account of my perceptions' (Strawson 1982, 87) necessarily 'goes beyond' the sensible experience which gives rise to it, we should not confuse perceptual experience with sensible experience. 'Going beyond' sensible experience does not mean 'adding' something to *perceptual* experience; nothing needs to be added as whatever is 'added' is an integral part of perceptual experience. In other words, to have perceptual experience, Strawson tells us, means just *seeing what* meets the eye.[1] Strawson's defence for this is elliptical. While he argues in great detail how perceptual experience is necessarily not merely sensory but infused with 'concepts', it is less clear what allows him to argue that such concepts are part of our perceptual experience and not imposed by the understanding.

Furthermore, Strawson has a very fixed idea of what the perceptual experience involves. He assumes that perceptual experience is necessarily epistemic as it involves the *recognition* of an object as an enduring object that is distinct from my subjective experiences. We necessarily distinguish between appearance and reality and are conscious that things exist unperceived. Indeed, his work

---

[1] The point is not that sense-data theorists are wrong in arguing that what 'actually' meets the eye are just sensations, but they are wrong in assuming that this is what we 'see'. I should like to thank Sybren Heyndels for helping me in articulating this point.

on perceptual experience has been instrumental for advocating the view that perceptual experience provides support for the naive realist theory that perceptual experience is a form of 'openness to the world' (McDowell 1994), which involves the presentation of ordinary mind-independent objects to a subject.

The aim of this chapter is to question this claim. While I agree with Strawson that what meets the eye is much richer than what sense-data theorists tell us, I do not believe that perceptual experience entails a commitment to a commonsense realism where we take ourselves to be immediately aware of real, enduring physical things in space and take it for granted that these enduring things are causally responsible for our interrupted perceptions of them (Strawson 2011, 51f.). Strawson, I should like to argue, and here I echo Tyler Burge, conflates the phenomenological description of how objects constitute or present themselves as structured with the epistemic aim of explaining the constitutive conditions of our conception of objectivity[2] (Burge 2010, chap. 4), namely the belief that these objects refer to ordinary mind-independent objects that exist unperceived—a conflation that I believe distorts Strawson's account of perceptual experience.

2. 'Seeing More' Is Seeing What Meets the Eye

For Strawson, seeing what meets the eye is epistemic or knowledge-giving as we are conscious of the subjective side of experience (the way in which things appear to me), which we see as distinct from the object of experience (the way in which things actually are).[3] Perceptual experience thus looks further than the subjective side of experience. It provides us with a direct awareness of a mind-independent world that reflects the way the world in fact is. Take the following passage as an example. Strawson says: 'When I naively report what I see at a moment (say, as a tree or a dog), my mind or my report certainly "looks further" than... the merely subjective side of the event of its immediately appearing to me. Of a fleeting perception, a subjective event, I give a description involving the mention of something not fleeting at all, but lasting, not a subjective event at all, but a distinct object' (Strawson 1982, 87).

'Seeing what meets the eye', for Strawson thus involves recognizing an object *as* an object, for instance my recognizing the strange dog I see, as a dog. And it involves my recognizing that what I continuously or interruptedly observe to be the same dog. Seeing thus involves some form of synthesis or binding activity: It requires the ability to use concepts that involve the combination of a certain type. I can see the stray dog *as* a dog only if I am able to see other dogs as dogs as well.

---

[2] For the purpose of this chapter 'our conception of objectivity' stands for the commonsense realist position.
[3] Snowdon (2008, ix) refers to the 'knowledge-giving role of perception'.

And it involves my ability to combine past perceptions with my present one and to see them all to be perceptions of one and the same object of a certain kind. It thus involves my ability to reidentify objects across time, i.e. my ability to identify objects as the same objects despite lapses in my perceptions of them. This leads Strawson to conclude that we necessarily see objects and their properties as distinct from our particular experiences of them (which are fleeting) and we take them to exist unperceived.

If I understand Strawson correctly, he assumes that *everyone* has to accept this description as this is what a 'natural and unforced account of my perceptions' (Strawson 1982, 87) reveals. After all, it reflects what Hume calls our 'implanted disposition to belief in distinct and enduring bodies' (Strawson 2008, 13). (I shall question this assumption later.) Disagreement arises only when we try to find out what *causes* us to see more than what sense-data theorists believe meets the eye. It is here where the novelty of Strawson's position comes to the fore. He departs from David Hume and commonsense theorists, insofar as he does not wish to understand the question as inquiring about what needs to be *added* to perceptual experience to arrive at the belief in the existence of enduring and distinct objects, but he understands it as an inquiry about *how* we can account for the fact that such a belief is an *integral* part of perceptual experience.

Strawson thus broadens how we should understand perceptual experience. It should not be thought of as a series of successive impressions, each having its own intrinsic instantaneous moment, but it should be thought of as entailing the necessary *connections* of our perceptions that give rise to the experience of distinct and enduring objects. Strawson thus questions Hume's view that nothing can be present to the mind that is not actual because (1) we cannot observe the connection between perceptions that are present to the mind and those that are absent, and (2) we cannot observe the connection between perceptions and the objects that are meant to be distinct from my perceptions of them. Hume, according to Strawson, is mistaken to treat the ideas of such necessary connections like those of secondary qualities that are formed by the mind. A 'natural and unforced' account of perceptual experience tells us otherwise: necessary connections are present to the mind. The mind does not need to look 'further than what immediately appears to it' (Hume 1978, 189) as the 'connecting and uniting power', i.e. *synthesis* is part of our perceptual experience.

To account for this, Strawson takes Kant's insight that the 'imagination is a necessary ingredient of perception itself' (Kant 1933, A 120) as his cue and makes the ingenious claim that we should read this to mean that the 'power of connection', which Hume also attributes to the imagination, *belongs* to perceptual experience and not, as Hume assumes, to a faculty that is distinct from it. This is why the imagination *must* be an essential ingredient of perception as it is impossible 'to give accurate, plain reports of our perceptual experience which did not already incorporate those beliefs' (Strawson 1982, 86). A 'natural and unforced' account of perceptual experience proves Kant right: our perceptual experience *necessarily involves* what Hume believes the imagination can only feign, namely our belief in the existence of continued and distinct objects.[4]

To understand why this is so, let us briefly recall how Kant arrives at this view. Kant argues that three forms of synthesis must be in place to experience something as an object.

First, I must be able to run through a manifold of perceptions and they must all be held together in order to represent a unity. Kant gives the example of drawing a line in thought. I grasp my perceptions consecutively. I see first the first part, and then the second part, and then the third and fourth part of the line, and so forth. Kant calls this the **synthesis of apprehension**. Another way of putting this is to say that my perceptions are temporally indexed and fleeting. (They conform to the forms of Intuition [Space and] Time.)

Second, and this is important to Strawson, Kant maintains that I experience continuity only if I am able to run through these individual perceptions. They must not only be held together but also need to be reproduced. For if I was always losing the previous perceptions, while moving from one perception to the next, I would not be able to see any connection between my perceptions. The problem is that *mere apprehension does not by itself yield connections between perceptions.* I must *perceive* my current perception in *relation* to previous ones, otherwise I am not able to refer to *consecutive* perceptions of a line. What is required is the **synthesis of reproduction**: I must *reinstate* previous perceptions so that I can compare and combine my current perceptions with the previous one. This then makes it possible for me to refer to a series of perceptions. It is in this context that Kant introduces the imagination: it refers to the power of representing in intuition an object that is not itself present (Kant 1933, B 151). By this Kant means that the imagination refers to our ability to present directly a sensory content that is not presently being apprehended. In other words, it refers to unseen parts of objects, be it the spine of a book, which is not currently visible to me, or the back of a box, or the previous points of the line.[5]

---

[4] This seems at odds with Strawson's initial hostility to Kant's doctrine of synthesis, which he believed leads to the model of a 'mind producing nature' where the 'understanding, the active faculty, with the help of its no less active lieutenant, imagination...' structures our experience under the auspices of 'the imaginary subject of transcendental psychology' (Strawson 1966, 97). It is this hostility that led Strawson to argue that it might be true that we can be self-conscious only if we experience a world of objects, but then the best explanation of the fact that we are self-conscious is that there really is a world of objects, independent of any imposition of intuitional and conceptual form on it by us. But he came to realize that this criticism was not justified as he admits in his intellectual autobiography: in '"Imagination and Perception", first published in 1970 and subsequently reprinted, I made some amends for my cavalier treatment of the notion of synthesis in *The Bounds of Sense*' (Strawson 2011, 237-8). Indeed, here he accuses Hume, and not Kant, for interpreting synthesis as *constituting* the objects of experience. This is because Hume, and not Kant, understands synthesis as a product of the imagination which is distinct from the faculty of perception.

[5] Indeed, Strawson is not mistaken in his comparison with Hume as Kant compares the synthesis of reproduction with what the empiricists call association and argues that the laws that govern association

So the argument against Hume is that we cannot have a series of subjective representations if we do not already see them in relation to one another and, indeed, as being of one and the same object. But, and this is what interests Strawson throughout his work, Kant does not leave it at this. Rather, he claims that to see my subjective representations *as* being of one and the same object, a third form of synthesis is required: the **synthesis of recognition**. I need to *recognize* that it is of one and the same object. As Kant says: 'Without consciousness that that which we think is the very same [for example, the same book, box or line] as what we thought a moment before, all reproduction in the series of representations would be in vain' (Kant 1933, A 103). In view of this, Kant holds that we must operate with a concept of 'an object corresponding to and therefore also distinct from the cognition' (Kant 1933, A 104). It is this concept that structures and, indeed, guides my perceptions. It is because it is a house or a box that I am able to have particular perceptions *of* it. In contemporary jargon, this shows that perceptual experience is *intentional* (Strawson 1982, 97). It is necessarily *about* something that is *distinct* from my subjective perceptions.

Strawson interprets this as showing that our subjective perceptions are blind, i.e. not recognized as such, unless we are in 'possession and application of concepts of a certain kind, namely concepts of distinct and enduring objects' (Strawson 1982, 87) that structure and organize our perceptions. So what Strawson seems to find appealing about Kant's account of the imagination is that Kant shows that we see more than the subjective side of experiences, which are fleeting, as we necessarily see also distinct and enduring objects that exist unperceived. This confirms the reciprocity thesis, which Strawson espouses throughout his work, namely that we see something as objective only if we are conscious that we are one and the same subject having these different perceptions. And having different perceptions, in turn, is possible only if we recognize them as being connected and thus relating to something objective (Strawson 1966, 97). The unity of consciousness thus requires the experience of something objective.[6]

If I read Strawson correctly, by drawing on Kant, Strawson turns Hume's natural disposition to belief into a transcendental argument. Namely, he begins with the premise the sceptic does not question: that we have self-conscious (subjective) thoughts and experiences, and he then proceeds to show that such experience is possible only if it is of enduring and distinct objects (Strawson 2008, 9). This allows him to argue that the application of concepts is necessary for

are empirical, that is based on what Hume calls custom and habit (Kant 1933, A 100). But Kant believes that association and the empirical synthesis of reproduction are made possible by the transcendental synthesis of productive imagination which makes experience in general possible. Kant thus draws a distinction between productive and reproductive imagination. The productive imagination makes particular experiences or experience in general possible; the reproductive imagination, in turn, is limited to past experiences.

[6] Objective here means: if it is not constitutively dependent for its existence on a subject's act of awareness (Strawson 1966, 98–101).

experience and further that we do not experience occurrent reportable perceptions if they have not been synthesized in one way or another (Strawson 1982, 90). These claims alone are not that different from the observations Strawson made in his earlier writings.

But it seems to me that Strawson, in his later essays on perceptual experience, is committed to something quite different. The focus is not the epistemic one 'explaining constitutive conditions for having a conception of mind-independent entities as mind-independent' (Burge 2010, 156) but the phenomenological one: how objects, i.e. the things themselves, constitute themselves as they are in themselves. Strawson does not seem to acknowledge the shift or recognize that it is necessary to distinguish between the two approaches. If I understand him correctly, he assumes that an account of perceptual experience is just an account of the possibility of operating with a conception of mind-independent objects that exist unperceived. But clearly there is a difference between showing how objects constitute themselves and asking if we have an epistemic warrant that justifies us in seeing them *as existing* unperceived.[7] Strawson seems to slide between the two projects: one is phenomenological, which seeks to give a 'natural and unforced' account of perceptual experience, namely how phenomena constitute themselves. The other, an epistemically motivated one, tries to tease out the constitutive conditions of my understanding of something as objective, namely my understanding of objects as representing the way in which things in fact are. Surely, one should not be confused with the other.

This conflation already comes to the fore in Strawson's appropriation of Kant's account of the imagination.[8] As I have argued above, there are three forms of synthesis and Strawson seems to attribute all three to the imagination. But not Kant. Kant *only* attributes the synthesis of recollection to the imagination and realizes that the synthesis of *recognition* needs to be attributed to the understanding instead. Kant thus realizes that it is one thing to see things as related to one another and quite another to recognize them as related.

Strawson does not draw such a distinction and, I assume, he probably feels he does not need to do so either, as in the end he is in agreement with Kant

---

[7] I am here in agreement with Tyler Burge when he argues that Strawson fails to distinguish between two projects. The first is the one that I have been discussing: the project of explaining constitutive conditions of experience which comprises certain structures. 'The second project is that of explaining constitutive conditions for having a conception of mind-independent entities as mind-independent. I call this second project that of explaining conditions for our conception of objectivity' (Burge 2010, 155). For Burge it is important to draw this distinction because he wishes to show that non-human animals also experience objects even if they do not have the epistemic capacity or self-conscious understanding to regard such objects *as* objective. This leads him to claim that it is the empirical and not the transcendental method that genuinely answers constitutive questions about the nature of perceptual states. My focus is a different one. I wish to argue that even for us language users, perceptual experience does not necessarily involve a self-conscious understanding of something *as* objective.

[8] This may indeed also explain why Strawson does not draw a distinction between the productive and reproductive imagination (see footnote 5 above).

that without the synthesis of recognition we would not experience any order whatsoever.[9] However, if correct, this just confirms that Strawson conflates two issues: one, what an 'unforced' account of perceptual experience involves, namely, seeing things in relation to one another, and two, how we can recognize them as related to one another. The latter involves self-consciousness, namely the conscious understanding that my subjective perceptions are distinct from the objective ones. It thus addresses the epistemic question how we can recognize objects as existing unperceived. However, when we try to answer constitutive questions about the nature of perceptual experience, no such recognition needs to be in place. Studying 'the way things appear to us' (Strawson 1966, 15ff.) is not explaining necessary constitutive conditions for our conception of objectivity.

3. A Genuine Account of Perceptual Experience

If we seek to answer genuinely constitutive questions about the nature of perceptual experience, then we need to accept that the question is not 'how do we come to recognize something as objective i.e., as existing unperceived?', but 'how objects constitute or present themselves'. And I believe this question must lead Strawson to part company with Kant. Once we reject what J.J. Gibson calls 'the sensation-based theories' (Gibson, 1972), we necessarily arrive at a different understanding of what is *given*. Indeed, as we have shown above, this is reflected in Strawson's account of perceptual experience. We no longer regard the sensations of light as 'the fundamental basis of *visual* perception, the data, or what is given', but the object as such. But this must mean that 'the data, or what is given' is not, as Kant saw it, 'blind', but structured. It involves 'connections', which are not *imposed* onto experience by the understanding. Strawson seems to suggest as much when he argues, as we have shown above, that the 'connecting and uniting power', i.e. *synthesis*, is part of our perceptual experience. Or when he claims that our commonsense realist commitment that there is a world of independently existing things 'is not properly described, even in a stretched sense of the words, as a theoretical commitment. It is, rather, something given with the given' (Strawson 2011, 47).

But if this is the view that Strawson wishes to advance, then he can no longer claim that 'Kantian synthesis is something necessarily involved in, a necessary condition of, actual occurrent reportable perceptions having the character they do have' (Strawson 1982, 90). Or that 'the three forms of synthesis could be understood as a kind of information processing that is taking place in our mind' (see Strawson 2011, 164). For this would suggest that synthesis is necessarily brought about by the subject. This is indeed how Kant sees it: 'We can represent nothing as

---

[9] Kant regards the third synthesis as the most fundamental one as it unifies the threefold synthesis and indeed makes the experience of apprehension and reproduction possible. The concept is a regulative rule, which allows for the unity between apprehension and reproduction (Kant 1933, A 104). I must be conscious of this unity otherwise all the apprehension and reproduction would be meaningless.

combined in the object without having previously combined it ourselves...' (Kant 1933, B 130). But it seems that when we try to provide a genuine account of perceptual experience, we arrive at the opposite view. What we perceive is not how the mind structures information but how objects constitute themselves as structured.

Take Strawson's description of the dog as an example: When I see a strange dog for the first time, Strawson argues, I see an unfamiliar thing of a familiar kind. There is no question of past perceptions of that thing being alive in the present perception. 'Still, one might say, to take it, to see it, as a thing of that kind is implicitly to have the thought of other possible perceptions related to your actual perception as perceptions of the same object. 'To see it as a dog, silent and stationary, is to see it as a possible mover and barker, even though you give yourself no actual images of it as moving and barking;... again, as you continue to observe it, it is not just a dog, with such and such characteristics, but the dog, the object of your recent observation, that you see, and see it as' (Strawson 1982, 90). What is striking about the description is that Strawson claims that seeing the dog *in relation* to other possible manifestations is not due to any *activity* on our part or the fact that we give ourselves an 'actual image'. As he says: 'It seems, then, not too much to say that the actual occurrent perception of an enduring object as an object of a certain kind, or as a particular object of that kind, is, as it were, soaked with or animated by, or infused with—the metaphors are *à choix*—the thought of other past or possible perceptions of the same object. Let us speak of past and merely possible perceptions alike as "non-actual" perceptions'. So Strawson claims that the non-actual perceptions are present in perception. They are as Strawson puts it 'in a sense represented in, alive in, the present perception' (Strawson 1982, 89). As we said, Strawson seeks to attribute this to the imagination. The claim is that the non-actual perceptions are present in perception 'just as they are represented, by images, in the image-producing activity of the imagination' (Strawson 1982, 89).

Strawson's account is ambiguous here. On the one hand he seems to echo Kant's account of the schema, namely the claim that we need to appeal to an image or rule that exhibits the structure of 'combinability' of what is given. On the other hand, he suggests that such an appeal is not necessary as what is given is already saturated with meaning and thus structured.

Let us look at this in more detail. Kant needs to appeal to a schema because he treats concepts and intuitions as heterogenous (see Kant 1933, A50–51/B74–76). He thus needs to show how the intuitions which are necessarily unconnected can fit the categories. The problem is that combination (synthesis) is possible only if the given is formed in such a way that it is *conceptualizable* or 'determinable' (Kant 1933, A266/B322). It has to *conform* to rules (i.e., it has to be unitary). This however demands that a sensible manifold must present itself (to us) in a particular combination which reflects the categories. (Kant 1933, B161) In other words, what is given must *present* itself as conforming to rules, i.e. as combinable. Only this can ensure that there is an intuitive a priori agreement with the categories prior to being categorised.

The problem however is that Kant believes that intuitions are particular and unconnected. This is why he must argue that even the perception of something given must involve some activity or cognitive operation on the side of the perceiving subject without which we would not be able to become aware of objects of perception. But because perception must be the primary stage in cognition, such a cognitive operation must be in place *before* we are conscious of it. This is why Kant refers to a spontaneity that is unacknowledged when he attributes the operation to the productive imagination which he calls 'a blind but indispensable function of the soul, without which we should have no knowledge whatsoever' (Kant 1933, B 103). "Blind" here means that it rests on a synthesis that is undetermined by concepts. The imagination thus provides us with the structure of unity that makes combination possible. It ensures that what we experience as given expresses or better exhibits rules which are not yet conceptually determined but make possible the subsequent application of concepts. Kant calls these rules the schema. A schema functions like a 'rule for the imagination,' it makes possible the application of a general (empirical) concept, like that of a triangle or that of a dog, to objects of intuition' (Kant 1933, A 140/B 179 f.). The schema connected with the concept of a dog thus provides me with a 'rule in accordance with which my imagination can specify the shape of a four-footed animal in general, without being restricted to any single particular shape that experience offers me or any possible image that I can exhibit *in concreto*' (Kant 1933, A 141/B 180) By 'rule' Kant does not mean a conceptually articulated regularity or instruction, but the capacity for a rule-governed manner of performance. i.e., its combinability. In many ways Strawson's account above echoes that description when he refers to the 'type' and image producing activity of the imagination.

Indeed, it seems that he, just like Kant, needs to appeal to such an architectonic as he repeats Kant's claim that different perceptions are blind and thus demand concepts as the senses themselves cannot bring about synthesis (Strawson "1982, 86-7). In view of this like Kant, he has to attribute the operation to the understanding or thought as we are referring to rules and concepts that are made sensible. But, on the other hand, his description defies such an account as he refers to the structures as given with the given. This suggests that he cannot argue that concepts and intuitions are radically heterogenous. Rather his account suggests that there are no gaps that need to be bridged as our perceptions are already *infused* with concepts and alive and given with the given. Strawson description is thus moving away from Kant by adopting a more phenomenological account which argues precisely what Strawson alludes to, namely that intuitions are not 'blind' but saturated with structures. To put it otherwise Strawson falls prey to the same critique that phenomenologists launch against Kant. It is because Kant treats intuitions and concepts as radically heterogenous that he fails to account for what a natural unforced account of perceptions reveals – namely, that what is given is rich and structured. Or to put it otherwise, he fails to acknowledge that the understanding is operative in intuition and thus an essential ingredient of the given (intuitions) (cf Merleau-Ponty 2002, 200, Husserl (Crisis 104) Heidegger 1997, 212 (312–13).)[10]

But this returns us to the question how can we account for the connection between what we actually perceive (the spine of the book) and what is not actually given (the book as such, its side, and its front, etc.)? It is one thing to argue that there is a spatially and temporally structured world and quite another to ask how we can perceive its structure or unity. This, indeed, is the question Strawson, in line with Kant tries to address when he appeals to the imagination. For the imagination, as Kant understood it, can produce a 'presentation', i.e. a sensible representation of an object that is not directly present. It can thus bridge the gap between what is sensible, on the one hand, and what is non-sensible or conceptual, on the other. But phenomenology claims that the question is wrong-footed. *There are no gaps that need to be filled or bridged.* This is because we *intuit*, i.e. perceive more than sensible data. We perceive *connections*, i.e. *synthesis*, between my different perceptions *as* perceptions of the same object before we recognize any gaps as gaps.

This comes to light when we try to account for how we perceive time. We never perceive a now-moment in isolation, but our experience of time (what Kant called the synthesis of apprehension) involves the recollection that Kant attributes to the imagination. We necessarily perceive the now-moment in relation to what is no longer and not yet. What is given, and thus *present* in perception, is both what is actual and what is not actual, i.e. the past and future perceptions. A phenomenological description of perceptual experience thus shows, contrary to Kant, that the mere apprehension by itself yields connections. In other words, synthesis constitutes itself in experience, it is given and requires no additional activity on our part.[11]

Take music as an example. I have cited Husserl at the outset of the chapter stating that we do not hear tone sensations but a singer's song. The claim is that we do not hear individual notes, namely sense-data, but we necessarily *hear*, i.e. *apprehend*, them in relation to one another. To do so, we do not need to 'bridge the gap' and bring past or future notes into the presence through acts of remembrance or imagination. We do not bring anything to the presence. No re-presentative act is required. Indeed, if we made all the notes present, we would not hear a tune at all, but simply noise. We would hear the present, past, and future notes in one go, as all notes would have been made present again, i.e. re-presented. But this is not what is happening. We hear a melody, and this means

---

[10] As Heidergger observed: 'viewed as a *quaestio juris*, the transcendental deduction is the most disastrous segment of teaching in Kantian philosophy to which one can refer' (Heidegger 1997, 209 (309)) Heidegger's concern is that this leads Kant to strengthen the separation between intuitions and concepts and fails to see that 'concepts of thinking are fundamentally grounded in the pure intuition of time' (Heidegger 1997, 212 (312–13)).

[11] In view of this Husserl refers to a passive synthesis (Husserl 2001).

that we hear the notes consecutively in relation to past notes that are no longer and future ones that are not yet. The past is *not* made present or re-presented, rather, as Husserl would put it, past and future notes are *presentative* as absent (Husserl 1991, §17, 41/401). They are *given* as past (no longer) and future (not yet). They are given as a presentative co-appearance.[12]

It is important to understand how they are given. For they are not given in a determinative way. When I listen to music, I do not need to determine what exact notes preceded the ones I currently hear, or what exact notes will follow. On the contrary, as we said, I do not hear individual notes in isolation but a melody. The structure of expectation is an indeterminate part of my perceptual experience. I have a sense that the music will go on without necessarily knowing exactly how it will continue. I become aware of this when the music suddenly stops playing, or when the object turns out not to be a book but a box. At such moments my expectations are being dashed. Even when I am not familiar with the particular musical piece, when the music abruptly ceases, I jolt, as I expected the music to continue in one way or another without being able to tell you exactly how it would have continued.[13] The surprise expresses that certain expectations were in place. If I had no implicit expectations, I would not be surprised. However, I become conscious of this only when things go wrong. It is then that I reflect and become conscious of the rules that structured my experience *as* rules.[14] But prior to that I just see things in relation to one another without recognizing them as related to one another.

Here, we clearly depart from Kant. Kant needs to appeal to the imagination to fill the *gap* and *explain* the perceptual *presence* of aspects of an object that are not actually present. Strawson echoes this view when he says that the role of the imagination is to 'exercise the power of concept application' (Strawson 1982, 96). But a phenomenological or descriptive account of perceptual experience shows that no such 'filling in' is required. I do not hear an individual tone say D and then A, which I need to combine with one another, but I hear a melody (i.e. the synthesis), in the same way as I see a unitary object, be it the box or a cathedral. I do not need to run through each individual moment and 'synthetically bring into being a determinate combination of a given manifold' (Kant 1933, B 138) and ascribe them to the identical self as *my representation*. I do not need to identify myself as the identical self that thinks A1 and A2 to be conscious of that unity. Rather I hear notes in relation to one another in the same way as I perceive a side of a box in relation to perspectives that are not actually present.

---

[12] For a more detailed analysis see Alweiss (1999a, 1999b, and 2000).

[13] See Heidegger (1962, 105E). Clearly this is only the case if I have some familiarity with the musical genre. So if I am familiar with Western music, I hear a tune or melody when I hear a pop song or Bach's Cantata but I may not hear a melody (i.e. detect a structure) if I listen to non-Western music for the first time. Atonal music by Stockhausen or Schoenberg or Escher's impossible objects play with this structure of expectation.

[14] As Heidegger (1962) puts it: when the hammer breaks, I become conscious of its assignment structure, as a structure.

Perception provides me with a field of presence that does not 'link' disparate moments with one another, but it provides me with a field that entails such a 'transition-synthesis'.[15] The presence is, to borrow Strawson's terminology, 'infused', 'saturated', and 'alive' with possible past and future perceptions. They are part of what is given in experience. No active synthesizing activity on the part of the subject is necessary. I am not experiencing discrete moments, but moments that are folded into a structure of expectation and remembrance that are an inalienable dimension of the present. They are given with the given. The argument is thus that what are *given* are not instances but structures, indeed synthesis. And the task of a philosophy of perception is to disclose or describe how they manifest themselves.

A phenomenological description of perceptual experience thus clearly departs from Kant. For Kant, perceiving unity involves running through all individual moments and recognizing that they can all be attributed to the same 'I think'.[16] Synthesis of perceptions, such as is required for the possibility of experience, thus involves the unification or combination of temporally successive items. This can be brought about only by the 'I think'. To cite Kant:

> [I]t is obvious that if I draw a line in thought, or think of the time from one noon to the next, or even want to represent a certain number to myself, I must necessarily first grasp *one of these manifold representations after another in my thoughts*. But if I were always to lose the preceding representations (the first parts of the line, the preceding parts of time, or the successively represented units) from my thoughts and not reproduce them when I proceed to the following ones, then no whole representation and none of the previously mentioned thoughts, not even the purest and fundamental representations of space and time, could ever arise.   (Kant 1933, A 102 emphasis added)

This is why the role of self-consciousness is central to Kant. I must be able to keep track of my experiences as they must all be 'combined in one consciousness' (Kant 1933, B 136). So, when I draw a line, I am thinking of different moments, my pen slowly moves from left to right. To see the relation between these moments, it is not sufficient to say that they are related, but I must be conscious that I am the same subject experiencing these different moments. This has led Kant to argue that self-consciousness requires both that experience is unitary (lawful) and that the manifold by means of which an object is given is united in one and the same consciousness.

---

[15] Merleau-Ponty (1962, 35 & 309) attributes this term to Husserl.
[16] In other words, synthesis is active: for the manifold to be known 'the spontaneity of our thought requires that it be gone through in a certain way, taken up, and connected. This act I name *synthesis*' (Kant 1933, A 77/B 102).

For Strawson, this means that when we think about physical bodies, we necessarily think also about ourselves and about the independence of physical bodies from minds (e.g. Strawson, 1959, 61). This leads Strawson to articulate the reciprocity thesis: I can think the unity only by thinking the combination of its parts, and I recognize particulars as being of a general kind only if I am able to refer the different experiences to a single thinking subject. This allows us to draw a distinction between the way things appear to us and the way things are (Strawson 1966, 100ff.).

Yet, we have argued that there is no need to 'run through' or combine experience. We can experience the unity without thinking the combination of its parts. Indeed, we do not begin with parts. I hear the melody before I can discern its parts and abstract the individual moments or tones. But this means that I can have experience of something as an object, indeed, as unified, without needing to attribute different experiences to a single thinking subject and without drawing a distinction between the way things appear to me and the way things are. Strawson indeed seems to acknowledge as much when he says: 'It is not necessary, in order for different experiences to belong to a single consciousness, that the subject of those experiences should be constantly thinking of them *as* his experience (Strawson 1966, 98). In other words, Strawson realizes that we do not always ascribe experience to ourselves. Rather, he is only committed to the claim that we must be able to do so. But, if we can account for experience without ascribing it to ourselves, then Strawson must grant that we can have experience without yet drawing a distinction between this is how things appear to me and this is how they are, and this means *without yet endorsing commonsense realism*, i.e. the thought that objects exist unperceived and are not in any way dependent upon them being perceived or thought about.

4. An 'Unforced' Account of Perceptual Experience

Perceptual experience is quite different from the way Strawson wants to understand it. For Strawson seems to believe that describing how objects constitute themselves, which in my view is the task of a genuine account of perceptual experience, is just articulating the necessary conditions for our conception of objectivity. But our analysis has shown that it is one thing that we necessarily perceive the world as structured, and quite another that we *recognize* it as existing unperceived.

This is not to deny that I necessarily see objects in relation to me and can discern their spatio-temporal position only in relation to where I find myself in the world. The desk is in front of me and the lamp to my left. Indeed, I necessarily see objects as *transcending* my particular point of view. When I see the desk from the back, I am aware that I am seeing only one particular perspective of the desk and I am thus aware that there are other possible perspectives which are occluded from my sight. This means I perceive the desk as a unitary object, that is, not only in relation to me but also in relation to other perspectives that are currently not available to me but are in principle available to others who occupy a different position to mine. Seeing a spatial object thus necessarily involves acknowledging that there are other routes from which the object can be accessed.

To this extent, I see an object as having a certain *independence* from my particular perspective and perceptual route. As I move around, I have different sense modalities, perspectives, and modes of apprehending one and the same object. Indeed, I can only refer to a particular perspective if I recognize that there are other actual and possible viewpoints on one and the same object. Strawson is right, recognition of different sense modalities or perspectives is just recognition of 'objectivity'. There are different perspectives and modalities of experience only if the same object can be encountered in different ways, and it is our ability to encounter the same object in different ways that enables us to experience it as the same object. Clearly, in these instances we are presented with mind-independent objects. But this does not mean that we necessarily assume that these objects exist.[17] 'Objectivity' here does not entail the epistemic claim that the object *exists* unperceived, after all there can be illusions of 'objectivity'. What I take to be a book may turn out to be a box. So, 'objectivity' refers to a mind-independence, in this case the identical book, which need not exist. In other words, perceptual experience taken by itself, though it is of something 'objective', is not epistemic; it merely describes how objects constitute themselves as they are *in themselves*; i.e. as mind-independent. But it does not entail the evaluative claim that this 'objectivity' reflects the way the world in fact is.[18]

I must make it quite clear what I am saying and what I am not saying here. I am not denying that experience is necessarily of something objective, but what I am concerned to dispute is that this entails the *recognition* and thus self-conscious understanding of something as objective, i.e. as existing unperceived. Perceptual experience does not involve any kind of epistemic justification. To use Kant's terminology, the synthesis of recognition is not required to have perceptual experience.

Ordinary experience confirms as much. Although there are clearly gaps in my perceptions, I do not need to reidentify objects in order to see the same lamp I saw yesterday. I am just seeing spatio-temporal continuous objects. Another way of putting it: I do not recognize the gaps *as* gaps and thus do not see a need to make the judgement that I am seeing the same lamp that I saw yesterday. In ordinary

---

[17] Jennifer Church (1990) develops a similar criticism of Strawson, by asking whether the ability to make judgements presupposes an ability to make distinctions between appearances and reality which leads her to question whether self-consciousness is necessary for perception.

[18] Indeed, this claim fits well with Strawson's observation that 'the immediacy which common sense theorists attribute to perceptual awareness is in no way inconsistent...with the occurrence of perceptual mistake or illusion' (2011, 128f.). The point is that perceptual experience is intentional. It is necessarily *of* something and it is *of* something 'objective', this is the case independently of whether the object exists or not (Husserl 1970, vol. 2, V, 99). For a detailed discussion of how we can make sense of non-existence see Alweiss (2010, 2013). See also Crane (2013).

perception there is no need to compare the perceptions I had of the lamp an hour ago with the perceptions I have of it now, but this means I do not need to attribute each one of these perceptions to myself either. Experience is only about the object and does not include thought about myself, or the thought about the independence of physical objects from my mind. Such thoughts become vital only when I see a need to assess the *validity* of my perceptual experience. It is then, and only then, that Strawson's epistemic concerns kick in. When things are put into question, we ask what are the constitutive conditions for the experience of something *as* mind-independent and enduring? But perceptual experience taken by itself requires neither an act of assent nor an epistemic justification.

Perceptual experience to this extent does not have a knowledge-giving role in the way Strawson wants it to. Strawson is mistaken when he claims that 'we could *not* explain all the features of the concept of sense perception without reference to the concept of knowledge' (Strawson 1992, 19). Perceptual experience does not involve the claim that mind-independent objects exist. Indeed, it does not involve any claim whatsoever. It is epistemically neutral. It merely discloses how objects constitute themselves as they are in themselves, namely, as spatio-temporal objects and includes no epistemic justification about their existence.

5. A Response to Scepticism

If this is correct, we have done away with the so-called problem of perception. The problem of perception asks 'whether we can ever directly perceive the physical world', where 'the physical world' is understood in a realist way: as having 'an existence that is not in any way dependent upon its being...perceived or thought about' (Smith 2002, 1). But we have argued that perceptual experience does not involve the claim that we can represent mind-independent objects. Once we realize this, I believe, as I shall show in more detail below, that we have *reasons to* maintain that there is no problem of perception.

Where does this leave Strawson? Strawson argues that we can directly perceive the physical world. This also leads him to conclude that there is no problem of perception. But it seems to me that as long as Strawson conflates his account of perceptual experience with the epistemic claim that we perceive objects that exist unperceived, the problem of perception persists. The worry is that Strawson can at most show that we must *conceive* our experience as being of spatially located objects existing independently of our perceptions of them and obeying causal laws. However, this in itself is not a proof that there *are* such objects. In fact, the world could in principle be totally different from the way we must conceive it.[19]

---

[19] To block such criticism some form of transcendental idealism must be invoked. See Alweiss (2005).

Indeed, what is striking, and a bone of contention for many, is that Strawson is not trying to present a philosophical theory that provides such a proof that such objects exist. Strawson, and here he alludes to Hume, seems to think it is sufficient to argue that the necessary belief 'in the existence of body' is 'ineradicably planted in our minds by Nature' (Strawson 2008, 10). But if that is all that Strawson is saying, then his justification of why we can sidestep the problem of perception treads on thin ice as it rests on a sentiment rather than an argument. The worry is then that *mind-independence* may well be necessary for *our conception of* perceptual experience but this is not a philosophical argument that provides sufficient proof that mind-independent objects *exist* (Stroud 1968). Surely, we are 'interested in how things are, not only in how certain standpoints or sets of beliefs say things are' (Stroud 2000, 187).

Strawson acknowledges as much but believes that he can sidestep sceptical concerns. Citing Hume, Strawson argues "'tis vain to ask Whether there be body or not? That is a point which we must take for granted in all our reasoning' (Strawson 2008, 11). Sceptical concerns are out of tune with the way we experience the world.[20] This is why we can *neglect* them, not because we have *reasons* to show why the sceptical position is inconsistent, but because it is 'idle' for us to concern ourselves with 'arguments'. We are *entitled* to ignore it because we 'simply *cannot help* believing in the existence of body' (Strawson 2008, 11). This, so Strawson says, is a sufficient *reason* **not** to meet sceptical doubts by argument. The appropriate response to scepticism is thus to bypass sceptical doubt rather than to attempt to argue with it on its own terms.

No sceptic would be content with such a position, as Strawson is simply avoiding the challenge without however having *reasons* to rebut the sceptic. *Ignoring* or *sidestepping* sceptical concerns seems more like a cowardly and unphilosophical move that does not solve the problem of perception. J. J. Valberg must be right, when he observes that as long as we believe that the sceptic's argument is right or unrefutable, we have no *reason* to ignore it. The problem is that Strawson seeks to provide *reasons* that do not rest on arguments (Valberg 1992, 172). All Strawson can say is that he is not convinced by them—they don't have a 'pull' insofar as they cannot undo our propensity to belief. But if this is the *reason* why they are not correct, then Strawson must be advancing an absurd position. He ends up arguing that 'he *cannot help believing* that they are false' (Valberg 1992, 173) even though he sees no fault in the argument as such. No sceptic would accept such a rebuttal. 'Who needs Nature when you have Reason on your side?' (Valberg 1992).

---

[20] Strawson's attitude to persistent scepticism reflects that of Spinoza when he observes in 'On the Improvement of the Understanding': 'I speak of real doubt existing in the mind, not of such doubt as we see exemplified when a man says that he doubts, though his mind does not really hesitate. The cure of the latter does not fall within the province of method, it belongs rather to inquiries concerning obstinacy and its cure' (Spinoza 1955, 29). I should like to thank Jim Grant who drew my attention to this passage.

This criticism seems justified if we conflate perceptual experience, which describes how objects constitute themselves, with the epistemic claim that such objects exist unperceived. If Strawson conflates the two claims, I believe he cannot refute the sceptic's charge, and the problem of perception persists. But I believe our analysis has shown that Strawson can avoid such a charge. Once we realize that perceptual experience is not knowledge-giving in the way Strawson understands it, we are *justified* in sidestepping sceptical concerns. This is not because perceptual experience *rebuts* the sceptic but because perceptual experience is distinct from an analysis that seeks to account for our conception of objectivity. As we have argued, perceptual experience is not evaluative. But this means that we do not operate with the premise that the sceptic seeks to question, namely, that we experience enduring objects that exist unperceived. When we are concerned with describing the nature of our perceptual experience, we take *no* position on whether our experiences represent mind-independent entities. This is not a concession to the sceptic. The claim is not that the problem of perception persists because we cannot prove that our experiences represent mind-independent objects, but the argument is that the sceptic has no *basis* to raise the question in the first place as we have neither asserted nor denied the *existence* of mind-independent bodies but are just describing how things constitute themselves. Perceiving the desk in front of me does not entail knowing that there is a desk that exists unobserved. Perceptual experience taken by itself is epistemically neutral. This is why there is nothing to doubt as nothing has been affirmed.[21]

So Strawson is correct that: 'If we asked a non-philosophical observer gazing idly through a window to give a description of her current visual experience of how it is with her, visually, at the moment, she would naturally provide the following answer: "I see the red light of the setting sun filtering through the black and thickly clustered branches of the elms; I see the dappled deer grazing in groups on the vivid green grass..."' (2011, 43). Her description would thus be 'rich' and structured. The observer would use concepts like *deer* and *elms* and the *setting sun* and would not only refer to shapes or colours. But we have argued that Strawson is mistaken when he claims that the observer necessarily believes that the objects and the properties that she describes, as distinct from her particular experiences, *exist* unperceived. If she remains faithful to the experience she actually enjoyed, such a *belief in existence* is not part of her perceptual experience.

Strawson seems to recognize as much, *but* he interprets this as a concession to the sceptic. As he puts it, *we*, as *philosophers* do not remain satisfied with this description. We 'want him [i.e. the observer, LA] to amend his account so that, without any sacrifice of fidelity to the experience as actually enjoyed, it nevertheless sheds all that heavy load of commitment to propositions about the world

---

[21] For an excellent discussion on the nature of doubt see Held (2000).

which was carried by the description he gave' (Strawson 2011, 43). The fictive observer would thus assume that *we* are looking for a different type of answer: one that focuses on how things are experienced within the limits of the subjective episode, 'an account which remains true even if he had seen nothing of what he claimed to see, even if he had been subject to total illusion' (Strawson 2011, 43). Strawson is keen to show that the description of experience which does not involve a commitment to the existence of things outside of experience remains unchanged. The observer 'does not start talking about lights and colours, patches and patterns. For he sees that to do so would be to falsify the character of the experience he actually enjoyed' (Strawson 2011, 43). Rather, he merely adds: 'It sensibly seemed to me just as if I were seeing such-and-such a scene' or 'My visual experience can be characterized by saying that I saw what I saw, supposing I saw anything, *as a* scene of the following character...' (Strawson 2011, 44) and then she would add the previous description of the trees and the deer, etc. In other words, Strawson contends that she would provide a description of our experience in terms of the ordinary objects of the world which *must* include our belief in the existence of things outside us. But as she realizes that philosophers would argue that this reflects a *belief* that cannot be grounded in reason, the observer makes a concession. She is aware that she cannot provide a good argument to counter the sceptic and thus modifies her account: she no longer claims that the objects she sees are mind-independent but understands that she can only say that it *necessarily* seems to her *as if* she was seeing mind-independent objects.

But we have argued no such commitment is involved in perceptual experience, but this means no concession is necessary. I do not necessarily see objects as existing unperceived. I simply see 'the dappled deer grazing in groups on the vivid green grass' and nothing more nor less. On the level of perceptual experience, I am making no evaluative claims as to their existence. We should not understand this as a concession to the sceptic. It does not render sceptical arguments into *good* arguments but shows that they are *redundant* as we do not operate with the belief that the sceptic wishes to attack, i.e. the belief that our experience corresponds to things outside us which exist unperceived. If we are *open* to the world describing the way in which things show themselves as they are in themselves, without *imputing* how they *must* show themselves, we realize that perceiving does not require believing that there is a world that exists unperceived. Such a belief requires a commitment and *evaluation* that is not yet present in perception.

I believe this shows that evaluative claims, even the claim that things exist unperceived, are second order acts. They cannot be, as Strawson seems to assume, primitive. This is because an endorsement is necessarily an endorsement of something that has already been presented, namely the things themselves as they show themselves. We can thus only accept or endorse *something* and argue that things exist unperceived, if we are presented with something, the things themselves, that facilitate such an evaluation. To this extent, perceptual experience, taken by itself, is not epistemic. It does not provide us with the certainty of particular *facts*, i.e. 'this is how things are' in contrast to 'this is how they appear to me', but it discloses a structure of the world that secures the ground or *possibility* of knowing something as something in the first place. It is because I perceive the things themselves that I can assess the validity of my experience of the things themselves. Perceptual experience, to this extent, provides the *route* for knowledge as it forms the basis upon which we can establish something about it and assess our knowledge claim. But this means its knowledge-giving role is derivative rather than primitive (Cassam 2008).

The knowledge-giving role of perception is realized only when there are reasons to question the validity of my perceptual experience. Be it when we regard things as problematic, when things go wrong, or when we have contradictory information. In such instances, there are reasons to question the validity of my perceptual experience, and I experience the disparity between appearance and reality as a result, feel a need to take a stand, and *evaluate* or assess my perceptual experience. But no such *evaluation* takes place in my unforced account of perceptual experience.

Had Strawson acknowledged that a faithful account of perception requires neither an act of assent nor an objective justification, he would have realized that he can provide after all an *argument* why the problem of perception is not primitive. It is not primitive because evaluative epistemic claims are second order acts. What is primitive instead is our trust or perceptual faith in experience: the things themselves that present themselves as they are in themselves, namely, as infinitely rich and structured. Perceptual experience thus discloses a realm that lies beyond doubt. It lies beyond doubt not because it provides the proof the sceptic is seeking, namely, that what we perceive exists unperceived, but it makes doubt and consequently such a proof possible in the first place. In other words, it provides the grounds for doubt and the possibility of assent.[22] Perceptual experience thus reveals a realm that is more primitive than doubt. To put it in another way, what cannot be doubted is that objects constitute themselves in a certain lawful way. And it is because they constitute themselves as such that we can evaluate them. Perceptual experience thus provides the *route* to epistemic questions which allows us to assess the validity of our experience. But this means we do not begin with an understanding of existence and non-existence but can only arrive at it. Contrary to Strawson, I think this is what Wittgenstein had in mind when he observed: 'If the true is what is grounded, then the ground is not *true*, nor yet false' (Wittgenstein 1975, sects. 205, 202). The claim is not that that ground that is 'not true, nor not yet false' refers to our natural disposition to belief in existence which we 'do *not* choose' (Strawson 2008, 17) and which we take as given in all our reasonings

---

[22] To this extent they provide the transcendental ground, i.e. the condition of possibility for knowledge claims.

(Strawson 2008, 18–20).[23] But the argument goes deeper. What precedes any questioning and affirmation of truth is perceptual experience, objects that disclose themselves as they are in themselves. Such objects lie beyond affirmation or negation, as they provide the ground for any kind of assessment. This is what I think we could have learned from Strawson's account of perceptual experience, had he not conflated the phenomenological project to describe the things themselves as they show themselves with the epistemic endeavour to explain the constitutive conditions for having a conception of mind-independent entities that exist unperceived.[24]

This may well tell us something important about the nature of perceptual experience. Perceptual experience is rich and meaningful. It opens a vista to the wonders of the world, disclosing the deepest meanings of objects, gradually leading us close to the heart of things. It is on the basis of perceptual experience that we can then come and evaluate the appearances and recognize the possibility of error and be willing to revise our judgements, but for this the world must first disclose itself in all its wonders and mysteries. That world is there before all belief (Heidegger 1985, 295).[25]

References

Alweiss, Lilian (1999a), 'The Enigma of Time', *Phänomenologische Forschungen*, 4(3): 150–203.

Alweiss, Lilian (1999b), 'The Presence of Husserl', *The Journal of the British Society for Phenomenology*, 30(1): 59–75.

Alweiss, Lilian (2000), 'On Perceptual Experience', *The Journal of the British Society for Phenomenology*, 31(3): 264–76.

Alweiss, Lilian (2005), 'Is there an "End" to Philosophical Scepticism?', *Philosophy* 80: 395–411.

Alweiss, Lilian (2010), 'Thinking about Non-Existence', in Carlo Ierna, Hanne Jacobs, and Filip Mattens (eds.), *Philosophy, Phenomenology, Sciences: Essays in Commemoration of Edmund Husserl*, Phaenomenologica 200 (Dordrecht: Springer), 695–721.

---

[23] I think that Strawson is mistaken when he claims that we can '"yoke" Wittgenstein to Hume' (2008, 24) as both 'refuse' the sceptical challenge. He fails to see that only Strawson's Hume refuses to engage with the sceptic; Wittgenstein in turn, does not refuse to engage with the sceptic but makes such an engagement impossible as he pulls the rug from under their feet.

[24] Elsewhere I have shown that a faithful account of perceptual experience thus turns out to be a form of transcendental idealism as it describes the conditions of possibility of experience both of objects that exist and of object that do not exist (Alweiss 2010; Alweiss 2023).

[25] I am indebted to extensive comments from Jim Grant on an earlier draft of this chapter and to students of my MPhil class at Trinity College Dublin. I should also like to thank William Lyons for a careful reading of the chapter and Steven Kupfer whose insightful and critical thoughts continue to inform my writing. Finally, I am grateful to the editors of this edition, Audun Bengtson, Benjamin De Mesel, and Sybren Heyndels, for their helpful comments.

Alweiss, Lilian (2013), 'Beyond Existence and Non-Existence', *International Journal of Philosophical Studies Special Issue: Intentionality* 21(3): 448–69.

Alweiss, Lilian (2014), 'Kant's Not so "Logical" Subject', *Harvard Review of Philosophy* 21: 87–105.

Alweiss, Lilian (2023), 'Third Cartesian Meditation: Ontology *after* Kant'. In Daniele de Santis (ed.), *Edmund Husserl's Cartesian Meditations: Commentary, Interpretations, Discussions*. Verlag Karl Alber: 91–112.

Burge, Tyler (2010), *Origins of Objectivity* (Oxford: Clarendon Press).

Cassam, Quassim (2008), 'Knowledge, Perception and Analysis', *South African Journal of Philosophy* 27(3): 214–26.

Church, Jennifer (1990), 'Judgment, Self-Consciousness, and Object Independence', *American Philosophical Quarterly* 27(1): 51–60.

Crane, Tim (2013), *The Objects of Thought* (Oxford: Oxford University Press).

Gibson, James J. (1972), 'A Theory of Direct Visual Perception', in Alva Noe and Evan Thompson (eds.), *Vision and Mind: Selected Readings in the Philosophy of Perception* (Cambridge, MA: MIT Press), 77–89.

Heidegger, Martin (1962), *Being and Time*, trans. John Macquarrie and Edward Robinson (New York: Harper & Row).

Heidegger, Martin (1977), 'The Origin of the Work of Art', in *Martin Heidegger: Basic Writings*, trans. David Farrell Krell (New York: Harper & Row).

Heidegger, Martin (1985), *History of the Concept of Time: Prolegomena*, trans. Theodore Kisiel (Bloomington, IN: Indiana University Press).

Heidegger, Martin (1997), *Phenomenological Interpretation of Kant's Critique of Pure Reason*, trans. Parvis Emad and Kenneth Maly (Bloomington: Indiana University Press)

Held, Klaus (2000), 'The Controversy Concerning Truth: Towards a Prehistory of Phenomenology', *Husserl Studies* 17(1): 35–48.

Hume, David (1978), *A Treatise of Human Nature*, ed. Lewis A. Selby-Bigge and P.H. Nidditch (Oxford: Clarendon Press).

Husserl, Edmund (1970), *Logical Investigations*. Vols. I & II, trans. John Niemeyer Findlay (London: Routledge & Kegan Paul).

Husserl, Edmund (1991), 'On the Phenomenology of the Consciousness of Internal Time (1893–1917)', in *Collected Works IV*, trans. John Barnett Brough (Dordrecht: Kluwer Academic Publishers).

Husserl, Edmund (2001), *Analyses Concerning Passive and Active Synthesis: Lectures on Transcendental Logic*, trans. Anthony J. Steinbock (Dordrecht: Kluwer Academic Publishers).

James, Henry (1891), 'Henry James to Robert Louis Stevenson, January 12, 1891', in Leon Edel (ed.), *Henry James: Selected Letters* (Cambridge, MA: Harvard University Press, 1987).

Kant, Immanuel (1933), *Immanuel Kant's Critique of Pure Reason*, trans. Norman Kemp Smith (London: Macmillan).

McDowell, John (1994), *Mind and World* (Cambridge, MA: Harvard University Press).

Merleau-Ponty, Maurice (1962), *Phenomenology of Perception*, trans. Colin Smith (London and New York: Routledge).

Merleau-Ponty, Maurice (2002), *The Structure of Behavior*, trans. Alden Fisher. (Pittsburgh: Duquesne University Press).

Rothko, Mark (1943), 'A Letter from Mark Rothko and Adolph Gottlieb to the Art Editor of the *New York Times*', 7 June 1943.

Smith, Arthur David (2002), *The Problem of Perception* (Cambridge, MA: Harvard University Press).

Snowdon, Paul F. (2008), 'Foreword', in P. F. Strawson, *Freedom and Resentment and Other Essays* (London: Routledge).

Spinoza, Benedict (1955), *Works of Benedict de Spinoza*. Vol. II, trans. Robert H. M. Elwes and Abraham Wolf (*Short Treatise*), and Halbert H. Britan (*Metaphysical Thoughts*) (New York: Dover Publications).

Strawson, Peter F. (1959), *Individuals: An Essay in Descriptive Metaphysics* (London: Methuen).

Strawson, Peter F. (1966), *The Bounds of Sense: An Essay on Kant's Critique of Pure Reason* (London: Methuen; reprinted London: Routledge, 1989).

Strawson, Peter F. (1982), 'Imagination and Perception', in Ralph C.S. Walker (ed.), *Kant on Pure Reason* (Oxford: Oxford University Press), 82–99.

Strawson, Peter F. (1992), *Analysis and Metaphysics: An Introduction to Philosophy* (Oxford: Oxford University Press).

Strawson, Peter F. (2008), *Scepticism and Naturalism: Some Varieties* (London: Routledge).

Strawson, Peter F. (2011), *Philosophical Writings* (Oxford: Oxford University Press).

Stroud, Barry (1968), 'Transcendental Arguments', *The Journal of Philosophy* 65: 241–56. Reprinted in Ralph C.S. Walker (ed.) (1982), *Kant on Pure Reason* (Oxford: Oxford University Press), 117–31.

Stroud, Barry (2000), *The Quest for Reality: Subjectivism and the Metaphysics of Colour* (New York: Oxford University Press).

Valberg, Jerome J. (1992), *The Puzzle of Experience* (Oxford: Clarendon Press).

Wittgenstein, Ludwig (1975), *On Certainty, Über Gewissheit*, bilingual ed., ed. Gertrude Elizabeth Margaret Anscombe and Georg Henrik von Wright, trans. Denis Paul and Gertrude Elizabeth Margaret Anscombe (Oxford: Basil Blackwell).

9
To Reply, or Not to Reply, That Is the Question
Descriptive Metaphysics and the Sceptical Challenge

Giuseppina D'Oro

1. Introduction

Since Barry Stroud (1968) articulated his influential criticism of transcendental arguments a consensus has grown that the choice between refuting scepticism by invoking a robust Kantian notion of the synthetic a priori and disregarding the sceptical challenge in the manner of the Humean naturalist is too stark. There are more options available than is suggested by what is often (rightly or wrongly, possibly wrongly) taken to be Strawson's intellectual trajectory from *Individuals* and the *Bounds of Sense* to *Scepticism and Naturalism* (Stern 1999a). One need not choose between a robust form of transcendental argument that seeks to defeat the sceptic head on and conceding defeat altogether: there is an intermediate logical space between these two extremes (Stern 1999b, 2000). This chapter locates Strawson's descriptive metaphysics in the debate concerning the scope of transcendental arguments, how much or little they can achieve, and how they position themselves vis-à-vis the sceptical challenge. I argue that descriptive metaphysics occupies an intermediate logical space between the confrontational posture assumed by the sort of transcendental arguments which were the target of Stroud's criticism and the quietist stance of the Humean naturalist, but also that descriptive metaphysics claims this logical space in a very distinctive way, one that differs from the way in which this middle ground has recently been appropriated by advocates of modest transcendental strategies. Modest transcendental strategists accept the sceptical challenge as meaningful and partially (but only partially) rebut it by developing transcendental arguments with modest epistemic goals that curb the ontological ambitions of truth-directed transcendental arguments. They distinguish between the (justification) sceptic who claims one has no good reason to hold certain structural beliefs (e.g. in the existence of the external world or in causal connections) and the (knowledge) sceptic who claims that one

Giuseppina D'Oro, *To Reply, or Not to Reply, That Is the Question: Descriptive Metaphysics and the Sceptical Challenge* In: *P. F. Strawson and his Philosophical Legacy*. Edited by: Sybren Heyndels, Audun Bengtson, and Benjamin De Mesel, Oxford University Press. © Oxford University Press 2024. DOI: 10.1093/oso/9780192858474.003.0010 cannot know whether such justified beliefs are true. Having drawn this distinction, modest transcendental strategists argue that transcendental arguments can answer the justification sceptic but not the knowledge sceptic. This chapter argues that although descriptive metaphysics has a great deal in common with modest transcendental strategies, there are small and yet very significant differences in the way in which the modest transcendental strategist and the descriptive metaphysician position themselves in relation to the sceptical challenge. In particular, the distinction between internal and external reasons/justification, which is invoked by modest transcendental strategies to distance themselves from ambitious truth-directed transcendental arguments (arguments that seek to address the knowledge sceptic), does not play a role in the descriptive metaphysician's 'response'[1] to the sceptic. Rather than distinguishing (as modest transcendental strategies do) between the sceptic who claims there is no justification to believe, for example, in the existence of the external world, and the sceptic who claims that we cannot know whether our justified beliefs in the existence of the external world are true (and therefore amount to knowledge of the external world's existence), descriptive metaphysics seeks to show that the sceptic has cornered herself into a position from which she can make no reasonable contribution to debate and is therefore not a genuine partner in conversation.

Section 2 considers Barry Stroud's original criticism of transcendental arguments and how modest transcendental strategists have revised the goals of transcendental arguments in the wake of this criticism. Sections 3 and 4 discuss what I take to be the descriptive metaphysician's strategy, how it differs from the modest transcendental strategy, and whether it ultimately collapses into a form of Humean naturalism. I argue that the descriptive metaphysician neither *replies* to the sceptic in the manner of the modest transcendental strategist nor concedes unqualified defeat to the sceptic in the manner of the Humean naturalist. Unlike the modest transcendental strategist, the descriptive metaphysician does not espouse the distinction between internal and external reasons/justification on which the divide between modest and ambitious transcendental arguments rests. Unlike the Humean naturalist, the descriptive metaphysician takes scepticism to be idle, *not* because the sceptical challenge has no influence on the way in which we are inclined to think and what we are inclined to believe, but rather because in denying the conditions for any reasoned argument to occur, the sceptic has placed herself outside the space of reasons. Scepticism should be ignored not because it is powerless to affect the way we think and what we believe, but because it undermines the conditions of the possibility for rational argument. Section 5 illustrates how the ambitious transcendental strategist, the modest transcendental strategist,

---

[1] I use the term 'response' rather than 'reply' to signal a form of engagement which does not necessarily require a reply in the standard sense in which, for example, Descartes is deemed to be 'replying' to the sceptic.

the Humean naturalist, and the descriptive metaphysician would engage with the sceptic through a concrete example.

My view is that the characterization of the intermediate logical space occupied by descriptive metaphysics offered here captures the spirit of Strawson's project (to some extent, if not in every respect), but if I were to be mistaken about ascribing this conception of descriptive metaphysics to Strawson, I would be content with advancing this reconstruction as a normative claim about how the descriptive metaphysician should position herself vis-à-vis the sceptical challenge.

2. The Parting of the Ways: Modest and Ambitious Transcendental Arguments

Transcendental arguments are often classified according to whether their goal is to establish conclusions about an external, mind-independent world, or about the belief structures of the epistemic subject. Those transcendental arguments which aim to establish ontological conclusions concerning the necessary structures of reality are said to be 'ambitious' and transcendental arguments which aim to establish claims concerning the necessary structures of our beliefs are said to be 'modest'. Both kinds of argument make necessary claims, the former about the nature of reality, the latter about the nature of experience. This external/internal divide between so-called 'ambitious' or 'truth-directed' and 'modest' or 'belief-directed' transcendental arguments (Stern 2000, 10) is largely the legacy of Stroud's attack on what *he perceived* to be Strawson's attempt to defend a robust Kantian notion of the synthetic a priori in his earlier work (*Individuals*, 1959 and especially *The Bounds of Sense*, 1966).

Stroud (1968) mounted an important challenge to what have since come to be known as 'ambitious' or 'truth-directed' transcendental arguments. Transcendental arguments, he argued, aim to establish anti-sceptical conclusions. They try to do so indirectly by arguing from a fact of experience to the conditions of its possibility. It is a fact of experience, for example, that we make a distinction between inner and outer objects; space is a condition of the possibility for making the distinction between inner and outer objects. Therefore, space must be real, or one would not be able to distinguish between inner and outer representations. Of course, this is not the conclusion that Kant drew in the Transcendental Aesthetic. Kant thought that space is a form of representation which is transcendentally ideal. Stroud was concerned with the ways in which transcendental arguments are appropriated to develop robust anti-sceptical conclusions concerning the nature of things, rather than the nature of our representation of them. Having construed transcendental arguments as establishing substantive claims about the nature of reality rather than idealist conclusions about the nature of our experience, Stroud objected that transcendental arguments leave open a gap between what must be believed to be the case for certain claims or distinctions to be possible, and what must be the case. Exposing the conceptual connection between the ability to distinguish inner from outer objects and the conditions that make it possible (space), for example, has no implications for the way things are independently of how objects have to be represented in order to be experienced as external. The sceptic, he argued, 'distinguishes between the conditions necessary for a paradigmatic or warranted (and therefore meaningful) use of an expression or statement, and the conditions under which it is true' (Stroud 1968, 255). One cannot, therefore, defeat scepticism by invoking the conditions of the possibility of meaningfulness or intelligibility (as transcendental arguments do) without covertly presupposing the ability to verify the claims arrived at transcendentally, thereby rendering the oblique way in which transcendental arguments reach their conclusions effectively superfluous. If one could verify the conclusions of transcendental arguments by checking them against a mind-independent reality, then one would not need to appeal to transcendental arguments in order to vindicate our entitlement to make certain distinctions. Transcendental arguments are therefore either redundant, because the conclusions they establish could be arrived at by other means, or they deliver only meagre epistemic conclusions (for a discussion of Stroud's criticism see Stern 2000, 44; Stern 1999a, 6).

Stroud's original criticism took all transcendental arguments to be ambitious, truth-directed arguments intent on refuting the knowledge sceptic by establishing synthetic a priori claims which, in his view, cannot be arrived at by means of conceptual analysis. This criticism prompted a reconsideration of the goal of transcendental arguments which resulted in the establishment of a distinction between 'ambitious' or 'truth-directed' and 'modest' or 'belief-directed' transcendental arguments, a distinction that had played no role at the time of Stroud's original 1968 criticism of Strawson.

Modest transcendental arguments, like ambitious ones, address the matter of our entitlement or right to hold certain beliefs, the *quid iuris* question, but they take the task of validation to be directed at beliefs rather than knowledge. They tell us what structural beliefs one must necessarily hold in order for some less structural beliefs to be possible but stop short of making the further inference that such structural beliefs are true. They do not, therefore, seek to close the gap between what one is justified in believing and genuine knowledge. On the contrary, they deliberately remain epistemically humble: modest transcendental strategies accept that the gap between justified belief and knowledge (justified true belief) cannot be closed and that, while it remains open, the sceptic can exploit this gap to raise doubts concerning our ability to provide external validation for our justificatory practices.[2] The divide between modest and ambitious transcendental

---

[2] Stern describes the kind of sceptic who doubts our beliefs are justified as the Humean sceptic and the sceptic who doubts whether the norms of justification are true as the Cartesian sceptic.

arguments may therefore be said to hinge on a distinction between internal justification (a notion of justification that invokes the coherence of our beliefs) and external justification, which requires more than mere coherence between beliefs.

Advocates of modest transcendental arguments tend to concede Stroud's criticism but argue that transcendental arguments can succeed in the more modest aim of vindicating the epistemic right or entitlement to have certain structuring beliefs. One need not give up hope of answering the normative question of one's entitlement to hold certain beliefs (the *quid iuris* question) and thus espouse a naturalism with a Humean flavour, as the later Strawson (allegedly) did in *Scepticism and Naturalism* (1985), in order to heed Stroud's renewal of Hume's admonition that no ontological conclusions follow from conceptual analysis. What needs to be done instead is to acknowledge that the necessary conclusions arrived at by means of transcendental argumentation concern only the structure of our beliefs about reality. For the modest transcendental strategist, the later Strawson's naturalistic turn is therefore an unwarranted overreaction to Stroud's criticism of his earlier work: the thing to do is to concede a partial defeat to the knowledge sceptic in order to claim a partial victory over the justificatory sceptic (Stern 1999b).

While modest transcendental strategies avoid Stroud's criticism, the contrast between an internalist and externalist notion of justification that they invoke to distance themselves from ambitious transcendental strategies ultimately raises the worry that too much has been conceded to the sceptic. For example, Robert Stern's claim that all that remains of Kant's idealism in the modest transcendental strategy 'is a kind of epistemological humility characteristic of this purely justificatory claim, that though our beliefs are warranted and rational in this "internal" sense they may still fail to correspond to how things really are in themselves, so that scepticism is still viable at that level' (Stern 1999b, 58) concedes precisely that our justified beliefs do not amount to knowledge because they lack 'external' validation. It is therefore not altogether surprising to find that modest transcendental arguments are sometimes described as articulating a strategy of 'sophisticated capitulation' (Sacks 1999, 67) to the sceptic, a criticism that echoes the charge of subjective idealism and higher-level scepticism that Hegel raised against Kant's transcendental idealism.[3]

3. Descriptive Metaphysics and Modest Transcendental Strategies

Stroud's criticism of transcendental arguments was influential in establishing a distinction between truth-directed and belief-directed transcendental arguments

[3] Only echoes as modest transcendental strategies are not committed to transcendental idealism in Kant's sense.

which has since become canonical. It is unclear, however, that the argument Strawson developed in *Individuals* was obviously aimed at rebutting the sceptic in the manner of ambitious transcendental arguments, as Stroud assumed (Hacker 2003, 52ff.). At the beginning of *Individuals* Strawson makes it clear that descriptive metaphysics differs from conceptual analysis not 'in kind or intention, but only in scope and generality' (Strawson 1959, 9). The difference is one of scope rather than kind because descriptive metaphysics aims to expose the most general features of our conceptual system. By characterizing the difference between descriptive metaphysics and conceptual analysis as one of scope, rather than intent or kind, Strawson distances himself from the view that the task of conceptual analysis in metaphysics is to advance empirical knowledge by making factual claims. This of course is a statement of intent, and many philosophers have failed to live up to their stated goals, but what it signals is that Strawson did not envisage the sort of conceptual analysis practised by the descriptive metaphysician to be advancing factual claims about reality; descriptive metaphysics does not aim at delivering the kind of synthetic a priori knowledge which, by Stroud's light, is sought by ambitious transcendental arguments. If anything, Strawson's statement of intent may give rise to the opposite suspicion, namely that descriptive metaphysics is epistemically humble in the manner of modest transcendental arguments and, for this very reason, does not even try to provide the sort of 'metaphysical' knowledge which Stroud thought transcendental arguments aim (but fail) to provide without having to exceed the bounds of experience.

In the following I consider whether the sort of transcendental argument that Strawson adopts in *Individuals* may be regarded as a modest transcendental strategy. I argue that while descriptive metaphysics has much in common with modest transcendental arguments it differs from them in one crucial respect. Rather than taking a position on either side of the modest/ambitious fence, descriptive metaphysics rejects the contrast between internal and external justification on which the distinction between modest and ambitious transcendental arguments hinges. Rejecting the divide between internal and external justification therefore enables Strawson's descriptive metaphysics to circumvent the need to choose between modest and ambitious transcendental arguments. I begin by outlining the Kantian-inspired transcendental strategy that Strawson develops in *Individuals* to uncover the conditions of the possibility for the reidentification of particulars, and then consider how Strawson addresses the Carnapian framework question, which Stroud claims transcendental arguments cannot answer. I argue that when Strawson addressed this question, in 'The "Justification" of Induction' (Strawson 1952), he answered it in a way that suggests descriptive metaphysics does not pursue a strategy of epistemological humility.

Strawson's discussion of the conditions for the identification and reidentification of particulars in *Individuals* takes its cue from Kant's discussion of the representation of space in the *Critique of Pure Reason* (1985 A 23/B 48). In the transcendental aesthetic Kant argued that the representation of space is necessary in order to make the distinction between inner and outer objects and between objects which are qualitatively identical and yet numerically distinct. Without the representation of space, Kant argued, we would be unable to distinguish between, say, the *representation of a chair* and *the chair*; we would also be unable to distinguish numerically objects that are qualitatively indiscernible, such as two qualitatively indiscernible copies of Da Vinci's *Mona Lisa*. For objects can be said to exist independently of me only if they occupy a portion of space other than mine; and qualitatively identical objects can be said to be numerically distinct from one another only if they are thought of as occupying different portions of space. Having argued that the representation of space is a condition of the possibility for making such distinctions, Kant inquired into the status of the representation of space and claimed that it is a transcendentally ideal form of sensibility, a feature of *our* way of representing objects. Strawson's discussion focuses on how claims concerning the numerical identity of objects which are not continuously perceived are possible. Consider, for example (not Strawson's example), Leonardo da Vinci's *Mona Lisa*. Is the painting of the *Mona Lisa* that I am looking at now the *same* painting that was in the Louvre yesterday? When we ask questions of this kind, we assume that what is meant by 'same' is not *qualitatively* same but *numerically* same. In doing so, we invoke a distinction between qualitative and numerical identity that cannot be read off the nature of our experiences of the *Mona Lisa* (assuming, for the sake of argument, that there is nothing that would differentiate our experience of the *Mona Lisa* today from our experience of the *Mona Lisa* yesterday from a qualitative point of view). If the distinction between numerical and qualitative identity cannot be read off the appearances, Strawson asks how such a distinction is possible:

> Where we say 'the same' of what is not continuously observed, *we think* we can as clearly make just this same distinction [between numerical and qualitative identity, my note]. But can we? Since spatio-temporally continuous existence is, by hypothesis, observed *neither* in the case where we are inclined to speak of qualitative identity *nor* in the case where we are inclined to speak of numerical identity, by what right do we suppose that there is a fundamental difference between these cases, or that there is just *the* difference in question?
>
> (Strawson 1959, 34)

This distinction is possible, he claims, because we operate with the idea of a single spatio-temporal system. That we operate with the conceptual scheme of a single spatio-temporal framework is confirmed by the fact that we are committed, at least in some cases, to claims concerning the numerical identity of objects which are not continuously observed (such as the case of the *Mona Lisa*). As Strawson says:

> There is no doubt that we have the idea of a single spatio-temporal system of material things; the idea of every material thing at any time being spatially related, in various ways at various times, to every other at every time. There is no doubt at all that this *is* our conceptual scheme. Now I say that a *condition* of our having this conceptual scheme is the unquestioning acceptance of particular-identity in at least some cases of non-continuous observation.
> (Strawson 1959, 35)

The conceptual scheme of a single spatio-temporal system is entailed in a Carnapian way (Carnap 1950) by a commitment to the identification of objects as numerically the same at least in *some* cases. By Strawson's lights one cannot simultaneously hold (a) that there are some cases of numerical identity and (b) reject the conditions (the conceptual scheme) that makes the reidentification of particulars as *numerically* the same possible.

Strawson further claims that sceptical questions concerning the numerical sameness of temporarily unobserved particulars, questions such as 'Is the *Mona Lisa* that I am admiring now numerically the same as that which was in the Louvre yesterday?' invoke the conceptual scheme of a single spatio-temporal framework. For he claims:

> There would be no question of *doubt* about the identity of an item in one system with an item in another. For such a doubt makes sense only if the two systems are not independent, if they are parts, in some way related, of a single system which includes them both. (Strawson 1959, 35)

Doubt concerning the numerical identity of this or that particular could not arise independently of the possession of the conceptual scheme of a single spatio-temporal system. Strawson's transcendental argument asks two questions. The first is: 'How are claims concerning the numerical identity of particulars which are not continuously observed possible?' The second is: 'How can the (sceptical) question "how do you know that this is a case of numerical identity rather than mere qualitative sameness" arise in the first instance?' His reply to the first question is that the distinction between qualitative and numerical identity is possible against the background assumption of a single spatio-temporal scheme. His reply to the second is that the sceptical question could not arise unless the sceptic invoked the framework of a single spatio-temporal system that allowed him to conceive of the distinction between qualitative and numerical sameness in the first instance. The very possibility of sceptical doubt concerning the numerical identity of particulars therefore presupposes possession of the criteria for making the distinction between numerical and qualitative identity which is being put into question:

> This gives us a more profound characterization of the sceptic's position. He pretends to accept a conceptual scheme, but at the same time quietly rejects one of the conditions of its employment. Thus his doubts are unreal, not simply because they are logically irresolvable doubts, but because they amount to the rejection of the whole conceptual scheme within which alone such doubts make sense.... For the whole process of reasoning only starts because the scheme is as it is. (Strawson 1959, 35)

This reminds us of the rejoinder often given to the sceptic in the first Meditation of Descartes, namely the sceptic who claims that it is not possible to distinguish between dreaming and waking experience. Such a doubt seems to be self-defeating because the very fact that one is making such a distinction (between being awake and being asleep) implies that one is in possession of criteria for making the distinction. Of course, unless these criteria are deemed to be infallible, replying to the sceptic in this way cannot show whether or not we have got things right in this or that case, whether one can know, in any specific instance, that one is not dreaming, or, in Strawson's case that the reidentification of a temporarily unobserved particular as numerically the same was in fact successful. Is the *Mona Lisa* that I saw in the Louvre yesterday the same *Mona Lisa* I am looking at now? It is conceivable that a thief could have broken in the museum overnight, evaded all the alarm systems, and replaced it with a qualitatively identical copy that occupies the very same spatial coordinates, and that I may be none the wiser. Strawson's claim that the sceptical question is hypocritical, however, shows two things. First, that arguing one way or the other, providing reasons for one scenario rather than the other, requires endorsing the conceptual scheme of a single spatio-temporal framework (just as being able to identify certain experiences as waking experiences requires criteria for so doing). Secondly, that the question which the sceptic claims cannot be answered ('is this the numerically same *Mona Lisa* as opposed to one that is qualitatively identical to the one that was here yesterday?'—'is this particular reidentification true/correct?') could not arise if one did not operate with the framework of a single spatio-temporal system that the sceptic puts into doubt. Without the framework in place, the conceptual distinction between qualitative and numerical identity which the asking of the question implies could not be made.

The sceptic, however, could go a step further. She could renounce the commitment to a single-spatio-temporal framework altogether. What would Strawson say to the sceptic who is willing to forfeit the commitment to a single spatio-temporal scheme? Since operating with the background assumption of a single spatio-temporal framework is the condition of the possibility for reidentifying temporarily unobserved particulars as numerically the same, forfeiting the commitment to a single spatio-temporal framework entails abandoning the assumption that there are at least *some* cases of successful reidentification and accepting the more radical possibility that there are no cases of successful reidentification, not merely that particular reidentification is imperfect and not infallible. This kind of consistent sceptic questions not individual cases of particular reidentification, but the criteria that make such individual reidentifications possible by renouncing the commitment to a single spatio-temporal framework, the very framework that enables the asking of the question 'is the particular I am observing now numerically the same one I saw yesterday?'

Strawson considers this consistent sceptic in 'The "Justification" of Induction' (Strawson 1952),[4] where 'justification' is aptly placed within quotation marks. Strawson suggests that doubt concerning whether induction is a justifiable procedure may seem to have sense but is not a meaningful doubt. For, he says:

> ...it is generally proper to inquire *of a particular belief*, whether its adoption is justified; and, in asking this, we are asking whether there is good, bad, or any, evidence for it. In applying or withholding the epithets 'justified', 'well founded', &c., in the case of specific beliefs, we are appealing to, and applying inductive standards. But to what standards are we appealing when we ask whether the application of inductive standards is justified or well grounded? If we cannot answer, then no sense has been given to the question. Compare it with the question: Is the law legal? It makes perfectly good sense to inquire of a particular action, of an administrative regulation, or even, in the case of some states, of a particular enactment of the legislature, whether or not it is legal. The question is answered by an appeal to a legal system, by the application of a set of legal (or constitutional) rules or standards. But it makes no sense to inquire in general whether the law of the land, the legal system as a whole, is or is not legal. For to what legal standards are we appealing?   (Strawson 1952, 257)

The question makes no sense because to ask whether induction itself is either justified or reasonable is like asking 'whether it is reasonable to proportion the degree of one's convictions to the strength of the evidence. Doing this is what "being reasonable" *means* in such a context' (Strawson 1952, 257). Rather than conceding that one's reliance on inductive inferences cannot be externally validated, Strawson argues that it makes no sense to seek the sort of external validation that would enable one to move from the claim that our inductive inferences are justified by the inductive principle to the claim that the inductive principle itself is justified because reality is uniform and amenable to being known inductively. The rationality of induction, he claims, 'is not a fact about the constitution of the world. It is a matter of what we mean by the word "rational" in its application to any procedure for forming opinions about what lies outside our observations' (Strawson 1952, 261–2).

---

[4] This the second part of chapter 9, 'Inductive Reasoning and Probability' in Strawson (1952).

Once the assumption that it is meaningful to ask whether rules of inference such as induction or deduction (Strawson only discusses induction) could be justified is set aside, it no longer makes sense to speak of the kind of connective analysis that descriptive metaphysics engages in as providing *merely* internal justification, i.e. reasons for *merely* believing something to be the case in contrast to reasons for something being the case. Reasons can be dismissed as *merely* internal, as providing *merely* coherentist justification, only if one assumes there is a different (and superior) kind of justification that is exempt from operating against certain background rules of inference. To illustrate: consider the contrast between good and bad friends. If a true friend is a good friend, then there is no such thing as a bad friend. And if the contrast between 'good' and 'bad' does not apply to friends, then we should speak of friends *simpliciter* for, when we talk about good and bad friends we are not really distinguishing between kinds of friends, but between people who are friends and people who are not. Analogously, if all reasons operate against the background of certain rules of inference, then the distinction between internal and external reasons/justification is spurious. We should treat the distinction between internal and external reasons in the same way in which we treat the distinction between good and bad friends and speak of reasons *simpliciter*.

This explains why descriptive metaphysics does not make heavy weather of the distinction (invoked by the modest transcendental strategist) between the challenge posed by the (justification) sceptic who doubts whether our beliefs can be justified, and the (knowledge) sceptic who doubts whether our justified beliefs are true. Rather than responding to Stroud's criticism by conceding to the sceptic that one must remain agnostic about whether the structuring beliefs that are justified transcendentally are true, descriptive metaphysics rejects the suggestion that the question 'are the fundamental rules of inference justified?' can be meaningfully asked. Since the demand for validation cannot be legitimately extended to the structures which make knowledge claims possible, the question concerning the validity of the framework which Stroud claims transcendental arguments cannot answer without going beyond a form of connective or conceptual analysis does not arise. And if it is actually asked, then it is a nonsense question, like asking 'is the Law legal?' (Strawson 1952, 257). Strawson advances these considerations in the context of his discussion of scepticism concerning induction, but they could be applied, *mutatis mutandis*, to his claims concerning the 'justification' of a single spatio-temporal framework which enables the reidentification of particulars in *Individuals*. Such a response to the sceptical challenge suggests that the distance between the modest transcendental strategy and Strawson's descriptive metaphysics is at once minimal and very significant. It is minimal because both approaches agree that the task of transcendental arguments is to trace the entailment relations holding between our putative knowledge claims and the conditions which make them possible. They agree that any validation of the structures of knowledge is backhanded. Where they disagree is in where they stand in relation to the sceptic's demand that the structures of knowledge could receive more than a coherentist/backhanded validation. The modest transcendental strategist thinks that it is not possible to go beyond coherentist justification to produce a transcendental argument to the effect that 'coherence yields correspondence' (Stern 1999b, 59) and holds that transcendental arguments fail to answer the sceptic, at least in that respect. The descriptive metaphysician goes a step further and casts doubt on the legitimacy of the demand that a justification for the norms which govern our inferences should be provided in order to invoke them in argument. Strawson might therefore agree that the demand that one should check whether the criteria of knowledge are adequate before deploying them is, as Hegel would put it, 'as absurd as the wise resolution of Scholasticus, not to venture into the water until he has learned to swim' (Hegel 1975, §10).

Both the descriptive metaphysician and the modest transcendentalist hold that the connections which transcendental arguments establish have modal force and are not merely psychological connections. But unlike the defender of modest transcendentalism, the descriptive metaphysician does not characterize the kind of connective analysis which exposes the necessary connections between the different parts of our conceptual scheme as *merely* internal. For, as we saw earlier, reasons can only be articulated against the background of certain rules of inference so that the expression 'internal reasons' is permissible only as a pleonasm which adds nothing to what it means for something to count as a 'reason'.

Descriptive metaphysics therefore responds to the sceptical stance in a very distinctive way, one that differs from the sort of reply articulated by ambitious and modest transcendental strategies alike. Descriptive metaphysics neither seeks to defeat the sceptic in the manner of ambitious transcendental arguments, nor endorses a form of epistemic humility which concedes partial defeat to the knowledge sceptic while claiming partial victory over the justification sceptic, as the modest transcendental strategy does. Rather, descriptive metaphysics endeavours to show that by doubting the criteria which enable knowledge claims to be made the sceptic silences herself and that rejecting the conditions that make knowledge claims possible leaves one with no place to argue from. This response closely resembles what Ralph Walker calls transcendental arguments in the second personal stance (Walker 1999, 20). To take an argument in the second personal stance 'is to place it in the context of trying to convince an interlocutor of something'. The second personal stance enables transcendental arguments to catch the sceptic red-handed in the act of a performative self-contradiction where they simultaneously seek to make a claim and reject the very conditions which make the claim possible. To illustrate (not Walker's example), consider the case of the climate change sceptic who questions the idea that global warming is a man-made phenomenon. This sceptic could be doubting either of two things. She could be doubting whether the claim that global warming is caused by anthropogenic emissions is true. Or she could be doubting the authority of the scientific criteria by which such claim is established. If the former is the case, the sceptic is engaging in a debate by advancing a claim, albeit a negative one and, in so doing, she will be invoking some form of inference through which such claim could in principle be corroborated. If the latter is the case, then she is not advancing any claim of her own. If the first kind of sceptic, the one who advances a claim, albeit a negative one (global warming is not caused by...), denies the authority of science, she is caught red-handed covertly invoking this authority to establish the claim, for example, that global warming is a cyclical phenomenon and not one affected by human activity. Transcendental arguments in the second personal stance expose the hypocrisy involved in denying the very criteria one deploys in argument. They do not address, on the other hand, the framework sceptic who is willing to forfeit the framework and is consistent in refusing to advance any claim of her own. This kind of sceptic, as Walker argues, cannot be defeated, but they should not be taken seriously either, because they do not advance (and cannot advance on pain of hypocritically invoking the criteria whose legitimacy they deny) any claims whatsoever and are therefore not genuine partners in conversation:

> Such people cannot be argued with. Anyone who refuses to rely on modus ponens, or on the law of non-contradiction, cannot be argued with. If they insist on their refusal there is therefore nothing to be done about it, but for the same reason there is no need to take them seriously. From a third-personal stance we can argue that unless they do have experience, and accept some elementary kind of inference, they cannot frame intelligible thoughts, and we may find that sort of argument convincing. It will not however convince them, since they are not open to conviction by argument. (Walker 1999, 20–1)

There is a difference between stating that the knowledge sceptic remains undefeated because one can never obtain external justification for the framework one adopts to advance one's knowledge claims and stating that since there is no knowledge independently of the adoption of some form of inference or other, the knowledge sceptic is not a genuine partner in conversation. It is this subtle difference that tells the descriptive metaphysician apart from the modest transcendental strategist.

In the next section I turn to the question as to whether the project of descriptive metaphysics as pursued by the later Strawson in *Scepticism and Naturalism* (1985) marks a break with the earlier conception of the task of descriptive metaphysics and the way in which the descriptive metaphysician positions himself in relation to the sceptical challenge.

4. Descriptive Metaphysics and Naturalized Epistemology

Both ambitious and modest transcendental arguments address the question of our entitlement either to hold certain beliefs (modest strategies) or to make certain knowledge claims (ambitious ones) and both approaches see themselves as providing a reply to the sceptic, either the sceptic about justification (in the case of modest strategies) or the knowledge sceptic (in the case of the ambitious strategy). They share a conception of the nature of epistemology as a normative inquiry that stands in sharp contrast to the one advocated by Hume. The Humean naturalist gives up altogether on the search for justification that characterizes normative epistemology. The question we should ask for Hume is not 'what justification do we have for holding beliefs in the external world or causation?' but rather 'what disposes us to have these beliefs?'. Philosophers should stop asking (and answering) the question of our right or entitlement to hold certain beliefs and dedicate themselves to a descriptive inquiry into human nature and the principles of association that govern the imagination. Hume's descriptive epistemology does not seek to answer the sceptical challenge by justifying certain structural beliefs. It turns instead to asking (and answering) a different question, namely, why are foundational beliefs in the existence of the external world or of causal connections so resilient in the face of the repeated failure of philosophy to provide adequate proof for the existence of the external world or of causal connections? Although for Hume the sceptical challenge cannot be met, it remains idle nonetheless because nature is too strong for it. As Strawson puts it:

> According to Hume the naturalist, sceptical doubts are not to be met by argument. They are simply to be neglected (except, perhaps, in so far as they supply a harmless amusement, a mild diversion of the intellect). They are to be neglected because they are idle; powerless against the force of nature, of our naturally implanted disposition to belief. (Strawson 1985, 10–11)

Strawson's rapprochement of the project of descriptive metaphysics with naturalism may appear to be signalling a departure from his earlier conception of descriptive metaphysics with its emphasis on the idea that metaphysics engages in conceptual analysis. Yet 'naturalism' is a potentially misleading label that Strawson attaches to his later views because the naturalism the later Strawson aligns himself with is very different from Hume's own brand of naturalism. In *Scepticism and Naturalism* Strawson continues to be committed to a notion of transcendental argumentation as a form of 'connective analysis' that characterizes his earlier conception of the task of metaphysics (Glock 2003, 40). He points out that the 'transcendental arguer' will always be faced with the challenge that:

> ...even if *he* cannot conceive of alternative ways in which conditions of the possibility of a certain kind of experience or exercise of conceptual capacity might be fulfilled, this inability may simply be due to lack of imagination on his part, a lack which makes him prone to mistake sufficient for necessary conditions. (Strawson 1985, 18)

But adds that, this notwithstanding:

> ...these arguments, or a weakened version of them will continue to be of interest to our naturalist philosopher. For even if they do not succeed in establishing such tight or rigid connections as they initially promise, they do at least indicate or bring out conceptual connections, even if only of a looser kind; and, as I have already suggested, to establish the connections between the major structural features or elements of our conceptual scheme – to exhibit it, not as a rigidly deductive system, but as a coherent whole whose parts are mutually supportive and mutually dependent, interlocking in an intelligible way – to do this may well seem to our naturalist, the proper, or at least the major, task of analytic philosophy. As indeed it does to me. (Strawson 1985, 18)

Then Strawson adds in parenthesis: 'Whence the phrase, "descriptive (as opposed to validatory or revisionary) metaphysics"' (Strawson 1985, 18).

Strawson acknowledges (in a nod to Stroud's 1968 criticism of ambitious transcendental arguments) that by means of transcendental argumentation one cannot rule out that there may be different conceptual schemes. This acknowledgement is however immediately qualified by the claim that transcendental arguments, even in a naturalistic key, do not cease to trace conceptual connections between the different parts of our conceptual scheme. It is clear from this, therefore, that Strawson's descriptive metaphysics, even in the later work, is not 'descriptive' in the same sense in which Hume's epistemology is 'descriptive'. For Hume the question one should ask is not the normative question of what entitles us to have certain beliefs, but the genetic question concerning why we form certain beliefs:

> The subject...of our present enquiry is concerned with the causes which induce us to believe in the existence of body. We may well ask, *What causes induce us to believe in the existence of body?* But 'tis in vain to ask, *Whether there be body or not?* (Hume 1740, I.4.2)

In Strawson's naturalism, unlike Hume's, the task of philosophical analysis is to understand how the elements of our conceptual system hang together, not what disposes us towards certain beliefs. For this reason, when in *Scepticism and Naturalism* Strawson says that he is about to consider 'a different kind of response to scepticism—a response which does not so much attempt to meet the challenge as to pass it by' (Strawson 1985, 3), he cannot mean that transcendental arguments, even in a naturalistic key, position themselves in relation to the sceptical challenge in exactly the same way as the Humean naturalist does: if transcendental arguments (even in a naturalistic key) engage in a form of connective analysis, then the sense in which the sceptical question is 'passed by' in Strawson's own naturalistic reply cannot be the same sense in which it is said to be idle for the Humean naturalist. For the Humean naturalist the sceptical challenge is idle because 'nature is too strong for it'; for the earlier Strawson, by contrast, the sceptical challenge is 'passed by' or not addressed head on because by refusing to accept the conditions of knowledge the sceptic has silenced herself and is therefore not a genuine partner in conversation. If the later Strawson still thinks of descriptive metaphysics as a form of connective analysis, then there seems to be no reason to think that Strawson fundamentally altered his views of how descriptive metaphysics positions itself vis-à-vis the sceptical challenge. If (a) Strawson's earlier conception of descriptive metaphysics is not 'validatory' in the sense of providing an ambitious transcendental argument (as in Stroud's reading of the earlier Strawson), and if (b) the sense in which Strawson's later metaphysics is 'descriptive' is not the same sense in which Hume's epistemology is 'descriptive', then there is less of a gap between the project of descriptive metaphysics as described in *Individuals* and in *Scepticism and Naturalism*. Nor perhaps is there such a gap in the way in which descriptive metaphysics positions itself vis-à-vis the sceptical challenge. In *Individuals* Strawson's emphasis is on the claim that the sceptic denies the conditions of the possibility for certain doubts to be raised; in *Scepticism and Naturalism* Strawson's emphasis is on the claim that scepticism should be passed by. But if the reason why scepticism should be passed by is not the Humean consideration that 'nature is too strong for it', then Strawson's stance on how descriptive metaphysics positions itself in relation to the sceptical challenge may not be fundamentally different from the earlier view that, having silenced herself, the sceptic cannot make any moves in the game of asking for and giving reasons. Since Strawson continues to be committed to a conception of descriptive metaphysics as conceptual/connective analysis, his use of the term 'naturalism' must be idiosyncratic and, as such, does not signal a radical conversion to Humeanism, but rather an attempt to claim an intermediate logical space between naturalism proper and robust transcendental arguments. I think that Stern is right in saying that one need not construe transcendental arguments in a naturalistic key in order to ascribe weaker conclusions to them (Stern 2003, 232). Yet, if the argument of this chapter is correct, descriptive metaphysics claims this intermediate logical space in a different way, since it rejects the distinction between internal and external justification and does not pursue a strategy of epistemic humility (D'Oro 2019).

This chapter has explored the way in which descriptive metaphysics positions itself vis-à-vis the sceptical challenge in the epistemic context. But the interpretative suggestion it makes has broader implications and could be pursued in the practical context to clarify the nature of Strawson's argument in 'Freedom and Resentment' (Strawson 1962/2008). Benjamin De Mesel (2018) has recently extended the distinction between (a) claiming that a framework cannot be externally justified against the framework sceptic, and (b) denying that the notion of justification is applicable to the framework, to the moral context to undermine the claim that in 'Freedom and Resentment' Strawson deploys a modest transcendental strategy against the moral sceptic. De Mesel argues against Justin Coates (2017) that Strawson's strategy is not to develop a modest transcendental argument which concedes the moral practice of holding people responsible cannot be (externally) justified. Rather Strawson denies that the notion of justification can be legitimately applied to the moral practice/framework of holding people responsible, i.e. Strawson questions the very notion of external justification. The interpretative suggestion defended here may therefore have broader applicability and pursuing it across the epistemic and the moral context might have the added bonus of uncovering a coherent metaphilosophical vision.

In the next section we will consider how advocates of ambitious transcendental arguments, modest transcendental arguments, Humean naturalists, and our descriptive metaphysician might respond to the sceptic's challenge in a concrete scenario.

5. On a Walk with the Ambitious Transcendental Strategist, the Modest Transcendental Strategist, the Humean Naturalist, and the Descriptive Metaphysician

Once upon a time I went for a walk with a group of people. We parked the car in the car park at position a on the map (Figure 9.1) and started to walk heading north in direction c, walking along a cucumber-shaped lake with the shore of the lake on our right-hand side. As it started to get dark, we decided that we'd better get back to the car. This decision was made as we reached the northern tip of the lake at position b.

One member of the group suggested that we should take the path to the right and make a U-turn, circling the lake on the other side with its bank on our right-hand side but in the opposite direction, heading south. All but one agreed. This dissenting member of the group objected that we should not do that, but should continue straight (heading further north) in direction c. The rest of the group explained that after parking the car we headed north in direction c, coasting the lake even if the lake was not always visible because of the thick vegetation so that, if we wanted to return to the car, we could do so either by simply turning back on

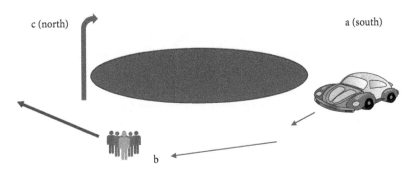

Figure 9.1 The Map

ourselves or by circling the lake as suggested. Since this particular group member insisted that we should continue heading north, a map was produced, which showed the lake, where we were in relation to it, and where the car was. This particular member of the group was not persuaded because they did not 'care' about the map and insisted that one should head in direction c irrespective of the map. What happened next? We did what I would take to be the sensible thing to do. We turned right and coasted the lake on the opposite bank heading south with that particular member of the group grudgingly following us and refusing to acknowledge the authority of the map, even when we reached the car just before dusk. On the way back we treated the protestations and moaning of this member of the party the way one treats a child's tantrums: by ignoring them. Were we right in doing what would seem to be the sensible thing to do? Was this response insufficiently philosophical? How would our philosophers, the ambitious transcendental arguer, the modest transcendental arguer, the Humean naturalist, and the descriptive metaphysician have responded?

The advocate of ambitious or truth-directed transcendental arguments might argue that it is in principle possible to persuade this person to accept the authority of the map by arguing that reality is as the map represents it to be and thus persuade them by means of argument that circling the lake is the correct thing to do. They would therefore stop the party in its tracks and spend as much time as needed arguing with the map-sceptic that the map is a true representation of reality. Being the transcendental philosophers that they are, they would argue not directly, by comparing the map with the reality it depicts, but indirectly by suggesting that the ability to discriminate between north and south presupposes that reality is as the map represents it. Their goal would be to persuade the map-sceptic that the map is a correct representation of reality and that they are not justified in dismissing the map as a potentially false or inaccurate representation of where the walking party stood in relation to the car and the lake. The modest transcendental strategist, unlike the ambitious transcendental one, would not be so adamant that the map is a true representation of reality and so would not set out to persuade the dissenting member of the group by arguing that reality is map-like. There is no way of knowing whether reality is indeed as the map represents it to be because our belief in the distinction between north and south cannot be externally validated by accessing reality independently of how the map represents it. No matter how carefully the members of the group read the map, they could be wrong in suggesting that the party should either turn back on itself or circle the lake heading south on the opposite bank, not because they had been guilty of careless map-reading, but because the map may be a systematically misleading representation of reality. They might add that they are nonetheless justified in believing in the map's ability to guide us because independently of a commitment to the way in which reality is represented by the map, they would not be able to navigate their way round the world, distinguishing between north and south, east and west and so forth. Yet, since there can be no way of checking whether what must necessarily be believed to be the case to navigate the world is actually the case, the modest transcendental strategist could at best dismiss the awkward member of the party as being unreasonable, not as being wrong or incorrect. Since modest transcendental strategies cannot rule out that reality may not be as the map depicts it to be, the suspicion of the dissenting member of the party that the map is an inaccurate representation of reality might actually be correct even if this appears unreasonable and unjustified by any supporting argument. Unlike the ambitious and the modest transcendental strategist, the Humean naturalist would not bother much with arguing. Any internal justification for believing in the map of the kind that the modest transcendental strategist might produce, would be circular and therefore question-begging. The Humean sceptic might agree with the modest transcendental strategist that one would not be able to distinguish between north and south, one direction and the other, without appealing to the authority of the map. But if one then tried to justify the map internally, by saying that one should accept its authority because it makes possible the distinction between north and south, one would simply be arguing in a circle (just as anyone attempting to justify the principle of induction by invoking specific inductive inferences would be). At the end of the day, however, all this would not really matter because (for the Humean naturalist) the belief in the map, held by the majority of people in the group, is not grounded in reason or argument; the map is just something that they are compelled to believe in by their nature and such natural dispositions are not open to refutation by rational argumentation. Perhaps the dissenting member of the party was not wired up to believe in the map, but there is little one can do about that faulty wiring because reasons are motivationally inert and they would be ignored even if they could ex-hypothesis be backed by sound rather than circular argument. The ambitious transcendental strategist, the modest transcendental strategist, and the Humean naturalist position themselves in different ways in relation to the sceptical challenge. The ambitious and modest transcendental arguers think of epistemology as a normative enterprise and they both take its task to be that of providing a justification for our beliefs against the sceptic, even if they differ as to how far justification can reach. The Humean naturalist, by contrast, abandons the search for justification altogether. Since reasons have no motivational power there is no point in trying to persuade the dissenting member of the group who has not been wired up to believe in maps. The dissenting member of the group (the sceptic) is ignored rather than engaged in rational argument.

Now, if the descriptive metaphysician had gone on a walk with the ambitious transcendental strategist, the modest transcendental strategist, and the Humean naturalist, how would she have handled the dissenting member of the group? The descriptive metaphysician, like the Humean naturalist, would not give the map-sceptic too much airtime but, unlike the Humean naturalist, would have reasons for dismissing the sceptic. For the descriptive metaphysician, the person who rejects the authority of the map is either caught red-handed invoking the map whose authority she ostensibly denies or she is silenced. If she suggests that one should move in direction c rather than a or b, then she is caught invoking the very criteria that she dismisses as dubitable and she can be argued with by consulting the map. If on the other hand she is consistent in her rejection of the map and any other criteria on the basis of which one could make any knowledge claims, then she can say nothing. And if she insists that one should go in direction c irrespective of the map, then she *should* be ignored for her claim is *not an argument but a mere assertion*. Just as the person who does not play by the rules of chess cannot be said to accomplish checkmate, so the person who claims one should go in a given direction, but rejects the conventions that enable us to determine whether one is moving north or south, *cannot truly be said to be disagreeing* with the remaining members about what direction to take because in order to genuinely disagree (or indeed to genuinely agree), they would have to accept that which they ostensibly reject: the authority of the map. The descriptive metaphysician, like the Humean naturalist, declines to reply. But unlike the Humean naturalist the descriptive metaphysician explains why we are *entitled* to ignore the sceptic, not why we are *inclined* to ignore him. Where the Humean naturalist explains what disposes us to ignore the sceptic, the descriptive metaphysician explains what grounds or reasons we have for declining to engage with the sceptical challenge.

References

Carnap, Rudolf (1950), 'Empiricism, Semantics and Ontology', *Revue Internationale de Philosophie* 4(2): 20–40.

Coates, Justin (2017), 'Strawson's Modest Transcendental Argument', *British Journal for the History of Philosophy* 25(4): 799–822.

De Mesel, Benjamin (2018), 'Are Our Moral Responsibility Practices Justified?', *British Journal for the History of Philosophy* 26(3): 603–14.

D'Oro, Giuseppina (2019), 'Between Ontological Hubris and Epistemic Humility: Collingwood, Kant and Transcendental Arguments', *British Journal for the History of Philosophy* 27(2): 336–57.

Glock, Hans-Johann (2003), 'Strawson and Analytic Kantianism', in Hans-Johann Glock (ed.), *Strawson and Kant* (Oxford: Clarendon Press), 15–42.

Hacker, Peter Michael Stephan (2003), 'On Strawson's Rehabilitation of Metaphysics', in Hans-Johann Glock (ed.), *Strawson and Kant* (Oxford: Clarendon Press), 43–66.

Hegel, Georg W. F. (1830/1975), *Hegel's Logic: Being Part I of the Encyclopaedia of the Philosophical Sciences*, trans. William Wallace (New York: Oxford University Press).

Hume, David (1740), *Abstract of the Treatise of Human Nature*, book 1. https://www.earlymoderntexts.com/authors/hume. Accessed 8 August 2021.

Kant, Immanuel (1985), *Critique of Pure Reason*, trans. Norman Kemp Smith (London: Macmillan).

Sacks, Mark (1999), 'Transcendental Arguments and the Inference to Reality: A Reply to Stern', in Robert Stern (ed.), *Transcendental Arguments: Problems and Prospects* (Oxford: Oxford University Press), 67–83.

Stern, Robert (1999a), 'Introduction', in Robert Stern (ed.), *Transcendental Arguments: Problems and Prospects* (Oxford: Oxford University Press), 1–11.

Stern, Robert (1999b), 'On Kant's Response to Hume: The Second Analogy as Transcendental Argument', in Robert Stern (ed.), *Transcendental Arguments: Problems and Prospects* (Oxford: Oxford University Press), 47–66.

Stern, Robert (2000), *Transcendental Arguments and Scepticism: Answering the Question of Justification* (Oxford: Oxford University Press).

Stern, Robert (2003), 'On Strawson's Naturalistic Turn', in Hans-Johann Glock (ed.), *Strawson and Kant* (Oxford: Clarendon Press), 43–66.

Strawson, Peter F. (1952), 'The "Justification" of Induction', in *Introduction to Logical Theory* (London: Methuen).

Strawson, Peter F. (1959), *Individuals: An Essay in Descriptive Metaphysics* (London: Methuen).

Strawson, Peter F. (1962/2008), 'Freedom and Resentment', Chapter 1 in *Freedom and Resentment and Other Essays* (Abingdon: Routledge), 1–28.

Strawson, Peter F. (1966), *The Bounds of Sense: An Essay on Kant's Critique of Pure Reason* (London: Methuen).

Strawson, Peter F. (1985), *Scepticism and Naturalism: Some Varieties* (London: Methuen).

Stroud, Barry (1968), 'Transcendental Arguments', *Journal of Philosophy* 65: 241–56.

Walker, Ralph (1999), 'Induction and Transcendental Argument', in Robert Stern (ed.), *Transcendental Arguments: Problems and Prospects* (Oxford: Oxford University Press), 13–29.

10
P. F. Strawson and Connective Analysis

A.P. Martinich

1. Introduction

P. F. Strawson's favoured method of philosophical analysis consisted of describing connections among concepts central to the way human beings grasp the world, such as the concepts of particulars and universals or attitudes about other people. He emphasized the connection among concepts rather than, say, among the supposed parts of an individual concept. Each concept and its connections with others help elucidate the other concepts that are analysed (Strawson 2011, 184).[1] He called his method 'connective analysis'. Method is used here in a loose sense since he did not describe any procedures or rules of thumb for performing connective analysis (see Grice 1989, 174). The term 'connective analysis' may even be a misnomer because far from being a kind of breaking down, it is the opposite in so far as it calls attention to things that do not noticeably go together. Strawson conceded the point but observed that the term 'analysis' was so entrenched that it was better to keep it than to multiply terms (Strawson 1992, 19).[2]

While one may think that straightforward description is sufficient for explaining something, or even that description is the best approach, I think examples are indispensable for at least two reasons. The first is that concepts without instances are empty. Examples show how concepts apply to the non-conceptual world (see Strawson 1974, 14; Strawson 2011, 83–4). The second reason is that many descriptions of new philosophical concepts rely to some extent on metaphor; and examples help detach the concepts from the metaphor. Even when description and examples are helpful, they may not completely distinguish one concept

---

[1] Although the origin and development of his conception of connective analysis is outside the scope of this chapter, a few comments may be made. It was not thematized to my knowledge until Strawson did so in 1992, but one can detect his use of it as early as 1948 in an unpublished paper, 'Formal Signs and Rules of Use' (Strawson, 1948). Could Strawson's idea have been influenced by the practice of his tutor Grice or J.L. Austin in the well-known 'Saturday playdates'? The word 'influenced' is vague enough to support assent. However, Grice says that Austin did not theorize his own or any other method (Grice 1989, 181–2; see Austin 1970, 175–85). And it is plausible that Strawson and Grice influenced each other since they did philosophy in tandem in the 1950s. Both Grice's analyses of meaning in 'Meaning' and 'In Defense of a Dogma', developed from discussions between them; and both articles contain connective analyses or parts of them, as I argue in Section 3.

[2] Paul Snowdon recommended the term 'relaxed analysis' for Strawson's method (Snowdon 2019).

from others in the same area because the description may be incomplete or vague, and the examples may not range as broadly as they should.

My goal in this chapter is to explain connective analysis in three ways: describing it (Section 2); discussing actual examples of the method (Section 3); and comparing reductive, connective, and modest conceptual analyses (Section 4). I then expand on my explanation in the remaining two sections. Section 5 shows that Grice's analyses of utterer's meaning or other sorts are not reductive in the sense of eliminating a kind of concept. Section 6 explains the relationship between 'modest' conceptual analysis and connective analysis. My attachment to Strawson's method will emerge throughout the chapter.

2. A Description of Connective Analysis

As mentioned above, Strawson said that his general aim in philosophy was to show the connections among a cluster of concepts that are related, with a particular interest in the concepts that apply most broadly to human experience such as those of bodies, persons, space and time, particulars and universals.[3] About his method, he wrote:

> Let us imagine... the model of an elaborate network, a system, of connected items, concepts, such that the function of each item, each concept, could, from the philosophical point of view, be properly understood only by grasping its connections with the others, its place in the system,... the picture of a set of interlocking systems of such a kind.   (Strawson 1992, 19; see also 24 and 46)

While simplicity is a virtue in other forms of analysis, connective analysis is comfortable with conceptual complexity, as long as it is illuminating:

> A concept may be complex, in the sense that its philosophical elucidation[4] requires the establishing of its connections with other concepts, and yet at the same time irreducible, in the sense that it cannot be defined away, without circularity, in terms of those other concepts to which it is necessarily related.
> (Strawson 1992, 22–3)

---

[3] An excellent example of the way Strawson explains interconnections of broad concepts is in Strawson (1992, 60–4 and 73–81). Concepts can also be arranged in a sort of hierarchy, with concepts that presuppose other concepts being higher in the sense of further from the foundational concepts than the presupposed ones (Strawson 1992, 21).

[4] 'Elucidation' is the word that expresses the favoured goal of connective analyses; David Wiggins used the concept in the 1980s and traced its origin to Frege and Wittgenstein. Like Strawson and Grice, Wiggins permitted circular elucidations of concepts (Wiggins 1991, 141–3 and 187–9; see also Helme 1979). (My thanks to Benjamin De Mesel for raising this issue and the connection to Wiggins.)

Connective analysis is consistent with or contains a large component of ordinary language analysis. A comment by Strawson suggests that J.L. Austin's meetings on Saturday mornings, as informal as they were, were exercises in connective analysis (Strawson 2011, 236–7). And Austin's article, 'A Plea for Excuses', especially when he contrasted excuses and justifications and related each to responsibility and action, is easily seen as an exercise in connective analysis (Austin 1970). (For the sake of brevity, I will sometimes omit the phrase 'concept of' where strictly it might be required.)[5] One difference between Austin's attitude and Strawson's is that the latter often had an eye for highly general concepts and systematization of them whereas the former did not, notwithstanding his work on speech acts (Chapman 2005, 62). Paul Grice seemed to occupy a middle ground. He never renounced the importance of ordinary language analysis, but he saw some limitations in it; and he pursued systematization more than Austin.[6]

A different objection is that 'connective' is inappropriate because it is metaphorical. Strawson himself occasionally criticized the use of metaphors in philosophy: 'The history of philosophy is full of unhappy or unsatisfactory metaphors' (Strawson 2011, 100). He objected to Gilbert Ryle's characterization of his philosophy as 'conceptual geography or conceptual mapping or charting' because it was 'uncomfortably metaphorical' (Strawson 1992, 3; see Ryle 1932).[7] He wrote that if the metaphorical element of geography, mapping, and charting is removed what remains is 'the notion of an abstract representation of certain relations between certain concepts made for a purpose' (Strawson 1992, 3). If I understand his criticism, it was unfair.[8] To remove the figurative element from a metaphor is to destroy it. Consider an analogous criticism of, say, cab drivers: 'they do no work because if you take away their driving, they are idle'. Well, yes; but their work is to drive vehicles, often on crowded or out-of-the-way streets for the benefit of their customers. The image from a metaphor is supposed to give the reader some sense of what something is like or of what doing something is like. Figuratively, of course.

Analytic philosophers other than Ryle, some well outside Oxford, thought the map-metaphor was useful. Following Frank Ramsey, David Armstrong analysed a

---

[5] Connective analysis may sometimes pry similar concepts apart; see 'Three Ways of Spilling Ink' (Austin 1970, 272–87). Another example is a paper in which Strawson showed that standard definitions and characterizations of logical form failed (Strawson 1948).

[6] Grice (1989, 171–85), and Petrus (2010, 4, 7–8); see Soames (2002, 2, 197–200). Grice criticized ordinary language analysts for sometimes confusing what the use of a word revealed about its meaning and what it revealed about what the speaker might be saying or implying with it.

[7] The issue of metaphorical terms in philosophy is fraught. If 'connective' in 'connective analysis' is metaphorical, so is 'analysis'; and the metaphor of connective taking apart or breaking down is inapt. I want to avoid pursuing this kind of dispute about metaphorical terms in philosophy. My goal is narrower.

[8] Strawson's critique of Ryle's account of categories was extended and not, I think, unfair (Strawson 1970; see 2011, 232, 239–40). Ryle's term, 'category mistake' has intuitive value, but lacked a sound theoretical account.

belief as a map that guides people through life (Armstrong 1973, 3–5). Naturally, this metaphor needs to be revised because no individual belief is a map; each belief is like a street name or address that helps one navigate (see Wittgenstein 1958, paragraphs 18 and 123). Getting to a particular place requires many interconnecting streets and addresses some of which immediately attach to one's destination. And here we seem to be back to Strawson's own conception of connected concepts. So, I think that this criticism of Ryle was unfair.

Beyond that, simply to say that some term is metaphorical is not a philosophical criticism, as Strawson knew (Strawson 2011, 100; see also Strawson 1992, 118–20). When Aristotle distinguished between form and matter, the matter (*hyle*) was literally raw wood. When Hume talked about impressions, impressions had to be in some medium, except that his impressions were not in anything, especially not minds.

Strawson was not averse to using metaphors himself and recommending some by others:

> Objects, he [Gottlob Frege] says, are *complete*, concepts *incomplete* or *unsaturated*. Not all parts of a thought can be complete; at least one must be 'unsaturated' or predicative; otherwise they would not hold together.
> (Strawson 1959, 153; see also Brown 2014, 7)

Strawson used a different metaphor for the same property of concepts. They are 'principles of collection', unlike individuals (Strawson 1974, 17; see also 18–19). In another place, he mentions other metaphors he used: 'the visual experience is "infused with" or "irradiated by" or "soaked with" *the* concept' (Strawson 1985, 82). Mentioning Strawson's use of metaphors is not criticism. I endorse his use of 'connective' to describe his method, and 'elucidation' as his goal. As for Ryle's metaphor of conceptual mapping, it is not worth giving an opinion partially because I have been talking about the use of metaphors in philosophy in general and only Strawson's in particular.

Metaphors have a place in philosophy. They can be the first word in philosophy ('Perception is saturated with concepts') and point in the direction of an answer. Teachers of philosophy invariably introduce the practice of analysis with the metaphors of the word's etymology, loosening, untying, and breaking down; in this way, the student is pointed in the direction of understanding what an analysis aims for. A metaphor can also be the last word of a particular treatment of a philosophical problem when literal talk gives out. A metaphor may be the best a philosopher can provide to give a glimpse of what needs to be explored next, but only as through a glass darkly.

It is hard to say when, if ever, philosophical metaphors become completely literal. Sometimes a metaphor that is just beneath the surface goes largely unnoticed for centuries. 'Concept' as used in philosophy is a dead metaphor for impregnation, and this latter sense derived from a metaphor that itself originated from *capere*, to grasp or seize something. Concepts metaphorically grab something. Like other technical words, it grows a literal meaning by acquiring properties through the literal use of expressions; concepts are general or universal; and when joined to another, form a new concept. As indicated earlier, Strawson's metaphorical term to explain the value of connective analysis is 'elucidation',[9] a trope that is close to one that has been used for almost two millennia. It is connected to the Neoplatonic and Christian concept of knowledge as illumination and of God's illumination of the human mind.[10] Notwithstanding Descartes's denigration of scholastic philosophy, he too used light as a metaphor, 'the light of nature', as others did. It is better to admit to one's dependence on a metaphor than to suppress or repress it. But ideally philosophy is getting rid of metaphors.

3. Examples of Connective Analysis

One way of moving away from metaphors in philosophy is to give examples of what ideally would be described literally. To this end, I will begin by discussing the connective analysis that is the focus of H. P. Grice and Strawson's article, 'In Defense of a Dogma'. The dogma defended was that the statement, 'Analytic propositions are true in virtue of their meaning, and synthetic propositions are true in virtue of facts', is intelligible and useful. It was one of the two dogmas that the philosophical heretic, W.V. Quine, had denied in 'Two Dogmas of Empiricism'. Logical positivists had reasoned that there were only two kinds of truths, tautologies, which are the domain of logicians and mathematicians, and empirical, synthetic truths, which are the domain of natural scientists. Looking for some distinctive and legitimate practice to follow, philosophers who felt the positivists' view was to be reckoned with, staked out an area that was neither trivial nor empirical. So, it would not be part of the purview of logicians or scientists. The analysis of concepts with wide application or importance in human lives seemed to be tailor-made for philosophers. Correct analyses would be necessarily true, as philosophical propositions had traditionally been claimed to be, and analytic. This conception of philosophy could sustain itself only if the distinction between analytic and synthetic propositions was legitimate. Quine's position in 'Two Dogmas of Empiricism', was that the distinction was not theoretically defensible (Quine 1961). He was not bothered by that result because he believed that philosophy was continuous with science. Grice and Strawson's

---

[9] Earlier, Strawson had used the word 'illumination' to express his philosophical method (Strawson 1963, 505). An excellent article on this and Strawson's criticism of Carnap is Pinder (2020).
[10] https://plato.stanford.edu/entries/illumination/#:~:text=Divine%20illumination%20is%20the%20oldest,in%20their%20ordinary%20cognitive%20activities

defence of the distinction was no small thing. They were trying to preserve a conception of philosophy that seemed to be a worthy successor to Plato's efforts to identify the definitions of such things as piety and justice and *also* Thomas Hobbes's analyses of desires, persons, and freedom.

Early in their article, Grice and Strawson made much of how easily the analytic/synthetic distinction is taught and uniformly applied to sentences not previously judged to be one or the other. So, the distinction must be a principled one that is not undermined by the existence of borderline cases. Their case for the intelligibility of the distinction depended in large part on its connections with other concepts expressed by words that seemed to be intelligible, such as 'synonymous' and 'means the same as'. Surely, a translation of a sentence from one language to another is synonymous if each has the same meaning; and if they have the same meaning, then they are synonymous. Moreover, it is easy to find ordinary sentences of the same language that have the same meaning (e.g. 'Lee has exactly one child' and 'Lee has one and only one child'). So both 'same meaning' and 'meaning' must be intelligible. Grice and Strawson wrote, 'We want only to point out that if we are to give up the notion of sentence-synonymy as senseless, we must give up the notion of sentence-significance (of a sentence having meaning) as senseless too. But then perhaps we might as well give up the notion of sense too' (Grice and Strawson 1956, 146).[11] Their strategy for vindicating the analytic/synthetic distinction was to show that it lived, and breathed, and had its being among a 'certain circle or family of expressions' (Grice and Strawson 1956, 147). When the elucidation of a group or cluster of expressions eventually results in a circle but is not objectionable because each member helps illuminate the others. Grice and Strawson mentioned two other clusters. One was the cluster which 'includes the propositional connectives and the words "true" and "false", "statement", "fact", "denial", "assertion"'. The other cluster 'includes "morally wrong", "blameworthy", "breach of moral rules"', and others (Grice and Strawson 1956, 148). A third worth mentioning includes rights, privileges, powers, claims, immunities, and duties (Waldron 1984, 10; other examples are implicit at Strawson 1992, 51–2, 59–60, 95–6).

Grice and Strawson pointed to only some of the connections among the a priori, the analytic, and so on. A few years after their article appeared, Anthony Quinton filled in many of the details of the intelligibility of those terms. He gave an account of the conceptual connections among the distinctions, a priori/a posteriori, analytic/synthetic, and necessary/contingent in his article, 'The *A Priori* and the Analytic'. He maintained in part that analyticity is an 'elucidation of the idea of necessity' and that the empirical is an 'elucidation of the concept of the contingent' (Quinton 1963–4, 109, 110). In an interim summary of the various connections of the three distinctions we have been discussing, he wrote:

---

[11] For a trenchant criticism of Grice and Strawson's argument, see Atlas (2010, 49–51, 53–6).

all and only necessary truths are analytic and all and only contingent truths are empirical. Since necessary and contingent truths are exclusive no truth is *both* analytic *and* empirical, since they are exhaustive every truth is *either* analytic *or* empirical. Since 'synthetic' means 'non-analytic' and '*a priori*' means 'non-empirical' every truth is synthetic or *a priori*, and no truth is both.

(Quinton 1963–4, 110; see also 112)

One objection that many philosophers would have raised in the 1950s to the supposed connections among 'a priori' and 'analytic', and the other terms mentioned above was that the analyses would turn out to be circular. To simplify greatly, the objection is that for example, analytic is analysed in terms of meaning, meaning in terms of necessary; necessary in terms of not synthetic... and eventually back to analytic. Two responses to this objection are worth considering.

The first is to accept the objection, as Strawson did. If analyses are provided to a set or cluster of terms that is large enough to elucidate most of them, then circularity is not objectionable. The second reply, which may bolster the first, can be put in two ways. Firstly, the circularity of a concept within a cluster does not hem it in. Concepts connect with actual or possible experiences of individual things and events; and those connections prevent the circularity of concepts from being vicious. So, if justice, obligation, and punishment are parts of a cluster, then instances of justice and injustice, obligation and permission, and reward and punishment indicate which individual things are being connected with which others. They also help track the consistency or coherence of the claims of connectedness. If punishment is rendered to someone who violated his obligation, then the asserted connections are confirmed. There is always the risk that asserted connections will not be confirmed. In such cases, the philosopher has various options to restore the equilibrium among the concepts and the instances; perhaps the supposed violation did not occur or that the person's action should be excused. The second way of putting the second reply draws on Grice and Strawson's point that the concepts of analytic and synthetic are taught through examples: The statements, 'The white chalk is white', 'Horses are horses', and 'Selfish people are not benevolent' are analytic. The statements, 'The chalk is white', 'Some horses are black', and 'Some people are selfish' are synthetic. And being able to understand those statements requires knowledge of instances of the topic specific words; and so the circle of interacting concepts is not vicious (see Grice 1989, 352).[12] In short, concept to concept connections are complemented by the connection between a concept and its instances.

A different objection to the position of Grice and Strawson is that they and Quinton were mistaken in thinking that necessity, the a priori, and other terms or

---

[12] Grice and Strawson were sensitive to the potential objection that an analysis was circular in some of their writings and occasionally criticized analyses on these grounds; see e.g. Grice (1975, 24–5). These analyses were not connective analyses.

concepts are mutually connected. Kripke argued convincingly that some necessary propositions are a posteriori (Kripke 1972). A reply is that while Kripke showed in effect that the connective analysis of Quinton was defective, he did not show that there was no connection among the terms.

Let's now consider a second example of connective analysis, Grice's analysis of meaning.[13] His analysis consists of many sub-analyses, such as natural, non-natural, and word-meaning (Grice 1989, 117–37, 213–23). His analyses constitute connective analysis because of the connections he makes among agents, their beliefs and intentions, the roles of persons directing intentions at an audience, the audience's recognition of those intentions, saying and implicating, rationality, certainty, and desire (Grice 1989, 3–143; Grice 1971, 1975; Neale 1992 notes the connection between meaning and conversation).[14]

Grice's intuition was that the sense of meaning applicable to a person's meaning something by some bit of behaviour, which includes but is not necessarily linguistic, was intending to get a person to believe or do something by getting that person to recognize that the utterer has that first intention. We can make this analysis clearer; and it is helpful to restrict it to the case of belief. In 'Meaning', Grice arrived at this:

A person A meant something by a bit of behaviour x if and only if A uttered x with the intention of inducing a belief in an audience B by means of B's recognition of A's intention.

In reply to various counterexamples, Grice revised his original analysis roughly to the following:

'U meant something by uttering x' is true if and only if, for some audience A, U uttered x intending:

(1) A to produce a particular response r

(2) A to think (recognize) that U intends (1)

(3) A to fulfil (1) on the basis of his fulfilling (2) (Grice 1989, 92).[15]

---

[13] Grice discussed his work on non-natural meaning with Strawson, who urged Grice to publish his thoughts: 'Unable to convince Grice to revise his paper and send it to a journal, he [Strawson] persuaded him to hand over the manuscript [of "Meaning"] as it stood. Strawson and his wife Ann edited it and submitted it to the *Philosophical Review*' (Chapman 2005, 63; the source is a tape recording of a discussion of Grice, Richard Warner, and Judith Baker; Siobhan Chapman provided me with the source; see Strawson 2011, 206).

[14] In Section 5, I shall grant for the sake of discussion that Grice's analysis of utterer's meaning is an example of conceptual analysis and even 'reductive analysis' in a Strawson's sense. The upshot will be that a modest conceptual analysis can be part a connective analysis.

[15] See Lycan (2008, 88). For a diagnosis of the problem with Grice's analysis, see Atlas (2005, 73–9).

Grice's analysis was elucidating in so far as it connected meaning with such familiar concepts as persons, intentions, beliefs, and recognition. In contrast, many previous philosophers had simply explained meaning as synonymous with some other concept, for Russell, denoting, and for others, representing or being a sign of. While the salient concept in Grice's analysis was intention, he did not say or imply that intentions are simpler or more basic than meaning; nor was he indicating that any of the other concepts in the analysans were simpler.

To forestall some misinterpretations, at least three more things should be noted. First, because Grice was analysing communicative meaning in its broadest form, the commonly used term 'speaker's meaning' to describe utterer's meaning is misleading or false.[16] Speaker meaning requires the utterance to be some elements of a human language, words or sentences.[17] Second, communicative acts have directed intentions, intentions aimed at one or more specific people. (Grice might have distinguished various kinds of observers of a speaker's meaning, such as an addressee, an audience whom the speaker knows is a witness, an unhidden overhearer who is not an addressee or audience, and an eavesdropper who surreptitiously overhears the speaker. The circle of relevant concepts could also be expanded to types of speakers.) Third, while Grice gives no indication that he is thinking of any kind of animal other than Homo sapiens, it is plausible that some primates instantiate utterer's meaning (Tomasello 2008).

Grice radically shifted the perspective of semantics from words and sentences meaning something to human beings or other agents meaning something. It was hard for philosophers of the time to appreciate that the fundamental idea is of a human being or agent meaning something. (See further the discussion in Section 5.) Before Grice, philosophers of language thought of meaning as the possession of individuals when they thought of meaning as anyone's possession. As a property of persons, meaning-something is a public action.[18] So, the elucidation of one person's meaning involves connecting it with other persons, at whom the intentions are directed. Although Grice's explanatory comments on intentions are not parts of an analysis, they are elucidations of them. His intentions are not necessarily parts of a plan formulated by the agent explicitly or

---

[16] Grice later attempted to analyse speaker's meaning in terms of the use of 'timeless utterances', and the attempt is generally regarded as a failure.

[17] Many of the supposed counterexamples to Grice's original analysis depend on settings in which the speaker is not trying to get the addressee to believe something, e.g. of a person talking to herself, or writing a private diary entry, or a student in answering a test. I think all of these cases should be considered as derivative upon the basic cases on which Grice was focusing. Talking to oneself, entering a thought in a private diary, and answering test questions could not exist unless the speakers had first learned how to communicate with others. Talking to oneself is talking as if the speaker is the hearer; the diarist is writing so that he or she will be able to recognize what she believed when she made the entry; the student answers with the intention of having the teacher recognize what the student knows or believes.

[18] One reason for the difficulty of seeing meaning as an action is that it is a highly unusual verb (Stampe 1968).

implicitly and not even fully present to consciousness. Their presence is subject to 'the same kinds of criteria as ... [are used] in the case of non-linguistic intentions', the default case is that people 'are presumed to intend the normal consequences' of their actions; and they depend on contextual features (a person does not intend to shoot a donkey if there is no donkey or donkey-like object present) (Grice 1989, 222). In some cases, a person who is asked what he intended by something, answers 'not based on what he remembers but is more like a decision, a decision about how what he said is to be taken' (Grice 1989, 222-3). Finally, the last sentence of 'Meaning' is proleptic: 'linguistic intentions are very like nonlinguistic intentions' (Grice 1989, 223). Its import could only be appreciated if the concept of nonlinguistic intentions is explicated, presumably by connective analysis.

My examples of connective analysis in this section belong to the philosophy of language. But connective analysis can be the goal of metaphysics, as Strawson showed in *Individuals* and other works, and even in philosophical logic. I think that Strawson's penchant for analysing highly general concepts such as subject and predicate and particular and universal was a personal preference. Connective analysis can be applied to philosophically interesting concepts of any generality. It will be discussed further in Section 6.

4. Reductive Analysis, Connective Analysis, and Modest Conceptual Analysis

Strawson contrasts connective analysis with reductive analysis,[19] hence the title of *Analysis and Metaphysics*, chapter 2, 'Reduction or Connection?' Although he does not define reductive analysis, his account has two features: (i) the search for concepts or other items that are simple in the sense of not being composed of other concepts or items, and (ii) the inclusion in one's ontology of only absolutely simple items (Strawson 1992, 20 and 45).[20] These two connote an analyst's attitude or background belief, namely, that ultimately there are simple concepts or items and that only these simple things properly exist. This attitude suggests a third features of reductive analysis: (iii) all apparent entities other than the simple

---

[19] Many more forms could be described. Analysis as therapy, invented by Ludwig Wittgenstein, was important to Strawson, but space does not permit a discussion of it here. See Strawson's review of *Philosophical Investigations* (Strawson 2011, 139-42) and in an article on Carnap. In the latter, Strawson wrote that therapy was appropriate when 'philosophical perplexity... is temporarily dominated by one' type or use of expressions to the exclusion of others of importance (Strawson 2011, 86; see also Strawson 1992, 8-10, and 13-14). Strawson may have been more sympathetic with Wittgensteinian 'therapeutic analysis' in the early 1950s than he was in the 1990s. He expressed some ambivalence in the 1990s: 'this picture of the therapist... is, in fact, exaggerated and one-sided. But... it too has merit' (Strawson 1992, 3; see also 3-5, 8-10, 13-14; and 2011, 36-7). (My thanks to Sybren Heyndels for comments on this point.)

[20] Later, I will quote Grice's denial that he was a 'reductivist'; this was his term for Strawson's 'reductionist'.

ones are eliminated from ontology. Feature (iii) is in line with (i) and (ii). Standard examples of reductive analysis involving the elimination of a concept or range of concepts are familiar from the history of philosophy. Materialist philosophers tried to show that the most basic kind of substances or entities are bodies, and non-material substances do not exist. In *Leviathan*, Hobbes analysed a large range of familiar psychological concepts without reference to minds or souls. He refers only to bodies moving very short distances, as 'endeavours'. Appetite, for example, is an endeavour towards the thing that causes the motion; aversion is an endeavour away from the thing that causes it. Hope is an appetite along with 'an opinion of attaining' it.[21] Despair is the same except that the opinion is that the object will not be attained (Hobbes 1651, 25; see also Martinich 2005, 24–53). Idealist philosophers try to show that only minds and their ideas exist; bodies are eliminated. Berkeley argued that the supposed concept of a body is incoherent, a product of confused thinking. A third example of reductivists bent on elimination are nominalists who maintain that the distinction between universals and particulars is bogus and eliminate universals. As these examples indicate, many reductive analysts aim at the elimination of some concept, not necessarily simplicity, *pace* Strawson.

Reductive analysis is serious philosophical analysis, which is supposed 'to find ideas that were completely simple, that were free from internal conceptual complexity', according to Strawson. But he concedes that philosophers typically proceed in 'a relatively modest spirit'. Such a philosopher who was to analyse knowledge as justified true belief might stop there even though she thinks that 'the concept of belief requires, and is capable of, analysis' (Strawson 1992, 17–18). In this way, he assimilates conceptual analysis, as practised by most Anglo-American philosophers in the second and third quarters of the twentieth century, to reductive analysis. But the assimilation works only with (i)–(iii) as background beliefs of the analyst, and those beliefs are not essential to what has usually been considered conceptual analysis.

It is an historical fact that many of the best-known analytic philosophers from 1940–80 thought that their remit was 'modest', solving or dissolving medium-sized conceptual puzzles (Passmore 1968, 363–4; and see Flew 1956 and 1965).[22] The goal of these analysts, piecemeal clarification of puzzling concepts, does not need to be supplemented with Strawson's requirement that simples are the ultimate stopping point. He was not justified in assimilating modest conceptual

---

[21] One might object that Hobbes's analyses are not completely successful because opining seems to be mental and he does not analyse it.

[22] Ramsey sometimes included 'elucidation' as an important part of philosophy; but he saw as a problem what Strawson saw as an opportunity. Ramsey wrote, 'we seem to get into the situation that we cannot understand e.g. what we say about time and the external world without first understanding meaning and yet we cannot understand meaning without first understanding certainly time and probably the external world which are involved in it. So we cannot make our philosophy into an ordered progress to a goal' (Ramsey 1990, 6; see also Passmore 1968, 362).

analysis to reductive analysis. My guess is that he was tempted by the desire to force his readers to choose between Quine's reductive analysis and his own connective analysis. He does his best to show that the latter is preferable (e.g., Strawson 1992, 37–50, 83–108).

One might object that Strawson himself says that a practitioner of conceptual analysis does 'not aim at including only concepts which are themselves absolutely simple (whatever they may be)' (Strawson 1992, 18). However, he quickly undercuts that statement with another: 'the philosopher in practice operates... with the reductive model or picture of reductive analysis' (Strawson 1992, 18). Why did he think this? The reason he gave was that 'the analytical philosopher hates to hear... the words, "Your analysis is circular"'; and if analysis is 'a kind of dismantling of a complex structure into simpler elements... [then] this process has not even begun if... [the analysans contains] the very thing, the very concept, that was to be dismantled' (Strawson 1992, 18–19).

Strawson's explanation is defective because the problem with circularity is independent of any assumption about the simplicity of concepts. The purpose of analysis is clarification (see Passmore 1968, 363–4). If an analysis is designed to clarify something x, then making x part of the analysans undermines the attempt to clarify x. Simples are not required unless the philosopher imposes that requirement on himself. None of (i)–(iii) above describes modest connective analysis.

Modest conceptual analysis can be further illuminated by considering knowledge as justified truth belief (hereafter: JTB).[23] The analysis is supposed to satisfy a person perplexed by the nature of knowledge. That perplexity fades or disappears with the clarification provided by the conjunction of justification, truth, and belief. No explicit assumption is made about simpler concepts being essential to clarification (Passmore 1968, 363–4). If simplification occurs, it is incidental to clarity.[24] One reason that simplicity is not required is that it may introduce additional complexity. Simplifying a propositional calculus by replacing two or three sentential connectives with, say, the Sheffer stroke, $\uparrow$ ('not both p and q'), makes the calculus psychologically more complex. Also, simplicity is undesirable when it misrepresents the phenomena, an objection that Strawson levels against Quine's ontology (Strawson 1992, 41–50).

If not for the counterexamples first imagined by Edmund Gettier (1963), the analysis of knowledge as JTB would be considered illuminating, but arguably not simpler than knowledge unanalysed. Consider first the notion of truth. For most

---

[23] Strawson considers the JTB analysis to be an example of his conceptual analysis (Strawson 1992, 17–18).
[24] Descartes is famous for recommending in *Discourse on the Method of Rightly Conducting the Reason* that problems be solved by resolving them into simple parts. However, the resolution into simple parts is not itself a solution. It is a means to achieving the goal of providing a solution, not the goal itself.

philosophers in the Western tradition, truth is not simple, for it consists of correspondence, a binary relation; correspondence is thought to hold between different kinds of things, a sentence (statement, proposition, or judgement), as one term and a fact as the other; and both terms are complex.[25] Finally, modest conceptual analysis does not have a way of comparing the simplicity of something of one kind with the simplicity of another.

What about justification? It seems to be more complex than knowledge, as indicated by the many complicated attempts to analyse it. One diagnosis of the failure of the JTB analysis is that a causal chain connecting the relevant fact to the acquisition of the true belief was deviant or unreliable. But it is hard to describe precisely the conditions for a reliable causal chain; and whatever description one settles on, it seems that it will not be simple.

That leaves the concept of belief. Prima facie, it may seem simpler because it is only one component of an analysis that consists of two others. But to assert that is to beg the question of whether it is supposed to be simpler. There are general reasons to question whether belief is actually simpler. Knowledge itself may be simple; and if so, belief probably cannot be so because then they would not share any property that would connect them; and most philosophers do think they are connected (Strawson 1992, 19).

One philosopher who believes that knowledge is simpler than belief is Timothy Williamson (Williamson 2000). His reasoning is roughly that intelligence requires consciousness; consciousness is awareness of one's environment; and awareness of one's environment requires knowledge of reality or at least knowledge of the way that reality appears. Belief does not appear in this genetic account of knowledge. The genetic account also suggests that knowledge may be independent of belief.[26] An analysis current in the late 1960s and early 1970s maintained that the proper analysis of knowledge is that x knows that p if and only if x has learned that p and not forgotten that p (Ryle 1949, 272; Ryle 1974; Lemmon 1967; Vendler 1972, 118; Wilson 1926, 98–100). Belief does not seem to be hidden within the concepts of learning and forgetting. It is not a part of or a necessary stage on the way to knowledge. An analysis of learning plausibly has to do with acquiring a skill in a sense broad enough to include intellectual skills. Once something is learned,[27] one knows it until one forgets it; and forgetting does not need to pass through a stage of believing to non-believing. Another reason for thinking that knowledge and

---

[25] If a person asked for an analysis of knowing that p was told that it is a justified belief that the belief itself corresponds with a fact might be criticized as providing more than the person wanted. Also, since some philosophers thought truth was simple (Plato, Anselm of Canterbury, and Frege), others that it involves coherence, and others that it is what survives investigation, an analysans that goes beyond what is needed may introduce a mistake or needless disagreement.

[26] Knowledge and belief may be independent in that neither entails the other but connected in that knowledge would be merely belief if circumstances were different, and similarly for belief and knowledge in different circumstances.

[27] I am using 'learn' in the factive sense: 'x learned that p' entails 'it is true that p'.

belief are independent of each other is their syntactic and semantic divergence (Vendler 1972, 89–119; cf. Dunn and Suter 1977). Knowledge that p and belief that p either have different contents—the content of knowledge is facts, and the content of belief is propositions—or they are contraries with respect to their cognitive attitude, as reflected in the colloquial comment, 'I don't believe that p; I know it'.[28]

One reason that these alternative analyses are possible, I think, is that while there is a definition for conceptual simplicity—something conceptual is absolutely simple if and only if no proper part of a concept is a concept—there is no criterion or test for it. As indicated above, it is not clear how to compare knowledge and belief with respect to simplicity. One attractive feature of connective analysis is that it need assume nothing about conceptual simplicity (see Strawson 1992, 19). It is easy to imagine that a connective analysis of either knowledge or of belief would eventually lead from one to the other through intermediate concepts.

The discussion of the JTB analysis of knowledge has led to considering some connections among learning, remembering, skill, awareness, and acceptance[29] (of a proposition). Other concepts, such as sense perception, may also be relevant to a connective analysis of knowledge, as Strawson suggested (Strawson 1992, 19; 2011, 125–45). Kantians, empiricists, and others would be sympathetic to that possibility. Delineating the connections among these concepts would illuminate not only the concept of knowledge, but also the other concepts connected with it.[30] These considerations indicate that the JTB analysis of knowledge is consistent with being a part of a connective analysis.

Rather than looking for simple concepts, connective analysis aims at rigour in the sense of giving precise, explicit, and linguistically clear descriptions (Strawson 2011, 225). By linguistic clarity it is meant that analysis should be orderly, concise, and to the extent possible in non-vague and non-equivocal words.[31] It should avoid the passive voice, circumlocutions, and so on. The difference between conceptual clarity, which cannot be measured, and grammatical clarity, which can, is vast.[32]

Connective analysis presupposes that concepts congregate. But it does not presuppose semantic holism, the view that the meaning of a word depends on the meanings of other words. The reason is that the connections among beliefs are of various kinds—causal, logical, associative—and strengths, of which a semantic

---

[28] An alternative analysis is to deny that belief and knowledge are contraries and to take 'I don't believe it', as negating its conversational implication that the speaker does not know it (Horn 1985).

[29] Of course, acceptance needs to be analysed or explained.

[30] Tracking the multiple connections among various concepts sometimes results in a rank ordering, although I do not think it needs to (see Strawson 1992, 33 and 20–7).

[31] I would prefer the term 'rhetorical clarity' but almost all philosophers consider 'rhetorical' pejorative.

[32] Strawson occasionally criticized clarity as a goal of competing types of analysis (e.g. Strawson 2011, 78–83).

connection is only one (see Williams 2001, 128-37). It is not an accident that we have returned to connective analysis from a discussion of modest conceptual analysis. (Their compatibility is a theme in Section 6.)

5. Is Grice's Analysis of Various Kinds of Meaning Reductive?

Strawson and others say that Grice's analysis of meaning is reductive (Strawson 2011, 184; Strawson and Wiggins 2001, 517; Neale 1992, 542; and Mrs J. Jack to whom Grice refers 1989, 350-1). They do not (or should not) mean by this that Grice tried to eliminate some particular entity or some kind of entity, for he did not. He begins with the sense in which a person means something by directing certain intentions at another person through some behaviour. He thinks that at some stage of greater sophistication, the person becomes a speaker because the behaviour relies on language. Linguistic meaning, meaning as intending, and meaning as necessary consequence of some kind, all remain. Nor is his analysis of utterer's meaning populated by simpler concepts. *X's meaning that p by an utterance u* is analysed in terms of belief, intending, and the nesting of intentions. All three have complexity.

Rather than being an eliminative reduction, Grice's analysis of utterer's meaning was a modest conceptual analysis that had the effect of reorienting the philosophy of language, as mentioned in Section 3. Before him, analytic philosophers conceived of meaning as primarily a property of either words (notably, Russell and Michael Dummett) or sentences (notably, Frege and Austin). Grice's analyses led philosophers *back from* (*reducere*) linguistic meaning to the meanings expressed in the actions of human beings or other agents. It was hard for philosophers of the time to appreciate this because pragmatics as a philosophical discipline hardly existed. Similarly, Strawson's article 'On Referring' was supposed to reorient philosophers of language, if not logicians. It is not words of a certain form or syntactic structure that refer but people with those forms of words. Grice (and Strawson's) discussions of meaning and referring were reductive only in the sense of leading one back to origins. It is ironic that Strawson criticized Grice for taking meaning to be essentially psychological, for that was Russell's accusation against Strawson. Instead of an analysis of language, Strawson gave 'an analysis of the state of mind of those who utter sentences containing descriptions' (Russell 1957, 388; see also Donnellan 2012, 3-45, 49-52, 115-19).

One might object that my position cannot be right because Grice says without elaboration that his analysis is reductive. But his remark is paradoxical because he immediately adds that it is not 'reductionist'. The way to dispel the air of paradox is to understand 'reductionist' in the etymological or originative ways just mentioned and not in the sense of eliminating any kind of entity. He never believed that 'semantic concepts are unsatisfactory or even unintelligible unless they can be provided with interpretations in terms of some predetermined, privileged, and favored array of concepts' (Grice 1989, 351). So Grice's conception of reductive analysis was different from Strawson's. While Grice, like Strawson, allowed circular analyses for clusters of concepts, he did not demand that concepts of the analysans be *simpler* than concepts in the analysandum. If Grice's analysis is reductive, it is 'reductive lite' (Grice 1989, 351).

Grice was always open to all sorts of concepts, even such 'intensional concepts as those of intending and believing'. He thought that 'one should at least *start* by giving oneself a free hand to make use of any intensional notions or devices which seem to be required in order to solve one's conceptual problems' (Grice 1989, 137). His reason was Strawsonian: 'If one denies oneself this freedom, one runs a risk of underestimating the richness and complexity of the conceptual field one is investigating' (Grice 1989, 137). In 'Method in Philosophical Psychology', he went on at some length about his philosophical liberality:

> I am not greatly enamoured of some of the motivations which prompt the advocacy of psycho-physical identifications [for psychological phenomena]; I have in mind a concern to exclude such 'queer' or 'mysterious' entities as souls, purely mental events, purely mental properties and so forth. My taste is for keeping open house for all sorts and conditions of entities, just so long as when they come in they help with the house-work. Provided that I can see them at work, and provided that they are not detected in illicit logical behaviour (within which I do not include a certain degree of indeterminacy, not even numerical indeterminacy), I do not find them queer or mysterious at all. To fangle a new ontological Marxism, they work therefore they exist... To exclude honest working entities seems to me like metaphysical snobbery, a reluctance to be seen in the company of any but the best objects. (Grice 1975, 30–1; see also Chapman 2005, 151–2; and Petrus 2010, 2)

6. Modest Conceptual Analysis and Connective Analysis

The point of emphasizing the difference between modest conceptual analysis and Strawson's conception of conceptual connective analysis was to show how the former could be part of the latter. While Strawson maintains that reductive and serious conceptual analysis aims at simplicity, Grice, in his description of 'conceptual analysis' does not. As he says, 'To be looking for a conceptual analysis of a given expression E is to be in a position to apply or withhold E in particular cases, but to be looking for a general characterization of the types of case in which one would apply E rather than withhold it' (Grice 1989, 174). Characterizations are not simplifications; and Grice neither says nor implies anything about 'simpler elements or constituents' or 'terms...[that] are more perspicuous' (Strawson 2011, 184). Were the astute reader to inspect the analysans for utterer's meaning in Section 3 above, they would see that Grice did not rely on simpler elements or constituents than those of the analysandum, *an utterer means something* (see Grice 1989, 92). One indication that he was not in search of simplicity is the way he justifies complicating his analysis by serially introducing examples (such as the purloined and planted handkerchief and the photograph of untoward affection) that require making the analysans increasingly complex. Another indication is that the analysis he gives for intending is even more complex (Grice 1971). A separate, relevant point is Grice's position that belief and intention are interconnected with 'the concepts of planning and of acting' (Grice 1971, 270).

Strawson disparages Grice's analysis as reductive when he refers to Grice's 'persisting attachment' to something like his original 'analysis in the case of the surely problematic concept of linguistic meaning' (Strawson 2011, 184). But in what sense is linguistic meaning a 'problematic concept'? It is not problematic in the way that Hobbes thought the concept of an immaterial substance was, or that Berkeley thought the concept of an unperceived substance was, or that Quine thought that analytic and synthetic sentences were. If linguistic meaning is problematic, it is so in the same sense as knowledge, justice, and morality. They are difficult to analyse successfully. Grice's persistent advocacy of his analysis of utterer's meaning and related concepts is no more a sign that his analysis is reductive than any other philosopher's persistent championing of an unpopular view is.

Strawson's last reason for thinking that Grice's analysis of meaning is reductive is that Grice analysed meaning 'in terms of non-semantic concepts of a psychological-cum-social order' (Strawson 2011, 184). But concepts belonging to psychology and society are part of the same range of concepts as meaning. They are no more reductionist in the philosophy of language than John Locke's explanation of the origin of property in terms of mixing one's labour with something unowned is reductionist in political philosophy. The psychological, social, and proprietary concepts remain in place.

When a modest conceptual analysis of a concept *c* is part of connective analysis, it may be expected that *c* will belong to a similar range of concepts and that its analysans will include concepts that belong to a different range of concepts. The JTB analysis of knowledge takes an epistemological concept and analyses it in terms of concepts of evidence, logic, and psychological commitment. The correct analysis of the numerous concepts of meaning includes concepts from diverse classes, such as nested intentions, mental states, actions, logical and causal relations precisely because 'meaning' is multiply ambiguous. However, Grice's analysis of utterer's meaning is more conservative; both it and the concepts of the analysans are psychological ones, namely, utterer's meaning, intending, believing, and recognizing.

Grice occasionally defended philosophical entities that had become disreputable such as sense-data in 'The Causal Theory of Perception' (Grice 1989, 224–47). In 'Meaning Revisited', he connected 'reality, thought, and language or communication devices' to 'a battery of psychological concepts, which we use both about ourselves and about...lower creatures' (Grice 1989, 284). Often, he said, we want 'to invoke the contents of a psychological theory in order to explain the transition from the creature's being in the presence of the object to its eating it' (Grice 1989, 284–5). The reason for using the concepts of believing and wanting is to formulate a 'vulgar, vernacular, psychological law', where 'vulgar' is not used pejoratively but means belonging to 'the rough kind of system with which we all work' (Grice 1989, 284–5).

Grice did not accept circular analyses for stand-alone modest conceptual analyses, for example his criticism of C.L. Stevenson's account of meaning (Grice 1989, 216). And he was concerned to explain why his analysis of the timeless meaning of utterances in terms of speaker's intentions was not circular (Grice 1989, 138). But, when a modest conceptual analysis of utterer's meaning was part of a connective analysis, circularity was permitted. An example is his analysis of believing in terms of wanting and wanting in terms of believing:

> x believes that p just in case x is disposed, whenever x wants (desires) some end E, to act in ways which will realize E given that p is true rather than in ways which will realize E given that p is false... x wants E just in case x is disposed to act in ways which x *believes* will realize E rather than in ways which x *believes* will realize the negation of E. (Grice 1975, 24)

So, Grice, like Strawson, objected to circular analyses only when the circle of concepts was too small, not when it was large enough for them to be mutually elucidating (Grice 1975, 24–5; and 1989: 138–9, 142–3, 201–3, 206, 216). His views about philosophical psychology are consonant with Strawson's own view of analysis:

> it seems at least questionable whether the reductive ideal is ever attainable in the case of any of those concepts which are of central philosophical importance: these latter, including the concept of meaning [and belief and wanting] tend to remain obstinately irreducible in the sense that they cannot be defined, or completely explained, without remainder or circularity, in terms of other concepts.... Each such concept has a complexity which can be elucidated by tracing its necessary connections with other complex concepts in a system or network of connected concepts... It is for this reason that I have long advocated the replacement of the *reductive* concepts of analysis by another, which I call the *connective* model. (Strawson 2011, 184; see also 2011, 102, and 1992, 22–4)

7. Conclusion

Connective analysis is valuable because it aims at describing the interrelationships among concepts that are important or essential to human abilities and relationships. The essential ones operate even when natural scientists are engaged in their most abstruse studies, though they may not be at the forefront of consciousness. Natural science 'requires theoretical sentences to remain answerable to observation sentences; and the latter are most conveniently understood as involving reference to bodies' (Strawson 2011, 167). While examples of connective analysis can be found in Strawson's numerous works, they were also important in Grice's work in philosophical psychology, which included communicative meaning.[33]

References

Armstrong, David (1973), *Belief, Truth, and Knowledge* (Cambridge: Cambridge University Press).

Atlas, Jay David (2005), *Logic, Meaning, and Conversation* (New York: Oxford University Press).

Atlas, Jay David (2010), 'Intuition, the Paradigm Case Argument, and the Two Dogmas of Kant'otelianism', in Klaus Petrus (ed.), *Meaning and Analysis: New Essays on Grice* (Basingstoke: Palgrave Macmillan), 47–74.

Austin, J.L. (1970), *Philosophical Papers*, 2nd ed., ed. James Opie Urmson and Geoffrey James Warnock (London: Oxford University Press).

Brown, Clifford (2014), *Peter Strawson* (London: Routledge).

Chapman, Siobhan (2005), *Paul Grice* (Basingstoke: Palgrave Macmillan).

Donnellan, Keith (2012), *Essays on Reference, Language, and Mind* (New York: Oxford University Press).

Dunn, Robert, and Geraldine Suter (1977), 'Zeno Vendler on the Objects of Knowledge and Belief', *Canadian Journal of Philosophy* 7(1): 103–14.

Flew, Antony, ed. (1956), *Essays in Conceptual Analysis* (London: Macmillan).

Flew, Antony, ed. (1965), *Logic and Language*, first and second series (Garden City, NY: Anchor Books).

Gettier, Edmund (1963), 'Is Justified True Belief Knowledge?', *Analysis* 23(6): 121–3.

Grice, Paul (1971), 'Intention and Uncertainty', *Proceedings of the British Academy* 57: 263–79.

---

[33] My thanks to Jay David Atlas, Audun Bengtson, Ryan Born, Siobhan Chapman, Benjamin De Mesel, Sybren Heyndels, Leslie Martinich, and an anonymous referee for Oxford University Press, for helpful suggestions.

Grice, Paul (1975), 'Method in Philosophical Psychology', *Proceedings and Addresses of the American Philosophical Association* 48: 23–53.

Grice, Paul (1989), *Studies in the Way of Words* (Cambridge, MA: Harvard University Press).

Grice, Paul, and Strawson, Peter F. (1956), 'In Defense of a Dogma', *The Philosophical Review* 65: 141–58.

Helme, Mark (1979), 'An Elucidation of *Tractatus* 3.263', *Southern Journal of Philosophy* 17: 323–34.

Hobbes, Thomas (1651), *Leviathan* (London). References are to chapter and paragraph, followed by the page number of a 1651 edition, numbers included in all good editions of the book.

Horn, Laurence (1985), 'Metalinguistic Negation and Pragmatic Ambiguity', *Language* 61: 121–74.

Kripke, Saul (1972), *Naming and Necessity* (Cambridge, MA: Harvard University Press).

Lemmon, Edward John (1967), 'If I Know, Do I Know that I Know', in Avrum Stroll (ed.), *Epistemology: New Essays in the Theory of Knowledge* (New York: Harper & Row), 54–82.

Lycan, William (2008), *Philosophy of Language*, 2nd ed. (New York: Routledge).

Martinich, Aloysius Patrick (2005), *Hobbes* (New York: Routledge).

Neale, Stephen (1992), 'H. P. Grice', *Linguistics and Philosophy* 15(5): 509–59.

Passmore, John (1968), *A Hundred Years of Philosophy*, 2nd ed. (Harmondsworth: Penguin Books).

Petrus, Klaus, ed. (2010), *Meaning and Analysis: New Essays on Grice* (Basingstoke: Palgrave Macmillan).

Pinder, Mark (2020), 'On Strawson's Critique of Explication as a Method in Philosophy', *Synthese* 197: 955–81.

Quine, Willard Van Orman (1961), *From a Logical Point of View* (New York: Harper & Row).

Quinton, Anthony (1963–4), 'The *A Priori* and the Analytic', in Peter F. Strawson (ed.), *Philosophical Logic* (London: Oxford University Press).

Ramsey, F. P. (1990), *Philosophical Papers*, ed. D. H. Mellor (Cambridge: Cambridge University Press).

Russell, Bertrand (1957), 'Mr. Strawson on Referring', *Mind* 66(263): 385–9.

Ryle, Gilbert (1932), 'Systematically Misleading Expressions', *Proceedings of the Aristotelian Society* new series, 32: 139–70.

Ryle, Gilbert (1949), *The Concept of Mind* (London. Hutchinson).

Ryle, Gilbert (1974), 'Mowgli in Babel', *Philosophy* 49: 5–11.

Snowdon, Paul (2019), 'P. F. Strawson', in *The Stanford Encyclopedia of Philosophy* (Spring 2019 Edition), Edward N. Zalta (ed.), https://plato.stanford.edu/archives/spr2019/entries/strawson

Soames, Scott (2002), *Philosophical Analysis in the Twentieth Century* (Princeton, NJ: Princeton University Press).

Stampe, Dennis (1968), 'Toward a Grammar of Meaning', *Philosophical Review* 77(2): 137–74.

Strawson, Peter F. (1948), 'Formal Signs and Rules of Use', P. F. Strawson Archives, used by permission of Galen Strawson.

Strawson, Peter F. (1959), *Individuals* (London: Methuen). Page references are to the Anchor edition, 1963.

Strawson, Peter F. (1963), 'Carnap's Views on Constructed Systems Versus Natural Languages in Analytic Philosophy', in Paul Arthur Schilpp (ed.), *The Philosophy of Rudolf Carnap* (LaSalle, IL: Open Court), 503–18.

Strawson, Peter F. (1970), 'Categories', in Oscar Wood and George Pitcher (eds.), *Ryle* (New York: Anchor Books), 181–212.

Strawson, Peter F. (1974), *Logico-Linguistic Papers* (London: Methuen).

Strawson, Peter F. (1985), *Skepticism and Naturalism: Some Varieties* (New York: Columbia University Press).

Strawson, Peter F. (1990), 'Review of *Studies in the Way of Words*', *Synthese* 84(1): 153–61.

Strawson, Peter F. (1992), *Analysis and Metaphysics* (Oxford: Oxford University Press).

Strawson, Peter F. (2011), *Philosophical Writings*, ed. Galen Strawson and Michelle Montague (Oxford: Oxford University Press).

Strawson, Peter F., and David Wiggins (2001), 'Herbert Paul Grice 1913–1988', *Proceedings of the British Academy* 111: 515–28.

Tomasello, Michael (2008), *Origins of Human Communication* (Cambridge, MA: MIT Press).

Vendler, Zeno (1972), *Res Cogitans* (Ithaca, NY: Cornell University Press).

Waldron, Jeremy (1984), 'Introduction', in Jeremy Waldron (ed.), *Theories of Rights* (Oxford: Oxford University Press), 1–20.

Wiggins, David (1991), *Needs, Values, Truth*, 2nd ed. (Oxford: Blackwell).

Williams, Michael (2001), *Problems of Knowledge* (New York: Oxford University Press), 128–37.

Williamson, Timothy (2000), *Knowledge and Its Limits* (Oxford: Oxford University Press).

Wilson, John Cook (1926), *Statement and Inference* (Oxford: Clarendon Press).

Wittgenstein, Ludwig (1958), *Philosophical Investigations*, 2nd ed., trans. Gertrude Elizabeth Margaret Anscombe (Oxford: Basil Blackwell).

11
Responsibility After 'Morality'
Strawson's Naturalism and Williams's Genealogy

Paul Russell

...there is a quite general ambiguity in the notion of 'our ordinary concept' of whatever it might be. Should the lineaments of such a concept be drawn exclusively from its use, from our ordinary *practice*, or should we add the reflective accretions, however confused, which, naturally and historically, gather around it?

– P. F. Strawson (1980, 265)

Scepticism about the freedom of morality from luck cannot leave the concept of morality where it was...

– Bernard Williams (1976/1981, 39)

1. Introduction

The views of P. F. Strawson and Bernard Williams on the subject of moral responsibility have both been highly influential. Strawson's influence drives largely from his 1962 British Academy lecture 'Freedom and Resentment', which has attracted a great deal of comment and criticism in the six decades that have followed its publication.[1] Williams's views have been presented in several different works, including two or three particularly significant papers published in the 1970s and 1980s, as well as his book *Shame and Necessity*, published in 1993.[2] It is, however, a striking and, perhaps, surprising fact that despite their overlapping concerns, and their considerable influence and profile on this subject, neither Strawson nor Williams directly engaged with each other's

---

[1] Collections on Strawson include: McKenna and Russell (2008/2016); Shoemaker and Tognazzini (2014).

[2] The papers I have particularly in mind are: 'Moral Luck' (1976/1981); 'How Free Does the Will Need to Be?' (1985/1995); and 'Internal Reasons and the Obscurity of Blame' (1989/1995). All these works are, in various ways, closely connected with each other and with *Ethics and the Limits of Philosophy* (1985/2011), which might be considered a pivotal work for a more general understanding of Williams's views on this subject. For an overview of Williams's views on ethics see Russell (2018).

Paul Russell, *Responsibility After 'Morality': Strawson's Naturalism and Williams's Genealogy* In: *P. F. Strawson and his Philosophical Legacy*. Edited by: Sybren Heyndels, Audun Bengtson, and Benjamin De Mesel, Oxford University Press.
© Oxford University Press 2024. DOI: 10.1093/oso/9780192858474.003.0012

views. Their views are, nevertheless, very relevant to one another and, depending on how they are read or interpreted, may be understood to be in direct opposition.

The central aim of Strawson's 'Freedom and Resentment' is to discredit scepticism about moral responsibility by employing a set of naturalistic arguments.[3] In contrast with this, Williams employs (Nietzschean-style) genealogy to raise sceptical worries and doubts about 'moral responsibility' and 'blame'.[4] Taken at face value, this suggests that they are at cross-purposes with each other. This is true, however, only on the assumption that the concept of moral responsibility that Strawson aims to defend is the same as the concept Williams aims to discredit. Another way of assessing this situation is to ask whether or not Strawson's naturalistic argument relies on the 'peculiar' assumptions and aspirations of 'the morality system', which is the more general target of Williams's (destructive) genealogical critique? It is this issue that is the central concern of this chapter.

2. Responsibility, Scepticism, and Strawson's Naturalism

Strawson's principal aim in 'Freedom and Resentment' is, as we have noted, to provide a naturalistic response to scepticism about moral responsibility. The source of the sceptical challenge is the claim that if the thesis of determinism is true then all our attitudes and practices associated with moral responsibility (praise and blame, rewards and punishments, etc.) are really unjustified. This sceptical challenge lies at the heart of the traditional free will problem. Strawson's naturalistic rejoinder is constructed around what he takes to be the (shared) flaws of the standard positions on this subject. As presented by Strawson there are two opposing positions on this subject: which he labels as the 'Optimist' and the 'Pessimist'. (Throughout this chapter these labels are capitalized to indicate their use.) The Optimist is essentially the classic compatibilist view. It maintains that the truth of determinism would in no way systematically discredit the concepts and practices associated with moral responsibility. The concept of moral responsibility that the Optimist is concerned with places heavy emphasis on the efficacy or utilitarian benefits of our practices of blame and punishment and the role that they play in 'regulating behaviour in socially desirable ways' (Strawson 1962/2013, 64). The Optimist's 'one-eyed utilitarianism', critics maintain, involves ignoring or eliminating any relevant role for *deserved* blame and punishment, along with notions of guilt, condemnation, and justice that rest on concerns about

---

[3] Strawson refers to his approach to the sceptical challenge as 'the way of naturalism' and he describes himself as following Hume's lead in this respect (Strawson 1985, esp. 10–14, 31–42).

[4] See, in particular, Williams's remarks in the opening chapter of *Shame and Necessity*, where he says that we have reason 'for being doubtful about "moral responsibility"' (Williams 1993, 7; see also Williams 1985/1995). Perhaps Williams's most sceptical remarks about moral responsibility and blame are presented in 'Interview with Bernard Williams' (1994, 4–5, 11–12).

desert (Strawson 1962/2013, 64–5, 79–81). Because they are heavily focused on 'forward-looking considerations', and give little weight to 'backward-looking' considerations relating to desert, views of this kind strongly encourage a policy of 'treatment and control'. From this perspective the agent is viewed as someone 'to be managed or handled or cured or trained', a person who we respond to in detached, instrumental terms (Strawson 1962/2013, 69, 79).[5]

The Pessimist, as Strawson understands this view, is an incompatibilist and finds the Optimist approach not only inadequate but inhuman (Strawson 1962/2013, 71–3, 79–80). According to the Pessimist there is 'something vital' left out of the Optimist's account. This 'gap' in the Optimist's account 'can be filled only if some general metaphysical proposition is verified' (Strawson 1962/2013, 64, 81–2). Although this proposition has proved difficult to state it is generally taken to involve a kind of 'freedom' that requires the falsity of determinism (e.g. contra-causal freedom of some sort). According to some Pessimists (i.e. libertarians) we can rescue desert-involving responsibility only if a freedom of this nature is possible for human beings. If we are to remedy 'the conceptual deficiencies' of the Optimist account, then we must have 'recourse to the obscure and panicky metaphysics of libertarianism' (Strawson 1962/2013, 83).

Strawson rejects both the Optimist and Pessimist accounts. He believes, nevertheless, that with suitable modifications and adjustments, we can arrive at a position that can 'reconcile' them (Strawson 1962/2013, 63). The shared error in the Optimist and Pessimist accounts, Strawson suggests, is that both 'over-intellectualize the facts' (Strawson 1962/2013, 81). The right place to begin is not with either utilitarian benefits or forms of contra-causal freedom but rather with the fundamental and ordinary fact of 'the very great importance that we attach to the attitudes and intentions towards us of other human beings, and the great extent to which our personal feelings and reactions depend upon, or involve, our beliefs about these attitudes and intentions' (Strawson 1962/2013, 66). Our concern with the value that we place on the attitudes and intentions of others takes the form of a general demand for good will or regard (Strawson 1962/2013, 67, 68, 74). The making of this demand is itself manifest or expressed in the form of our proneness to reactive attitudes, such as resentment and gratitude, or moral indignation, guilt, hurt feelings, and shame (Strawson 1962/2013, 66, 68, 69, 74, 79–80). It is in respect of these universal and fundamental features of human (moral) psychology that we need to locate the foundations of what is involved in holding others responsible and viewing a person as a member of the moral community (Strawson 1962/2013, 80). It is these facts about our proneness to reactive attitudes of 'moral sentiments' which serve to fill the gap in the Optimist's account.

---

[5] One obvious target of Strawson's criticism is Schlick (1939/1966). More recent versions of views of this kind can also be found. See, for example, Dennett (1984) which presents an 'engineering' model of responsibility (esp. 139–44, 153–69).

Once the 'complicated web of attitudes and feelings which form an essential part of moral life as we know it' is restored to its proper (foundational) place, we are better placed to address the question concerning the implications of the thesis of determinism for moral responsibility (Strawson 1962/2013, 80). The right way to approach this problem, Strawson argues, is to ask if the truth of determinism would require us to entirely abandon our commitment to the reactive attitudes, such as praise and blame, along with the practices of rewards and punishments that rest upon them. The theory of excuses and exemptions provides the relevant framework for assessing this issue.[6] The Pessimist maintains that if determinism is true, excusing considerations will (somehow) apply to all human action or hold universally. In reply, Strawson points out that excusing considerations apply when they indicate that the agent's will was such that it does not display any malice or lack of due care and concern. In cases such as ignorance, accidents, or coercion, we see that any injury caused is not due to objectionable motivations or an absence of good will. Nothing about the thesis of determinism implies that excuses of some kind apply universally or that in these circumstances we could no longer draw relevant distinctions along these lines (i.e. between actions that do or do not manifest ill will) (Strawson 1962/2013, 68–71). Where excuses do apply the agent is still an appropriate target of reactive attitudes but we have no reason to believe that the basic demand has been violated.

In the case of exemptions our reasoning is different. Exemptions are based on considerations that show that in some way the agent concerned is not an appropriate target of reactive attitudes. In cases of this kind we cannot reasonably expect the agent to comply with the basic demand because the agent is either psychologically abnormal or immature (Strawson 1962/2013, 68–71). The agent cannot, in these circumstances, effectively participate in the human (moral) community (Strawson 1962/2013, 72, 75–6, 80). Nothing about the thesis of determinism implies that every agent is in some relevant way abnormal or immature (e.g. mentally ill, a child). It follows from this that, contrary to the claim of the Pessimist, no relevant excusing or exempting considerations can be generalized on the basis of considerations of determinism.[7]

Strawson's naturalist response to scepticism leads to the conclusion that 'if we sufficiently, that is *radically*, modify the views of the optimist, his view is the right one' (Strawson 1962/2013, 82, Strawson's emphasis). The radical modification is that the compatibilist claim that is at the core of the Optimist's position can be

---

[6] Strawson speaks of 'two kinds' of consideration that might lead us to modify or withdraw our reactive attitudes (Strawson 1962/2013, 68). The excuse/exemption contrast marks this distinction.

[7] There is, of course, a second (and stronger) line of argument that Strawson advances in response to the sceptical challenge. This is based on his claim that whatever theoretical or philosophical objections may be advanced, it would be *psychologically impossible* for us to entirely suspend or 'systematically dislodge our commitment to reactive attitudes' (Strawson 1962/2013, 71–2, 77); see also Strawson (1985, 32–3, 39). For criticism of this (distinct) line of argument see Russell (1992/2017; 2011/2017, esp. 74–7; 2017c, 98–101).

accepted only if we reject the inadequate forward-looking, utilitarian oriented concept of moral responsibility that they rely on. Let us call the Optimist's conception U-responsibility (or the U-concept). Strawson agrees with the pessimist that there is 'a lacuna in the optimist's story' and that the crucial missing element involves desert (Strawson 1962/2013, 7, 65, 79, 80–1; see also Strawson 1980, 261–2). A credible compatibilism must, therefore, secure a desert-based conception of moral responsibility. Let us call this D-responsibility (or the D-conception). The mistake that the Pessimist makes is to assume that the only way to 'plug the gap' and provide some relevant foundation for desert is on the basis of 'the panicky metaphysics of libertarianism' and related claims about 'the falsity of determinism' (Strawson 1962/2013, 64, 81, 83). The Pessimist advances a particular interpretation of D-responsibility—let us call it D*-responsibility (or the D*-conception)—that is simply incoherent and unintelligible (Strawson 1962/2013, 81; see also Strawson 1980, 264–5).

The force of Strawson's naturalist alternative is that any relevant account of responsibility, one that is adequate to 'the facts as we know them', must begin with the value we (naturally and inescapably) place on 'the quality of others' wills towards us' (Strawson 1962/2013, 73, 81). The importance that we attach to this is manifest, and is of a (psychological) piece, with our liability or proneness to reactive attitudes or moral sentiments (Strawson 1962/2013, 80–1). Beyond this, however, these general facts about the conditions and circumstances of D-responsibility, 'neither call for, nor permit, an external "rational" justification' (Strawson 1962/2013, 81). While there remains 'endless room' for modification, redirection, criticism, and justification within this 'web of attitudes and feelings', there is no question of us being required to (or capable of) altogether discarding this psychological apparatus and the forms of human (moral) life based upon it.

3. Responsibility, 'Morality', and Williams's Genealogy

Bernard Williams's views about moral responsibility are intimately connected with his more general critique of what he refers to as 'the morality system'.[8] In respect of his concern with the morality system Williams is rightly regarded as a (deeply) sceptical or 'negative' thinker. A central feature of the morality system, as Williams understands it, is its particular conception of moral responsibility.[9] Much of Williams's discussion of responsibility is devoted to discrediting the account of it advanced by the morality system. A particular target of Williams's

---

[8] Williams (1985/2011, esp. chap. 10). For a general account of Williams's critique of 'the morality system' see Russell (2018).

[9] Along with *Shame and Necessity* and the papers mentioned in note 2 above, see also Williams (1995b, 575–8). See also Williams's remarks at (1985/2011, 41–4, 216–18). For an overview of Williams's views on this topic see Russell (2022b); and Queloz (2022).

various sceptical arguments in this direction is the 'purified conception of blame' that morality attaches special importance to (Williams 1993/1995a, 72-4; 1985/1995, 14-19). Williams regards blame and guilt as the most 'characteristic' reactions of morality (Williams 1985/2011, 197, 215-16; 1993, 91-3; 1985/1995, 15-16). Related to this observation, Williams also suggests that morality is prone to 'binary judgements' that flatten 'the range of attitudes, both positive and negative' (Williams 1985/2011, 42-3; also 1976/1981, 38). To understand all this we need to describe the most general features of the morality system.

The morality system is not, Williams suggests, a creation of philosophers but 'part of the outlook... of almost all of us' (Williams 1985/2011, 194). As such, it is embodied in our actual attitudes and practices. Although its exact nature is not easily summarized, its essential conceptual features can be described. The most fundamental of these is 'morality's' special notion of obligation (Williams 1985/2011, 7-9, 193). The obligations that morality is concerned with assume a sharp distinction between 'moral' and 'non-moral considerations' and give overriding weight to the former (Williams 1985/2011, 209, 218). These moral obligations serve as 'practical necessities' for the agent and are bound up with two other key concepts: voluntariness and blame. Moral obligations are grounded in reasons that are available to all (i.e. to 'the universal constituency') and they impose demands that attract blame and retribution when they are voluntarily violated (Williams 1985/2011, 200; 1993/1995a, 72-4). Blame carries the heavy baggage of retribution, holding that those who violate (moral) obligations *deserve* to suffer as a matter of justice (i.e. this is a requirement of a just moral order). Williams suggests that 'the most thorough representation of morality is Kant' and allows that, in this respect (i.e. retribution) utilitarianism is 'a marginal member' (Williams 1985/2011, 194, 197). Utilitarianism remains, nevertheless, 'deeply entangled with morality' (Williams 1985/1995, 17).

With this conceptual apparatus in place, other key features of morality that Williams rejects fall into place. This includes 'the purity of morality', which holds that it must not be tainted or corrupted by 'other kinds of emotional reaction or social influences' (Williams 1985/2011, 17-18, 43, 216; see also 1993, 91-5, 158). Most importantly morality must be immune to the influence of luck. This is essential if morality is to satisfy its ideal of 'ultimate justice' (Williams 1985/2011, 43, 216-17). The requirement that agents be (somehow) able to 'transcend luck', Williams argues, 'puts too much pressure on the voluntary' (Williams 1985/2011, 215-18; 1985/1995, 16-17; 1993/1995a, 72-5; 1993/1995b, 241-2). In order to satisfy these demands, and morality's 'peculiar' conception of moral responsibility—let us call this M-responsibility (or the M-concept)—we need to further refine or 'deepen' the idea of 'the voluntary'.[10] Judged by this ideal

---

[10] Understood this way, M-responsibility aims to deliver *pure* desert—untainted by contingency, luck, or fate. Any form of *just* retribution needs to be grounded in this (pure) source.

standard, the mundane materials provided by intentions, choice, deliberation, and related concepts of this (psychological) kind are insufficient and 'not what we really need' (Williams 1993, 40, 67-8; 1985/1995, 8-9). The 'metaphysical fuel' required to satisfy this ideal is 'limitless freedom' or 'total control' of some kind (Williams 1985/2011, 63-5, 216; 1993, 7, 94-5, 152-4, 158; 1994, 4-5, 11-12; 1995b, 578; 2002/2009, 203). As Williams sees it, all this is entirely 'illusory' and a 'fantasy'.[11]

The morality system, and the conception of M-responsibility that is essential to it involves, according to Williams, 'a powerful misconception of life' (Williams 1985/2011, 218). Its origins are heavily steeped in Christianity and suggest an untruthful picture of our ethical predicament (Williams 2002/2009, 203; 1993, 4, 9-12, 94-5; 1993/1995a, 72-4; 1994, 11-12).[12] All things considered, we are 'better off' without morality (Williams 1985/2011, 193; 1994, 9-10). Williams's principal method for exposing the falsity of this picture of human ethical life is through a (Nietzsche-style) genealogy, which is presented in the greatest detail in *Shame and Necessity*.[13] It is evident that there is a strong sceptical thread running through Williams's position on this subject. A prime target of this scepticism is M-responsibility and the assumptions and aspirations that are essential to it. What does not follow from this, however, is that Williams was a sceptic about responsibility *tout court*.[14]

Williams describes genealogy as 'a narrative that tries to explain an outlook or a value by describing how it came about' (Williams 2002/2009, 210).[15] When we consider a concept or value in these terms our confidence in it may be strengthened or weakened. If the former, we may describe our genealogical reflections as being 'vindicatory'; if the latter, they are 'critical' or 'destructive' (Williams 2002/2009, 198-9, 210; 2002, 35-8; 2002/2014, 409-12; 1998, 258). The question arises, therefore, is Williams's genealogy of our concepts related to responsibility vindicatory or destructive? The answer to this question turns on what concept (or concepts) of responsibility we are concerned with. With respect to M-responsibility the answer is clear: Williams's genealogical critique aims to discredit 'responsibility' and 'blame' as morality understands them. In taking this view Williams follows the footsteps of Nietzsche (Williams 1993, 9; 1994, 4-5;

---

[11] The key additional item required for 'morality' to secure its ideal of ultimate justice is the (rational) 'will', understood as the essential instrument of 'total control' (Williams 1993, 36, 40, 46).

[12] Williams points out that although the terms 'moral' and 'ethical' are often used interchangeably, they have different origins and different connotations. Williams uses the term 'moral' to flag its specific associations with the 'distinctive content' of 'the morality system'. See Williams (1985/2011, 7-13).

[13] Also relevant is Williams (1993/1995a, esp. 75 n.12) and Williams (2002/2009, 198-9, 210). For an account of this aspect of Williams's methodology see Russell (2022b).

[14] There are, nevertheless, some passages that may encourage the view that he was an unqualified sceptic about responsibility: e.g. Williams (1985/1995, 6-7; 1986/2014, 264-5).

[15] And see, more generally, Williams (2002, chap. 2).

1993/1995a, 72–5).¹⁶ The target here is not, as Williams points out, 'a universal human phenomenon but a particular historical formation' (Williams 2002, 38).¹⁷

There is, nevertheless, another side to Williams's genealogical critique of responsibility that is *vindicatory*, not destructive. This non-sceptical side of his genealogical narrative relies heavily on reflections on 'the Greeks' and tragedy. When we look to the Greeks, we find that they lacked the distinctive conceptual apparatus and aims of 'morality'. But this does not mean that they lacked any conception of responsibility. Nor does it imply, contrary to what the 'progressivist' account suggests, that their way of interpreting it was far removed from our own (modern, Western) view (Williams 1993, chap. 1; 1994, 11–12; 2002/2009, 203). What they share with us are the same essential psychological materials or 'elements' required for human ethical life, including intention, belief, and desire (Williams 1993, 33–4, 55, 67–8, 152). These 'universal materials' and shared elements are not interpreted in the same way in all cultures and societies but we should not suppose that there is one 'correct' interpretation or concept of responsibility (Williams 1993, 55–6). In this way, what we learn from the Greeks, Williams argues, is not only that our own conception of M-responsibility is not self-evidently superior, but that in important respects it is actually in much worse condition and much less truthful about human ethical life.¹⁸ What follows from this is that while Williams was a sceptic about M-responsibility, he was not a sceptic about responsibility in more general terms—it is only our 'local' (modern, Western) conception that he calls into question.¹⁹

It might be tempting to present the split between the destructive and vindicatory dimensions of Williams's genealogy in terms of the divide between libertarianism and compatibilism. It is certainly true that the aspirations of libertarian metaphysics to secure some form of 'ultimate' agency or 'limitless freedom' is motivated by the concerns of morality (Williams 1985/2011, 63–5, 196–8; 1976/1981, 20–1; 1994, 4–5; 1985/1995, 6–7, 17; 1993/1995a, 72; 1993, 66–8, 152, 158). It is also true that in rejecting M-responsibility Williams is rejecting libertarian understandings of moral responsibility, much as Strawson rejects D*-responsibility. It is not true, however, that his critical genealogy is directed exclusively against libertarianism and its metaphysically extravagant claims. On the contrary, as Williams makes clear, most compatibilists are also 'wedded' to M-responsibility (Williams 1985/1995, 7, 19; 1995b, 578). The question arises, therefore, what is the

---

¹⁶ On the Williams–Nietzsche relationship see Clark (2001), and (the contrasting views of) Leiter (2022).
¹⁷ And see, more generally, Williams (1993, chap. 1).
¹⁸ This aspect of Williams's genealogical critique is discussed in more detail in Russell (2022b).
¹⁹ Among the universal materials of responsibility that Williams identifies are reactive attitudes (Williams 1985/2011, 41–4). The point that Williams would emphasize, in relation to reactive attitudes, is that they vary a great deal, depending on our particular ethical culture. The tendency of 'morality' is to reduce and impoverish the available range of such reactions, with a heavy emphasis on 'blame' and 'guilt' (Williams 1985/2011, 197, 212; 1993, chap. 4).

significance of Williams's genealogical critique of M-responsibility for Strawson's naturalistic account of D-responsibility?

4. The Basic Opposition

It is clear that if Williams's critique of M-responsibility was targeted only against (libertarian) D*-responsibility then there would be no conflict between his critique and Strawson's naturalism, since Strawson also rejects D*-responsibility. However, as we have noted, Williams argues that there are many compatibilists who are comfortable members of the M-responsibility family. Given this, it is possible to reject D*-responsibility without rejecting M-responsibility. With regard to Strawson's naturalism, we need to ask if he takes his naturalistic defence of D-responsibility (detached from 'the panicky metaphysics of libertarianism'), as still satisfying the aims and assumptions of morality and M-responsibility? If that is the case, then there would be a direct opposition between the views of Strawson and Williams (despite their shared scepticism about D*-responsibility).

Is there any evidence that Strawson's naturalist arguments should be read as supportive of M-responsibility? One reason for reading Strawson this way is that this is how some of his most prominent followers have presented and advanced his views. A notable example of this is found in R. Jay Wallace's *Responsibility and the Moral Sentiments* (1994). In this work Wallace defends and elaborates on a (neo-Strawsonian) naturalist account of moral responsibility, one that combines a Strawsonian account of holding responsible with a Kantian theory of moral agency (or rational self-control). Drawing on materials found in 'Freedom and Resentment', Wallace defends a 'narrower' interpretation of moral responsibility, where 'the basic stance of holding someone morally responsible involves a susceptibility to reactive attitudes [i.e. negative reactive attitudes such as resentment, indignation and guilt] if the person breaches moral obligations we accept' (Wallace 1994, 66; see also 29–33). Wallace goes on to point out, rightly, that his (narrower) construal of the Strawsonian view is consistent with the essentials of the 'morality system' and its (distinctive) understanding of M-responsibility (Wallace 1994, 39–40, 64–6). Where Wallace diverges from Strawson, apart from his narrower interpretation of reactive attitudes, is that he rejects the suggestion that M-responsibility (as he presents it) is a universal or 'inescapable' feature of human nature or society.[20] It is, Wallace suggests, 'at least conceivable that there might be cultures whose members do not have the stance of holding people to expectations in their repertoire' (Wallace 1994, 38–9, 64–5).[21]

---

[20] See Strawson (1962/2013, 71–3, 81; 1985, 32–39, 41).

[21] This is not, of course, a minor deviation from the original Strawsonian programme. Suffice it to say that if we assume, with Wallace, that the Strawsonian programme should be (narrowly) construed

On the sort of 'modified reading' of Strawson that Wallace proposes, Strawson's concept of D-responsibility more or less converges with M-responsibility. More generally, Strawson's arguments are understood to be drawing on and defending the morality system by placing its (distinct) conception of moral responsibility on naturalistic foundations. How credible is this reading of Strawson?[22] There is certainly much in Strawson's discussion that lends itself to this interpretation. An important feature of Strawson's system is the emphasis that he places on our concerns with 'quality of will' (Strawson 1962/2013, 65, 68, 73, 80). An agent's quality of will is assessed in relation to the relevant 'moral demands' and 'obligations' that they are subject to and expected to comply with (Strawson 1962/2013, 74; see also 1961/1974, 30–3, 35–8). As Strawson sees it, any functioning human society requires a system of 'socially sanctioned' demands or rules such that 'the generality of those subject to moral demands must genuinely recognize some obligations under the system of demands' (Strawson 1961/1974, 36–7, Strawson's emphasis).[23] Consistent with the orientation of M-responsibility, Strawson places heavy emphasis on 'negative' moral emotions, such as blame, moral condemnation, indignation, and guilt (Strawson 1962/2013, 63, 64, 65, 74, 79, 80–1). He also ties these (negative) moral emotions to our retributive dispositions and propensities. Punishment and our willingness to 'acquiesce' to the suffering of the offender are, Strawson maintains, 'all of a piece with this whole range of attitudes' (Strawson 1962/2013, 80). Clearly, then, on this account responsibility and retribution are tightly woven together and part of our natural, universal human psychology.

Perhaps the most striking evidence that Strawson does not share Williams's sceptical attitude with regard to M-responsibility is that he expresses few if any doubts about the conceptual apparatus involved, much less shows any general discomfort with our 'ordinary' moral concepts and practices. Strawson does express doubts about D*-responsibility and accepts that notions of this kind may 'infect' our 'ordinary concept'. To this extent, he allows that confusions of this kind may have 'naturally or historically' gathered around our ordinary concept (Strawson 1980, 265). He insists, nevertheless, that 'the lineaments of such a concept... [should] be drawn exclusively from its use, from our ordinary *practice*' (Strawson 1980, 265, Strawson's emphasis). This concept, which is built

in terms of M-responsibility, and we also accept, with Wallace (and Williams), that M-responsibility is a local, contingent cultural achievement, then key elements of the original Strawsonian programme collapse. For a more detailed discussion of this see Russell (2013/2017).

[22] As I explain below, even if this a reasonable *interpretation*, it still may not be the best way to advance or develop Strawson's arguments from a *critical* perspective. It may be that the best way to advance Strawson's naturalistic programme is to move it in the *opposite* direction—i.e. *away* from the morality system.

[23] Strawson acknowledges that the specific demands in question may well vary from one community to another. Such variation, however, should not be exaggerated. 'It is important to recognize', he says, 'that certain human interests are so fundamental and so general that they must be acknowledged in some form and to some degree in any conceivable moral community'.

around the 'complicated web of attitudes and feelings' that he describes, forms 'an essential part of moral life as we know it' (Strawson 1962/2013, 80). Understood this way, our 'ordinary concept' is not only unproblematic, it is indispensable to human existence. All this suggests that Strawson's arguments are not unfriendly to 'the morality system' and M-responsibility. If this is correct, then Strawson's naturalistic vindication of D-responsibility may be interpreted as a vindication of M-responsibility, unencumbered by the obscure and incoherent metaphysical baggage of D*-responsibility. Clearly, however, this reading would return us to a direct *opposition* between Strawson and Williams on this subject.

5. The Case for Reconciliation

While there is some basis for reading Strawson as a proponent of 'morality', there are several considerations that tell against it.

(1) Consider, first, the issue of freedom. In 'Freedom and Resentment' Strawson says very little about the problem of freedom as it concerns moral responsibility. Although he makes a few passing remarks about it the focus of his attention lies elsewhere, with his account of the reactive attitudes and excusing considerations.[24] Nor does he attach much importance to the debate about 'alternate possibilities' or the requirement that the responsible agent 'could have acted otherwise', even though this is a topic that has dominated much of the debate. To the extent that Strawson has anything to say about this matter, he suggests that it can be easily interpreted within the framework of various excusing considerations of a more particular kind, unrelated to determinism.[25] Beyond this, Strawson also makes no effort to provide for forms of 'self-creation' of any kind.[26] Strawson, like Williams, is entirely satisfied with the mundane, familiar materials of human agency

---

[24] For Strawson's remarks relating to freedom in 'Freedom and Resentment' (1962/2013, 64, 65, 78, 81; also 1985, 32, 40–1; 1992, 133–42). See also Strawson (1962/2013, 80).

[25] This response is implicit in his (cursory) remarks in 'Freedom and Resentment' (1962/2013, 68). In his later writings, coming after 'Freedom and Resentment', Strawson does say a bit more about this issue in the context of responding to several of his critics. Ayer argues, for example, that the thesis of determinism implies that no agent could have acted otherwise and that this implies that agents lack the sort of freedom required for desert (Ayer 1980, 6–9; Strawson 1980, 261–2). Strawson's basic reply to this line of criticism is to deny that the ordinary or common moral requirement that an agent could have acted otherwise, concerning '*certain specific kinds of natural impediments*', is equivalent to a more general requirement concerning the absence of sufficient natural impediments '*of any kind whatsoever*' (Strawson 1983/2011, 150; 1992, 136–7). In general, Strawson aims to *deflate* this whole issue, while adopting a familiar (classical) compatibilist line on it. For a helpful analysis of Strawson's later comments on this issue, including interesting criticism coming from Rajendra Prasad (1995), see De Mesel (2022).

[26] Strawson's lack of concern with this issue contrasts sharply not only with libertarians (who aim to 'deepen' moral freedom in these terms) but also with both sceptics and other compatibilists. See, e.g., Dennett (1984, chap. 4) and G. Strawson (1994/2013).

and moral psychology, such as belief, desire, intention, and choice. With regard to familiar incompatibilist (i.e. 'Pessimist') concerns about 'conditioning' and 'manipulation', Strawson is casually dismissive of sceptical objections developed along these lines. 'We can', he says, 'cheerfully acknowledge that conditioning by reinforcement and its contrary is, and always has been, in full operation upon us anyway; though not, mercifully, under the direction of omnipotent authority' (Strawson 1980, 264).[27] None of this is what we should expect from someone who aims to defend a conception of M-responsibility. It suggests that Strawson believes that D-responsibility need *not* meet the standards of morality and M-responsibility. Contrary to Ayer and others, Strawson is arguing that (moral) desert should not be interpreted in terms of M-responsibility and the assumptions and aspirations that it rests on—not the least because this only encourages the 'ultimately unintelligible' D*-conceptions, which then leads on to undiluted scepticism (Strawson 1980, 264–5; 1992, 133; 1998, 261).

(2) Closely related to Strawson's lack of interest in 'refining' or 'deepening' our concept of freedom is his attitude to the issue of moral luck and an agent's history. In 'Freedom and Resentment' he does mention the problem of an agent's 'formative circumstances', which may be unfortunate. The relevance of this, according to Strawson, is limited to the way in which it may indicate that the agent's ability to effectively participate in the moral community is somehow damaged or impaired (i.e. on analogy with cases of mental illness or immaturity) (Strawson 1962/2013, 66–7). That is to say, agential history (e.g. childhood deprivation) serves as an exempting condition only in so far as it provides evidence of impaired moral competence.[28] Being determined is not, by itself, a relevant exempting consideration.

In *Scepticism and Naturalism* Strawson mentions Thomas Nagel's (admirable) paper 'Moral Luck' and its concluding worry that if we see agents and their actions as simply part of the natural causal order 'then the veil of illusion cast over them by moral attitudes and reactions must, or should, slip away' (Strawson 1985, 32). This sort of (Pessimistic) worry encourages theories of self-determination (i.e. D* views) that are not only unintelligible, they are, Strawson claims, misguided because they incorrectly assume that we can be 'reasoned out' of our moral reactive attitudes by sceptical reflections of this kind. At no point, however, does Strawson engage with the sort of specific worries about luck that Nagel mentions, relating to the limits on our forms of self-control or the circumstances of (moral) choice that we may confront in life. Those who are committed to M-responsibility cannot be so easily satisfied with a response that simply *ignores*

---

[27] Contrast Ayer's objection to Strawson's position: 'let us suppose that a theory of conditioning were developed...' (Ayer 1980, 9). See also Strawson's (unconcerned) remarks concerning the suggestion 'that a multitude of influences in the agent's past...made the agent just what he currently is' (Strawson 1998, 261).
[28] Wallace pursues and further develops this line of reasoning in *Responsibility and the Moral Sentiments* (1994, 166, 214, 231–5).

the concerns being raised.[29] The general stance that Strawson takes with respect to issues about luck and fate (or agential history) is that sceptical concerns of this kind are a clear case of philosophical extravagance and excessive over-intellectualization of moral life and practice. Our actual practices, Strawson maintains, avoid all this and we should not attempt to cater to it (Strawson 1980, 265).

(3) For the morality system, in its purest Kantian form, the relationship between blame and retribution is tight. Blame has 'positive' retributive force, whereby justified blame implies an *obligation* to punish the wrongdoer.[30] On this view, *justice* demands that those who violate their obligations receive a due measure of retribution (i.e. imposed suffering or pain of some kind). Strawson shows no inclination to endorse any such view. Although Strawson insists that justified punishment needs to be deserved and properly supported by (backward-looking) considerations relating to the (intentional) violation of moral norms, he also emphasizes the importance of 'social utility' as a check or constraint on such practices (Strawson 1962/2013, 80).[31] Strawson in no way endorses any form of 'positive' or 'pure' retributivism on the basis of his naturalistic arguments (e.g. in contrast with Mackie). Clearly, then, while D-responsibility, as Strawson presents it, denies that justified punishment can be understood 'in terms of social utility alone' (i.e. contrary to U-conceptions), there is no evidence that he accepts principles of positive retribution of the sort associated with 'morality' and M-responsibility.

(4) In the closing paragraphs of 'Freedom and Resentment' Strawson turns his attention to the relevance of moral variation and relativism for his account of the reactive attitudes. He begins by noting that, with regard to the 'network of human attitudes' which he has been describing, there is much greater 'historical and anthropological awareness of the great variety of forms which [they] may take at different times and in different cultures'. He continues:

> This makes one rightly chary of claiming as essential features of the concept of morality in general, forms of these attitudes which may have a local and temporary prominence. No doubt to some extent my own descriptions of

---

[29] This is true not only of Nagel but is also evident in Watson's (mostly sympathetic) discussion of Strawson's views (Watson, 1987/2013).

[30] A clear example of M-responsibility understood this way is presented in G. Strawson (1994/2013). See, in particular, his account of the relationship between 'true moral responsibility' and justified punishment as it concerns 'the story of heaven and hell' (366–7). A similar view is presented by J. L. Mackie (1982/1985). Mackie argues that 'the principle of positive retributivism' or 'retaliation' is essential to our reactive attitudes and ordinary moral thinking. According to Mackie, we should not aim to justify this connection between our reactive attitudes and positive retribution but rather *explain* it in biological, evolutionary terms.

[31] It may be argued that Strawson's (brief) views concerning punishment and retribution are suggestive of a 'mixed' or teleological-retributivist view, as developed and articulated by Hart (1959/1968). (There are some strong affinities between Hart's and Strawson's views relating to responsibility and punishment, especially as this relates to their shared aim of preserving a robust role for the concept of desert.)

human attitudes have reflected local and temporary features of our own culture. But an awareness of variety of forms should not prevent us from acknowledging also that in the absence of *any* forms of these attitudes it is doubtful whether *we* should have any thing that we could find intelligible as a system of human relationships, as human society.

(Strawson 1962/2013, 82, Strawson's emphasis)

The fundamental point that Strawson is insisting on here is that underneath the considerable diversity and variations of forms of moral life there remains something constant and universal that unifies them. Any functioning human society requires reactive attitudes, in *some* form or other, to support and sustain the moral norms and expectations that bind that community together (Strawson 1985, 41, 46–7). While we should not assume that our own (local) conceptions are universal, we should not conclude from this that there are no relevant universal or constant features for us to identify and describe.

How does Strawson's concession regarding the limits of his own descriptions and interpretation of the reactive attitudes relate to 'morality' and M-responsibility? From the genealogical perspective, Strawson's remarks serve to show that the 'local and temporary features of our culture' take the particular form of 'morality' and its accompanying view of 'responsibility' and 'blame'. Strawson's description of our reactive attitudes no doubt reflects these 'local' prejudices—but this *particular form* of moral life is not what he is concerned to secure against sceptical critique. His fundamental concerns lie deeper than this, with the claim that any recognizable, intelligible form of human ethical life still requires *some form* of these attitudes, even if they take a different form than 'morality' suggests.

Read this way, Strawson's naturalism can allow for a considerable degree of pluralism about how we might interpret the concept of responsibility (i.e. consistent with Williams's observations). It is not so liberal, however, as to allow for the *complete absence* of reactive attitudes in human life (e.g. as advocated by U-conceptions). According to this reading, Strawson does not have any ambition to vindicate (or discredit) M-responsibility by means of his naturalistic arguments. His naturalistic arguments are targeted against the sceptic about D-responsibility. On the broader reading, therefore, it is essential that these targets be distinguished, since it is possible to reject M-responsibility without rejecting D-responsibility (as we find in Williams's account).

Clearly the above considerations suggest a very different understanding of the Strawson–Williams relationship on this subject. Granted that Strawson's naturalistic arguments do not aim to vindicate M-responsibility but only D-responsibility, more broadly understood, there is no direct opposition or conflict between their views. Both reject U-responsibility as an inadequate account of moral responsibility on the ground that they fail to capture our universal and essential concern with desert (as explained in terms of backward-looking considerations and the emotional responses that this involves). Both also reject D*-responsibility as an incoherent and unintelligible effort to capture the relevant features of desert that we are concerned with. From Williams's genealogical perspective, Strawson is still not sceptical *enough* (i.e. in relation to M-responsibility). This gap between them does not, however, discredit Strawson's core naturalistic claims understood in broad terms. When Strawson is read in broad terms his arguments serve neither to vindicate nor discredit M-responsibility. While he may present the case for D-responsibility in terms that draw on the conceptual apparatus of 'morality'—consistent with 'local and temporary features of our own culture'—it is not his concern to show that D-responsibility must take this particular form or satisfy its assumptions and aspirations.

6. The Limits of Reconciliation

It is evident that there are two quite different ways of reading Strawson's 'Freedom and Resentment', depending on how we understand the relationship between D-responsibility and M-responsibility in this context. On the narrow understanding, Strawson's aim to secure D-responsibility involves defeating scepticism about M-responsibility (i.e. D-responsibility and M-responsibility are not distinguished). Strawson is read as employing the psychological materials provided by his naturalistic descriptions in a way that will satisfy the aims and assumptions of M-responsibility within compatibilist constraints (i.e. without falling back on D*-conceptions). Followers of Strawson, such as Wallace, have further developed and advanced this way of defending his naturalistic programme.

The alternative way of reading 'Freedom and Resentment' accepts that he is trying to provide an account of moral responsibility that falls between the inadequate account of U-responsibility and the incoherent account of D*-responsibility but rejects the (narrow) suggestion that this should be understood in terms of accepting or endorsing the various assumptions and aspirations of M-responsibility. On the broader reading, Strawson's naturalist argument may be formulated and presented in terms of the conceptual apparatus of 'morality' but he (explicitly) allows for variations or differences in cultural forms of reactive attitudes that do not conform to the model of M-responsibility. Strawson's broad naturalism, uncoupled from M-responsibility, is entirely consistent with the naturalistic presuppositions of Williams's *vindicatory* genealogy of moral responsibility.

Although the broad interpretation certainly brings Strawson and Williams closer together on this subject, the possibilities for a complete 'reconciliation' should not be exaggerated. There remain substantial points of divergence, even on the broad account of Strawson's naturalism. In the first place, as already emphasized, although the broad interpretation does not take Strawson to be employing naturalistic arguments in defence of M-responsibility, it does not take him to be a sceptic about M-responsibility either. This is an important difference, since scepticism about 'morality' and M-responsibility is central to the negative aspect of Williams's genealogical account. For Williams there is no prospect of sustaining M-responsibility once its 'illusions' and 'fantasies' are exposed through genealogical reflections and observations. This point of divergence is connected to two other significant differences between Strawson and Williams on the issue of moral responsibility.

One obvious feature of Strawson's discussion of this issue is that he regards his naturalistic account of responsibility as being reliably descriptive of our (current) 'ordinary practice' (Strawson 1980, 265). His account is not intended to be in any way 'revisionary'. This way of presenting his views in 'Freedom and Resentment' reflects his preference for 'descriptive' over 'revisionary' metaphysics. Strawson first introduced this distinction in *Individuals*, published three years before 'Freedom and Resentment'.[32] Descriptive metaphysics, he says, 'is content to describe the actual structure of our thought about the world, revisionary metaphysics is concerned to produce a better structure' (Strawson 1959, 9). Unlike its revisionary counterpart, descriptive metaphysics does not aim to produce conceptual change. There is 'a massive core of human thinking which has no history...there are categories and concepts which, in their most fundamental character, change not at all' (Strawson 1959, 10). It is this same 'descriptive' orientation that informs 'Freedom and Resentment'. Strawson's naturalism aims to uncover and reveal the essential, universal features of our human psychology and conceptual repertoire as manifest in our attitudes and practices related to moral responsibility. Although there are 'local and temporary' variations in our moral sentiments and reactive attitudes, the existence and influence of some form of these attitudes, Strawson argues, 'remains relatively constant' (Strawson 1962/2013, 82; 1985, 47–9; 1980, 265). The variation and genealogy of the particular concepts involved is no part of his concern—even less is any effort to revise or reform our current (or local) ways of thinking about ethical life.

Williams accepts that there are 'universal and unifying' features to be found in any conception of moral responsibility (*qua* D-responsibility) and also accepts that reactive attitudes of some kind are essential to this (Williams 1985/2011, 40–4; 1993, 55–6). This is not, however, the focus of his own concerns and interest. On the contrary, it is precisely cultural variation and genealogy—especially as this relates to 'morality' and M-responsibility—that he is mainly concerned to explain and describe. His negative genealogy, as targeted against

---

[32] Although Williams never directly engages with Strawson on the issue of moral responsibility, he did publish a lengthy review of Strawson's *Individuals*. Williams's remarks concerning Strawson's views on 'descriptive metaphysics' are brief, but he describes the questions raised as of 'great importance' (Williams 1961, 310).

'morality' and M-responsibility, has two especially important tasks. The first is that it makes clear that 'morality' and its associated conceptions of responsibility and blame, although deeply embedded in our current (modern) forms of ethical thought and practice, have no claim to being universal or inescapable features of human ethical life.[33] Second, when we compare our own views to alternative conceptions and practices, as presented in history and literature (e.g. via the Greeks), we come to recognize that much of our own outlook is untruthful and based on illusion and self-deception (Williams 1993, chap. 1). Taken together, these two components of Williams's negative genealogy serve to discredit any *naturalistic* defence of M-responsibility (i.e. developed along narrow lines).[34]

Williams, in contrast with Strawson, emphasizes that the compatibilism that he defends in no way 'leaves everything more or less where it was' (Williams 1985/1995, 19–20; 1986/2014, 264–5; 1995b, 578).[35] In particular, once we abandon the illusions and ideals attached to M-responsibility we will 'need to recast our ethical conceptions' (Williams 1985/1995, 19). We should not expect, in light of these genealogical reflections and observations, that we will be in any position 'to keep the morality system in adequate business' (Williams 1985/1995, 19). It is evident, therefore, that in contrast with Strawson's neo-Wittgensteinian 'quietism', Williams is fully committed to a 'revisionary' programme. There is nothing conservative or complacent about Williams's attitude to our existing (modern) ethical ideas. In this his concerns contrast sharply with Strawson's general comfort with the current status quo.[36]

Along with what we may describe as Strawson's 'conservative bias', there is an accompanying commitment to vindicating 'optimism' (Strawson 1962/2013, 82). The basis for Strawson's optimism is that the naturalist approach that he advocates serves to defeat the threat of scepticism about moral responsibility. On the narrow interpretation, defeating scepticism about D-responsibility involves defeating scepticism about M-responsibility (since, on this view, there is no distinction to be drawn between them). On the broad interpretation, however, defeating scepticism about D-responsibility does not imply or require defeating scepticism about M-responsibility. According to the broad view, D-responsibility

---

[33] As already noted, this is a genealogical point that even some adherents of 'morality' accept (e.g. Wallace).

[34] In general, Williams's negative genealogy is developed with a view to exposing the forms of illusion and self-deception that 'morality' and 'progressivism' encourages. This is why, following Nietzsche, he describes his genealogical investigations as 'untimely' (Williams 1993, 4).

[35] See also Williams's remarks in *Ethics and the Limits of Philosophy* (1985/2011, 166, 177), and 'Making Ends Meet' (1986, 207).

[36] In conversation with Bryan Magee, Strawson denies being 'conservative' in any sense that implies 'resistance to change' (Magee 1971, 158–9). What he is resistant to, he says, is 'ineffective philosophical dreaming'. However, while it is true that Strawson allows for the possibility of revision and criticism *internal* to 'the web of attitudes and feelings' he is describing, he expresses no dissatisfaction with our existing notions and practices—much less does he challenge or question them. It is here that the contrast with Williams is especially sharp and clear.

without M-responsibility still supports optimism. The relevant source of pessimistic concern about scepticism, Strawson maintains, rests with its bleak and inhuman implications leading to a universal 'objective stance'. All this is still avoided on the D-conception, even if the requirements of M-responsibility are not satisfied. All that is lost, according to Strawson, is the obscure and unintelligible notion of 'ultimate freedom' (e.g. as associated with D* conceptions), which is not anything that we have reason to care about or value (Strawson 1980, 265).

Williams does not share or endorse any sort of unqualified 'optimistic' stance with respect to D-responsibility of the kind that his own vindicatory genealogy describes. On the contrary, there are important and significant sources of 'pessimism' that Williams is concerned with and identifies. When our concept of responsibility dispenses with the illusions and fantasies that 'morality' encourages, we need to face or acknowledge some troubling and disturbing truths about the human ethical predicament—in particular, our exposure to luck and fate. These are truths that 'morality' seeks to deny or conceal from us. Contrary to the optimistic and complacent tone of Strawson's naturalistic arguments in 'Freedom and Resentment', defeating scepticism (*qua* D-responsibility) does not serve to deliver undiluted 'good news'.[37] One of the benefits of turning back to the Greeks and ancient tragedy—as Williams's genealogical methods suggest we should do— is that we will find that they were more *truthful* about such matters and less disposed to self-deception.

For Williams it is essential that we carefully distinguish D-responsibility from M-responsibility, since he is sceptical about the latter but not the former. Strawson's naturalism, as we have noted, leaves it unclear how he understands the relationship between these two (distinct) concepts of responsibility. One reason that this matters, as Williams emphasizes throughout his writings on this subject, is that 'morality' and M-responsibility carry 'optimistic' baggage that is not only untruthful but that we are better off without. Separating D-responsibility and M- responsibility is not just a matter of getting rid of 'the panicky metaphysics of libertarianism', since many (most) compatibilists also aspire to satisfy the assumptions and aspirations of 'morality'.[38] What we need, Williams argues, is a compatibilism that does not aim to deliver the optimistic good news' that the morality system is committed to.

When we reflect truthfully on our situation and predicament as human agents in this world we must acknowledge, with the Greek tragedians, that significant forms of fate and luck are intertwined with the exercise of human (moral) agency. There are, for example, significant limits to our powers or abilities to shape our

---

[37] 'Philosophy, and in particular moral philosophy, is still deeply attached to giving good news' (Williams 1996/2006, 49).

[38] One notable exception to this is Hume who, as Williams points out, shows 'striking resistance to some central tenets of... "morality"' (Williams 1985/1995, 20 n.12). For a more detailed examination of Hume's compatibilist views in relation to this matter see Russell (1995, esp. chaps. 6–9).

own motivations and character. We are certainly not 'self-creators' in these (ultimate or absolute) terms. There are similar limits to our control over the (specific) ethical choices that we must face and confront. Nor do we have complete control over the consequences that may flow from our action even when these consequences may have obvious, and perhaps dramatic, ethical significance. There is, in short, no perfect or ideal equality of moral opportunity. The aspiration to 'ultimate' or 'final' control over the particular trajectories that our ethical lives may take is—however attractive or consoling as a self-image—still a delusion. We cannot, therefore, hope to secure an ethical world that is so 'pure' and 'untainted' by contingency and luck that we preserve absolute fairness all the way down.[39]

The form of D-responsibility that Williams describes rejects or dispenses with these optimistic assumptions and aspirations of morality. This has, however, pessimistic implications of a distinct kind. The source of pessimism operating here is not scepticism about (moral) responsibility but, on the contrary, an acceptance that responsible moral agency is vulnerable to luck, contingency, and the limits of control. Strawson, unlike Williams, shows no obvious sign of being troubled or disturbed by pessimistic reflections of this kind. Along with his conservative bias he retains an easy optimism which the broad interpretation of D-responsibility cannot support or sustain.[40]

7. The Limits of Strawson's Naturalism

We now have before us two quite different interpretations of Strawson's core intentions in 'Freedom and Resentment'. Which of them is the most accurate? Given the (sparse) evidence available, we can conclude only that Strawson's position in 'Freedom and Resentment' is *indeterminate* between these two readings, as a good case can be made for each of them. What really matters here, however, is not which way we interpret Strawson but rather what the *critical significance* of these two interpretations comes to. Let us consider, first, the narrow account. If Strawson is advancing his naturalistic arguments with a view to defeating or discrediting scepticism about M-responsibility then, for reasons already mentioned, his project fails. It fails, most importantly, because it does not significantly engage with or even address concerns about luck, history and fate—as Watson (1987/2013) and others have pointed out.[41] Nor is it obvious that Strawson's naturalistic arguments can be modified or expanded in a way that

---

[39] Perhaps the most influential contemporary statement of this outlook (i.e. the perspective of 'morality') is presented in Nagel (1976/2013).

[40] For an exploration of the pessimistic implications of this conception of D-responsibility, separated from optimistic aspirations of M-responsibility, see Russell (2000/2017, 2008/2017, 2017a, 2022a).

[41] This line of criticism is, of course, central to Williams's genealogical critique.

convincingly meets these (sceptical) objections.[42] It may be argued, on this basis, that the broad account offers us a more plausible way of reading Strawson's naturalistic arguments.

The broad account, as we have noted, encounters its own difficulties. When we abandon M-responsibility and embrace a conception of D-responsibility that is uncoupled from M-responsibility, this will not, as Williams points out, 'leave everything where it was'. Moreover, accepting a conception of D-responsibility detached from the metaphysical and conceptual baggage of M-responsibility cannot secure any sort of unqualified optimism. Conceptions of D-responsibility, so understood, bring with them reflections about the limits of human agency and the way in which fate and luck are infused into human ethical life. Strawson's presentation of his naturalist arguments suggests that he aims to dismiss or minimize (or simply ignore) the significance of all this.[43]

Perhaps the most important limitation to be found in the central argument of Strawson's 'Freedom and Resentment' concerns its basic understanding of the free will problem itself. Here the contrast with Williams is, perhaps, especially significant. Strawson presents his case for naturalism about moral responsibility squarely within the framework of the opposition between compatibilists and incompatibilists (i.e. Optimists and Pessimists). This is the crucial philosophical fault line that he is concerned with. In respect of this, although he seeks some sort of 'reconciliation' between the two sides, he comes down decisively on the side of compatibilism (i.e. the side of 'Optimism' suitably modified). In taking this stance, however, Strawson's specific commitments in relation to 'the morality system' remain, as we noted, undecided or indeterminate. This leaves the crucial question unanswered: Does Strawson's understanding of our 'ordinary concept' of moral responsibility concern M-responsibility or not? Until these matters are clarified and explained, it remains unclear what the actual *significance* of Strawson's proposed reconciliation comes to.

For the genealogical account, as Williams presents it, the fundamental philosophical fault line that is relevant here falls not between compatibilism and incompatibilism, it falls between those who accept and those who reject the aims and assumptions of the morality system. This genealogical perspective

---

[42] The most obvious example of such a neo-Strawsonian project, as mentioned above, is Wallace's *Responsibility and the Moral Sentiments* (1994). Doubts about this project are presented in Russell (2011/2017, 2013/2017).

[43] It might be argued that we are vulnerable or prone to this form of 'pessimism' only as long as we continue to harbour the (optimistic) illusion about 'absolute fairness' and 'the purity of morality'. Once freed from this illusion, the critic may argue, any lingering pessimism should evaporate. But this need not be the case. Even when such illusions are thoroughly discredited and/or shown to be incoherent, confronting the limits of human agency, and how this influences the trajectories of our ethical lives, remains a (reasonable) basis for being 'troubled' or 'disconcerted'. Although some may claim to face this situation with complete tranquillity, this (optimistic) attitude may be taken as a sign of evasion or as a failure to sufficiently reflect on our ethical predicament. On the analogy between mortality and human agency (as both concern the issue of finitude) see Russell (2000/2017, 202–4).

suggests a very different picture of the free will problem from the one that Strawson presents. There is a free will problem for us (now), according to the genealogical account, because we (moderns) are committed to the illusions and fantasies of the morality system.[44] This, as we have pointed out, is true not just of libertarians but also of compatibilists and sceptics.[45] What all these parties share is an optimistic view—fundamental to 'morality'—that ethical life can and must be pure and untainted in these terms. If this ideal cannot be met, then our ethical world will collapse in upon itself. There is no credible 'solution' to the free will problem as long as we share the faulty views and ideals of 'morality'.[46] Naturalist observations and considerations of the general kind that Strawson draws attention to may well serve as the relevant *platform* on which the free will problem as we now confront it has *arisen*. By themselves, however, the naturalist claims that Strawson advances cannot effectively describe or remove our current confusions, nor identify our (viable future) options, without the resources of genealogical reflection and historical understanding.[47]

What is the significance of this genealogical interpretation of the free will problem for Strawson's naturalist project? A narrow reading of Strawson's arguments suggests that he does not reject the assumptions and aspirations of 'morality' and that he endorses an understanding of the free will problem in these terms (i.e. with regard to the sceptical threat to M-responsibility). If this is his project then genealogical considerations (e.g. of the kind that Williams describes) suggest that it fails. On a broader reading, Strawson is no more concerned to 'solve' the free will problem than Williams is. The fundamental point that Strawson (read this way) and Williams converge on is that we can vindicate robust forms of moral responsibility (*qua* D-responsibility) without accepting the task of defeating scepticism about M-responsibility. Nevertheless, for reasons that Williams makes clear in *Shame and Necessity* and other related contributions, when we leave behind the aims and assumptions of 'morality', with a view to making sense of our ethical lives in a more truthful manner, we (moderns) will need to 'recast our ethical conceptions', particularly as this concerns responsibility

---

[44] Williams employs the analogy of the problem of evil, since it is a problem 'only for those who expect the world to be good'. Similarly, 'there is a problem of free will only for those who think that the notion of the voluntary can be metaphysically deepened' (Williams 1993, 68).

[45] Even the sceptic, working within this framework, assumes that where M-responsibility is not satisfied there is no 'true' or 'genuine' responsibility. This conclusion, it may be argued, leaves the sceptic wholly complicit in the distortions and self-deceptions of 'morality'.

[46] In especially revealing remarks about his core philosophical concerns and aims, Williams suggests that they have been concentrated on making '*some* sense of the ethical as opposed to throwing out the whole thing because you can't have an idealized version of it' (Williams 2002/2009, 203). This is, in nutshell, the essence of his objection to scepticism as generated by 'morality'.

[47] The importance of historical understanding and cultural sensitivity for philosophy—particularly as it concerns ethics—is a central theme in a number of Williams's writings. See, e.g. Williams (1991/1995, 2000/2006).

and blame. This is a task that Strawsonian naturalism cannot itself help us with. For this task we need to turn to the resources of genealogy.[48]

References

Ayer, Alfred Jules (1980), 'Free-Will and Rationality', in Zak van Straaten (ed.), *Philosophical Subjects: Essays Presented to P. F. Strawson* (Oxford: Oxford University Press), 1–13. Reprinted in McKenna and Russell (eds.), *Free Will and Reactive Attitudes*, 37–46.

Clark, Maudemarie (2001), 'On the Rejection of Morality: Bernard Williams's Debt to Nietzsche', in Richard Schacht (ed.), *Nietzsche's Postmodernism* (Cambridge: Cambridge University Press), 100–22.

De Mesel, Benjamin (2022), 'Taking the Straight Path: P. F. Strawson's Later Work on Freedom and Responsibility', *Philosophers' Imprint* 22: 1–17.

Dennett, Daniel (1984), *Elbow Room: The Varieties of Free Will Worth Wanting* (Oxford: Clarendon Press).

Hart, Herbert L. A. (1959/1968), 'Prolegomenon to the Principles of Punishment', *Proceedings of the Aristotelian Society* 60 (1959), 1–26. Reprinted in Hart, *Punishment and Responsibility: Essays in the Philosophy of Law* (Oxford: Clarendon Press), 1–27.

Leiter, Brian (2022), 'Bernard Williams's Debt to Nietzsche', in Andras Szigeti and Matthew Talbert (eds.), *Morality and Agency: Themes from Bernard Williams* (New York: Oxford University Press), 17–35.

McKenna, Michael, and Paul Russell, eds. (2008/2016), *Free Will and Reactive Attitudes: Perspectives on P. F. Strawson's 'Freedom and Resentment'* (Farnham: Ashgate; reprinted London and New York: Routledge).

Mackie, John Leslie (1982/1985), 'Morality and the Retributive Emotions', in Timothy Stroup (ed.), *Edward Westermarck: Essays on his Life and Works* (Helsinki: Acta Philosophia Fennica). Reprinted in Mackie, *Persons and Values: Selected Papers Volume II* (Oxford: Clarendon Press), 206–19.

Magee, Bryan (1971), 'Conversation with Peter Strawson', in *Modern British Philosophy* (New York: St. Martin's Press).

Nagel, Thomas (1976/2013), 'Moral Luck', *Proceedings of the Aristotelian Society*, Supp. Vol. 1: 137–51. Reprinted in Russell and Deery (eds.), *The Philosophy of Free Will*, 31–42.

---

[48] A version of this chapter was presented at the conference 'P. F. Strawson at 100' held at KU Leuven (November 2019) and also at Aarhus University (October 2021). I am grateful to those who were present on those occasions for their comments and suggestions relating to this chapter. I would particularly like to thank Lucy Allais, Stefaan Cuypers, Tori McGeer, Helen Steward, Somogy Varga, and, especially, the editors of this volume—Audun Bengtson, Benjamin De Mesel, and Sybren Heyndels—for their helpful comments and criticisms.

Prasad, Rajendra (1995), 'Reactive Attitudes, Rationality and Determinism', in Pranab Kumar Sen and Roop Rekha Verma (eds.), *The Philosophy of P. F. Strawson* (New Delhi: Indian Council of Philosophical Research), 346–76.

Queloz, Matthieu (2022), 'A Shelter from Luck', in Andras Szigeti and Matthew Talbert (eds.), *Morality and Agency: Themes from Bernard Williams* (New York: Oxford University Press), 184–211.

Russell, Paul (1992/2017), 'Strawson's Way of Naturalizing Responsibility', *Ethics* 101: 287–302. Reprinted in Russell, *The Limits of Free Will*, 29–45.

Russell, Paul (1995), *Freedom and Moral Sentiment: Hume's Way of Naturalizing Responsibility* (New York: Oxford University Press).

Russell, Paul (2000/2017), 'Compatibilist-Fatalism: Finitude, Pessimism, and the Limits of Free Will', in Ton van den Beld (ed.), *Moral Responsibility and Ontology* (Dordrecht: Kluwer), 199–218. Reprinted in Russell, *The Limits of Free Will*, 187–208.

Russell, Paul (2008/2017), 'Free Will, Art and Morality', *The Journal of Ethics* 12: 307–25. Reprinted in Russell, *The Limits of Free Will*, 134–58.

Russell, Paul (2011/2017), 'Moral Sense and the Foundations of Responsibility', in Robert Kane (ed.), *The Oxford Handbook of Free Will*, 2nd ed. (Oxford: Oxford University Press), 199–220. Reprinted in Russell, *The Limits of Free Will*, 67–96.

Russell, Paul (2013/2017), 'Responsibility, Naturalism and "The Morality System"', in David Shoemaker (ed.), *Oxford Studies in Agency and Responsibility* (Oxford: Oxford University Press), 184–204. Reprinted in Russell, *The Limits of Free Will*, 97–118.

Russell, Paul (2017a), 'Free Will Pessimism', in David Shoemaker (ed.), *Oxford Studies in Agency and Responsibility*, Volume 4 (Oxford: Oxford University Press), 93–120. Reprinted in Russell, *The Limits of Free Will*, 243–75.

Russell, Paul (2017b), *The Limits of Free Will* (New York: Oxford University Press).

Russell, Paul (2017c), 'Free Will and Moral Sentiments', in Kevin Timpe, Meghan Griffith, and Neil Levy (eds.), *The Routledge Companion to Free Will* (New York and London: Routledge), 96–108.

Russell, Paul (2018), 'Bernard Williams: Ethics from a Human Point of View', *Times Literary Supplement* [*Footnotes to Plato*—18 December 2018]. https://www.the-tls.co.uk/articles/bernard-williams-ethics-human-point-view/

Russell, Paul (2022a), 'Moral Responsibility and Existential Attitudes', in Dana Kay Nelkin and Derk Pereboom (eds.), *The Oxford Handbook of Moral Responsibility* (Oxford and New York: Oxford University Press), 519–41.

Russell, Paul (2022b), 'Free Will and the Tragic Predicament: Making Sense of Williams', in Andras Szigeti and Matthew Talbert (eds.), *Morality and Agency: Themes from Bernard Williams* (New York: Oxford University Press), 163–83.

Russell, Paul, and Oisin Deery, eds. (2013), *The Philosophy of Free Will* (New York: Oxford University Press).

Schlick, Moritz (1939/1966), 'When Is a Man Responsible?', in *Problems of Ethics*, trans. David Rynin (New York: Prentice-Hall), 143–56. Reprinted in Bernard Berofsky (ed.), *Free Will and Determinism* (New York: Harper & Row), 54–63.

Shoemaker, David and Neal Tognazzini, eds. (2014), *Agency and Responsibility, Vol. 2: 'Freedom and Resentment' at 50* (New York: Oxford University Press).

Strawson, Galen (1994/2013), 'The Impossibility of [Ultimate] Moral Responsibility', *Philosophical Studies* 75: 5–24. Reprinted in Russell and Deery (eds.), *The Philosophy of Free Will*, 363–78.

Strawson, Peter F. (1959), *Individuals: An Essay in Descriptive Metaphysics* (London: Methuen).

Strawson, Peter F. (1961/1974), 'Social Morality and Individual Ideal', *Philosophy* 36: 1–17. Reprinted in Strawson, *Freedom and Resentment and Other Essays* (London: Methuen), 26–44.

Strawson, Peter F. (1962/2013), 'Freedom and Resentment', *Proceedings of the British Academy* 48: 187–211. Reprinted in Russell and Deery (eds.), *The Philosophy of Free Will*, 63–83.

Strawson, Peter F. (1980), 'Replies', in Zak van Straaten (ed.), *Philosophical Subjects: Essays Presented to P. F. Strawson* (Oxford: Oxford University Press), 260–6.

Strawson, Peter F. (1983/2011), 'Liberty and Necessity', in Nathan Rotenstreich and Norma Schneider (eds.), *Spinoza, His Thought & Work* (Jerusalem: Israel Academy of Sciences and Humanities). Reprinted in Strawson, *Philosophical Writings* (Oxford: Oxford University Press), 146–56.

Strawson, Peter F. (1985), *Scepticism and Naturalism: Some Varieties* (London: Methuen).

Strawson, Peter F. (1992), *Analysis and Metaphysics: An Introduction to Philosophy* (Oxford: Oxford University Press).

Strawson, Peter F. (1998), 'Reply to David Pears', in Lewis Edwin Hahn (ed.), *The Philosophy of P. F. Strawson* (Chicago and LaSalle: Open Court), 259–62.

Wallace, R. Jay (1994), *Responsibility and the Moral Sentiments* (Cambridge, MA: Harvard University Press).

Watson, Gary (1987/2013), 'Responsibility and the Limits of Evil', in Ferdinand Schoeman (ed.), *Responsibility, Character and the Emotions: New Essays on Moral Psychology* (Cambridge: Cambridge University Press, 1987). Reprinted in Russell and Deery (eds.), *The Philosophy of Free Will*, 84–113.

Williams, Bernard (1961), 'Mr. Strawson on Individuals', *Philosophy* 36 (138): 309–32.

Williams, Bernard (1976/1981), 'Moral Luck', *Proceedings of the Aristotelian Society*, Supp. Vol. 1, 115–35. Reprinted in Williams, *Moral Luck: Philosophical Papers 1973-1980* (Cambridge: Cambridge University Press), 20–39.

Williams, Bernard (1985/1995), 'How Free Does the Will Need to Be?', Lindley Lecture, University of Kansas. Reprinted in Williams, *Making Sense of Humanity*, 3–21.

Williams, Bernard (1985/2011), *Ethics and the Limits of Philosophy*. With a commentary by A.W. Moore and a foreword by J. Lear (London and New York: Routledge [Routledge Classics edition 2011]).

Williams, Bernard (1986), 'Making Ends Meet', *Philosophical Books* 27(4): 193–208 (with Simon Blackburn).

Williams, Bernard (1986/2014), 'A Passion for the Beyond', review of Thomas Nagel, *The View from Nowhere*, *London Review of Books* 8.14 (1986). Reprinted in Williams, *Essays and Reviews 1959-2002*, foreword by Michael Wood (Princeton, NJ: Princeton University Press), 261–6.

Williams, Bernard (1989/1995), 'Internal Reasons and the Obscurity of Blame', *Logos* 10: 1–11. Reprinted in Williams, *Making Sense of Humanity*, 35–45.

Williams, Bernard (1991/1995), 'Making Sense of Humanity', in James Sheehan and Morton Sosna (eds.), *The Boundaries of Humanity: Humans, Animals, Machines* (Berkeley, CA: University of California Press). Reprinted in Williams, *Making Sense of Humanity*, 79–89.

Williams, Bernard (1993), *Shame and Necessity* (Berkeley, CA: University of California Press).

Williams, Bernard (1993/1995a), 'Nietzsche's Minimalist Moral Psychology', *European Journal of Philosophy* 1(1): 4–14. Reprinted in Williams, *Making Sense of Humanity*, 65–76.

Williams, Bernard (1993/1995b), 'Moral Luck: A Postscript', in Daniel Statman (ed.), *Moral Luck* (Albany, NY: State University of New York Press). Reprinted in Williams, *Making Sense of Humanity*, 241–7.

Williams, Bernard (1994), 'Interview with Bernard Williams', *Cogito* 8(1): 3–19.

Williams, Bernard (1995a), *Making Sense of Humanity and Other Philosophical Papers 1982-1993* (Cambridge: Cambridge University Press).

Williams, Bernard (1995b), 'Ethics', in Anthony Clifford Grayling (ed.), *Philosophy: A Guide Through the Subject* (Oxford: Oxford University Press), 545–82.

Williams, Bernard (1996/2006), '*The Women of Trachis*: Fictions, Pessimism, Ethics', in Robert B. Louden and Paul Schollmeier (eds.), *The Greeks and Us: Essays in Honor of Arthur W.H. Adkins* (Chicago: University of Chicago Press). Reprinted in Williams, *The Sense of the Past: Essays in the History of Philosophy*, ed. and introd. Myles Burnyeat (Princeton, NJ: Princeton University Press), 49–59.

Williams, Bernard (1998), 'Seminar with Bernard Williams', *Ethical Perspectives* 6 (3–4): 243–65.

Williams, Bernard (2000/2006), 'Philosophy as a Humanistic Discipline', *Philosophy* 75: 477–96. Reprinted in Williams, *Philosophy as a Humanistic Discipline*, ed. and introd. Adrian William Moore (Princeton, NJ: Princeton University Press), 180–99.

Williams, Bernard (2002), *Truth & Truthfulness: An Essay in Genealogy* (Princeton, NJ: Princeton University Press).

Williams, Bernard (2002/2009), 'A Mistrustful Animal', in Alex Voorhoeve (ed.), *Conversations on Ethics* (Oxford: Oxford University Press), 195–212. Interview dated December 2002, first published in *The Harvard Review of Philosophy* 12(1).

Williams, Bernard (2002/2014), 'Why Philosophy Needs History', *London Review of Books* (2002). Reprinted in Williams, *Essays and Reviews 1959–2002*, foreword by Michael Wood (Princeton, NJ: Princeton University Press), 405–12.

12
Navigating 'Freedom and Resentment'

Lucy Allais

1. Introduction

'Freedom and Resentment' is an extraordinary paper. It is one of only a handful of papers P. F. Strawson wrote touching on moral philosophy, yet it has changed philosophy of emotion and moral psychology, as well as having a huge impact on the free will debate.[1] The notions of reactive attitudes and quality of will, introduced by Strawson in this paper, are now standard terms in philosophical discussion of forgiveness, moral emotions, and moral responsibility, to the extent that it is hard to see how we could do without them.[2] The paper is rich, suggestive, fascinating, and frustrating—the last of these because it is notoriously hard to pin down and to work out what the argument is supposed to be. It sometimes seems to me to be like a philosophical inkblot test in which we all find our preferred view of moral responsibility and free will. The arguments seem tantalizingly deep but elusive, and then sometimes when you try to pin them down they seem disappointing or question-begging. It has been interpreted in an enormously wide range of ways, from Victoria McGeer's utilitarian, Humean compatibilist reading, my Kantian incompatibilist-compatibilist and non-consequentialist reading, to expressivist and Wittgensteinian readings.[3] Rather than arguing for a particular

---

[1] E.g. Michael McKenna's and Derk Pereboom's 2016 book on free will, which gives an overview of different positions in the free will debate, devotes a chapter to Strawson's paper, as one of the key topics in the free will debate (McKenna and Pereboom 2016). For a variety of discussions of Strawson's paper, see McKenna and Russell (2008) and Shoemaker and Tognazzini (2015), two collections containing papers discussing 'Freedom and Resentment'.

[2] I have argued elsewhere that simply in virtue of the *content* of reactive attitudes, on Strawson's rich account, the notion solves some of the problems philosophers have been concerned with in relation to forgiveness. E.g. many people think that forgiveness includes giving up or overcoming reactive attitudes like resentment, but many also hold that not just any overcoming of blaming reactive attitudes counts. I could get rid of anger by, e.g. forgetting or by putting you out of my mind. I may have no *resentment* towards you because I have come to regard you as *beneath contempt*. If you want me to forgive you, my having no anger towards you in any of these ways would not be what you want. In response to this problem, one strategy discussed in the literature is to see forgiveness as requiring the meeting of further conditions, in addition to the overcoming of anger and resentment. I have argued that a number of attempts to add extra conditions do not work (Allais 2008) but that we can avoid the need for extra conditions by having the details of the intentional content of resentment in clearer view; this is where Strawson's analysis makes all the difference.

[3] See McGeer (2015); Allais (2015); Wallace (1994); De Mesel and Heyndels (2019); De Mesel (2018); Bengtson (2019).

interpretation, my aim in this chapter is to show that the text is consistent with a range of different interpretations. To do this, I aim to bring out some key choice points at which interpretations can diverge: the central moves or ideas in Strawson's text which, depending on how we read them, result in radically different understandings of the paper. The idea is to pay attention to the places where our interpretation of an initial idea leads us down a path that puts the next idea in a particular light, but where a different starting interpretation could have led to an alternative picture, equally coherent and apparently compatible with the text.

In Section 2 I give a brief overview of Strawson's strategy, and then, in Section 3, note some key ideas in the paper which seem to me to be subject to radically different interpretations. I sketch broadly Humean, Wittgensteinian, and Kantian ways of understanding the key ideas and the overall picture they result in, and note some common features shared by these readings. In the final section, I look in more detail at a key idea with respect to which, I argue, Strawson's lack of precision makes an enormous difference: the question of what the thesis of determinism is. Here I draw on Pamela Hieronymi's recent book (Hieronymi 2020), which seems to me to give overall the most convincing reading of the text— but also one which brings out why different ways of understanding the thesis of determinism matter to our interpretation of the argument as well as to its strength.

2. Strawson's Strategy in 'Freedom and Resentment'

Strawson famously opens the paper with two characters who have different views of the threat determinism may pose to our freedom—or, more centrally, to our practices of moral appraisal, praise, blame, and punishment. Strawson's optimist thinks that if determinism were true, it would not undermine our having freedom, while his pessimist worries that it would and thinks that the optimist has an inadequate account of what it is to see people as responsible for their actions. Strawson thinks both sides have something right and something wrong. He thinks that the optimist is right that there is not any general thesis of determinism that threatens the coherence and justifiability of our practices of moral appraisal. But the pessimist who thinks that the truth of determinism would mean that our moral appraisals are not really justified or deserved and are merely manipulative strategies for bringing about desirable outcomes, has a legitimate concern about what it is to see ourselves and each other as responsible agents. Strawson's strategy is to attempt to bring about a reconciliation. In particular, his idea is that if we can make the optimist's opening view of responsibility and moral appraisal more adequate, by 'radically' changing it, we can show the pessimist that we do not need to bring in 'obscure and panicky metaphysics' to make sense of the freedom needed for moral responsibility (Strawson 1962, 25). In particular, he argues that making the optimist's view of moral responsibility more adequate does not require the falsity of determinism. He argues that the optimist is right that 'the facts as we know them' do not show determinism to be false, and right that 'the facts as we know them' do supply an adequate basis for meaningful moral responsibility attributions. But the optimist has an inadequate view of 'the facts as we know them', which needs to be radically altered.

The optimist's initial—inadequate—view is that our responsibility attributions are primarily a matter of social regulation: praise and punishment are ways of training people to be better, so their being 'deserved' is not to the point. The pessimist thinks this leaves out the crucial centre of what it is to see ourselves and each other as responsible. Strawson's radical alteration of the optimist's account appeals to the idea that the moral life as we know it is essentially constituted by a complicated web of attitudes and feelings which are fundamentally different from strategies of management or training in how they reveal our caring about each other's attitudes to us and express our views of each other's (and our own) responsible agency. Furthermore, these attitudes and feelings constitute our practice of holding people responsible. Central examples of these 'reactive attitudes' are gratitude and resentment, both of which reveal our caring about the attitude towards us that another has expressed in their actions, as well as our seeing the act as attributable to them in the way constitutive of holding them responsible. He argues that by attending to this range of attitudes we can recover all we need of responsibility practices from 'the facts as we know them'.

In developing this account of moral-emotional responsibility practices Strawson draws a contrast between two ways in which or two 'views' from which we can think about people when we interact with them: what he calls the participant view and what he calls the objective view. The participant view is the view we have of people with whom we are embedded in relationships: as co-participants in relationships we care about the attitudes to us expressed by other co-participant's actions, and this caring is expressed by our responding to them with such attitudes as gratitude and resentment. The objective view is the view we take of people when we see someone as an object of social policy, treatment; something to be taken into account, managed, handled, cured, or trained. The mistake in the optimist's opening position is to understand punishment, moral praise, and blame from the perspective of the objective view, which loses much of what we humanly care about, and even loses sight of the point of view from which we understand people as responsible. Crucially, Strawson holds that we can switch between the objective and the participant views, and that they do not exclude each other, though they are 'profoundly opposed' (Strawson 1962, 9).

In order to argue that the truth of determinism could not be relevant to our responsibility attributions, Strawson considers two broad ways in which we come to withdraw or modify the way we see people as responsible in our reactive responses to their actions. One involves, while continuing to see someone from the participant view, changing our understanding of what they did and their intentions in such a way that we no longer see them as having acted with ill will—coming to see, for example, that what they did was justified in the circumstances, or that the action is excusable. This is a change in our understanding of the nature of their willing, which makes blame no longer appropriate, but it does not involve a change in seeing the action as flowing from them or expressing their will as a free and responsible act. In contrast, the other way of ceasing to blame involves shifting to seeing someone from the objective view, from which we no longer see them as an appropriate object of moral appraisal. Most commonly, this is a function of understanding someone as in some way 'abnormal' or incapacitated, which makes holding them responsible seem inappropriate, such as '[t]hat's purely compulsive behaviour on his part' (Strawson 1962, 8). These cases involve no longer seeing the person as having had bad will because of no longer seeing what they did as fully an intentional action at all. Intriguingly, Strawson holds that we can also make the shift from the participant to the objective view in 'normal' cases, as a 'relief from the strains of involvement' (Strawson 1962, 12).

Strawson argues that neither of these two types of reasons for seeing people as not responsible and subject to blame have anything to do with the thesis of determinism. The possible truth of determinism would neither imply, in the first case, that everyone acts with good will, nor, in the second case, that everyone is abnormal. He argues that when we do switch to the objective view on particular occasions, it is never because of thinking that someone's act is determined in a way in which all behaviour would be determined if determinism were true. Strawson argues that this shows determinism not to threaten our moral responsibility attributions. This is one of the places in which his argument is in danger of seeming question-begging: it is unclear why the considerations we ordinarily take to warrant revisions in judgement about people's will should have much weight in relation to a metaphysical thesis which is not meant to be an ordinary consideration. In response to this, two further moves are crucial to his case. One is that Strawson argues that the web of attitudes and feelings that constitute our responsibility practices are humanly real and cannot be given up, and that they are neither capable of nor admit of external justification. The other is that he argues that there is no possible sense of determinism of which all the following things are true: (1) when we see people as incapacitated in the way that undermines reactive attitudes we see their behaviour as caused in this sense, (2) that if determinism is true all behaviour is caused in this way, and (3) the possibility of all behaviour being caused in this way is consistent with the facts as we know them (Strawson 1962, 12).

Strawson concludes that the optimist is wrong to think that the objective view leaves out nothing important, because responsibility attributions do not make sense from the objective view, but that the pessimist is wrong to think that what it leaves out requires a metaphysical solution, or the falsity of determinism. The participant view is fundamental to us, is different from the objective view, and would not be undermined by the truth of determinism.

3. Choice Points and Different Interpretations

There are a number of features of this argument which, it seems to me, are both central and also particularly open to being interpreted in different ways. In this section I shall discuss different ways of reading his appeal to 'the facts as we know them'; his notion of 'quality of will'; his contrast between the 'objective' and 'participant' attitudes and his claim that the responsibility practices revealed and expressed by our reactive responses are neither capable of nor in need of external justification. In the next section, I shall argue that his claim that he does not know what the thesis of determinism is can be understood in radically different ways which are compatible with very different accounts of the relation between free will and determinism.

Strawson's emphasis on 'the facts as we know them' suggests an anti-sceptical Humean approach, which seems further to combine with a Humean naturalism in his rejection of the need for external justification for our responsibility practices.[4] His discussion of our ordinary human practices can be taken as claiming that we are simply psychologically incapable of giving up our general responsibility attributions; this is what Hieronymi calls the simple Humean interpretation, which holds that *since* we are not naturally capable of abandoning the reactive attitudes, speculating about whether they are justified is idle (Hieronymi 2020, 2, 58–9). A broadly Humean approach seems further supported by the fact that he wants to show the pessimist that we do not need the 'panicky metaphysics' of libertarian 'contra-causal' freedom (Strawson 1962, 24–5). And it fits with his emphasis on the centrality of emotions to moral life—on people's benevolence, good will, affection or malice, contempt, indifference towards us being what we centrally care about. Furthermore, it might seem that a broadly Humean sceptical attitude to metaphysics combined with an anti-sceptical approach to the empirical facts is indicated by Strawson's saying that he does not know what the thesis of determinism is, but that no general thesis such as determinism could be relevant to our responsibility attributions. There are, therefore, multiple pieces that cohere nicely in a broadly Humean, naturalistic, and emotivist picture.

A possible concern about a broadly Humean reading is that it is not obvious what kind of account it can give of Strawson's claiming that the objective and the participant views are profoundly opposed. Strawson says that the prestige of the theoretical sciences should not lead us to think their detached perspective is able to capture all the facts in all their bearings, and we are neither required nor permitted to regard ourselves as 'detached from the attitudes which, as scientists, we study with detachment' (Strawson 1962, 25). In Strawson's contrast between the objective and participant views, a very complex part of his account, the

---

[4] How to understand Strawson's naturalism is the subject of debate. See, e.g. Russell (1992).

explanations of action we give in terms of people acting for reasons seems to be situated in a fundamentally different order of explanation than the causal explanations studied by the empirical sciences. But this is not how either Hume or contemporary compatibilists tend to think about action, since they typically take it that the way to naturalize human action is to think of it as caused by reasons understood as psychological states that fit into an empirical causal story. Perhaps it could be argued that the participant view is characterized by feelings rather than facts, but this seems to take it insufficiently seriously.[5] Strawson takes the reality of people acting responsibly to be part of 'the facts as we know them', not to be part of a non-factual emotional view of the world. Another way to make this point is that many contemporary compatibilists of a roughly Humean orientation do take the free will question to be a metaphysical question, which seems to be part of what Strawson is denying.

An alternative way of understanding what Strawson takes to be the profound contrast between the participant and objective views is in terms of a broadly Wittgensteinian characterization of our responsibility practices as an autonomous 'way of life', where Strawson is seen as providing a 'grammatical analysis of our moral responsibility language-game' (Bengtson 2019). A Wittgensteinian approach fits with a quietist attitude to metaphysics, and seems well suited to capture the idea that our responsibility practices neither need nor admit of external justification, something Hieronymi describes as 'the broadly Wittgensteinian point' that you cannot support or question a practice using notions that are constituted by that practice (Hieronymi 2020, 2). A broadly Wittgensteinian approach avoids the danger of losing a contrast between the objective and the participant views by having a too reductive emphasis on the empirical facts.

While Strawson's emphasis on the centrality of emotions in our moral lives initially seems Humean, this becomes much less obvious when we pay attention to the extremely complex intentional content he attributes to the reactive attitudes—which are not simply emotions. The expression 'quality of the will' can be taken to express the idea of acting with feeling (the benevolence, malice, etc., with which someone acts), but it is crucial that Strawsonian reactive attitudes have extremely complex intentional content, and include a careful consideration of what the agent took themselves to be doing in acting. Strawson says:

> If someone treads on my hand accidentally, while trying to help me, the pain may be no less acute than if he treads on it in contemptuous disregard of my existence or with a malevolent wish to injure me. But I shall generally feel in the second case a kind and degree of resentment that I shall not feel in the first. If someone's actions help me to some benefit that I desire, then I am benefited in any case; but

[5] But see Zimmerman (2016).

> if he intended them so to benefit me because of his general goodwill towards me, I shall reasonably feel a gratitude which I should not feel at all if the benefit was an incidental consequence, unintended or even regretted by him, of some plan of action with a different aim.   (Strawson 1962, 6)

The contrasts between these two cases do not just concern brute feeling, but clearly involve the reactor's understanding of the conception the person they are reacting to has of what they are doing, and the way this takes into account other people—what Kantians would call the agent's maxim. Furthermore, Strawson thinks that reactive attitudes evaluate this in the light of a legitimate demand for a minimal (and context-specific) degree of good will (Strawson 1962, 6). So reactive attitudes express an evaluation of a person in the light of what their action expresses about the way they regarded another person in what they took themself to be doing, in the light of a legitimate demand for a minimal degree of good will. While broadly Humean and Wittgensteinian approaches are often taken to fit more naturally with the text, this is in fact a highly Kantian account of the evaluation of action. In the *Groundwork to the Metaphysics of Morals* (Kant 1785/1996), famously, Kant's opening and central notion is the quality of an agent's will, which is revealed in what the agent takes themself to be doing (their maxim), evaluated in relation to a legitimate demand for them to recognize the claims of other persons. Taking feelings and emotions as central to moral life is of course a fundamental part of a Humean approach; but feelings also have a role in Kant's moral philosophy,[6] and the idea of responses to other persons which evaluate them in the light of the way they conceived of what they were doing, how this expressed regard for some other person, and seeing this in the light of a legitimate demand for what is owed to persons, are central to a Kantian moral psychology, as well as to Strawson's notion of reactive attitudes.

It might be objected that even if Strawson's quality of the will thesis, as well as the details of the intentional content of reactive attitudes, were seen in this way, a broadly Kantian reading would be incompatible with other central features of Strawson's position: his naturalism, his anti-metaphysical stance, and his rejection of the idea that our moral practices are susceptible to or in need of external justification. But there are versions of a Kantian position that are very similar to all these features of Strawson's account. On common ways of understanding Kant's positive characterization of freedom in terms of practical reason and rational capacities, it does not involve metaphysics—including obscure and panicky metaphysics.[7] Kant takes us to know our freedom in recognizing moral reasons, and

---

[6] Kant's central moral motivation—respect—is a feeling.

[7] See, e.g. Korsgaard (2009). Kant's metaphysical conception of freedom as a distinct kind of causality, does I think, involve metaphysics, but it is less obvious it plays a role in his positive characterization of freedom. He argues that it is a transcendent metaphysical idea, and transcendent metaphysical ideas, in going beyond the bounds of experience, go beyond human cognition.

in our moral judgements about ordinary human actions—plausibly part of Strawson's 'facts as we know them'. Since he thinks all humans recognize moral reasons, and in recognizing moral reasons we understand ourselves as free, he does not take our understanding of ourselves in this way to be subject to 'external' justification, or to follow from some metaphysical thesis. I noted that on the Humean approach it is not entirely obvious how to cash out the contrast between the objective and the participant views, nor to explain why they should be thought to be profoundly opposed. In contrast, Kant's account of the way we characterize autonomous action in terms of its being governed by reason puts it in an entirely different space of explanation from empirical causal explanation. Strawson's characterization of the objective view is in terms of explanations of behaviour that make it not explicable in terms of rational intentions: if your attitude to someone is wholly objective 'you cannot reason with him' (Strawson 1962, 9). This is clearly opposed to explanations that see action within 'the space of reasons'. And, like Strawson, Kant thinks that we can shift between the two ways of seeing actions, since he thinks we can look at actions both from the point of view of empirical causal explanation and from the (entirely different) point of view of intentions governed by reason.

It might be objected that Kant's moral philosophy, and therefore also his view of responsibility attributions, is objectivist in a way that seems at odds with Strawson's approach. Strawson is sometimes taken as having an expressivist or 'response-dependent' view of moral responsibility, which holds that *being* responsible is a matter of *being held* responsible, and that *being held responsible* is a matter of being subject to a reactive attitude (see Wallace 1994). But this might be reading more into the text than is explicitly stated, and the text supports alternative readings. Strawson says that 'attitudes of disapprobation and indignation are precisely the correlates of the moral demand in the case where the demand is felt to be disregarded. The making of the demand *is* the proneness to such attitudes' (Strawson 1962, 22). What he characterizes as constitutively linked are our making moral demands and our being prone to reactive responses in relation to these demands being violated (or exceeded). But our *making* moral demands and the *validity* of these demands need not be equated, so characterizing our *making* of the moral demand in terms of our proneness to certain responses to its being violated is entirely compatible with moral demands having some kind of objective validity, as well as with there being a fact of the matter as to whether someone is rightly held responsible for an action. He does not say, note, that the validity of the moral demand is a matter of our proneness to such attitudes, nor does he say that being responsible just is a matter of being subject to such reactive responses. Rather, it is the *making of* the demand which is inseparable from the proneness to the attitudinal responses in response (in the case of blame) to violations of the demand: holding someone to be validly subject to a demand for a certain degree of good will is, he thinks, inseparable from being prone to indignation, resentment, and other reactive responses to their not showing good will.

It might be thought that seeing limitations of broadly Humean, Wittgensteinian, and Kantian approaches to interpreting Strawson's paper suggests that we should, in addition, return to paying attention to the details of Strawson's own comments on methodology (including on where he draws on these various philosophical traditions), rather than trying to read him in the light of some other framework (Heyndels 2019). While I think this is right, it is worth noticing the extent to which these different interpretations can be made consistent with the text. For those who have their own preferred reading, I recommend taking seriously thinking about how a different interpretation of what is meant by the 'quality of the will' with which someone acts, or of how we should understand what is included in 'the facts as we know them', can lead to a gestalt shift in interpretation, in which the other pieces of the argument appear in a different, but still mutually coherent light.

If broadly Humean, Wittgensteinian, and Kantian approaches all seem to have some basis in the text, one way to move forward could be to see whether there is something common to these ways of reading Strawson that we can take away. All the interpretations I have mentioned so far agree on finding in Strawson the idea that our approach to the free will problem should start by taking seriously how deeply we believe we act with whatever kind of freedom is needed for moral responsibility, how fundamental this is to the way we see ourselves and each other, and what we humanly care about. We simply do see ourselves and each other as having whatever freedom is needed for responsibility. Another thing common to the three approaches I have mentioned is the idea that there is no general metaphysical doctrine that threatens this view of ourselves. Here, however, I think we run into a further, deep lack of clarity in Strawson's argument, that turns, I shall argue, on his leaving open what the thesis of determinism is. How we understand the status of this disavowal, and what versions of the thesis of determinism we read into the argument, will lead to very different understandings of the claim that no general metaphysical doctrine could threaten the view we have of ourselves in our ordinary responsibility attributions.

4. The Thesis of Determinism

One of the most striking features of Strawson's paper is his saying, right at the beginning, that of all the disputants in the free will debate, he takes himself to be most closely aligned with those who say they do not know what the thesis of determinism is supposed to be. But how can we reconcile freedom with determinism without knowing what is claimed by the thesis of determinism? Strawson says that despite not knowing what the thesis is, we can proceed to make progress, and even to show that determinism (whatever it is) would not undermine responsibility attributions. He argues that while he doesn't know what determinism is, he does know that if there is a coherent thesis of determinism, there must be a sense of 'determined' such that, if the thesis is true, then all behaviour whatsoever could be determined in that sense (Strawson 1962, 10). Furthermore, in a series of claims the joint truth conditions of which are not easy to understand, Strawson says that there is no possible sense of determinism of which all the following things are true:

(1) when we see people as incapacitated in the way that undermines reactive attitudes we see their behaviour as caused in this sense;
(2) that if determinism is true all behaviour is caused in this way;
(3) the possibility of all behaviour being caused in this way is consistent with the facts as we know them (Strawson 1962, 12).

I shall refer to these as Strawson's three claims about determinism.

Hieronymi provides what seems to me a convincing reconstruction of how the argument could proceed in the absence of an account of what the thesis of determinism is. As she sees it, Strawson's argument turns on the claims that determinism is a *general* thesis, and that no general thesis could show our responsibility practices to be inappropriate. The cases we regard as exempt as a result of considering them from the objective view are typically cases of abnormality, and, as Strawson famously says, 'it cannot be a consequence of any thesis which is not itself self-contradictory that abnormality is the universal condition' (Strawson 1962, 11). This step—Strawson immediately acknowledges—seems facile. As Paul Russell argues, the hard determinist thinks that determinism would mean that we are all, in a sense, *incapacitated*, and while *abnormality* cannot be the normal case, it is not obvious that *incapacity* could not be (Russell 1992, 299). In response to the concern about being facile, Hieronymi argues that the way to understand Strawson's argument is to put together two parts of his position. The first is his claim that 'we never shift to a more objective attitude because we believe the person's behaviour was determined in some sense (forced, caused, fated, out of their control) in which all behaviour is determined, if determinism is true' (Hieronymi 2020, 39). The second is what she calls Strawson's 'social naturalism' (the idea that 'some or other such system of expectations and reactions, demands and attitudes, is, as he puts it, "given with the fact of human society"') (Hieronymi 2020, 27). Hieronymi argues that we can see Strawson as making a transcendental argument that moves from the existence of society to the satisfaction of the conditions required for it (Hieronymi 2020, 27–8). When we see a person as somehow abnormal or incapacitated, we exempt them because their behaviour was brought about in some way that renders them incapable of ordinary interpersonal relationships (at least in regard to this action). But, she suggests, given the actual existence of human society, nothing could show that we are *all* incapable of ordinary interpersonal relationships, since ordinary adult relating is actual—it is among the facts as we know them—and humanly impossible to abandon. Since human social interaction is actual, no general thesis can undermine it, rather, responsibility attributions can be undermined only in individual contrastive cases. She says that if determinism (whatever it is) is true, it is already true, so being determined in whatever way it specifies does not render us incapable of ordinary adult relating.

I find Hieronymi's reconstruction compelling both as a reading of Strawson and as a transcendental argument for the satisfaction of the conditions required by ordinary relating, but I find it much less obvious that it proves the thesis of metaphysical compatibilism: that metaphysical determinism would not rule out human free agency. Let us grant what she calls Strawson's social naturalism—the actuality of human society, including the responsibility attributions expressed in the reactive attitudes and the way this relates to our natural capacities. Or, as Strawson puts it, that it is part of the facts as we know them that 'people often decide to do things, really intend to do what they do, know just what they're doing in doing it' (Strawson 1962, 3). The transcendental argument Hieronymi invokes says that because we know ordinary human relating to be actual, we know that any general metaphysical thesis which is inconsistent with it is not actual.[8] But this does not show that metaphysical determinism is compatible with ordinary agency, rather, it shows that either metaphysical determinism is compatible with agency, or metaphysical determinism is not actual. And, more generally, it shows of any general metaphysical thesis about agency that it is either compatible with agency (which is actual) or is not true. To say, as Hieronymi does, that if determinism were true it would already be true, is not an argument which shows determinism to be compatible with the fact of ordinary human interacting and nor does it give any grounds for thinking determinism *is* true. Consider, by way of comparison: if I were a victim of a Cartesian demon it would already be true that I am the victim of a Cartesian demon, and if I were a victim of a Cartesian demon perhaps I would be the only person who existed, which is clearly not compatible with ordinary human agency as we know it. Since I take the world and ordinary agency to be actual, I take the worry that I could be the victim of a Cartesian demon to be idle. But this does not show that my being a victim of a Cartesian demon is *compatible* with the facts of ordinary agency as we know them. The transcendental argument tells us that whatever is inconsistent with actual agency is not the case, but this says nothing about whether any particular metaphysical hypothesis is compatible with actual agency. If something we know to be actual is incompatible with determinism, then determinism is *not* already true (even though, if it were true

---

[8] I would prefer to state this more weakly, as saying that we have such a strong commitment to the reality of ordinary human relating that we know it more strongly than any reason we could have to believe in any metaphysical thesis that seems to be inconsistent with it.

it would already be true). Similarly, if (as I assume) my agential interactions with other persons are actual, I am not a victim of a Cartesian demon. So I agree with Hieronymi that we could construct a transcendental argument from the actuality of our responsibility practice to the actuality of the conditions of its possibility. But the strength of this case as an argument for the reality of free will is separable from its strength as an argument for metaphysical compatibilism.

Unpacking this in more detail, notice the difference between the claim that no general metaphysical thesis could convince us that we do not have the ordinary powers we take ourselves to have and the claim that no general metaphysical thesis could be incompatible with our ordinary agential powers. The former is a statement about certain sceptical hypotheses being idle; the latter is a metaphysical thesis, and a surprisingly strong one, since it seems to imply that agency does not have a metaphysics. If we take the former as expressing the results of a transcendental argument for the actuality of the conditions of our ordinary powers,[9] it seems to me that it leaves it open what metaphysical theses are compatible with our actual powers. Surely there are sceptical possibilities—no matter how remote—that are inconsistent with human agency being what we ordinarily take it to be, such as the hypothesis that I am a victim of a Cartesian demon. To say that these sceptical hypothesis are *idle* and do not undermine our commitment to our actual agential powers is different from saying that their being true would be *compatible* with our ordinary agential powers. In order for it to be true not just that no metaphysical thesis could give us reason to believe we do not have ordinary agential powers, but that no metaphysical thesis could be inconsistent with ordinary agential powers, it would have to be that agency could not have any metaphysical conditions. This seems implausible. If agency involves causal powers, it surely has metaphysical conditions, and there are ways of understanding the causal powers agency involves that are incompatible with one or other general metaphysical thesis, including, perhaps, metaphysical determinism.[10]

It is at this point in the argument that, it seems to me, Strawson's vagueness about what the thesis of determinism is makes a crucial difference. In the rest of the chapter I will present two very different ways determinism can be understood, and then evaluate these in relation to a conception of the metaphysics of agency which I take to be inconsistent with one understanding of determinism but not the other. By relating these to Strawson's argument, I will conclude that to the extent that Strawson's argument is compelling, it does not in fact show anything about the metaphysical compatibility of responsibility attributions and metaphysical determinism.

---

[9] An alternative is to take it as a claim about our psychological limitations.
[10] I am not sure whether Wittgensteinian quietists would align themselves more closely with the idea that such general metaphysical theses as metaphysical determinism are idle because we have no reason to believe them, or with the idea that they are idle because agency has no possible metaphysics.

While Strawson says he doesn't know what the thesis of determinism is, in the contemporary free will debate it is often understood in a clearly specified way. Hieronymi opens her interpretation with a precise statement: determinism is the thesis that 'the complete physical state of the world at any one point in time, together with the laws of nature, determines the complete physical state of the world at all other points in time' (Hieronymi 2020, xi–xii). It is important to notice that, understood in this way, metaphysical determinism does not appear to be an empirical claim, nor anything a naturalist has reason to believe is true, nor part of 'the facts as we know them'. It is not a claim within science, but a philosophical interpretation of science.

An alternative way to understand determinism is as a thesis about what kind of scientific laws there are at some particular level or domain of scientific investigation, so as a substantive empirical possibility. For example, it could that the laws of sub-atomic physics will turn out to be deterministic.

It is crucial to see that these ways of understanding determinism are different: physics could discover that the laws describing sub-atomic particles are deterministic without this showing that at any one moment in time there is only one possible future. In order to take the physical, empirical hypothesis about deterministic laws in some domain to show that there is only one possible future it would need to be shown not just that laws governing matter at some particular level (say, the sub-atomic laws) are deterministic, but furthermore, that these laws are the only thing that explains why anything happens. But this further claim goes beyond the content of the laws, and denying it does not involve invoking 'panicky metaphysics' or anything 'contra-causal'—it is denied, for example, by scientists who think that biological phenomena cannot be understood without top-down or whole-part causation.[11] Another way to put the point is that there being only one metaphysically possible future follows from certain physical laws being deterministic only if we are dealing with a system closed under those laws. That the system is closed under those laws is not part of the content of the laws, or of the claim that they are deterministic, so is not established by the science that establishes the laws.

I have suggested that determinism can be understood either as a substantive empirical hypothesis about the nature of some physical laws or as a general metaphysical thesis about the total unfolding of events in space and time. We can now ask whether Strawson's argument that no possible sense of determinism is compatible with his three claims is meant to apply to only one, or to both of these senses of determinism. In terms of empirical determinism, we can see Strawson as arguing that no matter what we find out about the laws of nature—the kind of causation science investigates—this will not undermine the idea that,

---

[11] See Murphy and Brown (2007); Juarrero (2002); Steward (2012); Cartwright (1999).

roughly, people act for reasons.[12] If physics discovers that matter is governed by probabilistic laws or deterministic laws, this has nothing to do with and will not affect the idea that people act for reasons, and in this sense our agency is compatible with deterministic causation in nature. If we read the argument in terms of metaphysical determinism, he is saying that if at any moment in time there is never more than one thing that could happen, this has nothing to do with and does not affect the idea that people act for reasons. On the former reading, the argument seems to me plausible, but does not touch debates about metaphysical compatibilism and incompatibilism—the metaphysical free will debate that Strawson aims to dissolve. I will argue that on the second reading, his argument is not compelling.

Strawson says that while we do not know what the thesis of determinism is, we do know that if there is a coherent thesis of determinism, there is a sense of 'determined' of which it is true that all behaviour could be determined in this sense. He says that there is no such thesis which is also compatible with his three claims. I will argue that whether this is plausible cannot be evaluated independent of an account of the metaphysics of agency, and depends on deciding whether determinism is an empirical or a metaphysical claim. To show this, I will very briefly sketch an account of the metaphysics of agency which I take to be coherent (though I do not try to show that it is true), and which takes determinism not to be compatible with all of Strawson's three theses, if determinism is understood as the metaphysical thesis specified by Hieronymi.

A way of understanding the metaphysics of agency which is incompatible with metaphysical determinism is the idea that agency requires the possibility of more than one course of action being open to the agent. Helen Steward presents such a view, arguing that agency constitutively involves what she calls 'two-way powers', which she understands as the power to do or refrain from doing things, or, as she puts it, to settle what happens in the world: 'the power to make the course of worldly events go one way at a given point in time (or perhaps just to permit it to go one way at that point in time), when it could (at that very time) have gone differently in some respect' (Steward 2020, 344). As she argues, it follows from this conception of agency that actions are 'things whose occurrence is always non-necessary relative to the totality of their antecedents—things such that they might either occur or not occur, for all that has thus far been settled at the time at which they occur' (Steward 2020, 345). While incompatible with metaphysical determinism, this conception of agency says nothing about what the laws governing sub-atomic particles are like, and whether they are deterministic or

---

[12] This point could also be put in terms of the idea that people's actions are appropriately subject to reactive responses, but I take this not to be separable from the idea of intentional action, and Strawson says: 'people often decide to do things, really intend to do what they do, know just what they're doing in doing it' is part of the facts as we know them (Strawson 1962, 3).

indeterministic, so seems compatible with determinism about some domain of physical laws. Furthermore, Steward's picture is naturalistic in the sense that she is centrally concerned with animal agency, which she argues is not compatible with metaphysical determinism because understanding animals as agents requires thinking of them as having two-way powers. She says:

> [e]very point in an animal's waking life, I argued, is a point at which that animal settles, by means of the exercise (or nonexercise) of each of the myriad capacities which together constitute its executive agency, how things will be in respect of the particular portion of the world it is able to affect.... It follows from this conception of what agency involves that actions cannot be merely the inevitable event-consequences of sets of antecedent causes. If they were, there would be nothing left for anyone to do, for there would be nothing left for anyone to settle at the time of action.   (Steward 2020, 344)

This account of our agency as involving two-way powers which settle how things will be is not an account involving occult 'contra-causal' powers outside of nature, but rather one which sees our agential powers as continuous with those of other animals. Two-way agential powers, on this picture, are natural, and are the powers of ordinary agency. Of course there is the crucial difference between us and other animals in our having the capacity to direct our agential powers in response to reasons—in line with rational abilities—and this makes us liable to being held morally responsible for our actions in a way in which other animals are not. But here it is reason, not occult causal powers, that makes the difference for the possibility of attributing moral responsibility to our exercises of our agential powers.

Not only is this a possible view of agency, crucially for our purposes, it seems compatible with the reactive practices on which Strawson puts so much emphasis. Indeed, it is arguable that a conception of agency as involving such two-way powers is embedded in our ordinary practices of moral appraisal, praise, and blame. I shall not attempt to demonstrate this here; I simply want to say enough to make plausible that it *might* be. The idea is that our ordinary practices of moral appraisal involve seeing agents as, typically, having more than one course of action available, and our practices also involve thinking that by acting, agents exercise the power to make things go one way rather than another. Furthermore, it seems to me that the ordinary thought that a person could have acted differently than they did is embedded in the content of the reactive attitudes. When we feel resentment towards someone, we think that they should not have acted the way they did; when we feel guilt, we think that *we* should not have acted the way we did; when we feel gratitude, we think that the person to whom we feel gratitude did more than they had to. This suggests that it is part of the content of resentment, guilt, and gratitude that the agent could have acted differently than they did.

In response to this, it might be pointed out that compatibilists have worked hard to show that metaphysical determinism allows for the possibility of having acted differently in a conditional sense: roughly, if an agent's beliefs and desires had been different they would have acted differently. But showing that there is a way of making sense of such conditional alternative possibilities is different from showing that conditional alternative possibilities are part of the ordinary responsibility attributions expressed in reactive attitudes. The latter would require that, for example, when I hold someone responsible in the way contained in resentment, I think not 'they could have not done that', but rather, 'if they had been different they wouldn't have done that'. This does not strike me as capturing the responses contained in our ordinary practices. Similarly it seems to me that feeling gratitude does not involve thinking of someone: had they had different beliefs and desires they would have acted differently, but rather that they could have acted differently but chose to act like this. This, it seems to me, is why some philosophers who are convinced by metaphysical determinism argue that we need to radically revise our reactive practices (see Pereboom 2002). This is all very quick, and I have of course neither established a two-way powers metaphysical conception of agency, nor that this conception of agency is embedded in our ordinary moral appraisals. My argument simply requires the coherent possibility of this combination.

The next step is to relate this to Strawson's discussion of the kinds of contrastive cases we use to undermine responsibility attributions. The first two of his three claims say that there is no sense of determinism of which it is both true that when we see people as incapacitated in the way that undermines reactive attitudes we see their behaviour as caused in this sense, and also that if determinism is true all behaviour is caused in this way. However, the two-way powers understanding of agency just sketched seems to me to question this. Among the considerations that Strawson considers to undermine responsibility attributions he includes: he could not help it, he was pushed, he had to do it, it was the only way, they left him no alternative. These directly invoke the agent's having had no possibility of having acted differently than they did, suggesting, contrastively, that ordinary moral appraisal involves the idea of alternative possibilities. Coming to regard people as not having had alternate possibilities for acting is one way we come to cease to blame them; if metaphysical determinism is true, all 'behaviour' is such that people did not have alternate possibilities. Thus, in relation to a two-way powers understanding of agency, there is a way in which people's 'behaviour' could be determined (their having no options for acting differently) which in our ordinary practices we take to undermine responsibility attributions, and which is a way in which all 'behaviour' could be determined, if metaphysical determinism is true.[13]

Strawson says that determinism is not a threat because there is no coherent sense of determinism which is compatible with all three of his claims. I have suggested a possible view of the metaphysics of agency, plausibly embedded in our

---

[13] If the two-way powers view of agency is correct, there is nothing that can really be called behaviour or action if metaphysical determinism is true.

reactive practices, which would take metaphysical determinism to be consistent with his first two claims. But there is still one more claim: this sense of determinism must be compatible with 'the facts as we know them'. So now the question is whether the possibility that at any one time there was only ever one thing that could have happened is compatible with the facts as we know them. On the one hand, since many philosophers seem to accept that metaphysical determinism is or might be true, it seems that it could be consistent with at least some of the facts as we know them. On the other hand, if the facts as we know them include people's acting, then, according to a two-way powers view of agency, metaphysical determinism is not consistent with the facts as we know them. This means that metaphysical determinism is not a sense of determinism which is consistent with Strawson's three claims, and therefore not one his argument counts against.

The upshot of all this is that because he does not specify how he understands determinism, Strawson's argument is ambiguous. On the one hand, if the idea of robust alterative possibilities is embedded in ordinary responsibility attributions, and if one way we exempt involves coming to see people as having had no alternatives, then Strawson is wrong in claiming that there is no possible sense of 'determined' which is both a way behaviour is determined when we exempt people and also a way in which all behaviour would be determined if determinism is true. On the contrary, one reason for exempting people is their having had no alternative, and if determinism is true, no one has ever had an alternative. On the other hand, Strawson's claims can be made consistent by saying that metaphysical determinism is not a possible sense of determinism we need to worry about, because it is a highly general thesis which we have no reason to accept if it is inconsistent with the facts as we know them—including the actuality of human agency. This could be Strawson's intention if he were understanding determinism as an empirical hypothesis about the nature of laws in some domain, but then it leaves the question of metaphysical compatibilism untouched by his argument.

I have not attempted to establish a conception of agency as involving the kind of two-way powers Steward appeals to, and I have also not given reasons for thinking Strawson had anything like this two-way powers view of agency in mind. On the contrary, I think Hieronymi's reading is more plausibly what he had in mind. Rather, my point is that, perhaps surprisingly, Strawson's conditions can be read in a way consistent with the two-way powers conception, since someone who supports this conception can agree that there is no sense of determinism that simultaneously is a way we see people's actions as determined when we exempt them and is consistent with the facts as we know them. But if this is true, then the transcendental argument for the reality of human freedom simply leaves the questions about the compatibility of ordinary agency and metaphysical determinism where we started—in dispute—because it is compatible with radically different views.

I agree with Strawson, on Hieronymi's reading of him, in thinking that the ordinary agential powers that reactive attitudes respond to are actual, and that we do not believe in them on the basis of being persuaded by arguments, including arguments about what metaphysics of causality they involve. And I agree that this places limits on what we should take metaphysics to be capable of undermining. But this is different from claiming that no *possible* general metaphysical way the world could be would make it the case that we do not in fact have the ordinary agential powers we take ourselves to have. In my view, Strawson's argument is most successful if we take him to be showing that determinism about some laws, such as those governing sub-atomic particles (and empirical possibilities about the nature of the laws) is no threat to human agency, while metaphysical determinism, as a general metaphysical thesis ruling out the possibility of anything have ever happened differently, is something we have no reason to think is the case.[14] But precisely because of the way he leaves open what the thesis of determinism is supposed to be, the text is compatible with different interpretations, and what is required to resolve disputes between these is more details about the metaphysics of agency and how it relates to various possible ways of understanding determinism. Appealing to the reality of our practices of treating each other as responsible, and the commitment to ordinary agential powers that is part of this, can feature in a transcendental argument showing that no metaphysical thesis incompatible with these powers is actual, but without detailed attention to the actual metaphysics of agency, this does not tell us which metaphysical theses are inconsistent with the metaphysics of agency. It just tells us that any that are inconsistent with it are not actual—including, perhaps, metaphysical determinism.

5. Conclusion

I have argued that the very wide range of extant interpretations of Strawson's famous paper has an explanation: the paper is genuinely compatible with very

---

[14] The Kantian approach I mentioned in the previous section seems to fit together well with this, because, as I understand him, Kant's aim in dissolving the free will problem is not to provide a metaphysics of 'contra-causal freedom', but to show that we do not have reason to think that metaphysical determinism threatens our freedom. Part of his strategy for doing this, as I understand it, involves showing that metaphysical determinism is a transcendent metaphysical claim (one tempting to empiricists) that goes beyond what we can demonstrate or what we need to make sense of science. Understanding this means we do not have to take it as a threat to the ordinary responsibility attributions embedded in our moral judgements, which involve thinking that a person should have— and could have—acted differently than they did. Thus, the Kantian approach fits with the idea that no general metaphysical thesis could undermine our ordinary responsibility attributions. We are wrong to think general metaphysical theses are a threat, because we are wrong to think that we have stronger grounds for believing in them than we do in ordinary agency. Furthermore, this Kantian approach is, in Strawson's terms, optimistic (it takes freedom to be actual), and it also involves, as Strawson wants to do, radically changing his initial optimist's view of the facts as we know them.

different interpretations. Key notions in the paper, such as Strawson's appeal to 'the facts as we know them'; his notion of 'quality of will'; his contrast between the 'objective' and 'participant' attitudes and his claim that the responsibility practices revealed and expressed by our reactive responses are neither capable of nor in need of external justification, can be understood in very different ways. Most participants in the free will debate are trying to give different accounts of a group of concepts concerning moral responsibility and free will, and, in my view, different ways of understanding these can be read into Strawson's picture. An interpretation of a key concept will lead to a particular understanding of the argument, and of the next key concept, resulting in the possibility of completely different, yet coherent, and textually grounded, readings of the paper. Finally, I have argued that Strawson's explicit vagueness about the thesis of determinism means these indeterminacies cannot be resolved on the basis of the text alone.

While this may seem a disappointing result, it in no way diminishes the achievement of Strawson's paper in terms of his introduction of the crucial notion of reactive attitudes, and his explication of the relation between these, our practices of holding responsible, and our belief in human free agency. Furthermore, it seems to me that the differences between the understandings of the crucial notions that I have highlighted play an important role in ongoing philosophical disputes about how to understand free will, and thus that the focus Strawson's paper brings to the relations between these notions, and the implications of different ways of understanding them, enable us to make genuine progress in this debate—even if not exactly the progress he had hoped to bring about.

References

Allais, Lucy (2008), 'Wiping the Slate Clean: The Heart of Forgiveness', *Philosophy & Public Affairs* 36(1): 33–68.

Allais, Lucy (2015), 'Freedom and Forgiveness', in David Shoemaker and Neal A. Tognazzini (eds.), *Oxford Studies in Agency and Responsibility: 'Freedom and Resentment' at 50*, vol. 2 (Oxford: Oxford University Press), 33–63.

Bengtson, Audun Benjamin (2019), 'Responsibility, Reactive Attitudes and Very General Facts of Human Nature', *Philosophical Investigations* 42(3): 281–304.

Cartwright, Nancy (1999), *The Dappled World: A Study at the Boundaries of Science* (Cambridge: Cambridge University Press).

De Mesel, Benjamin (2018), '"Are Our Moral Responsibility Practices Justified?" Wittgenstein, Strawson and Justification in "Freedom and Resentment"', *British Journal for the History of Philosophy* 26(3): 603–14.

De Mesel, Benjamin, and Sybren Heyndels (2019), 'The Facts and Practices of Moral Responsibility', *Pacific Philosophical Quarterly* 100(3): 790–811.

Heyndels, Sybren (2019), 'Strawson's Method in "Freedom and Resentment"', *The Journal of Ethics* 23(4): 407–23.

Hieronymi, Pamela (2020), *Freedom, Resentment, and the Metaphysics of Morals* (Princeton, NJ and Oxford: Princeton University Press).

Juarrero, Alicia (2002), *Dynamics in Action: Intentional Behaviour as a Complex System* (Cambridge, MA: MIT Press).

Kant, Immanuel (1785/1996), *Groundwork to the Metaphysics of Morals*, Cambridge Texts in the History of Philosophy, ed. and trans. Mary Gregor (Cambridge: Cambridge University Press).

Korsgaard, Christine (2009), *Self-Constitution* (Oxford: Oxford University Press).

McGeer, Victoria (2015), 'P. F. Strawson's Consequentialism', in David Shoemaker and Neal Tognazzini (eds.), *Oxford Studies in Agency and Responsibility: 'Freedom and Resentment' at 50*, vol. 2 (Oxford: Oxford University Press), 64–92.

McKenna, Michael, and Derk Pereboom (2016), *Free Will: A Contemporary Introduction* (New York and London: Routledge).

McKenna, Michael, and Paul Russell (2008), 'Perspectives on P. F. Strawson's "Freedom and Resentment"', in Michael McKenna and Paul Russell (eds.), *Free Will and Reactive Attitudes: Perspectives on P. F. Strawson's 'Freedom and Resentment'* (Farnham: Ashgate), 1–17.

Murphy, Nancy, and Warren Brown (2007), *Did My Neurons Make Me Do It? Philosophical and Neurobiological Perspectives on Moral Responsibility and Free Will* (Oxford: Oxford University Press).

Pereboom, Derk (2002), *Living Without Free Will* (Cambridge: Cambridge University Press).

Russell, Paul (1992), 'Strawson's Way of Naturalizing Responsibility', *Ethics* 102(2): 287–302.

Shoemaker, David, and Neal A. Tognazzini, eds. (2015), *Oxford Studies in Agency and Responsibility: 'Freedom and Resentment' at 50*, vol. 2 (Oxford: Oxford University Press).

Steward, Helen (2012), *A Metaphysics for Freedom* (Oxford: Oxford University Press).

Steward, Helen (2020), 'Agency as a Two-Way Power', *The Monist* 103: 342–55.

Strawson, Peter F. (1962), 'Freedom and Resentment', *Proceedings of the British Academy* 48: 1–25.

Wallace, R. Jay (1994), *Responsibility and the Moral Sentiments* (Cambridge, MA: Harvard University Press).

Zimmerman, Dean (2016), 'Thinking with Your Hypothalamus: Reflections on a Cognitive Role for the Reactive Emotions', in Paul Russell and Michael McKenna (eds.), *Free Will and Reactive Attitudes: Perspectives on P. F. Strawson's 'Freedom and Resentment'* (London: Routledge), 255–73.

13
Between Exemption and Excuse
Exploring the Developmental Dimensions of Responsible Agency

Victoria McGeer

1. Introduction

This chapter will focus on what is probably the most celebrated essay in Strawson's corpus, 'Freedom and Resentment' (Strawson 1974), originally presented to the British Academy in 1962. There is an interesting and open question as to how it connects with Strawson's other concerns and projects; but considered simply in itself, it is surely one of the most remarkable and groundbreaking essays written on the topic of moral responsibility in the last half-century. It has certainly spawned an enormous body of secondary literature and, given its iconoclastic suggestiveness, continues to intrigue philosophers with regard to its core commitments and implications. As R.J. Wallace remarks, 'there is no fixed and stable view that might be labeled the Strawsonian account of responsibility. Strawson's original lecture contains a wealth of ideas, and many philosophers who have been influenced by the lecture have naturally chosen to develop and defend different ones among them, and to develop them in different ways' (Wallace 1994, 10).

Impossible, then, to avoid controversy in unpacking Strawson's ideas. So far as one finds them attractive, the best one can hope to achieve is an account of responsibility—and, of course, our responsibility practices—that resonates with salient claims that Strawson makes and is also worth taking seriously on its own merits. It turns out that this is easier said than done. Like other philosophers working in this space, my goal has been to preserve the central tenets of Strawson's view while adding sufficient detail to make those tenets philosophically defensible. However, such details have a way of highlighting problems inherent in the general approach, and the challenge is to find a way to solve such problems without substantially undercutting the original view. In this chapter, I focus on two related problems. The first is to flesh out in general terms how we should understand Strawson's distinction between agents who are fit to be held responsible and those who are not (i.e. those who are properly exempted from our accountability practices). The second is how to manage the grey area invariably created by

Victoria McGeer, *Between Exemption and Excuse: Exploring the Developmental Dimensions of Responsible Agency* In: *P. F. Strawson and his Philosophical Legacy.* Edited by: Sybren Heyndels, Audun Bengtson, and Benjamin De Mesel, Oxford University Press. © Oxford University Press 2024. DOI: 10.1093/oso/9780192858474.003.0014

Strawson's naturalistic account of what makes for responsible agency—a complex and murky terrain that David Shoemaker has aptly dubbed 'responsibility from the margins' (Shoemaker 2015).

This second problem has drawn more attention of late, with critics rightly pointing out that the bulk of Strawsonian scholarship has focused on delineating the conditions that make someone a (fully) responsible agent, appropriately subjected to an unqualified range of our accountability practices (see, for instance: Brandenburg 2018, 2019; Brandenburg and Strijbos 2020a, 2020b; Kennett 2020; Pickard 2013; Shoemaker 2015). Individuals who do not meet these conditions are simply viewed as exempted. Of course, there is philosophical controversy about how precisely to specify these responsibility-constituting conditions, with significant implications for what sort of agents fall within the charmed circle (this is the first problem my chapter will address).[1] But the assumption has been that this is where all the action lies. There is not much for Strawsonians to say about those who fail to meet these conditions, so no harm is done in treating this distinction as presumptively binary: either the agent is *fully* responsible and thereby subject in an unqualified way to our accountability practices, or the agent is not fully responsible and thereby appropriately exempted from such practices.

The critics just referenced insist that there is more to say. As they rightly point out, there is a whole class, or even classes,[2] of agents who do not fit comfortably into one or other of these categories (the 'fully responsible' versus the exempted). They are somewhere in between. And the question is: Are there resources within Strawson's general approach to accommodate such agents? And if not, how must Strawson's approach be filled out or modified to provide a truly comprehensive account of responsible agency? I shall come to these questions by the end of this chapter, defending a view that I think is commensurate with Strawson's sketchy remarks on this topic. Moreover, this view is commensurate with maintaining the overall shape of our reactive attitudes and practices even in this grey zone of 'proximal' responsible agency[3]—including, for instance, the much debated and much criticized phenomenon of affective blame. However, this is not to say that no modifications are in order. They are, but the modifications I recommend are more in keeping, so I maintain, with Strawson's overall approach to responsible

---

[1] It is important to note that here and throughout this chapter I mean responsibility in the 'accountability' sense. A number of theorists maintain that there are other normatively significant conceptions of responsibility (e.g. responsibility in the 'attributability' sense; responsibility in the 'answerability' sense); and that agents who fail to be (fully) responsible in the accountability sense might still be responsible in one of these other senses (for further discussion, see Shoemaker 2011, 2015; Watson 2004). I put these nuances aside. Adopting Shoemaker's term 'responsibility from the margins', I mean only to be talking about agents in the margins of *accountability* responsibility; hence, agents who are not fully exempted from our accountability practices. I remain neutral on what other notions of responsibility it makes sense to employ in these or other contexts.
[2] I say 'classes', as there may be substantially different kinds of diminished responsible agency (e.g. as found in children versus cognitively atypical adults).
[3] This phrase is inspired by Vygotsky's notion of a 'zone of proximal development' (Vygotsky 1978).

agency, where that agency is understood to be ever a work in progress. Thus, I lead up to this topic by way of a more general discussion and elaboration of Strawson's overall view.

The chapter will proceed as follows. In Section 2, I highlight three signature theses from Strawson's essay that together suggest a naturalistically plausible and attractive view of what it takes to be a responsible agent—namely, to have a capacity for responding to moral reasons (or, as I shall sometimes say, a capacity for normative self-governance). The next two sections delve into some sticky details, considering two rather different versions of this 'capacitarian' approach to responsible agency. Section 3 examines the 'dispositionalist' approach, a view standardly found in the literature, but which I argue encounters fatal problems. Section 4 considers a 'skills-based' alternative that avoids these problems. However, it also entails a more radical view of what it means to be a 'fully responsible' agent, along with a distinctive view of the point and purpose of our accountability practices. On the skills-based approach, there is a sense in which we are *all* 'responsible-agents-in-the-making'; and this in turn puts pressure on the idea that agents in the proximal zone of responsible agency deserve differential treatment in terms of our accountability practices. I address this problem in Section 5, drawing inspiration from Strawson's sketchy remarks on these penumbral cases to outline a distinctive sense in which such differential treatment is mandated, as well as the kind of differential treatment it makes sense to require.

2. Three Signature Strawsonian Theses

First signature thesis: Responsible agency consists in a naturalistically respectable (metaphysically inexpensive) property made salient to theorists by attending to our ordinary attitudes and practices of holding responsible.

Strawson is deservedly famous for his methodological recommendation that philosophers give up their preoccupation with abstract worries about whether the metaphysical thesis of determinism threatens the very idea of responsible agency.[4] The question of what it takes to be such an agent cannot, and should not, be settled on such abstract intellectualist grounds. Instead, we should turn our attention to our everyday attitudes and practices of holding responsible, where the problem of responsible agency has real and pressing significance for us. Indeed, the problem is so pressing and significant that our attitudes and practices are infused with a range of powerful emotions that only seem appropriate in relation to the attitudes and doings of responsible agents. These are what Strawson calls

---

[4] The thesis that all events in the universe, including human decisions and actions, are entirely governed by determinate causal laws.

'reactive attitudes', including in his long and fairly heterogeneous list of such attitudes: gratitude, resentment, indignation, hurt feelings, certain types of adult love, moral approbation, shame, guilt, and remorse. Notably, emotions such as repulsion, fear, pity, and other kinds of love are explicitly excluded (Strawson 1974, 4–6, 9). We may debate the proper extension of the list of reactive attitudes, but once again, what distinguishes them as a class is that we direct them—or feel we ought to direct them—only towards certain kinds of agents.

But what kind of agents are these? I said above 'responsible agents', but in fact this is tendentious shorthand for agents that are *fit to participate* in a wide array of interpersonal relationships 'ranging from the most intimate to the most casual', but which are nevertheless distinctive in so far as they are permeated by our reactive attitudes and practices (Strawson 1974, 6). Strawson's substantive claim is that this is all it takes *to be* a responsible agent: a person fit to participate in such relationships; hence, to be held responsible in the manner of our reactive attitudes and practices. Yet, why should philosophers look here for the distinguishing features of responsible agency? What makes these relationships so special, as distinct from other kinds of relationships in which these attitudes and practices are substantially absent?

The first thing to note is that these other kinds of relationships—or, perhaps better, 'ways of relating' to other human beings—depend on taking a distinctively 'objective' stance towards the person in question. In Strawson's description, it involves seeing that person, 'perhaps, as an object of social policy; as a subject for what, in a wide range of sense, might be called treatment, as something certainly to be taken account, perhaps precautionary account, of; to be managed or handled or cured or trained' (Strawson 1974, 9). And, importantly, although Strawson allows that the objective stance can be emotionally toned in many ways, it cannot be so in all ways:

> ... [i]t may include repulsion or fear, it may include pity or even love, though not all kinds of love. But it cannot include the range of reactive feelings and attitudes which belong to involvement or participation with others in interpersonal human relationships; it cannot include resentment, gratitude, forgiveness, anger, or the sort of love two adults can sometimes be said to feel reciprocally, for each other. (Strawson 1974, 9)

So here we have two very different stances, 'objective' and 'participant', that we can take towards other people. They are stances that engage our emotions in quite different ways and that Strawson sees as 'profoundly *opposed* to each other', though, interestingly 'not altogether *exclusive* of each other' (Strawson 1974, 9, emphasis in the original). I will come back to what Strawson might mean by this remark in my final Section 5 below. But the fundamental question Strawson's observations now press upon theorists is simply this: What would make us take one stance or the other? Strawson's response to this is nuanced, but his key observation is that we sometimes regard taking the objective stance towards someone as *mandated* precisely because they are not 'fit to participate', or participate fully, in ordinary interpersonal relationships: they are 'warped, or deranged, neurotic or just a child' (Strawson 1974, 8). In short, we do not regard them as 'responsible agents'. Hence, we exempt them, and judge that we ought to exempt them, from 'normal participant reactive attitudes' (Strawson 1974, 9).

Now to Strawson's deeper metaphysical point. There is clearly a distinction to be made between agents who are responsible in this sense versus those who are not. This is a distinction that matters enormously to us in our practical lives; and it is one that we are reasonably good at making in our dealings with one another. As Strawson would say, it is grounded in the 'facts as we know them' (Strawson 1974). In making this distinction, we are responding to some feature of agents that may be present or lacking, as the case may be. But this feature has nothing to do with the truth or falsity of the metaphysical thesis of determinism. For, in the first place, the truth or falsity of the thesis is certainly not apparent in the facts as we know them. And, in the second place, even if the thesis is true, it characterizes a universal condition that applies to all human behaviour. Hence, it can have no bearing on the *particularity* of the features on which we rely—and, more importantly, which *matter* to us—in making the relevant practical distinction between agents who are fit to be held responsible and those who are not.

And so we arrive at the positive face of Strawson's novel methodological recommendation: If we want to gain some theoretical purchase on the substantive feature of agents that make them fit to be held responsible, then we should delve more deeply into the nature of our reactive attitudes and practices and see what we can learn from them. This takes us to Strawson's next signature thesis.

Second signature thesis: Our reactive attitudes and practices express a normative demand/expectation for due moral regard.

In excavating our accountability practices, Strawson begins by noting a distinctive feature of human beings: that we care enormously whether others treat us with 'goodwill, attention or esteem, on the one hand or contempt, indifference and disregard on the other' (Strawson 1974, 5). Indeed, we care so much about this that we are prepared to 'demand some degree of goodwill or regard on the part of those who stand in [various] relationships to us', modulated to suit the particular kinds of relationships in question (e.g. as between family, friends, or relative strangers) (Strawson 1974, 6). But this feature of our interpersonal ways of relating to one another is naturally expressed in and through our reactive attitudes. As Strawson says, 'the making of the demand *is* the proneness to such attitudes' in all their rich complexity (Strawson 1974, 22).

The thesis that our reactive attitudes express—and indeed communicate (Watson 1987)—a demand for (contextually modulated) moral regard is attractive on three counts. In the first place, it jibes with the phenomenology of the relevant emotions. For instance, when we feel resentment or gratitude, we experience these emotions as merited or deserved in light of how someone behaves towards us relative to the demand for due regard: if they intentionally (or negligently) flout that demand, we think they deserve our resentment; if they intentionally exceed the demand, they merit our gratitude.

Secondly, the thesis explains why our reactive attitudes and practices are central to some kinds of human relationships, but not to others. They are central to those human relationships which depend, in their very nature, on all parties in the relationship making and respecting the demand in question. Friendship, for instance, is not a conceptual possibility without a particular framework of friend-regarding normative demands that all parties to such relationships are generally expected to respect. But this is not true of other relationships: for instance, with pets. We may love our pets dearly, and society may impose various normative demands on *us* with regard to the kind of treatment we owe to our pets. But we impose no such normative demands and expectations on our pets for obvious reasons. Of course, we may attempt to regulate their behaviour via a training regimen. But we do not expect our pets to understand the importance of showing us due moral regard in how they comport themselves in relation to us, and, hence, our reactive attitudes and practices are quite out of place with respect to them.

Finally, the thesis is attractive because it has substantive implications for what it takes to be a responsible agent. This takes us to Strawson's third signature thesis, constituting the crux of his approach to this entire debate. For, contrary to the arid speculations of the metaphysicians he disdains, the kind of feature we arrive at via a consideration of our reactive attitudes and practices has two main attractions: (1) it is naturalistically intelligible; and (2) it is evidently the kind of feature that makes possible the normatively enriched field of interpersonal relationships that lies at the heart of human sociality; thus, it wears its practical importance on its sleeve.

Third signature thesis: To be a responsible agent—i.e. to have what it takes to be an *appropriate* target of reactive attitudes and practices—is to have the capacity for responding to moral reasons.

Gary Watson is deservedly famous for drawing attention to the 'incipiently communicative' nature of our reactive attitudes and practices as Strawson presents them (Watson 1987, 264). But his interpretative essay goes further in drawing an obvious implication from that view. In order to sensibly impose normative demands on someone, they must have what it takes, psychologically speaking, to understand the nature of those demands and govern themselves accordingly (Watson 1987, 263–5). And so we come to the third signature thesis of Strawson's essay: to be a responsible agent is to have the capacity to understand and live up to the core demand expressed in our reactive attitudes and practices; namely, that we treat one another with due moral regard, as required by the relationships and circumstances in which we find ourselves. In short, it is to have a capacity for responding to moral reasons—or, as I shall sometimes say, a capacity for normative self-governance. Call this the 'capacitarian' approach to responsible agency.[5]

Is this really Strawson's view of what it takes to be a responsible agent? No doubt there are Strawsonians who would disagree. But I think it is a reasonable and attractive interpretation of his view, again on three counts. In the first place, as Watson so ably emphasizes, it fits nicely with Strawson's explicitly articulated view that our reactive attitudes and practices make normative demands.

Secondly, while a number of Strawson's observations concern agents who are *incapacitated* in some or all respects for ordinary interpersonal relationships' and therefore inappropriate targets of our reactive attitudes and practices (Strawson 1974, 12), his tendency is to supply descriptive examples of such agents, rather than an explicit characterization of what they share in common; e.g. 'the agent... is warped, deranged, neurotic or just a child' (Strawson 1974, 8). Still, given the general drift of his remarks, it is not much of a stretch to identify this common element as a substantial incapacity to respond to the moral reasons. This would certainly help pinpoint the kind of 'psychological abnormality' or 'moral under-development' that Strawson insists prevents such agents from (fully) participating in ordinary interpersonal relationships.

A third and final reason to endorse this capacitarian interpretation is that it presumptively satisfies Strawson's desiderata on providing an adequate philosophical account of responsible agency. The capacity for normative self-governance looks to be the kind of agential feature that is practically important, reasonably detectable in our day-to-day experience with one another, and plausibly naturalistic (i.e. metaphysically undemanding). Hence, discerning the presence, or absence, of such a capacity need not go beyond the 'facts as we know them'.

Advocates of this approach to responsible agency are particularly keen to stress its naturalistic bona fides. But fleshing out the capacitarian view in suitable naturalistic detail gives rise to certain problems that are hard to square with the central tenets of Strawson's view. In the following sections, I discuss two possible ways of elaborating the view: one that I call a 'dispositionalist' approach (Section 3) and the other a 'skills-based' approach (Section 4). Both approaches encounter difficulties, but I shall argue that they are insurmountable for the

---

[5] Although they each develop it in their own way, notable advocates of this general view include: Fischer and Ravizza (1998); Pettit and Smith (1996); Vargas (2013); Wallace (1994); Wolf (1987, 1990). This is by no means an exhaustive list.

dispositionalist. Admittedly, the skills-based approach has some presumptively radical implications. But as will I go on to suggest in Section 5, these are in fact congenial with Strawson's overall view and, indeed, allow for an interesting development of the sketchy remarks he makes in connection with that under-discussed class of agents who fall within the grey area between excuse and exemption.

3. The Dispositionalist Approach to Responsible Agency

One way to vindicate the claim that having a capacity for responding to moral reasons is a naturalistically intelligible property of human agents is to model it on the dispositional properties of everyday physical objects (Fara 2008; Smith 2003; Vihvelin 2004). There is nothing metaphysically mysterious, for instance, in attributing the dispositional property of 'fragility' to a glass vase. Of course, dispositional properties can *seem* mysterious in so far as they are essentially connected with something's propensity or 'power' (as is sometimes said) to manifest some characteristic behaviour under a range of counterfactual conditions. For instance, we say a vase is 'fragile' just in case we assume that *here and now* it has a propensity/power to break under a range of (relevant) counterfactual conditions (droppings, strikings, throwings, heatings, etc.). But we explain this mysterious-sounding propensity by reference to some quite unmysterious, naturalistically respectable (albeit scientifically arcane) physical property the vase possesses here and now: its underlying molecular structure. In short, we have a perfectly intelligible naturalistic account of what it means for the vase to possess the dispositional property of 'fragility':

> a vase is 'fragile' just in case it is, here and now, physically structured so that, under a range of relevant counterfactual conditions (strikings, droppings, heatings, etc.), it would (typically) break under those conditions.

Notice that the above characterization stipulates that the fragile vase would 'typically' break under the specified counterfactual conditions. This is to embrace the widely accepted view that dispositional properties are never 'sure-fire'. Fragile vases do not invariably break when dropped. This may be due to a variety of interfering factors, such as an uncharacteristic soft spot in the floor just at the point of impact, or someone's incredibly fast reflexes in grabbing the vase mid-fall. But it may also be down to a random, fluke event: a chance resilience in the vase's inter-atomic bonds that kept it from breaking when it normally would. Be that as it may, the key point on which dispositionalists insist is that none of these possibilities undermines the propriety of attributing the dispositional property of 'fragility' to the vase, for such properties characterize real and robust patterns in possible behaviour thanks to how the vase is physically structured, minor perturbations in those patterns notwithstanding.

Let us turn now to the responsibility-conferring capacity for responding to moral reasons. According to the dispositionalist, this too should be understood as a propensity or power; in this case, an agent's propensity or power to understand and govern themselves in accord with the moral reasons, not just in the actual circumstances, but under a relevantly wide range of counterfactual circumstances as well. Does exercising such a power require any untoward metaphysical hocus-pocus? Not at all, the dispositionalist claims; for, just as in the case of the vase, this so-called power can be modelled as a naturalistically grounded dispositional property, where the relevant grounding is some fiendishly complex neural and ultimately physical property of the agent's brain; a property that I shall henceforth simply refer to as 'psychological'.[6] Hence, and by analogy with the vase:

> a person has the (responsibility-conferring) capacity for responding to moral reasons just in case they are, here and now, psychologically structured so that under a range of relevant counterfactual conditions, they would (typically) respond to the moral reasons obtaining in those conditions.

Once again, this is not to suggest the dispositional property need be sure-fire in order to be appropriately attributed. And this is just as well, because it is a well-known fact that responsible agents sometimes fail to 'exercise their capacity' for responding to moral reasons, saying or doing things in consequence that are (prima facie) objectionable on moral grounds. On the dispositionalist approach, this simply means the agent fails to manifest the relevant dispositional property. Again, this failure may be due to various interfering factors, a point to which I shall return below. But the crucial thing to emphasize is that such failures do not necessarily indicate that the (responsibility-conferring) dispositional property is not in place. It is in place so long as the agent in question has the relevant psychological (i.e. neural and ultimately physical) grounding property at the time of their objectionable behaviour.

While a capacitarian approach of this sort is admittedly attractive on naturalistic grounds, it is not without problems. I here identify four key problems. The first two are not fatal to the position but require some finessing to resolve in a plausible way. By contrast, the last two seem to me much more problematic; indeed, problematic enough to suggest abandoning this approach altogether in favour of the skills-based alternative I shall discuss and defend in Section 4.

---

[6] All references to psychological properties in this chapter are to be read as ontologically reducible to complex neural, and ultimately physical, properties of the agent's brain. This is not to suggest they are likewise explanatorily reducible.

3.1 The Demarcation Problem

Recall that Strawson's fundamental objective is to identify a naturalistically plausible feature of agents, discernible in our day-to-day interactions with one another, that marks a principled distinction between agents who are fit to be held responsible and those who are not. We have seen why it makes sense to nominate a capacity for responding to moral reasons as the responsibility-conferring feature. However, as any capacitarian must acknowledge, having a capacity is not an on/off sort of thing. Capacities come in degrees; and this may seem to suggest there is no sharp distinction to be made between agents who are fit to be held responsible and those who are not.

Of course, many would insist that this is not a problem at all. It just acknowledges the facts on the ground; indeed, in a way that traditional metaphysicians are unable to do. After all, if responsible agency is linked with having some contra-causal metaphysical power, then presumably agents either have this power or they do not. And this would imply there really is a bright metaphysical line to be drawn between agents who are responsible and those who are not. But, in fact, this is not how we treat the distinction in day-to-day life. When bright lines are required, we legislate; and do so precisely because, for various pragmatic reasons, we need to impose some artificial structure on what is recognized to be a fundamentally messy empirical reality.

So, here the capacitarian may simply bite the bullet. True, there is no bright metaphysical distinction to be made between agents who are fit to be held responsible and those who are not. But this does not undermine the normative value in having a status conferring notion of a 'fully' responsible agent (Korsgaard 1996; Schapiro 1999). By that, we could simply mean someone who has earned the right to be treated as a responsible agent; to be granted the full rights and duties of such an agent, including the 'right' (as some consider it) to be exposed in an unqualified way to our reactive attitudes and practices. Of course, to have earned this right in a normatively just world, the agent must surely have a sufficiently well-developed capacity for responding to moral reasons in place; otherwise, it would seem intuitively unfair to expose them to such attitudes and practices in the ordinary way. Anyone who lies below this threshold of normative competence should be treated differently; and if they fall sufficiently below such a threshold, then they ought to be exempted. Determining where these various cut-off points lie may present us with some tricky practical issues; but the fact that we need to impose such structure on an essentially scalar feature of agents does not undermine the theoretical integrity of this general approach. And so, we may freely endorse the following dispositional characterization of a 'fully' responsible agent: a person has a sufficiently well-developed capacity for responding to moral reasons to count as 'fully' responsible just in case they are, here and now, psychologically structured so that under a sufficiently wide range of counterfactual conditions, they would (typically) respond to the moral reasons obtaining in those conditions.

3.2 The Epistemic Problem

As noted above, responsible agents sometimes fail to exercise their capacity for responding to moral reasons; and this is quite different from failing to have the capacity (to a sufficiently well-developed degree) in the first place. After all, agents who fail to exercise their capacity can be the appropriate target of reactive blame; not always, of course, as they may have some legitimate justification or excuse for failing to respond to the moral reasons. I shall come to this in a moment. But agents who do not have the capacity—or do not have it to a sufficiently well-developed degree—can hardly be faulted for failing to exercise it; hence, they seem inappropriate targets of reactive blame, or so common intuition suggests. In short, much seems to hang on this difference.

Fortunately, the dispositionalist can give us a clear articulation of what makes for this difference. At the time of their action, either the agent was psychologically structured so that they would (typically) have responded to the moral reasons obtaining in those conditions, or they were not. But short of seeing how the agent *would* behave under a range of sufficiently similar counterfactual conditions, it is hard to see how this determination could be made. At the very least, this suggests we should be epistemically extremely cautious in responding to people's putative wrongdoings with reactive blame, especially if we have not had many dealings with them. This conclusion may be very welcome to a number of philosophers who find Strawson's apparent endorsement of our readiness to experience resentment and indignation in our day-to-day interactions normatively objectionable. Be that as it may, this epistemological situation is hard to square with Strawson's vision of the relative ease with which we apparently discern one another's aptness to be targeted with such attitudes in our everyday interactions with one another. So, some alternation in that vision seems to be in order.

3.3 The 'Hard' Problem of Deserved Blame

This next problem seems to me fatal to the dispositionalist view.[7] Assume, for the sake of argument, that we are now confronted with a normatively competent agent who fails to respond to the moral reasons on a given occasion. As we have already noted, this is a familiar situation. Competent moral agents do fail in this way from time to time, injuring or harming another person in consequence. But, often in such cases, they can offer their victim a plea or excuse that effectively reassures the victim that their actions did not display any culpable lack of respect, concern, or good will; that it was an innocent or excusable mistake concerning the likely

---

[7] This argument is developed in McGeer (2018a, 2018b); McGeer and Pettit (2015); Pettit (2018, chap. 5).

consequences of their action (that it would cause harm); or perhaps it was something they were constrained to do, despite the harm it would cause. Hence, in acting as they did, they did not fail—or culpably fail—to be responsive to the moral reasons.

The case is quite otherwise when agents *culpably* fail to be responsive to the moral reasons, i.e. without any excuse or justification. Here we assume that, given the agent's normative competence, they could have shown their victim due moral regard. There was nothing getting in the way of their doing that; nothing that might reasonably let them off the hook. Hence, in Strawson's estimation—and by our commonsense lights—they are quintessentially appropriate targets of reactive blame for failing to exercise a capacity they palpably have.

Now, we ask, in what sense do these failing agents palpably have the requisite capacity in place? We noted above that to be judged 'normatively competent' (in that sense 'fully' responsible), an agent's capacity for responding to moral reasons must be one that is sufficiently well-developed to take them over some murkily specified threshold, at which point holding them to account for their behaviour in the manner of ordinary reactive attitudes seems normatively justified. On the dispositional view, we have taken this to mean the following: a normatively competent agent is (here and now) psychologically structured so that, under a sufficiently wide range of counterfactual conditions (stipulatively determined so as to satisfy these threshold requirements), they would be responsive to the relevant moral reasons obtaining in those conditions. And yet, here we have a normatively competent agent who nonetheless fails to respond to those reasons in the actual circumstances. How do we account for this failure?

One obvious explanation is that the actual conditions are sufficiently unlike the conditions in which they would be reasons-responsive as to fall outside the range of their normative competence. So, in effect, we would be blaming them for failing to manifest a disposition they do not in fact have: to respond to the moral reasons in the specific circumstances (or kind of circumstances) in which they behaved objectionably. But now, how is this any more normatively acceptable than blaming an agent who is not 'fully' responsible in the stipulated threshold sense? After all, both kinds of agents fail to have the kind of normative competence that would allow them to behave appropriately in the circumstances envisioned. So, both kinds of agents should really be let off the hook.

This is an unpalatable bullet for the dispositionalist to bite. But perhaps we have mischaracterized the situation at hand; perhaps there is a better way, on the dispositionalist approach, to understand how a competent agent could fail in a blameworthy way. To see why, recall that dispositional properties in general are never 'sure-fire' even when no interfering factors are present. The precious Ming vase was dropped on the tile floor, but, flukily, it didn't break; its interatomic bonds inexplicably held together, and everyone breathed a sigh of relief. Similarly, the dispositionalist might say, a normatively competent agent could be psychologically structured so that they typically would respond to the moral reasons in the specific circumstances in which they find themselves; i.e. those circumstances do not fall outside the range of their normative competence. Nonetheless, on this occasion, they simply fail to do what they should do, morally speaking. Hence, it is reasonable to blame them for that failure.

And now we come to the nub of the hard problem. Common sense dictates that agents must earn or deserve the blame they receive; that their moral failures are down to them in a normatively substantive way. This is what makes it appealing to source such failures in something like an agent's metaphysically unconstrained 'act of will'. Of course, the dispositionalist has ruled out this explanation as naturalistically unacceptable; but it seems they have nothing to offer in its place, at least at the level of agential responsibility and control. The agent simply and flukily failed to manifest the relevant dispositional property, despite circumstances being opportune for the agent to be reasons-responsive. Of course, analogous to the vase, we could point to some random subatomic events occurring in the relevant neural circuitry of the agent's brain. This might give us a naturalistically acceptable account of why the agent failed to respond to the moral reasons on this occasion; namely, a glitch in neural processing. But this explanation is hardly consistent with blaming the agent for that failure. Indeed, it would be more appropriate to extend our sympathy, given the untoward character of this specific failure in light of (what is assumed to be) their dispositionally robust normative competence.

So, it seems the dispositionalist is left with a stark choice. They can bite the bullet, retaining their naturalistic account of what it means to be a responsible agent, but at the seeming cost of providing no normatively acceptable defence of our attitudes and practices of holding one another to account (see, for instance, Smith 2003). Or they can abandon their dispositional view, hoping to find a naturalistic alternative that does a better job on this normative front. Shortly, I shall propose just such an alternative. But first, let me mention one final problem for the dispositionalist that will help motivate the alternative I propose.

3.4 The Dudley Do-Right Problem

The hard problem, as I mentioned above, seems to me sufficient to sink the dispositionalist view. But, even putting that aside, it has one curious implication that should not go unremarked. As we have just seen, the dispositionalist endorses a particular characterization of what it is to be a normatively competent agent: such agents are psychologically (neurally/physically) structured in such a way as to be reliably—indeed, *robustly*—responsive to the moral reasons under a sufficiently wide range of counterfactual conditions. Hence, when they fail to respond to those reasons under conditions that fall within their normative competence, they are (by definition) acting 'out of (dispositional) character'. But this implies that normatively competent agents are generally rather saintly characters; in effect, they have the normative dispositional profile of a Dudley Do-Right, who never intentionally swerves from doing his duty.[8]

The problem here is clear. While there may indeed be Dudley Do-Rights among us, this does not match our ordinary conception of what it takes to be a 'fully' responsible agent; one that is sufficiently normatively competent to be an appropriate target of everyday reactive attitudes and practices. We often take such agents to have moral flaws; indeed, sometimes *significant* moral flaws that not only account for their bad behaviour, but which we often regard as dispositionally resilient. (In fact, we often take ourselves to be such agents as well.) But these reflections do not lead us to judge that such agents (ourselves included) are appropriately exempted from ordinary accountability practices; that they lack what it takes to merit the kind of reactively infused blame that Strawson highlights as part and parcel of such practices. To the contrary. So, once again, dispositionalists are faced with a hard choice: they can hold on to their preferred naturalistic characterization of what it takes to be a normatively competent agent—a characterization that now seems quite eccentric—or they can search for an alternative characterization that promises to comport more nearly with, and ideally vindicate, our ordinary conception of what 'fully' responsible agents are really like. This is (partly) what motivates the skills-based approach I turn to next.

4. The Skills-Based Approach to Responsible Agency

The key insight driving the skills-based approach is that agential capacities, especially of the sort at issue here, are quite unlike the dispositional properties of non-agential objects; and to emphasize their distinctiveness, I shall henceforth refer to them as 'skills' in contrast with mere (object-centred) 'dispositions' (McGeer 2018a, 2018b; Ryle 1949). This is not to deny that skills share some superficial similarities with dispositions; but these pale in comparison to their distinctive features, which need to be highlighted if we are to make progress on the problems in question.

For instance, one superficial similarity is that dispositions and skills both come in degrees. A vase can be more or less fragile; a person can be more or less responsive to moral reasons. But notice that we also say, and perhaps more colloquially, that a person's capacity is more or less 'well developed'. Not so in

---

[8] For those deprived of the cultural experience, Dudley Do-Right is a cartoon character from the 1960s, described in Wikipedia as a 'conscientious and cheerful Canadian Mountie' (i.e. a member of the Royal Canadian Mounted Police), ever bent on bringing the evil Snidely Whiplash (and other miscreants) to justice (https://en.wikipedia.org/wiki/Dudley_Do-Right).

connection with a vase; we never say that its fragility is more or less 'well developed', even though its fragility can certainly increase over time (e.g. by acquiring stress-induced micro-fractures through negligent treatment).

This is not simply a quirk of the English language. Rather, it marks a fundamental difference between skills and dispositions; namely, that skills are essentially developmental in nature. To have a skill is to possess an inherently dynamic or labile capacity that takes agential work to develop and maintain. This becomes clear when we consider some examples: speaking a language, bike-riding, playing the piano, mountain-climbing, solving cryptic crossword puzzles; and generally being reason-responsive in a given domain. All of them take work to develop; and they all get rusty with disuse. They are, in effect, 'use it or lose it' agential properties. Needless to say, the dispositional properties of objects are not dynamic in this way. Fragile objects do not need to work at developing or maintaining their fragility. Rather, it takes external work—generally our work—to alter or change these relatively stable properties of things.

But what sort of work must agents do in order to develop and maintain their skills? The answer is 'practice', where practice involves repeated attempts to manifest some target behaviour under conditions that give agents feedback as to how well or badly they are doing, according to some standard of performance. If such conditions are relatively stable, practice may eventuate in a skill that is relatively easy to maintain (e.g. tying shoelaces). Ryle himself referred to such skills as 'habits' (Ryle 1949, 42). But more demanding skills—skills that must be exercised in a potentially open-ended variety of circumstances—require ongoing agential effort to develop and maintain (e.g. mountain-climbing, speaking a language, writing philosophy papers, responding to moral reasons). Indeed, the line between development and maintenance in such cases begins to blur, as agents must continue to test, probe, and explore different ways of exercising such skills, and then adjust what they do in light of the feedback they receive. Ryle called such open-ended skills 'intelligent capacities', noting that in and through their exercise the agent is 'still learning' (Ryle 1949, 42).[9]

Notice that feedback from the environment plays a critical and continuing role in this (ongoing) developmental process. In fact, it is a kind of external 'scaffolding' that cannot be thrown away. Of course, the kind of external feedback agents need to develop and hone their skills will depend significantly on the capacities in question. For instance, certain skills are essentially individualistic physical skills: walking, mountaineering, target-shooting. Instruction from others can certainly help in developing and maintaining such skills and is often pragmatically essential. But, in principle, such skills could be learned in isolation from others, simply by trying to walk, climb a mountain, hit a target, and getting corrective feedback

---

[9] For further discussion of the distinction between habits and intelligent capacities, see McGeer (2018a).

from the physical environment. But this is not the case with skills that are essentially *social* in nature, i.e. skills that involve operating within an interpersonal norm-governed environment: speaking a language, dancing the tango, playing soccer, dining in a restaurant. While such skills have their physical components, the crucial thing agents must learn is how to govern their own behaviour in accordance with socially regulated norms. For these norms are what constitute and constrain the very activities in which agents are learning to engage. Hence, social feedback from others regarding how well or badly they are doing in conforming to such norms is a critical part of the (ongoing) learning process.

There is one final point that deserves special emphasis. We have already noted that, according to the skills-based approach to (intelligent) capacities, there is no developmental endpoint. Agential capacities of this sort are always a work in progress, requiring ongoing corrective feedback from the physical and/or social environment to develop and hone them. But this is consistent with the observation that there are important differences between relative novices and relative experts. In particular, novices require a specially supported and structured environment in which to develop their skills to a level of sufficient competence that this requirement can be relaxed. I shall have more to say about the special nature of this learning environment in Section 5, as it is germane to the issue of responsibility in the margins. For now, however, I return to the main challenge of this section: providing a naturalistic characterization of a normatively competent agent that avoids the list of problems encountered by the dispositionalist view. How does the skills-based approach fare in this regard? I address the four problems raised for that approach here in reverse order.

4.1 Solving the Dudley Do-Right Problem

Dispositionalist and skills-based capacitarians can agree that agents count only as 'normatively competent'—hence, are fit and proper targets of our everyday accountability practices—just in case they have a 'sufficiently well-developed' capacity for responding to moral reasons. But there the agreement ends.

On the dispositionalist approach, as we have seen, attributing the requisite capacity involves viewing agents from an explicitly atemporal perspective. Specifically, at the very moment in which they act, they must be deemed to have a particular physical/psychological constitution such that they (typically) *would* respond to the moral reasons obtaining in a (sufficiently) wide range of counterfactual conditions, including especially conditions that are sufficiently like their actual circumstances. In short, they must be deemed to have a sufficiently robust—and, in my view, unrealistically saintly—dispositional profile at the very moment in which they act.

On the skills-based approach, by contrast, attributing the requisite (dynamic) capacity involves viewing agents from an explicitly inter-temporal perspective. Specifically, they must be deemed to have what it takes, psychologically speaking, to develop and maintain the skill of responding to moral reasons through practice. While this involves a richer conception of the agent's psychology in one respect, it is also far more modest in another. It is richer in so far as it presents normatively competent agents as agents who have the psychological wherewithal to take responsibility for (re)shaping their capacity for responding to moral reasons over time. But it is also far more modest in so far as there is no presumption that normatively competent agents will be such as to exercise their capacity well on any given occasion, whether for cognitive or motivational reasons. Indeed, given the demandingness of the skill involved, the presumption is they may often fail to show due moral regard, according to standards generally endorsed in the community (though of course failing to meet such standards is not always to fail egregiously, a point we should not forget). In short, on the skills-based approach, the Dudley Do-Right problem simply disappears. Normatively competent agents have room to be the morally flawed agents we all recognize ourselves to be, a fact certainly emphasized by Strawson through underscoring our everyday experience with the range of reactive attitudes and practices (negative ones included) that permeate our interpersonal relationships 'from the most intimate to the most casual' (Strawson 1974, 6).

4.2 Solving the Hard Problem of Deserved Blame

But can the skills-based approach make equally satisfying headway on the hard problem of 'deserved blame'; i.e. reconciling a naturalistic conception of what it takes to be a normatively competent agent with the commonsense view that such agents are sometimes justly blamed for failing to respond to the moral reasons? To be precise, they are justly blamed just in case they are *agentially* responsible for their failures, absent any acceptable excuse or justification. And the problem with the dispositionalist approach is that their failures are not only surprising given their normative competence (as characterized by the dispositionalist), but also completely outside of their agential control; a bad-luck, glitchy misfiring of underlying neural circuitry that otherwise operates in a fairly reliable way.

We have seen how the skills-based approach takes a step in the right direction; there is no presumption that normatively competent agents, whose dynamic capacity for responding to moral reasons is always a work in progress, will exercise that skill well on any given occasion. But how are agents *themselves* responsible for such failures, especially in such a way as to make blame a distinctively appropriate (i.e. 'deserved') response to such failures? Once again, the skills-based approach insists this question cannot be meaningfully addressed except from an inter-temporal/developmental perspective. But once that perspective is adopted, a satisfying answer to this question is readily available. The answer has two connected prongs.

The first prong is simply this: normatively competent agents are themselves responsible for their failures because they—and only they—are able to *take* responsibility for developing and maintaining their capacity for responding to moral reasons; a capacity which, on this occasion, has proved inadequate. They do so, as we have seen, not just by exercising that capacity well, but also (and primarily) by having what it takes, psychologically speaking, to interpret corrective feedback from others as relevant to their performance and adjust what they do in light of that feedback. Such feedback will certainly have an informational component; but if it is to do a good job of providing agents with the kind of external scaffolding they need to avoid such failures in the future, it must have a motivational component as well, encouraging agents to focus their energy on trying to do better going forward.

This takes us to the second prong of the skills-based reply; namely, vindicating blame as an appropriate response to (perceived) wrongdoing. The general idea is that blame is appropriate—and, in that sense, 'deserved'—in so far as it is particularly well-suited to giving agents the feedback they need to develop and/or bolster their capacity for responding to moral reasons. Indeed, all our reactive attitudes and practices can be seen in this light. Given their range and intensity, not to mention their significance for us in negotiating the complex terrain of our interpersonal relationships, they are, as Strawson characterizes them, precisely the scaffolding infrastructure we need to sustain these capacities more generally in the community at large.

But what is it about our reactive attitudes and practices that makes them particularly apt in this regard? To fill in these details, we should recall certain aspects of Strawson's analysis; in particular, the second and third signature theses from Section 1. The second thesis stresses what it is we communicate through these attitudes and practices, at least in a generalized sense: the standing demand for due moral regard. The third thesis reminds us that we only direct these attitudes and practices towards certain sorts of agents: those who have the capacity to live up to this normative demand. But now, taking these theses together, we arrive at the following implication: targeting particular agents with our reactive attitudes and practices provides them with a kind of exhortative feedback. We are effectively telling them that we do not despair of them as moral agents; that we do not view them 'objectively'; i.e. as individuals to be manipulated or managed or somehow worked around; indeed, that we hold them accountable to a standard of moral agency precisely because we think them capable of living up to that standard. So, reactive attitudes communicate a positive message even in their most negative guise; even in the guise of anger, resentment, indignation. The fact that we express them says to their recipients that we see them as individuals who, going forward, can certainly do better in understanding and living up to the norms that make for moral community. And, indeed, that we expect them to do better precisely because of the feedback we are now providing (see too, McGeer and Pettit 2015).

I said above that feedback of the relevant sort must be both informationally rich and motivationally salient if it is to do a good job of scaffolding the development/ maintenance of an agent's capacity for responding to moral reasons. This calls to mind a more controversial aspect of the reactive attitudes and practices as Strawson describes them; namely, their affective tone. The value of the blaming emotions in particular—resentment, indignation, moral outrage—has met with some scepticism (Brandenburg 2018; Nussbaum 2016; Pereboom 2014; Pickard 2011, 2013; Seneca 2010; Waller 2014).[10] But here, I think, the skills-based approach provides insight into why we should be hesitant to completely disparage this dimension of our reactive attitudes and practices. Of course, it may be true, as Strawson observes, that such emotions are practically unavoidable in the context of ordinary interpersonal relationships, signifying how much we care that others treat us with due moral regard. But, from the skills-based perspective, a crucial consideration is the impact that expressing such emotions has on others, signalling to them how much we care and, more importantly, how determined we are to bring them back, as Adam Smith says, 'to a more just sense of what is due to other people' (Smith 1759/1982, part I. chap. 3. sect. i). In short, it is the emotionality of our reactive attitudes that may help explain their distinctive power in scaffolding one another's moral capacities (McGeer 2013, 2018a).

There is one final point that deserves emphasis. So far, I have talked rather skeletally of what it takes to be a normatively competent agent on the skills-based approach; hence, a fitting target of our reactive attitudes and practices. But now, we can put more flesh on the bones. As suggested by the account so far, our reactive attitudes will be well targeted if their recipients have the psychological wherewithal to interpret and respond appropriately to the message these attitudes convey. But what does this imply? The competency requirement might suggest that agents should immediately understand why they have been targeted with the reactive attitude in question. But, on the skills-based approach, even this is not essential. All that matters is that agents have some basic normative awareness of the *significance* of being so targeted; specifically, that their actions have been subjected to normative review, which review now calls on them to provide some normatively relevant response. In my view, agents show such basic normative awareness simply by way of their own reactive sensitivities; i.e. their tendency to experience a relevant reactive emotion in response to the other's reactive attitude (e.g. guilt, shame, or even indignation in response to someone's blame). These

---

[10] But for resistance to such scepticism, see Cherry (2019); Lorde (1997); McGeer and McKenna (in prep); Muldoon (2008); Srinivasan (2016, 2018).

responsive reactive emotions are relevant in so far as they 'comment' on the normative propriety of the original reactive attitude (guilt acknowledges blame; indignation rejects it). But, more importantly, they are critical motivationally in so far as they promote further normative engagement with others, prompting agents to engage in 'reactive exchanges' (often involving third parties) that sometimes acknowledge, but very often challenge, the original person's normative judgement.

It is these reactive exchanges that constitute a particularly potent site of moral development. For this is where the normative feedback that agents supply to one another is discussed and negotiated, sometimes in fraught and unproductive ways, but often in ways that generate real moral insight and hence a better understanding of how to operate in accord with the moral reasons. Indeed, what is notable about such exchanges is their potential for supporting development on any given side of the exchange. In cases of blame, for instance, the blamer may have more to learn than the person blamed; for example, that their judgements were over-hasty, or harsh, or unduly moralistic, and, in fact, it is the blamer, rather than the person blamed, who owes the other contrition, apology, and a commitment to working on their own moral failings (of course, often it is the other way around).

Putting all these pieces together, we arrive at the following conclusion. On a skills-based account of responsible agency, normatively competent agents—agents who are fit and proper targets of our reactive attitudes and practices—are simply agents with the psychological wherewithal to engage in meaningful reactive exchanges. To be deemed 'normatively competent', they need not be highly skilled in responding to the moral reasons (i.e. 'above threshold' reasons-responsive). But they do need to be *reactively responsive* to other agents. This involves, first, an emotionally grounded, informationally attentive sensitivity to the reactive attitudes of others; and, secondly, the wherewithal to engage in a meaningful form of reactive exchange that potentially foments moral insight and development. In short, they must be responsive to the scaffolding power of reactive attitudes, for it is this very responsiveness that enables such agents to be responsible; that is, to maintain and develop the requisite capacity for responding to moral reasons.

4.3 Alleviating the Epistemic Problem

The epistemic problem, remember, is simply that of explaining how we could know that someone is sufficiently normatively competent to be a fit and proper target of our reactive attitudes and practices. This problem is challenging for the dispositionalist approach, since it involves assessing whether someone is psychologically structured *here and now* so that they would respond to the moral reasons in a sufficiently wide range of counterfactual conditions, including conditions that are very like the ones they are actually in. Dispositionalists might claim that we deal with epistemic problems like this all the time, as in determining whether a vase is fragile. But even they must concede that the two cases are massively different in complexity, if not in kind; hence, the epistemic problem remains highly challenging on their sort of approach.

But this is not the case in the skills-based approach. As the discussion above makes clear, the bar has been significantly lowered on what it takes to be a normatively competent agent; namely, a person who is reactively responsive to other agents and, thus, reactively sensitive to the scaffolding power of reactive attitudes. For this is what it takes to 'have'—in a dynamic, developmental sense—the requisite capacity for responding to moral reasons. Moreover, this is hardly an esoteric feature of agents that is difficult to discern in our everyday dealings with one another. Although there may be controversial cases, we are generally quite adept at detecting when individuals are substantially disabled in this regard; for instance, as Strawson says, if they are 'warped or deranged, neurotic or just a child' (Strawson 1974, 8). Such agents, we judge, are psychologically unfit to do the kind of normative work required of them in ordinary reactive exchanges. In sum, the epistemic problem seems far more tractable on the skills-based approach.

4.4 Revisiting the Demarcation Problem

The demarcation problem, recall, is one of identifying a naturalistically plausible feature of agents, discernible in our day-to-day interactions with one another, that marks a *principled* distinction between agents who are fit to be held responsible and those who are not. Capacitarians are generally bound to acknowledge that the very feature that makes for this difference is something that comes in degrees, creating a considerable grey area between those who are 'fully responsible'—i.e. sufficiently normatively competent to be exposed (in an unqualified way) to our reactive attitudes and practices—and those who are fully exempted. This generates two further problems: first, specifying what sufficiency amounts to in this context and, second, having something reasonable to say about how agents in the grey area should be treated that acknowledges both their in-between status and developmental potential.[11]

We have seen how the dispositionalist handles the first of these problems by specifying the degree of counterfactual robustness in the dispositional property that must be in place if agents are to count as having 'over the threshold' normative competence. Only then are they fit and proper targets of our reactive attitudes and practices. By implicature, agents falling below this threshold are not fitting targets of such attitudes and practices. Beyond that, dispositionalists do not have much to say. After all, from their explicitly non-developmental perspective,

---

[11] Of course, such potential may vary within subclasses of underdeveloped agency.

this second problem of navigating the grey area of in-between responsibility is not really germane to their primary task.

Things are not as straightforward on the skills-based approach. One of its primary virtues, as we have seen, is accommodating the commonsense view that 'normatively competent' agents can often fail—and even fail egregiously—in responding to moral reasons. But this means that normative competence is not so easily specified in terms of an 'above threshold' responsiveness to such reasons, especially if cashed out in dispositional terms (the Dudley Do-Right problem). The skills-based approach addresses this problem by linking normative competence to something more developmentally apropos; namely, 'reactive responsiveness'. Competent agents must have what it takes, psychologically speaking, to engage in meaningful reactive exchanges, enabling them to develop and maintain their capacity for responding to moral reasons. This approach is additionally attractive in making progress on both the hard problem and the epistemic problem. But the proposed specification of 'normative competence' now seems to have two counterintuitive implications that spell trouble for the approach as a whole: (1) it significantly increases the scope of 'normatively competent' agents, thereby possibly encompassing individuals who common sense dictates would fall more naturally into the grey area of those not quite fit to be held responsible; and (2) it further suggests that all such agents are appropriate targets of our reactive attitudes and practices, since these attitudes and practices play an essential role in supporting the development of the very capacity that makes for responsible agency. In short, the skills-based approach seemingly makes no allowances for agents with an underdeveloped capacity for responding to moral reasons. But this conclusion not only flies in the face of common sense, it constitutes a fairly radical departure from the letter, and spirit, of Strawson's text. So, unless its proponents find some way to ward off, or at least soften, these counterintuitive implications, it loses appeal both as an attractive account in its own right and as a viable elaboration of Strawson's view. The next and final section tackles this problem.

5. Navigating the Grey Areas of Responsible Agency

As an initial softening remark, it is worth emphasizing a point made earlier: that any capacitarian must legislate the appropriate application of concepts like 'normatively competent' and 'fully responsible', imposing this conceptual structure somewhat arbitrarily on an invariably messy underlying reality. The question for the capacitarian, then, is how best to impose this structure, given the kind of status-conferring normative work we get such concepts to do. And this means that the criteria by which we make such designations are up for negotiation. That said, it would be odd indeed if this negotiation resulted in a serious contraction of what is generally recognized to be a substantial grey area of 'borderline penumbral cases', to use Strawson's term; i.e. underdeveloped agents, such as children, with respect to whom our reactive attitudes and practices seem neither entirely appropriate nor entirely inappropriate.

Fortunately, this is not a consequence of the skills-based approach. Indeed, by renegotiating the criteria for ascribing 'normative competence', it promises to do more than preserve a sensible and significant grey area of penumbral responsibility. It provides a more nuanced and dynamic picture of how to characterize such 'underdeveloped' agents and, concomitantly, makes suggestions regarding the special modifications to our reactive attitudes and practices plausibly best suited to meeting their specific developmental needs. By way of conclusion, I briefly sketch these constructive implications, leaving their fuller development for another time.

As we saw at the end of the last section, the critical move for the skills-based approach is to focus less attention on agents' first-order responsiveness to moral reasons (especially as conceptualized in dispositional terms) and more on what enables them to take responsibility for developing and honing their skills in this regard. Essentially, this involves having the motivational and cognitive wherewithal to make good and appropriate use of critical feedback from others, delivered powerfully and primarily, so this chapter has argued, in the form of everyday reactive attitudes and practices. And so we arrive at the skills-based conception of 'normative competence': rather than having a suitably robust degree of *reasons* responsiveness, agents must have a suitably developed kind of *reactive* responsiveness: the kind of responsiveness that enables agents to capitalize on the scaffolding power of reactive attitudes.

The questions now facing the skills-based approach are simply these: What does it take to have a 'suitably developed' kind of reactive responsiveness? Is this something that we might plausibly attribute to agents who intuitively fall within the grey area of underdeveloped agency? If not, what modifications to our reactive attitudes and practices are called for in interacting with such agents, and why? I take each of these questions in turn.

In the last section, we saw that (suitably developed) reactive responsiveness has two components. The first is 'reactive sensitivity': agents must have an emotionally mediated, primary awareness of the normative import of others' reactive attitudes, as directed towards their own attitudes and behaviour. But the second is 'reactive engagement': agents must have the psychological wherewithal to respond appropriately to others' reactive attitudes, where this involves engaging in meaningful forms of reactive exchange– discussing, and sometimes disputing, the normative import of their own attitudes and behaviour. For these are the very processes that support moral insight and development. The suggestion made earlier is that the primary site of these exchanges is with other agents; but, as individuals develop, they become increasingly able to conduct meaningful forms of such exchanges in inner dialogue with themselves. Thus, while the need for external scaffolding never disappears, agents become increasingly able to guide and support the development of their own responsiveness to moral reasons by providing such scaffolding to themselves.

Now, what of agents who intuitively fall within the grey area of underdeveloped (or otherwise compromised) responsible agency, such as children or, as Strawson himself suggests, agents with certain psychological impairments? I hope the characterization of normative competence just reviewed makes clear why such agents might reasonably be judged to fall short of this standard. In addition, the skills-based approach adds nuance in suggesting that agents may differ in how they fall short of this standard, either from inadequate reactive sensitivity, inadequate reactive engagement, or both. This might help in grounding finer discriminations within the general class of underdeveloped and/or compromised agents that could be useful in guiding more supportive and appropriate interactions. To illustrate the general view, however, I shall here restrict myself to a consideration of one very large subset of such agents; namely, typically developing children.

The primary dimension of their failure, I submit, is not a matter of reactive insensitivity. Empirical evidence shows that even very young children are aware of the normative complexity of human interactions, to the point, for instance of robustly distinguishing between moral and conventional norms on a number of dimensions (Nucci and Turiel 1978; Turiel 1983). Moreover, they show such awareness in their distinctive emotional responses to these different kinds of norm violations and they are likewise sensitive to such emotional responses in others when directed at their own (and others') attitudes and behaviour (Blair 1999, 2003; Blair et al. 2006; Keupp et al. 2016). In short, they are by nature 'reactively sensitive' creatures, which should be no surprise to anyone endorsing a Strawsonian approach to responsible agency, since the natural reactive sensitivities of our species constitute the foundational touchstone of the entire approach.

But now, what of their capacity for reactive engagement? Do children have the psychological wherewithal (cognitively and motivationally) to engage in the kind of substantive reactive exchanges that enable them to take responsibility for developing and honing their skill in responding to moral reasons? I think the answer is 'no'. This is not to say that parents and other caregivers/educators do not often engage children in a form of these exchanges. They certainly do, and I shall come back to the significance of this in a moment. But it is to say that children do not have what it takes to hold up their end in such exchanges—or make use of them in a reflectively substantive way—without a great deal of support from their interlocutors.

But why? What is it that children are lacking in this regard, especially given their reactive sensitivity? My response to this draws heavily on Tamar Schapiro's insightful characterization of what she calls the 'normative predicament of childhood' (Schapiro 1999). Schapiro sets this predicament against the more general predicament we all face as mature agents; namely, managing our conflicting motivational impulses in a way that reflects a relatively coherent deliberative perspective. Such a perspective enables us to discriminate amongst those motivational impulses, enfranchising those that we can stand behind or endorse as manifesting our best reason for action. In so doing, we turn our actions into something more than mere agential doings; they become meaningful expressions of who we are as persons; they become expression of our character, or—as some might say—our 'will'. More to the point, they become the kind of actions for which we can answer in a deliberatively significant way (Smith 2008); hence, they become the kind of actions for which we can take responsibility, making us fit to participate in reactively permeated interpersonal relationships. However, in order to reach this stage of maturity, we need to have pulled ourselves together, as it were, finding our way to an established set of principles by which we can govern ourselves and through which we assume the mantle of an authoritative, self-legislating creature, responsible for who and what we are. But children are not yet in this position:

> ...the immature agent cannot adjudicate...conflicts [among conflicting motivational claims] in a truly authoritative way for lack of an established constitution, that is, a principled perspective which would count as the law of her will. Thus, the condition of childhood is one in which the agent is not yet in a position to speak in her own voice because there is no voice which counts as hers.
> (Schapiro 1999, 729)

The problem for children, then, is that their reactive sensitivities are only sufficient to ensure they are tuned into features of the world that matter for their developing a reasonably coherent and appropriately structured normative perspective. But, until they develop that perspective, the motivational impulses that derive from these reactive sensitivities have no more authoritative standing in the child's psychic economy than any other motivational impulses; or, if they do have authoritative standing, that standing will be externally imposed by way of an outwardly directed concern with pleasing, or displeasing, others. What must happen for children, instead, is the gradual development of conscience: an inner voice which is truly theirs, and theirs because, as Schapiro puts it, they have 'carve[d] out a space between themselves and the forces within them' (Schapiro 1999, 735)—a space in which their own deliberatively endorsed principles now become a compass by which they can steer. Moreover, their position with respect to others is correspondingly transformed in a way that enables normatively significant reactive exchanges. The developing agent now has the resources to understand others' critical or corrective input as targeting the adequacy of their own deliberative perspective; and, using the resources of that perspective, they are likewise empowered to debate and discuss the normative value of others' critical input. In short, such agents are well on their way to earning the status of being 'fully' responsible by way of their increasing sophistication in reactive responsiveness.

We come at last to the final question of the chapter: How should we engage with individuals who have yet to emerge from this grey area of underdeveloped responsible agency? Specifically, what modifications to our reactive attitudes and practices are necessary to support that emergence, where—as indicated by the above analysis—this involves cultivating the development of a well-formed deliberative perspective? My answer to this question reinvokes the observation made in Section 4 that novices require a specially supported and structured environment in which to acquire distinctively new skills. That environment generally involves the intervention of experts who direct, remind, model, and otherwise coach the novice into doing things conducive to developing a skill. The novice may have some insight into what they are doing and why. But this is not necessary. Indeed, when it comes to the early development of rudimentary skills, this is far from the case. Wood et al. (1976) introduce the idea of 'parental scaffolding' to characterize such learning environments, where young children have very little sense of the skills they are developing: e.g. emotion-regulation, decision-making, good manners (for further elaboration, see Bruner 1983, 1990). The key idea behind parental scaffolding is that a child's caregivers inculcate these skills by way of involving them in interactions that require the child to perform the skill in question; then, supporting them in the performance of their part by way of directing, modelling, reminding, and coaching. In short, caregivers themselves take on the role assigned to the child in supportive reinforcement of the child's efforts; and they slowly withdraw that role-playing support as the child becomes skilled enough to do it on their own.

I return now to the problem of what children must develop in order to become normatively competent agents; i.e. agents that can successfully participate in normatively significant reactive exchanges. The suggestion here is that this is precisely the kind of skill developed by way of parental scaffolding. Young children do not yet have a deliberative perspective of their own, which perspective is prerequisite for self-standing participation in reactive exchanges. But their caregivers can elicit this perspective in them by engaging them in reactive exchanges and then supporting them in playing their part as would be expected of them if they had a fully developed deliberative perspective of their own. So, for instance, if a child is naughty and the parent blames them for their naughtiness (perhaps by showing anger or irritation), it is up to the parent to assume a managerial role, orchestrating the child's response in such a way that it assumes the form of an appropriate response to another's blame. This will involve helping the child attend to the significance of what they have done; how and why it constitutes an unacceptable breach of normative expectations; why this involves others' feelings (their cares and concerns); how the child would feel if something similar were done to them; how to manage their own feelings of anxiety, guilt, or shame in the face of another's blame; how to offer apologies when apologies are due; how to better regulate their own behaviour going forward by consulting their own sense of what they should do (the inner voice of conscience); and, most important of all, how to accept that normative failures are part of everyday life. Indeed, 'since things go wrong and situations are complicated' (Strawson 1974, 8, 16), blamers themselves are not always in the right of it, and sometimes (though less often than putative wrongdoers might like) an acceptable plea or excuse is the appropriate response to someone's blame.

There is no determinate list of these scaffolded activities, but through them children gradually come into their own as normatively competent agents, increasingly able to perform such activities in propria persona as they develop a deeper appreciation of how their attitudes and behaviour are morally significant for others and vice versa. Hence, the dawning of this appreciation is properly tracked by the gradual withdrawal of managerial parental scaffolding, leaving in its place the unveiled version of something already present; namely, the full-blown edifice of ordinary peer-to-peer reactive scaffolding. Thus, we are left with the following view: interacting with underdeveloped agents does not require any dramatic modification in the affective tone or responsibility-attributing content of our everyday reactive attitudes and practices. But what it does require is an extra dimension of supportive managerial work on the part of agents already skilled in the practice to enable novices to play their allotted roles. This seems to me to fit with the spirit of Strawson's own remarks on the topic; so I here close with a final quotation from 'Freedom and Resentment':

> [P]arents and others concerned with the care and upbringing of young children cannot have to their charges either kind of attitude [objective or reactive] in a pure or unqualified form. They are dealing with creatures that are potentially and increasingly capable of holding, and being objects of, the full range of human and moral attitudes, but are not yet truly capable of either. The treatment of such creatures must therefore represent a kind of compromise, constantly shifting in one direction, between objectivity of attitude and developed human attitudes. Rehearsals insensibly modulate towards true performances.
>
> (Strawson 1974, 19)

References

Blair, Robert James Richard (1999), 'Psychophysiological Responsiveness to the Distress of Others in Children with Autism', *Personality and Individual Differences* 26: 477–85.

Blair, Robert James Richard (2003), 'Facial Expressions, their Communicatory Functions and Neuro-Cognitive Substrates', *Philosophical Transactions of the Royal Society of London Series B: Biological Sciences* 358(1431): 561–72.

Blair, Robert James Richard, Abigail A. Marsh, Elizabeth Finger, K.S. Blair, and Jun Luo (2006), 'Neuro-Cognitive Systems Involved in Morality', *Philosophical Explorations* 9(1): 13–27.

Brandenburg, Daphne (2018), 'The Nurturing Stance: Making Sense of Responsibility Without Blame', *Pacific Philosophical Quarterly* 99: 5–22.

Brandenburg, Daphne (2019), 'Inadequate Agency and Appropriate Anger', *Ethical Theory and Moral Practice* 22(1): 169–85.

Brandenburg, Daphne, and Derek Strijbos (2020a), 'The Clinical Stance and the Nurturing Stance: Therapeutic Responses to Harmful Conduct by Service Users in Mental Healthcare', *Philosophy, Psychiatry, & Psychology* 27(4): 379–94.

Brandenburg, Daphne, and Derek Strijbos (2020b), 'Reproach without Blameworthiness', *Philosophy, Psychiatry, & Psychology* 27(4): 399–401.

Bruner, Jerome (1983), *Child's Talk: Learning to Use Language* (New York: W.W. Norton).

Bruner, Jerome (1990), *Acts of Meaning* (Cambridge, MA: Harvard University Press).

Cherry, Myisha (2019), 'Love, Anger, and Racial Injustice', in Adrienne M. Martin (ed.), *The Routledge Handbook of Love in Philosophy* (New York: Routledge), 157–68.

Fara, Michael (2008), 'Masked Abilities and Compatibilism', *Mind* 117(468): 843–65.

Fischer, John Martin, and Mark Ravizza (1998), *Responsibility and Control: A Theory of Moral Responsibility* (Cambridge: Cambridge University Press).

Kennett, Jeanette (2020), 'Blame, Reproach, and Responsibility', *Philosophy, Psychiatry, & Psychology* 27(4): 395–7.

Keupp, Stefanie, Christine Bancken, Jelka Schillmöller, Hannes Rakoczy, and Tanya Behne (2016), 'Rational Over-Imitation: Preschoolers Consider Material Costs and Copy Causally Irrelevant Actions Selectively', *Cognition* 147: 85–92.

Korsgaard, Christine (1996), 'Two Arguments Against Lying', in *Creating the Kingdom of Ends* (Cambridge: Cambridge University Press), 335–62.

Lorde, Audre (1997), 'The Uses of Anger', *Women's Studies Quarterly* 25(1/2): 278–85.

McGeer, Victoria (2013), 'Civilizing Blame', in Justin Coates and Neal Tognazzini (eds.), *Blame: Its Nature and Norms* (Oxford: Oxford University Press), 162–88.

McGeer, Victoria (2018a), 'Intelligent Capacities', *Proceedings of the Aristotelian Society* 118(3): 1–30.

McGeer, Victoria (2018b), 'Scaffolding Agency: A Proleptic Account of the Reactive Attitudes', *European Journal of Philosophy* 27(2): 1–23.

McGeer, Victoria, and Michael McKenna, eds. (in prep), 'Moral Responsibility and the Attenuated Role of the Hostile Emotions'.

McGeer, Victoria, and Philip Pettit (2015), 'The Hard Problem of Responsibility', in David Shoemaker (ed.), *Oxford Studies in Agency and Responsibility*, vol. 3 (Oxford: Oxford University Press), 160–88.

Muldoon, Paul (2008), 'The Moral Legitimacy of Anger', *European Journal of Social Theory* 11(3): 299–314.

Nucci, Larry, and Elliot Turiel (1978), 'Social Interactions and the Development of Social Concepts in Preschool Children', *Child Development* 49: 400–7.

Nussbaum, Martha C. (2016), *Anger and Forgiveness: Resentment, Generosity, Justice* (Oxford: Oxford University Press).

Pereboom, Derk (2014), *Free Will, Agency, and Meaning in Life* (Oxford: Oxford University Press).

Pettit, Philip (2018), *The Birth of Ethics: A Reconstruction of the Role of Nature in Morality* (Oxford: Oxford University Press).

Pettit, Philip, and Michael Smith (1996), 'Freedom in Belief and Desire', *Journal of Philosophy* 93: 429–49.

Pickard, Hanna (2011), 'Responsibility Without Blame: Empathy and the Effective Treatment of Personality Disorder', *Philosophy, Psychiatry, & Psychology* 18(3): 209–24.

Pickard, Hanna (2013), 'Responsibility Without Blame: Philosophical Reflections on Clinical Practice', in K.W.M. Fulford, Martin Davies, Richard Gipps, George Graham, John Z. Sadler, Giovanni Stanghellini, and Tim Thornton (eds.) *The Oxford Handbook of Philosophy and Psychiatry* (Oxford: Oxford University Press), 1134–54.

Ryle, Gilbert (1949), *The Concept of Mind* (Chicago, IL: University of Chicago Press).

Schapiro, Tamar (1999), 'What Is a Child?', *Ethics* 109(4): 715–38.

Seneca, Lucius Annaeus (2010), *Anger, Mercy, Revenge*, trans. Robert A. Kaster and Martha C. Nussbaum (Chicago, IL: University of Chicago Press).

Shoemaker, David (2011), 'Attributability, Answerability, and Accountability: Toward a Wider Theory of Moral Responsibility', *Ethics* 121(3): 602–32.

Shoemaker, David (2015), *Responsibility from the Margins* (Oxford: Oxford University Press).

Smith, Adam (1759/1982), *The Theory of the Moral Sentiments* (Indianapolis, IN: Liberty Classics).

Smith, Angela M. (2008), 'Control, Responsibility, and Moral Assessment', *Philosophical Studies* 138(3): 367–92.

Smith, Michael (2003), 'Rational Capacities, or: How to Distinguish Recklessness, Weakness, and Compulsion', in Sarah Stroud and Christine Tappolet (eds.), *Weakness of Will and Practical Irrationality* (Oxford: Clarendon Press), 17–38.

Srinivasan, Amia (2016), 'Would Politics Be Better Off Without Anger?', *The Nation*, 30 November.

Srinivasan, Amia (2018), 'The Aptness of Anger', *Journal of Political Philosophy* 26(2): 123–44.

Strawson, Peter F. (1974), 'Freedom and Resentment', in *Freedom and Resentment and Other Essays* (London: Methuen), 1–25.

Turiel, Elliot (1983), *The Development of Social Knowledge: Morality and Convention* (Cambridge: Cambridge University Press).

Vargas, Manuel (2013), *Building Better Beings: A Theory of Moral Responsibility* (Oxford: Oxford University Press).

Vihvelin, Kadri (2004), 'Free Will Demystified: A Dispositional Account', *Philosophical Topics* 32(1/2): 427–50.

Vygotsky, L. S. (1978), *Mind in Society: Development of Higher Psychological Processes* (Cambridge, MA: Harvard University Press).

Wallace, R. Jay (1994), *Responsibility and the Moral Sentiments* (Cambridge, MA: Harvard University Press).

Waller, Bruce N. (2014), *The Stubborn System of Moral Responsibility* (Cambridge, MA: MIT Press).

Watson, Gary (1987), 'Responsibility and the Limits of Evil: Variations on a Strawsonian Theme', in Ferdinand Schoeman (ed.), *Responsibility, Character and the Emotions: New Essays in Moral Psychology* (Cambridge: Cambridge University Press), 256–86.

Watson, Gary (2004), *Agency and Answerability: Selected Essays* (Oxford: Clarendon Press).

Wolf, Susan (1987), 'Sanity and the Metaphysics of Responsibility', in Ferdinand Schoeman (ed.), *Responsibility, Character and the Emotions: New Essays in Moral Psychology* (Cambridge: Cambridge University Press), 46–62.

Wolf, Susan (1990), *Freedom Within Reason* (Oxford: Oxford University Press).

Wood, David, Jerome S. Bruner, and Gail Ross (1976), 'The Role of Tutoring in Problem Solving', *Child Psychology and Psychiatry and Allied Disciplines* 17: 89–100.

Index

For the benefit of digital users, indexed terms that span two pages (e.g., 52-53) may, on occasion, appear on only one of those pages.

agency 251-3, 270-8, 277n.14, 280-309
   animal agency 273-4
Allais, Lucy 146
Allison, Henry 147
alternative possibilities 244-5, 274-6
analysis 153, 155-60, 162, 195-7, 202-3, 205-7, 213-33
   connective vs. reductive 7, 122-4, 127, 202-3, 205-7, 213-33
analytic Kantianism 5-6, 8, 121-2, 153
analytic/synthetic distinction 3-4, 8, 140-3, 146-68, 218
analytic philosophy 120-1, 146, 157-8, 160n.25, 206
analytic truth 8, 150-1, 153-5, 157-9, 162
   see also necessary truth
   see also conceptual truth
animal 46-7, 121-2, 132-3, 135-9, 175n.7, 221
   see also agency, animal agency
Anscombe, Gertrude Elizabeth Margaret 86-7
a priori 8, 31, 122, 124n.3, 140-3, 146-68, 192-7, 218-20
apprehension 173, 176n.9, 179-80, 183
Aristotle 3-4, 123-4, 164-5, 216
Aristotelian(ism) 121, 125-6
assertion 2, 15-37, 39, 42-3, 48, 109, 211, 218
autonomy 122, 139-40
Austin, John Langshaw 1-4, 213n.1, 215, 227
Ayer, Alfred Jules 88, 89n.14, 90n.15, 92n.18, 244-5, 244n.25, 245n.27

basic particulars 59-78, 101-4, 110, 113, 115, 117-18, 124
   see also particulars
behaviour 8, 45-7, 79-98, 136-9, 220, 227-8, 284-5, 287, 291, 293-5, 302-3, 305-6
behaviourism 97, 138
Bennett, Jonathan 121, 153-5, 157
Berkeley, George 123, 222-3, 229
Bird, Graham 147
blame 235-6, 238-9, 241n.19, 243, 246, 249-50, 254-5, 261-3, 267-8, 274-5, 281-2, 290-3, 296-9, 305-6

body 4, 7-8, 59-78, 125, 129, 140, 162-4, 185, 206, 222-3
   see also material body
Brandom, Robert 136
Burge, Tyler 171, 175, 175n.7

Campbell, John 77n.9, 78, 81n.6, 95-6, 162
capacitarianism 282, 285-9, 295, 300-2
Carnap, Rudolf 3-4, 197, 199, 217n.9, 222n.19
Cartesianism 195n.2
   Cartesian demon 270-1
   see also Descartes, René
Cassam, Quassim 102n.5, 156-7, 187-8
categories 63, 70, 72-4, 76-7, 101, 124, 149-52, 177, 215n.8
causation 7, 121, 141, 143, 205, 272-3
certainty 142-3, 187-8, 220
Chesterton, G.K. 140
Chomsky, Noam 33
Christianity 240
circularity 7, 95, 103, 106, 110-11, 124, 156, 209-11, 214, 219, 224, 230
classification 99-100, 121-2, 124, 128-9, 140
coherentism 202-3
Collingwood, Robin George 81, 93-7
common sense 6, 125-7, 142-3, 158, 171-2, 171n.2, 176, 182
communication 6, 8, 38-58, 61, 63-4, 66-7, 72, 74, 76-7, 127
compatibilism 235-8, 241-2, 251, 253, 264-5, 270-6
conceptual analysis 7, 9, 122-3, 153, 155, 195-7, 202-3, 205, 213-33
   see also analysis
conceptualism 122, 135-6, 139
conceptual scheme 59-63, 66, 70-2, 74, 89-90, 101-4, 116-18, 121-6, 142-3, 198-200, 203, 206
conceptual truth 8, 87, 122, 134, 142-3, 157n.18,
   see also analytic truth
   see also necessary truth

connective analysis 7, 22–3, 122–4, 127, 202–3, 205–7, 213–33
    see also analysis, connective vs. reductive
    see also reductive analysis
consciousness 62–3, 79–98, 122, 127–8, 134–5, 153, 174–6, 181–2, 181n.17, 222, 225–6, 231
    see also self-consciousness
contingency 74, 76–7, 141, 252
control 251–2, 292, 296
conversation 16–17, 21–2, 31–2, 78, 192–3, 203–4, 206–7, 220
conversational tailoring 15–16, 32
criteria 8, 60, 71, 133–4, 199–204, 211

Davidson, Donald 1, 54, 96–7
definite descriptions 1–2, 15–37, 108n.12
demonstratives 16, 18, 27, 32
De Mesel, Benjamin 208, 241n.19
Dennett, Daniel 236n.5, 244n.26
Descartes, René 123, 193n.1, 200, 224n.24
    see also Cartesianism
desert 235–9, 239n.10, 244–8, 262, 284–5, 292, 296–7
descriptive metaphysics 4, 7–8, 75n.7, 101–4, 118, 120–5, 141–3, 164–5, 249
    see also metaphysics
description 67, 69–72, 132, 171, 179, 181, 192–212
determinism 4–5, 235–7, 244–5, 260–79, 282–4
dispositionalism 282, 286–8, 290–3, 295–6, 299–301
Donnellan, Keith 17, 227
Dorr, Cian 155–6
Dummett, Michael 40n.3, 43, 227

elucidation 7, 123, 214n.4, 216–18, 221–2, 223n.22
empiricism 3–4, 111n.15, 120–1, 124n.3, 132–3, 140
epistemology 1, 8, 49–50, 83, 86–7, 97, 124n.3, 151n.8, 196–7, 205–7, 209–11
essence 123–6, 160
Evans, Gareth 59, 62–3, 78, 87, 102n.5, 162
event 7, 20, 60, 63–4, 74, 76–7, 99–100, 124, 129, 137, 140–3, 171
experience 6–8, 62–4, 68, 80, 86, 88–9, 100, 104, 111, 120–91, 194–8, 200, 204, 206, 214, 216
explication 3–4
expressivism 267–8

fate 239n.10, 245–6, 251–3
first-personal perspective 159–63
forgiveness 260n.2
freedom 7, 140, 217–18, 228, 236, 244–5, 261–2, 266–9, 277n.14

free will 253–5, 260–1, 264, 268–73, 276–8
Frege, Gottlob 15–18, 40–1, 43n.4, 106–7, 214n.4, 216, 225n.25, 227

genealogy 9, 235, 240–2, 247–51, 253–5
Gettier, Edmund 224–5
Gibson, James 75n.7, 77nn.10,11, 176
given 140, 169, 176–91
Glock, Hans-Johann 153
grammar 6, 22, 28n.9, 34, 99–100, 122, 124n.3, 134, 157n.18, 265
gratitude 4–5, 18, 236, 262, 265–6, 274–5, 283–5
Grice, Herbert Paul 3–4, 15–16, 19–20, 32, 39–42, 44, 213–33
guilt 235–6, 238–9, 241n.19, 243, 274, 282–3, 298–9, 305–6

Hamann, Johann Georg 152
Hart, Herbert 246n.31
Heidegger, Martin 169, 178, 179n.10, 180nn.13,14, 189
Herder, Johann Gottfried 152
Herz, Marcus 147n.2
Hieronymi, Pamela 261, 264–5, 269–73, 276–7
hinge proposition 142–3
Hobbes, Thomas 222–3, 229
Hume, David 3, 6–9, 172–5, 173nn.4,5, 185, 188n.23, 192–4, 195n.2, 196, 205–11, 216, 251nn.37,38
Humean 264–8
Husserl, Edmund 8–9, 159–60, 162–3, 169, 178–80, 179n.11, 180n.15, 183n.18

idealism 5–6, 62n.2, 120–1, 141, 147–50, 152, 155, 157, 160, 162–5, 183n.19, 189n.24, 194–8
identification 8, 59–78, 104, 111, 132, 138, 140–1, 171–2, 197–203
    see also reidentification
identity 7, 65–6, 70–2, 78, 103, 115, 197–200
identificatory force 16–17, 27–31
imagination 95–6, 148, 161–4, 169–91, 205–6
incompatibilism 236, 250, 253–4, 272–3
indignation 267–8, 282–3, 290, 297–9
induction 197, 201–3, 209–11
inference 22–3, 53–7, 88, 124, 128, 201–4, 209–11
inferential dispositions 53–7
information structure 22–3, 29, 31, 34
intellect 122, 128, 132–3
intensional 54–5, 54n.8, 228

intention 6–7, 29n.10, 38–58, 86, 93–4, 174, 217–22, 227–30, 266–7
interpersonal 4–5, 63, 68, 70
introspection 159, 162–3
intuition 121–2, 132, 151–2, 173, 177–8, 179n.10
i-words 20, 27–8, 31

Jacobi, Friedrich Heinrich 152
James, Henry 170
James, William 132–3
judgement 121, 124n.3, 128–32, 134–6, 140, 151–2, 224–5
justice 217–19, 229, 235–6, 239–40, 246
justification 29–30, 88, 93, 95, 183–4, 188–9, 192–212, 215, 224–5, 263–7, 277–8, 290–1, 296

Kant, Immanuel 3–6, 8, 62n.2, 120–91, 194–8, 239–41, 277n.14
  Critique of Pure Reason 5–6, 8, 62n.2, 120–68, 197–8
  Groundwork of the Metaphysics of Morals 146, 266
Kantian(ism) 5–7, 62n.2, 120–68, 192–4, 197, 226, 266–8, 277n.14
Kitcher, Patricia 147
Kripke, Saul 1, 17, 160, 219–20

laws of nature 142, 272–3
Leibniz, Gottfried Wilhelm 123
libertarianism 241–2, 251, 253–4, 264
Lichtenberg, Georg Christoph 129
Locke, John 229
logic 1–3, 20, 29n.10, 33–4, 53n.7, 120–3, 124n.3, 131, 134, 146, 150–1, 157–8, 222, 229
logical atomism 123
logical positivism 123, 217–18
luck 234, 239–40, 245–6, 251–3

Mackie, J.L. 246n.30
material body 4, 8, 59–78, 103–4, 125, 129
  see also body
material object 4, 7, 124, 142, 199
  see also object
McDowell, John 44–8, 122, 136–7, 139–40, 153n.13, 170–1
McTaggart, J.M.E. 157
meaning 2, 6–8, 17, 38–58, 81–7, 123, 141, 146–7, 192–5, 201–3
mental state 8, 79–98, 135, 229
metacritique 152–3
metaphor 213–18

metaphysics 1, 101–4, 118, 120–5, 127–8, 131, 134, 141, 143, 147, 154, 192–212, 222, 266–7
  see also descriptive metaphysics
  see also revisionary metaphysics
mind 7, 79–98, 128, 128n.6, 141, 148–52, 164–5, 172, 173n.4, 176–7, 182–5, 184n.20, 216–17, 222–3, 227
mind-independence 122, 128n.6, 129–30, 132, 156, 162, 170–1, 175, 175n.7, 183–9, 194–5
Moore, G.E. 8, 123–4, 142–3, 148, 157–63
Moore's Paradox 43
moral appraisal 261–3, 274–5
moral development 299
moral psychology 236, 245, 260–1, 266
  see also psychology
moral reasons 266–7, 280–309
moral responsibility 4–5, 9, 208, 234–59, 261–4, 267–8, 274, 277–8, 280
morality 4–7, 208, 229, 234–59
morality system 235, 238–40, 242–4, 246, 250–1, 253–4
Moran, Richard 48, 50n.6
music 179–80, 180n.13
myth of the given 140
  see also given

Nagel, Thomas 245–6, 252n.39
naturalism 6–9, 192–4, 196, 205–11, 235–6, 235n.3, 242, 247–55, 264, 266–7, 280–1, 286–8, 292–3, 295–6
  see also social naturalism
necessary condition 15, 44, 82, 89–91, 125–7, 129–30, 132–4, 149, 156–8, 162–4, 194–5, 197–8, 206
necessary truth 149, 219
  see also analytic truth
  see also conceptual truth
Nietzsche, Friedrich 235, 240–1, 250n.34
nominalism 121–2, 222–3
nonsense 126, 142, 202–3
norm of representation 141
normative competence 289, 291–3, 296, 300–3

object 4, 6–7, 120–45, 149–52, 156, 160–1, 163–5, 194–5, 197–9
  see also material object
objectivity 62–3, 66, 74, 121–2, 128n.6, 129–32, 136, 139–40, 142n.14, 150–1, 153, 161–2, 171, 171n.2, 175–6, 175n.7, 182–3, 186
ordinary language 3–4, 107, 112–15, 120–1, 215
other minds 4, 21–2, 79–98, 130

parental scaffolding 305–6
particulars 59–78, 99–119, 121–2, 124n.3, 128–34, 140, 162, 182, 197–203, 213–14, 222–3
Peirce, Charles Sanders 48–9
perception 6–9, 46, 64, 68–9, 74, 76–8, 111n.14, 121–2, 127–8, 131–3, 136–9, 158–62, 169–91, 216
person 4, 28, 62–3, 72n.5, 79–98, 125, 129, 135n.10, 140
personal pronoun 20, 122, 131, 134
phenomenology 159–60, 171, 175, 178–81, 188–9, 284–5
philosophy of language 1, 8, 33, 38, 43, 60–1, 222
physics 272–3
Plato 217–18, 225n.25
Plutarch 138–9
praise 235–6, 261–2, 274
pragmatics 33, 227
practical reason 266–7
predicate 3–4, 16–17, 19–20, 22, 24, 32–4, 54n.8, 79–119, 124n.3, 128–30, 128n.6, 222
P-predicate 79–98
predication 4, 6, 27, 29, 31, 120–2, 132–3
see also subject-predicate distinction
presupposition 2, 6–8, 15–37, 110, 123, 125–6, 129, 131, 136n.11, 140, 194–5, 199, 209–11
process 60, 63–4, 74, 76–7, 100, 104, 129
proper name 2, 20, 27, 32, 64–5
proposition 17–18, 23, 29n.10, 39, 41–3, 48–50, 52–5, 57, 89, 103, 107–10, 110n.13, 113, 116, 122, 128–9, 131, 134, 136–7, 140–3, 151n.8, 153–5, 158, 186–7, 217–20, 224–6
psychology 33, 93–4, 120–1, 127–8, 141, 143, 147–52, 157–60, 160n.28, 162–4, 173n.4, 203, 296
see also moral psychology
psychologism 120–1
punishment 219, 235–7, 243, 246, 261–2
Putnam, Hilary 1, 146

quantifier 17
Quine, Willard Van Orman 1, 3–4, 33–4, 61–2, 110n.13, 111, 115n.17, 217–18, 223–4, 229
quietism 8–9, 192–3, 250, 265, 271n.10

Ramsey, Frank 2–3, 100, 101n.2, 104, 215–16, 223n.22
rationalism 120–1, 124n.3
reactive attitudes 4–5, 9, 23, 236–8, 241n.19, 242, 244–7, 249–50, 260–71, 274–5, 277–8, 280–309
reactive sensitivities 298–9, 302–5
realism 6–9, 157, 170–1, 176, 182

reality 100, 116, 118, 123–4, 124n.3, 128n.6, 136, 139, 141–3, 170–1, 181n.17, 188, 194–7, 201, 209–11, 225–6, 230
reciprocity thesis 174, 182
recognition 132–5, 170–1, 174–6, 183, 220–1
reductive analysis 7, 123, 220n.14, 222–8
see also analysis, connective vs. reductive
see also connective analysis
reference 2, 16, 18–22, 28, 31–2, 59–78, 106, 108–9, 114, 115n.17, 120–1, 132–4, 140, 222–3, 231
reference failure 15–16, 22–3, 25–6
reflection 159–64
reidentification 60, 70–2, 99, 104–5, 111–12, 114–15, 140, 162, 171–2, 183–4, 197–203
see also identification
relativism 6, 246
remembrance 179–81
representation 17, 46–7, 124n.3, 128–9, 132, 141, 151–2, 163–4, 174, 179–81, 194–5, 197–8, 209–11, 215
reproduction 173–4, 173n.5, 176n.9
resentment 4–5, 236, 260n.2, 262, 265–8, 274–5, 282–5, 290, 297–8
retribution 239, 239n.10, 243, 246
revisionary metaphysics 4, 101n.3, 104, 118, 122–3, 125, 164–5, 206, 249
see also metaphysics
Rorty, Richard 5–6, 134n.9, 153–4
Rothko, Mark 169–70
rule 2, 34, 38–9, 42–3, 55–7, 128–9, 141–2, 176n.9, 177–80, 201–3, 211, 218
Russell, Bertrand 1–3, 17–19, 32, 68, 107–9, 157, 221, 227
Russell, Paul 234–59, 269–70
Ryle, Gilbert 1, 6, 53, 215–16, 225–6, 293–4

scepticism 4–9, 60, 70–1, 79–80, 88–93, 124n.3, 125–7, 129–30, 184–9, 184n.20, 192–212, 235–8, 240–1, 244–5, 248–55, 271
Schlick, Moritz 129, 236n.5
self 150–1, 180
self-ascription 82–6, 89–91, 122, 130–5, 140, 153
self-consciousness 46, 64, 121–2, 124n.3, 127–31, 134–6, 139, 143, 150–1, 153, 156, 173n.4, 174–6, 175n.7, 181, 181n.17, 183
see also consciousness
self-knowledge 88–9
Sellars, Wilfrid 1, 136
semantics 33–4, 54n.8, 57, 129–31, 134, 221–2
formal 6, 38, 50, 55–6
sensation 86, 121, 127–8, 141, 169–70, 170n.1, 176, 179–80

sense-data 124n.3, 132–4, 158–9, 161–2, 169–72, 170n.1, 179–80, 230
sense-impression 149–50
sensibility 121–2, 128n.6, 147n.2, 151–2, 197–8
sensible experience 6, 170, 177, 179
sentience 127–8
shame 236, 282–3, 298–9, 305–6
simplicity 117, 214, 222–6, 228–9
skill 225–6, 280–309
social naturalism 269–71
　see also naturalism
solipsism 62–3, 81–2, 87, 89–90
sound 4, 45–7, 62–4, 66, 72–4, 104, 162
space 7, 59–64, 66–70, 73–7, 112–15, 121, 142–3, 151–3, 162, 171, 173, 181, 194–5, 197–8, 214
　see also spatio-temporal framework
spatio-temporal framework 59–62, 66–71, 75, 129, 132, 140–3, 198–203
　see also space
　see also time
speech act 8, 39–43, 45, 48, 50, 55–7, 215
spontaneity 122, 139–40, 178, 181n.16
state of consciousness 79–80, 83–4, 127–8
Steward, Helen 273–4, 276
stoicism 138–9
Strawson, Galen 118n.20, 246n.30
Strawson, P. F.
　'On Referring' 1–2, 8, 15–20, 33–4, 99–100, 118, 227
　'Truth' 2–3
　Introduction to Logical Theory 3, 197, 201
　'Carnap's Views on Constructed Systems Versus Natural Languages in Analytic Philosophy' 3–4
　'In Defence of a Dogma' 3–4
　'Social Morality and Individual Ideal' 4–5
　'Freedom and Resentment' 1, 4–5, 9, 208, 234–80, 306
　Individuals 4, 8, 59–146, 153–4, 162–5, 182, 192–212, 249
　The Bounds of Sense 5, 8, 120–68, 173n.4, 174–6, 174n.6, 182, 192–4
　'Meaning and Truth' 6, 8, 38, 41
　Subject and Predicate in Logic and Grammar 6, 8, 15–37, 101n.2, 128
　'Perception and Its Objects' 6, 8–9
　Scepticism and Naturalism 6–8, 80, 89, 91, 93–4, 172, 174–5, 185, 188–9, 188n.23, 196, 205–8, 245–6
　Analysis and Metaphysics 7, 9, 184, 222–3
Stroud, Barry 5–6, 90–1, 126n.5, 155n.16, 185, 192–7, 202–3, 206–7
subjective 128n.6, 130, 161–2, 164, 170–1, 174–6, 196

subject-predicate distinction 4, 6, 16–17, 22, 32, 100, 102–3, 105–10, 112–13, 115–16, 118
　see also predication
synthesis 148–53, 156n.17
synthetic a priori 8, 122, 124n.3, 140–1, 151–8, 163–4, 192–7

telling 8, 38–58, 84, 90
testimony 29–30, 46, 50
Theory of Descriptions 1–3, 17–18
time 7, 59–62, 66–73, 75, 105, 112–13, 115, 117, 121, 142–3, 151–3, 214, 223n.22
　see also spatio-temporal framework
topic-comment distinction 16, 22–3
transcendental arguments 5–9, 60, 71–2, 91n.16, 122, 125–7, 129, 131, 133, 135, 140–3, 163, 174–5, 192–212, 269–71, 276–7
transcendental deduction 148–52, 154, 156–7, 163, 179n.10
transcendental idealism 5–6, 120–1, 141, 147–50, 155, 164–5, 183n.19, 189n.24, 196
transcendental psychology 120–1, 127–8, 141, 147–52, 163–4, 173n.4
truth 2–3, 7, 15, 17–18, 20, 23, 26, 28–9, 38–40, 42–3, 43n.4, 46–57, 107, 110, 134, 140, 148–51, 153–63, 169–70, 192–7, 209–11
　see also conceptual truth
　see also necessary truth
truth-conditions 19–20, 28–9, 38, 43, 52, 54–7
truth-value gap 17–18, 20, 23, 26
trust 47–8, 188–9
trustworthiness 49, 51–2

understanding 20, 81, 94–6, 121–2, 128n.6, 136n.11, 140, 148, 151–2, 170, 173n.4, 175–6, 175n.7, 178, 183, 223–4
universals 99–119, 121–2, 124n.3, 128–9, 131–4, 213–14, 216–17, 222–3
unity 122, 127–8, 128n.6, 131, 134, 140, 148–51, 153, 173–4, 176n.9, 178–82
utilitarianism 235–9

verificationism 84, 86–7, 90–1
voluntariness 239–40

Walker, Ralph 153–5, 153n.13, 203–4
Wallace, R. Jay 4–5, 242–3, 245n.28, 250n.33, 253n.42, 267–8, 280, 286n.5
Watson, Gary 4–5, 246n.29, 252–3, 281n.1, 284–6
Wiggins, David 4, 78, 214n.4, 227

Williams, Bernard 9, 234–59
  Shame and Necessity 235n.4, 240, 254–5
  Ethics and the Limits of Philosophy 234n.2, 250n.35
Williamson, Timothy 163n.33, 225–6
Wisdom, John 158

Wittgenstein, Ludwig 3, 6–7, 80–1, 97, 116, 122, 129–30, 134, 141–3, 157n.18, 158, 188–9, 188n.23, 214n.4, 215–16, 222n.19
Wittgensteinian 18, 80–1, 122–3, 222n.19, 250, 265–6, 268, 271n.10